Cambridge
Footlights Dramatic Club

Pembroke College

Jan 12th

Dear Mr Bassett,

I should very much like to join you all for lunch on the 14th. What time and where? I can easily be anywhere by 11.30 but not before. Would you please write to me or phone a message to Pembroke as this will find me quicker than the "Footlights" address.

I look forward to seeing you on Thursday

Yours sincerely
Peter Cook.

Jan 12th   Pembroke College

Dear Mr Bassett,

   I would very much like to join you all for lunch on the 14th.
What time and where? I can easily be anywhere by 14.30 but not
before. Will you please write to me or phone a message to Pembroke as this will find me quicker than the "Footlights" address!

   I look forward to seeing you on Thursday,

   Yours sincerely,

   Peter Cook

HOW VERY INTERESTING

PETER COOK'S UNIVERSE AND ALL THAT SURROUNDS IT

snowbooks

LONDON

SNOWBOOKS

2 4 6 8 10 9 7 5 3 1

Excerpts from the the BBC Radio 4 programme *Cook's Tours* are reproduced
courtesy of the BBC. Excerpts from Kenneth Williams' Diaries are reproduced
courtesy of HarperCollins Publishers.

The editors and publisher gratefully acknowledge the permission granted to
reproduce the copyright material in this book. Every effort has been made to
trace copyright holders and to obtain their permission for the use of copyright
material. The publisher apologizes for any errors or omissions and would be
grateful if notified of any corrections that should be incorporated in future
reprints or editions of this book.

Proudly published in Great Britain by
Snowbooks Ltd.
120 Pentonville Road
London N1 9JN
www.snowbooks.com

A CIP catalogue record for this book is available from the British Library
ISBN 1 905005 23 7
ISBN-13 978 1 905005 23 9

CONTENTS

RANDOM THOUGHTS ON PETER COOK

'60s
Yeah
He used to wear
Italian suits
And Chelsea boots
Beyond the Fringing
E. L. Wistying
Bernard Bradening
Perfect genting
Establishmenting
Lenny Brucing
Cocking a snooting
Putting the boot in
Satirising
Private Eyeing
Elegant & slim & thinning
Liked a glass of Gordon's ginning

Bet he got an awful lot of what we might call nookie.
Who he?
Cookie

'70s
A touch of wiz
A bot of fizz
A show of biz
Not Only But Alsoing
Dudley Mooring
Eamonn Andrews
& Zsa Zsa Gaboring
Never boring
Jumping jiving
Thrilling thriving
Fridge behinding
In Americing
Clive & Dereking
Has us roaring
Then some moring
Till our sides
Were sore and soaring
Sorer than some school kid who got whipped for playing
    hooky
Who he?
Cookie

'80s/'90s
Years of bliss
With wife and kids
And cannabis
And getting pissed
What's wrong with this?
The choice was his

Greebling
Streebling
Svenning
Skiving
Ducking diving
And imbibing
Stephen Frying
Anderson Cliving
He was fucking fab
And trying
Now in Hampstead grave
He's lying
No denying
This is filthy rotten swizz
He's missed and missed and missed and missed
By me
By you
By Auntie Pru
By barman
Broad
And bookie
Who he?
Cookie

INTRODUCTION

PETER COOK: Oh dear... Oh dear, oh dear... Oh dear, oh dear, oh dear...
ELEANOR BRON: What's wrong?
PETER COOK: Oh, nothing... just thinking aloud.
> (From a writing session for an unfinished, unperformed Cook/Bron stage revue, 1994.)

'Just thinking aloud.' That is what Peter Cook did best and it was a gift (or curse) that never left him. It was there in the black-and-white Fifties when he developed his loner persona Arthur Grole (the twin brother, albeit from different parents, of E.L.Wisty), the solitary whining mine of ill-digested misinterpreted nuggets of information—his 'interesting facts' that were never entirely factual nor attention-grabbing ('Did you know the whale is not really a fish? It's an insect... and it lives on bananas'). It was there when he established the perfect attraction of opposites in his double-act with Dudley Moore when, for a decade (1965-1975), they huddled in their caps and raincoats and wittered endlessly about 'very important things like life, death, Heaven, the universe, swimming.'[1]

And it was still there in his 1993 radio series of improvised confrontations with Chris Morris, *Why Bother?* ('I feel nothing but pride; that's all I do feel. An empty pride, a hopeless vanity, a dreadful arrogance, a stupefyingly futile conceit... but at least it's something to hang on to') and his multi-guesting on the Christmas '93 edition of Channel 4's *Clive Anderson Talks Back*. One of his characters there, Norman House, the environs-of-Ipswich-based biscuit tester abducted by aliens, tells of the atmosphere on the planet Ikea being 'very thin'—luckily, he had some air stored in his jumper and socks—and one might reasonably assume Peter Cook pulled his comedic inventions out of similar thin air. Dudley Moore remembered them improvising the Frog And Peach interview for the 1966 *Not Only But Also* series—their chosen modus operandi was in extemporisation and then rigorous cutting of dead-ends and superfluous chaff; the physical act of writing slowed their ability and opportunity for invention—and was astounded by Peter's spontaneous description of how his character Sir Arthur Streeb-Greebling had met his wife during the war:

---

1 Peter Cook in his last TV appearance (Pebble Mill, November 1994). This utterance was echoed nine years later by Sacha Baron Cohen as Ali G who opened his *Ali G In The USAiii* TV series with, 'America 'as hinvented some of the bestest things in the world—McDonalds, gangsta rap, spaghetti and swimmin'.' An intentional, if cryptic, salute? Cook, with and without Moore, has permeated most subsequent comedy with his revolutionary influence. Michael Palin's *Monty Python* character, the timid tedious milquetoast Arthur Putey, is cut from the same voicecloth as Wisty; Simon Munnery's League of Tedium is an aggressive remake/remodel of Cook's parkbench philosophical bonehead megalomaniac, and lines like 'I can speak 35 languages. I am the inventor of 34 languages' are Wistyesque wonders. And who are Spinal Tap, at source, if not Dud and Pete in heavy metal bouffants and spandex pants? More than superficial links, Cook can be thanked or blamed for the abandonment of the traditional three-minute sketch with a strong punchline at its end. Cook and Moore also elevated the notion of the meaningless comedy catchphrase to new heights, or depths, by convulsing their audiences with the simple word 'Funny'.

'Yes, she blew in through the drawing-room window with a piece of shrapnel, became embedded in the sofa and, you know, one thing led to her mother and we were married in the hour.'

The casual throwaway elegance of that statement, blending ludicrous cartoon imagery, everyday objects ('drawing-room window', 'sofa'), the creative twist of the linguistic shortcut cliché 'One thing led to another' (perversely, a working-class phrase) and the logic-defying abandonment of real time ('we were married in the hour') culminate in nothing less than Comedy Poetry.

Peter Cook's preferred method of creating—winging it; 'daring to fail' as Alan Latchley, his football manager from the celebrated Anderson showcase, would have it—was not an entirely flawless one. Since it was a predominantly verbal invention, the power of Cook's humour is overwhelmingly reliant on one hearing it. When his riffs and skits are set down on the page, as they have been in two anthologies (*Tragically I Was An Only Twin* and *Goodbye Again*), they can seem the aimless, drifting flotsam and jetsam of an unconcentrated mind, self-indulgent maunderings or even lifeless. It's hard to see where the joke is, what the joke is, what the point is. Cook's comedy only works, makes sense and becomes outrageously vital when it is enacted. Compare the transcript of *Entirely A Matter For You* with the recording of Cook's cataclysmic reading of it. He was a bona fide performing genius, someone who knew to a shattering degree the value of the pause. He was blessed with an incalculable talent for vocal expression and the multi-layered meanings in his work only become apparent when he spoke them in his variety of tongues.

This book has a variety of tongues all 'just thinking aloud' about Peter Cook and what was about Peter Cook. These tongues first flapped around in the pages of *Publish And Bedazzled*, the (ahem) fagazine of the Peter Cook Appreciation Society, which ran for 34 issues—discounting special editions—between 1995 and 2004. As well as modestly undertaking to interrogate every single person who may or may not have been on the same planet as Cook, the *Pub & Bed* also set about trying to locate the rare examples of Cookiana—obscure records, unfilmed scripts, alternate or unedited takes of familiar material—in an attempt to piece together his psychic jigsaw or simply to amuse our readers, the upstanding members of The Seductive Brethren. Most of this unearthed treasure has been reprinted in ...*Only Twin* and *Goodbye Again* (*sans* credit, but enough of that).

How Very Interesting is the fourth Peter Cook book. First off the blocks was *Something Like Fire: Peter Cook Remembered*, a festschrift collated by Peter's widow, Lin. A wealth of fascinating, amusing and heartfelt testimony was devalued by the editor's natural insistence that her husband was some kind of saint, the overall effect of the book being a whitewash of the darker aspects to Cook's psyche. All references to Peter's beloved family and two former wives were either excised totally or briefly mentioned in minute catty or scatty asides. One of the book's contributors, Auberon Waugh, complained in *Pub & Bed* #6 that the tome was 'repetitive, as they all say the same kind of things about him.' Much better balanced was Harry Thompson's almost brilliant biography of the magic Wisty 'un, *Peter Cook: A Biography*. although its central flaw is the one common to most life stories—i.e. seeing it as a simple rise and fall. According to Thompson, Cook reached the apex of his private and creative life in 1970. The collapse of his first marriage and the catastrophic disaster that was his live TV chat show *Where Do I Sit?*—both in 1971—were the dual summits of the slippery slope of irreversible decline. This theory was merely a third-rate movie plot device; real life is just not like that.

Pete And Dud: An Illustrated Biography by Alexander Games happily eschewed chronology in favour of juxtaposing the nigh incompatible personalities of Cook and Moore and examining their unique chemistry in collaboration. Games' analysis of their work was right on the money but the text was marred by gossip columny twaddle about their showbiz lifestyles which was probably at the insistence of some *Hello!*-reading 19-year-old publisher.

This book differs from all the above titles in that *Publish And Bedazzled* was strictly a labour of love, a by-the-fans-for-the-fans enterprise, and within the loose structures and strictures of a fanzine we could afford to spend ten pages or more rambling about *The Rise And Rise Of Michael Rimmer*, Cook's 1970 flawed cinematic masterpiece, or his post-Punk music show *Revolver*. Indeed, we spent almost an entire issue dedicated to *Bedazzled*. And why not? In a positive sense, *How Very Interesting* is like a disc of DVD extras accompanying the main feature (the three previous books) although, in this particular case, one needn't necessarily have seen the prequels to this book to gain illumination and satori from its pages. ('Ho ho, very satorical' I hear a distant groan.)

To preserve the distinct flavour of these articles' origins, the jokey—if not completely idiotic—introductions have been retained. This decision is a conscious one arrived at through long discussions with this volume's co-editors Dan Kieran (who was named after the guitar riff of The Who's 'Baba O'Riley') and Peter Gordon, my old mucker at the *P&B*. We agreed that it lent the proceedings a merry air—and also spared us the agony of flogging our atrophied old peanut brains trying to conjure up new ones.

PAUL HAMILTON

SICOPHANT

To the pcas,

What the dickins are you trying (and I say again... Trying) to do here. The Peter Cook appreciation society my arse, more like the 'I am trying (very!) to write something in the style of the great man, but am trying far to hard' society. Stop it you childish moron...it is simply not working! Just live your own sad little life and stop living the life of someone you obviously regard highly, as do many many others, but by doing so, are ruining for = those with half a brain.

So please GROW UP and find your own style. Stop plagarising the form of others for everyone elses sake Good night.

GAZ LLOYD-HUGHES, via email.

THE STORY SO FAR...

GRAMS: *Dick Barton Special Agent Theme*

ANNOUNCER: We present: *Peter Cook, A Cautionary Tale*. The story so far... Peter Edward Cook is born 17 November 1937 in Torquay, Devon. Even at this young age he was already the eldest child of Alexander and Margaret Cook. Alexander was a diplomat, administering various sections of the glorious British empire and his son was expected to follow in his prestigious wake.

GRAMS: *All Things Bright And Beautiful*

ANNOUNCER: The young Peter is sent packing to Radley College, a public school near Oxford. Here he showed a flair for performance, playing in several school plays, and as a writer, penning the libretto to a musical for Radley's Marionette Society, *Black & White Blues*, and earning pocket money submitting snippets to humorous magazine *Punch*. But it was also here that he came into contact with the demon force that would bring his ultimate downfall... Comedy.

GRAMS: *Ying Tong Song*

ANNOUNCER: For it was now that he would encounter the heady

influence of The Goon Show. Obsessed by their madcap chatter-
ings, Cook would feign illness just so he could listen to their shows.
He even wrote a Goon Show all of his own and sent it to their
ringleader, Spike Milligan. Cook's experiments with low humour
led him to invent two routines; one a lampoon of a mesmerically
dull school servant Arthur Boylett, who wondered whether a stone
might be worth money because he thought he saw it move; and
another a piece of pseudo-hagiography about the Holy Bee of St
Ephesus.

It is now 1957 and time for young Cook to leave school and face
the responsibilities of adulthood at Pembroke College, Cambridge.
Will he grow sure and steady into the fine ambassador for Queen
and Country that duty and destiny demands? Or will he succumb
to his craven desire for comedy and cheap entertainments? Read
on...

FORTUNE: COOKIE

Way, way back about three seconds ago when some of you were as old as I am now, Alexander Games was a-pondering the question of comedy teams for his double-biography of Peter Cook and Dudley Moore. Who better to interrogate, then, than Tonybenn-eyed satire bwana John Fortune? Nowadays rightly acclaimed for his duologues with John Bird, Fortune also collaborated with Cook on comedy sketches when they were Footlights and fancy free students in Cambridge. Let's eavesdrop on Alex and John as they natter away a tea-punctuated Chiswick afternoon...

JOHN FORTUNE: The whole question of collaboration is very interesting because, I mean, I've done it all my life with, you know, Eleanor [Bron], John Bird, John Wells, Alan Bennett and, of course, Peter. I first met Peter at Cambridge. When I was in my second year I directed the Footlights revue and wrote most of it with Peter. David Frost was in the cast. It was a show called *Pop Goes Mrs. Jessop*, I remember. The first money I actually ever earned professionally was in writing a sketch with Peter for one of those West End revues—*One Over The Eight*, I think, with Fenella

Fielding. It was a sketch set down in a coalmine and the whole thing was the miners were Pakistanis for some reason and they had similar accents to the Welsh, so it was all: 'Have you seen my biryani?' Peter had written quite a lot of sketches for this show but that was the only one we wrote together for it, and it was very nice to get a cheque every couple of months.

ALEX GAMES: Was that subject matter—coalmining—the inspiration for the *Sitting On A Bench* monologue about he could've been a judge?

JF: No, but that 'I could've been a judge' monologue first appeared in [... *Jessop*]. It's quite interesting that the Footlights, which in my first year had been directed by John Bird [*The Last Laugh*] and in which every sketch in it ended with a death and was all about the end of the world, why suddenly the Footlights were doing these kinds of jokes rather than what had happened for generations beforehand—you know, jokes about punts and bedmakers and boys dressed up as girls—and after we left it went back to that for a while. I think the reason was we were all very interested in the class system—and we kind of had to be because John Bird and I came from very similar, lower middle-class, grammar school backgrounds, coming to Cambridge on scholarships. And Peter, because of his family's colonial experience, also saw British society somewhat from the outside.

Back to collaboration and the reason I think why in Peter and Dudley's work Dudley never got the credit that perhaps he deserves. Because if you ever tried to collaborate with Peter it was next door to impossible. The thing is, at the end of a successful collaboration, you always feel: 'Oh, I was the passenger: John Bird had all the ideas and all the jokes,' you know, 'I'm only there to make the tea and coax him into genius,' that sort of feeling. But when one actually looks at the material one thinks: 'Oh that was my idea.' Because we, John and I, improvise a lot, it has to be like that—otherwise it would be a monologue. But with Peter, it was a monologue because once he'd got going there was no way into his fantasy. It was almost like a disease, a mental disease, in that—going back to mining—he just mined a seam in his head, and there was no way you could be in it with him.

At the beginning of The Establishment, I remember by about teatime we'd have to beg Peter to stop because we'd be laughing so much it hurt. You actually got a stomach ache from it.

AG: But you and the others were comic writers yourselves, didn't you ever feel a kind of rivalry in those situations? Could you say to him: 'Stop! I can say something funny as well if only you'd let me?'

JF: Umm, yes, in a way. But the point I'm making about Dudley is, actually, Dudley could collaborate—a lot. I think part of the duets where they're in mufflers and caps, Dudley could draw on a lot of his experiences. A great strength and charm of Dudley's humour was that it does come from being the boy who was never picked for the football team. And having problems. Even at that time he was very troubled about who he was. Whereas my love of collaboration is that, you know, you only need half an idea, there was never any shortage of ideas with Peter. What you needed was an enormous courage to jump into the improvisation and contribute.

AG: And if you did, would he let you in?

JF: Yes, he was very generous and if you said something funny he would fall about. I'd done quite a bit with Peter, but I'd be The Straight Man, I'd be the person reading the newspaper when he comes up saying: 'I've got a viper in this box' kind of thing. And there the only skill required is to not corpse.

AG: Was he trying to make you corpse?

JF: Oh yes. This was why, in a way, I mean he was a genius but he was a terrible actor. [Laughing] I mean, embarrassingly bad. When he acted he'd look at you like that, always.

AG: A sideways stare.

JF: That's right and he'd challenge you to keep a straight face.

AG: This is one of the paradoxes—brilliant performer, terrible actor.

JF: It's the same with Rory Bremner. You know, get Rory to play Robin Cook and it's all there—the voice, the face, the works—and he's brilliant. But ask him to be the England cricket captain and say: 'I've got the batting order here,' he would be hopeless.

AG: But Peter wasn't really an impressionist –

JF: No, not really. He just had these voices. But those things he did [on *Clive Anderson Talks Back*, Xmas 1993], he was a wonderful actor there because you really believed in the character.

AG: So, what had happened there?

JF: I think that in his head he had done it so often that he became them and they became him.

AG: You said you directed *Pop Goes Mrs. Jessop* at Cambridge. What was it like directing him?

JF: Well, I had never directed before, really, so [*Laughs*] I didn't know what I was doing either. It was mainly issues of 'Where shall we put this bench?' and 'Do you want to stand further up-stage?' The title of the show was mine. It was just surreal—I just had this notion of a woman exploding. And 'Jessop' is a subconscious thing; I come from Bristol and one of the greatest cricketers ever to come out of Bristol was Gilbert Jessop. A big six-hitter.

I wrote one of the first reviews of *Beyond The Fringe*, when it played at The Arch [Arts] in Cambridge after the Edinburgh opening. That's when Peter went into full flight.

AG: Where did the review appear?

JF: The Cambridge Review, a sort of grown-up university, er, reviews of academic works. *Beyond The Fringe* was a revelation, because I had never seen Dudley, I knew Jonathan—slightly, and I'd never seen Alan, and I sort of knew what Peter did. The two things I remember about seeing *BTF* for the first time was Alan's sermon and Peter doing Macmillan, because nothing that we had ever done at Cambridge was political, really.

AG: But political cabaret was what you went on to produce at Peter's Establishment Club.

JF: Yes, Peter had the idea of a club because it meant you didn't have to submit scripts to the Lord Chamberlain's Office [*The LCO was the theatrical censor until 1968*—Ed.] and he wanted to do political jokes. The greatest disservice done to the Establishment was by Jonathan Miller in *The Sunday Times* the weekend before the club opened. Poor Jonathan, he thought—in his lofty way—he was doing us a favour, but we couldn't possibly live up to that kind of hype.

Also, something which we could not possibly have foreseen was—because it was a membership club—everybody would want to come to the opening night. I mean, we were very, very stupid. So when it opened, the show was two hours late because there were five times too many people who could get in wanted to get in. Comfortably it could have accommodated about a hundred. It was a long narrow room. I was very nervous and the first sketch was a crucifixion scene—it was a class thing—with me as Christ and Jeremy Geidt and John Bird as two crucified criminals moaning: 'Oh, why are you so much higher than us?' and so on. As the lights went out I noticed in the front row Harold Hobson [drama critic for *The Sunday Times*] whom I recognised because I knew he had a club foot encased in an enormous built-up shoe, and apparently was very religious. We had a small stage and in the black-out after the sketch I stepped on his club foot. I thought: 'Well, that's *The Sunday Times* gone for a start!' His review was pretty dismissive but then I think most of them said: 'Oh, I thought this was going to bring down the government.'

We used to do two shows a night and then John and I would go down to a snooker club in Windmill Street where all the cab drivers played, and play all night. Amazing to be young.

AG: What was the structure of the club? Was there a bar?

JF: There was a bar as you came in, and then it opened out a little bit and there were tables where people had dinner, and there was a stage. You could go downstairs to the basement where Dudley and his band would play jazz.

AG: Were Peter and Dudley bonding at this time?

JF: No, they were just the lads from *BTF*. Jonathan I don't recall ever going to the club and I don't think Alan ever went either. But Peter always said he and Dudley were the showbiz people whereas Jonathan's an intellectual snob and Alan wants to go home and have his cocoa. The success of their partnership and the seeds of its problems for both of them was due to their keenness to exploit the success of *BTF*. Because the other thing that went on—and you've got to remember we were all very young, just out of Cambridge—I never saw this as a career and certainly Eleanor didn't; I had to persuade her to give up a perfectly good job with De La Rue who make banknotes—that very soon we were all going to get a proper job. This feeling was partly reinforced by Jonathan being a doctor, as he never stopped telling you [*Chuckles*] and, for him, this was a brief hiatus. He was going to be the professor of neuro-physiology somewhere. Alan was then the most unlikely showbiz person. They were kind of examples of what the rest of us would have to be. So that when *BTF* eventually stopped and 'B' companies toured it round Australia—with Peter Bellwood and people like that—something had to happen to Peter [Cook]. The Establishment was bought from Nick Luard by a gangster called Raymond Naish who persuaded us to come back from New York and do another show. But the writing was on the wall for The Establishment because the reason Raymond Naish wanted it was so that he could open a casino upstairs and fleece the middle-class clientele, which I think he did in the end. It was terrible vandalism because the upstairs was [theatre set designer] Sean Kenny's studio...

There was this show called *Behind The Fridge* [starring Peter and Dudley] which was at The Cambridge [Theatre] and then they took it to America and started touring it, I dunno. That show was just the two of them. And Peter told me later on that it was desperate, you know? Because there are tensions between couples and playing exactly the same material every night with just the two of you. And travelling around. With Peter, one of his ambitions was always to be a rock musician and, you know, have groupies and all that sort of thing. And Dudley was a musician and did have groupies [*Chuckles*] and, erm, I think that kind of boredom and the fact that, y'know, given any kind of provocation, Dudley would tell you all about his psychological problems and his childhood bedwetting, whatever, and *Reader's Digest* psychobabble. And Peter, without much provocation, would go into one of his fantasies, and I'm sure Dudley, rather than say: 'Please stop, Peter, because it hurts too much to go on laughing,' he would just say: 'Oh no, not again.' I don't know, but I imagine that was the case. So the kind of stuff you're left with is getting pissed and fucking, really.

And the thing which did amaze me about Peter—and I don't know where it came from but I suspect it was from being an international celebrity and chat shows and having to advertise the show and having to go on radio and all that kind of thing—was that he seemed to lose all his curiosity about politics. Because one of the things Alan [Bennett] reminded me of at Peter's memorial was that in the early '60s whenever you saw Peter it was with every newspaper that had been published under his arm, and he just read newspapers like a madman. He was fascinated with politics. You know that *That Was The Week That Was* was originally going to be The Establishment On Television? And in fact we did a pilot in which that's what it was, really, and David Frost was in it but in a very marginal way. And Peter's contempt for David—which had started at Cambridge because David was treasurer of the Footlights Club and the editor of Granta and, um, very, very ambitious. He'd got a summer job with Anglia Television one year. But in the Footlights there was a big old box where people, when they had done a sketch, had chucked the scripts in, so there were sketches in there from the 18-whenever The Footlights started. And David, one summer, combed through these sketches and found the ones that he thought were commercial and either flogged them or kept them and used them himself. I remember when we had the club in New York, David coming over as—as now—a star. We had lunch together and the first thing that happened was David sent the food back because it wasn't good enough. I'd only ever seen that behaviour in the movies. And when better food was served he was talking about *TW3* and its millions of viewers and he said: 'I only see this show as a platform.' I said: 'A platform for what?' He replied: 'I'm very seriously thinking of going into politics and I think I may be offered a safe seat.' I've got the feeling it was for the Liberals but the only safe seat for the Liberals is in the Orkneys or somewhere. I told Peter this and I remember him falling down with laughter.

AG: How did The Establishment fare with American audiences?

JF: It was a wonderful success because nobody in New York was doing that sort of thing. We did topical political jokes about America. We only performed the crucifixion scene once, on the opening night. The next day we had the most amazing reviews; you couldn't have written them for yourself. We went into the club for a drink before the show, full of ourselves, when two of the biggest men you've ever seen in the biggest overcoats you've ever seen, arrived and said: 'We're from Cardinal Spellman's office and you won't be doing the crucifixion scene tonight.'

AG: And, of course, [in April 1962] you had an American appear in the London Establishment: Lenny Bruce.

JF: I was very fond of Lenny. Together with Peter, he was the best

I ever saw. He stayed with me when he first was in London and it was very funny because he'd gotten this doctor in Harley Street to prescribe him heroin, and we used to go to John Bell & Croyden [*Large pharmacy in Wigmore Street, round the corner from Harley Street*—Ed.] with his prescription—that he had to get every day. He could get it at midnight so we'd go in about 10 to 12. By that time only the pharmacy was open—the rest of the shop was shut off by these hospital folding screens. And we'd go in and see all these twitchy people hanging around—addicts, most of them—and Lenny would go up to them and say: 'What are you so miserable about? Christ, in five minutes you're gonna get some heroin! Isn't that wonderful?' Then, after he's obtained his heroin, we're going out and Lenny pulls one of these screens aside and there's someone getting a fix, and Lenny's: 'Grrr, can't you wait until you're in the cab?' He was wonderful!

AG: Peter was a fan of Lenny Bruce too, wasn't he?

JF: Yes. How could one not be? He was a revelation. To have someone onstage saying: 'Did someone say "Fuck you"? "Fuck me"? That's not an insult, man, that's beautiful! If you wanna insult me, say "Un-fuck you."' I've never seen people—respectable middle-class—leave a place fast enough. Just hilarious.

AG: Peter, with Dudley, attempted something similar in terms of language and attitude with *Derek & Clive*. Were you exposed to that?

JF: Yeah! Yeah!

AG: And what do you think of it?

JF: Yeah, I think it's very good. I think, at the time, they thought, by the lobsters and Jayne Mansfield and all the rest of it, they could get some kind of jazzy improvisation by using material that had to be completely fresh because nobody did it. I mean, nobody talked like that. I think that's a good thing to do.

AG: It's interesting you use the adjective 'jazzy' because, for Cook, it's as if it was jazz.

JF: Yeah, yeah.

AG: About Peter's political comedy: He seemed to lack the antipathy one senses in the socio-political sketches by John Bird and yourself.

JF: That's true. John has a visceral antipathy to some politics and some politicians. I used to be pretty indifferent, really, to the government—I just considered political comedy to be as good as any other kind—but since this government's come to power [*Laughs*] I feel much more strongly about it. It's weird.

Peter saw politicians as innately absurd. We were talking once about some minister—it might have been Michael Howard—who had gone on TV to defend the indefensible, and we were both saying: 'They don't have to do it. They can say "No, I'm opening a fête, I'm busy," but they're so vain that, even to be made to look stupid, they can't resist.' I don't find that disgusting like John perhaps would.

The difference between my collaboration with John and Peter's collaboration with Dudley is that we—John and I—share political beliefs broadly and had similar upbringings, although we are very different personalities. But we are close friends. He's not only my oldest friend, I suppose, apart from one or two from school, but my closest friend. If I was in real trouble he'd be the first person I'd go to. But you couldn't say that about Dudley and Peter.

AG: Did Peter have that relationship with anyone?

JF: Not really, no.

AG: Something you said once about your difficulty in making yourself lovable to an audience is interesting because Cook had a similar trouble. He wasn't as lovable as Dudley.

JF: That's right. What I was talking about was that when we do our bits on Rory Bremner's show, we never address the audience—ever. But then we did a stage show last year where we had to, for the first time, and it was actually quite liberating. But no, Peter could never be Bob Monkhouse. Because Peter always gave people that sideways look, and people would feel alarmed that they were being scrutinised.

AG: Right. You once said that when you and John are working, occasionally an idea would come up and you'd say: 'That's a Peter Cook one.'

JF: Yes. I remember John and I once did a whole thing about going out in the morning and seeing this flying insect going past with black and yellow stripes and follow it for miles and miles, desperately hoping that it would lead us to some honey, but alas it was not a bee. That is a very Peter Cook kind of construction and you occasionally find yourself doing that sort of surreal thing. We did another one about the Millennium and how the focus of the Millennium was going to be the Queen Mother and, you know, she's 99 and what would happen if she died and one of the suggestions was a 300-foot-long inflatable Queen Mother that would be towed along by a Spitfire. The ghost of Peter hovers over that kind of idea.

THE MIDWIFE OF SATIRE

A guy called John Bassett—who never gets any credit: JOHN BASSETT! is the name—was the one who put [*Beyond The Fringe*] together. It was his idea.

Peter Cook, 1979

All my life I've been an impresario but never taken or made any money out of it—which is a very good way to keep friends but not a way to make a living.

John Bassett, 1999

*Born in October 1934 in Hampstead, John Bassett has acted as literary agent for Coward, Maugham and Beckett, discovered scriptwriter Eric Chappell (*Rising Damp*, etc.), worked and played in TV for 25 years ('director, producer, voice-over, any old thing') before he went freelance and 'promptly fell apart'. It was while running a barge in France for seven years that he admits to 'never having been so happy'. He is currently involved in 'doing up' his son's flat. 'It's been a rewarding life,' he says with no trace of bitterness but perhaps a truckful of irony.*

Enormous fangs are extended to Harry 'TV' Thompson who arranged a meeting in November 1998 betwixt the Paul Hamilton and John Bassett over nibbles'n'slurps at fashionable Charlotte St scrannerie Bert O'Riley's ('Shurely "Bertorelli's"?'—Ed.). John, as no one knows, was the catalyst of Beyond The Fringe, *the show that won the 1962 World Cup, cured baldness, invented colour and singlehandedly started the Vietnam war. Most of the following interview took place after burps in TalkBack Productions' office, a vomit's fling from Charlotte St, with ickle-wickle bits and bobs included hith and thith from a January '99 yak in a boozeslurpey in NW3.*

PAUL HAMILTON: Where does it all begin?

JOHN BASSETT: 1960. I was Assistant Artistic Director of the Edinburgh Festival, under Robert Ponsonby, from 1959. *Beyond The Fringe* was 1960—August 22nd, 10.45 at the Lyceum Theatre, Edinburgh.

What is absolutely fantastic about that was it opened to 32% capacity, which is nothing; 1300, 1400 seats and only 200 people. But from word of mouth from the first night, the remaining performances played to 120% capacity.

PH: What was your intention behind *BTF*? Bringing together Oxford and Cambridge?

JB: It was just an extension from my part of all the sketches and cabaret items that Jonathan, Alan and Dudley had done. Jonathan was eager to make money at the time as he was a doctor and very badly paid.

PH: Was he at UCH [University College Hospital, off Tottenham Court Road]?

JB: That's right. Which is why our first meeting with Peter was in the Italian restaurant—now destroyed, but roughly where Thames Television was, next to the old Capital Radio building—so that

Jonathan could dash out for lunch. But Robert Ponsonby deserves a lot of credit. It's all very well for me to introduce him to funny young guys but it was he who took the chance in putting it on. It was his reputation on the line. It was only one of who-knows-how-many shows in the Festival but it was an important one because the whole point was to do late-night entertainment and get some of the business that up till then the fringe—the non-Festival events—had been getting.

PH: Is it true Jonathan Miller was once called 'The Danny Kaye Of Cambridge'?

JB: Yes, I'm sure he was. He had the manic thing; he flails his arms; he's Jewish, like Danny Kaye was; he does stream-of-consciousness stuff, though on a higher plane, I think, than Danny Kaye. It seems to me an entirely appropriate analogy, except I'm sure Jonathan feels he has a far more educated mind and that his talents are infinitely more widespread than just flailing round the stage and doing streams of gibberish.

PH: You knew Dudley from way back.

JB: I first met Dudley in the cloisters and silent echoing empty spaces of the chapel in Magdalen College. Dudley was the Magdalen organ scholar, which meant he got free tuition for the four years he was there in return for playing the organ at all the church services. Anthony Page, now a famous theatrical director but then an undergraduate, heard that I could play the trumpet. Dudley needed a trumpet player to play the score he had written for a production of *The Changeling*, to be performed at the abbey there. Little did he know I was musically illiterate—I was 95% jazz, so the dots befuddled me. So all Dudley's writing went for naught and he very kindly said, 'Just play what you feel like and I'll follow along behind you on the organ'. He obviously understood that I was keen on jazz and played it, and he had a reasonable collection of Erroll Garner, the pianist he admired most. But Dudley hadn't then twigged how jazz is put together and, indeed, improvising on a chord sequence is something that has usually escaped most classical musicians, if that's the right name for them. The pianist in my band, in effect, turned the key for Dudley to learn how to play jazz and Dudley never looked back. I am convinced that once Dudley learned to play jazz, as he did in my band, his whole social life changed and, from that day, his reputation with women started. When I first met him, a quieter, shyer, more private, timorous individual it would be hard to think of... John Bassett & His Band played Union cellars and May Balls, plus the Dorchester and Savoy hotels. We began getting recording contracts, none of which have been issued because, just as we were taping the last tracks for a lovely LP, The Beatles burst upon the scene and nobody wanted jazz anymore.

PH: Amongst all this activity you were the Assistant Artistic Director at the Edinburgh Festival, of course.

JB: Hmm. My first year there, 1959, I was finding my feet and the second year was when Robert decided on late-night entertainments. Les Freres Jacques, a group from France, was booked, and I can't recall the second act, but I had fairly intentionally overspent the budget so there wasn't enough real money for another act of standing which, to a certain degree, forced Robert's hand to accept the four guys. They got £100 each for the week, but then Donald Langdon, Peter's terrible agent, came in and insisted on £110 for Peter. This naturally soured relations between the four of them. But the net result was, after Langdon took his agent's fee of 10%, Peter was left with £99. Quite why Peter stuck with Langdon after that... I mean to say, everyone's entitled to make mistakes, but Langdon, all along, was insisting Peter should have nothing to do with the show: 'It's only a lot of tatty undergraduates and it would ruin your career.' That's not apocryphal, if I'm using the word rightly: that is absolutely true. So quite why Peter carried on using him, I don't know, except Peter had a wonderful theory that I think is quite right, that human beings always do make mistakes so by definition your agent is going to make mistakes, therefore he's going to screw your career up at some point so you might as well have someone you can't stand so you can scream and shout at them.

PH: A strange thing about their first meeting at the restaurant is that none of the quartet can remember the type of food—Chinese, Indian—but they all agree the food was ghastly.

JB: Oh! [*Giggles*] No, the restaurant was quite definitely Span—er, Italian. Absolutely definitely Italian. And I do recall Dudley doing a Groucho Marx act, following a rather sexy waitress out through those swing-doors and re-enter following another waitress and copying her walk. Peter was exceptionally funny, which was both a challenge and a relief. He was easily as funny as any of them had thought and maybe, in a large number of areas, much funnier. They all had their specialities though it is true to say that Peter's humour was a much broader, scattergun effect because he read every single newspaper every single day. He picked up thousands of little-known facts, idiosyncrasies, one-liners, all of which widened his comic vision. I can't begin to think how he got any work done at all at Pembroke College. Tons of newspaper used to flood out of his house every day and he had read them all. Items in the more lightweight tabloids would form the basis of his humour. But actually physically reading all this stuff! Even speed-reading is time-consuming, on the scale he read.

PH: And the others, were they, back then, just like the public perceives them to be? Like, was Alan Bennett shy and subdued?

JB: Alan was shy and sharp. He comes out with good one-liners but he bides his time. He doesn't believe in gabbing for the sake of it. Every word has got to count for Alan and that is totally apparent in his writing.

PH: Is it true Dudley had a mime act where he had a violin that, er, behaved like a baby?

JB: Oh yes!!

PH: Did he perform that at the restaurant?

JB: No, he wouldn't have taken his violin along.

PH: Oh, I see. I understood it was a mime—not with a real violin.

JB: No, it's because he could make a violin sound like a crying baby. Now this is years ago but I do recall he creates this baby-crying noise on the violin and then starts cuddling the violin as if it were a baby.

PH: Did Dudley audition that piece for inclusion in the show?

JB: No. They were all quite shy of demonstrating their talents. In fact, I have maintained that the main basis of 16 of the sketches is Peter. But that wonderful speech in the Shakespeare parody—'Get thee to Gloucester, Essex. Do thee to Wessex, Exeter. Fair Albany to Somerset...'—that is a Jonathan insertion. Dudley's contributions are mostly musical ones, from the Colonel Bogey solo to the very good incidental music that occurs in the poignant moments of Aftermyth Of War.

PH: How much of *BTF* had already been written before they all met up?

JB: Quite a lot. Peter had a lot of sketches scudding about. Jonathan was, and remains, a very dominant personality and he was very dominant in the Edinburgh rehearsals when there was no real director other than me, and all I was doing was coordinating and dashing back to the office to do other things for the Festival. Jonathan was the great one for the visual ideas and the show's bare simplicity—like a hat to suggest an RAF officer rather than a full uniform. In Edinburgh they all wore grey trousers and jumpers, not suits like they did in London. A piano, a table and four chairs was practically the entire inventory of the prop list.

PH: Was there any conflict between the writers as to what sketches should be used and what should be dropped?

JB: No. I think when you're dealing on the level of talent they had—they don't mind if an idea doesn't quite come off because they recognise it themselves; so they're not defending a thing. It's a lesser talent who would spend a long time thinking up a joke who will then defend it and be upset when it's cut. On the level of those four, they recognise the greater good of everybody—and, many times, a first attempt at a good line was cut and rewritten to the eventual benefit of everyone.

PH: Yes, I've had a butcher's at the original scripts submitted to the Lord Chamberlain's Office for censorship, and there are plenty of rewrites—T.V.P.M. for example, and a few versions of Alan's 'Vicar' monologue.

JB: I've certainly heard about eight or ten versions of that sketch. I'm sure that's how Alan works... Everything was stacked against us at Edinburgh what with the actual fringe revues and events going on and our show having no publicity at all and being on late at night. No one had heard of the four boys and why should they? But it was cataclysmic, that first night. It really was unbelievable. They performed roughly 20, 25 pieces.

PH: What's that, about an hour?

JB: Yes, it was a short hour. The show was expanded at the Fortune Theatre in London. The Edinburgh show hadn't an interval. If you see the original programme, none of the sketch titles seem to have any reference to anything at all. Then there was the fight to obtain the rights to bring the show to London, which Willie Donaldson won—for all the wrong reasons, although he's a very sweet guy.

PH: He's the *Henry Root* man.

JB: He is *Henry Root*. I think it was four or five months before we went to London, and that was preceded by try-outs in Brighton and

Cambridge. And Willie, because he didn't quite have the confidence in himself—

PH: Didn't he lose a fortune on *Here Is The News*, the John Bird revue?

JB: He lost a fortune on a vast number of things. He has always maintained that he put on a revue with John Bird and Eleanor Bron which was very mishandled but, had it come to London, then *BTF* never would have. Or certainly wouldn't have had the effect that it did. Anyway, that show folded in Blackpool or Oxford, I don't know; John Bird or Eleanor Bron could tell you more about it, but the scenery didn't arrive on time and the venues they played weren't suitable to their kind of humour, Willie ran out of money—oh, disaster!

PH: So how did he become involved?

JB: The big reason was that he had made the offer before *BTF* had even opened in Edinburgh. He had bought a small management called Jack Waller Limited and there was an old boy who came with the furniture; this old boy was always there, and Willie was so sweet he couldn't tell him to leave. This old boy came in and it's, 'Oi remember the old days'n'rrraahhhhhhhn.' He went on and on and did absolutely nothing. But he was very sweet... However, we said to Willie if he could match the top price offered for the show by the London managements he could have it. In a sense, I'm very glad we did because, for my part, Donald Langdon rode me out of the show very quickly. I got £40 a week for two weeks to do the publicity as it arrived in London, whereas I'd normally expect 2% of the gross, which would've been Big Money. But Willie voluntarily gave me 1% of the gross which was a totally uncalled-for and generous gesture. It is said that Willie had given bits and pieces away to investors to such an extent that eventually he was giving away more than the show could take—like the film *The Producers*, where they're paying out more than they earn. Whether that's true or not I don't know but certainly he didn't make a fortune out of it and he should've. Willie also produced *The Gingerbread Man* and *The Bedsitting Room*, and Spike Milligan always maintained that it was Willie who saved his life when he was terribly depressed. It was Willie who put Milligan into *The Bedsitting Room*, showed confidence in him and turned up every night to see him. But I don't think Willie made a bean out of that show, either.

PH: *Beyond The Fringe*, prior to London, played in Brighton.

JB: Yes, the famous bad review—and, indeed, it nearly killed the show because Willie, insofar as he lacked self-confidence, took on Sir Donald Albery as a co-producer, who had promised us the Wyndham Theatre, which would have been magical. But he then betrayed us, as he [*giggles*] had a reputation for doing. Wyndham's is more than treble the size of the Fortune Theatre, so you can imagine the box-office takings over a two-year run. Albery never liked the show, didn't understand it, but that never stopped him constantly taking credit for it. But this one—God almighty!—bad review in Brighton was hysterical because it was very, very, very bad but, in the guarded tones of the '60s, it sort of said things like 'Why make fun of Mr. Macmillan? Either you like him, in which case you keep quiet and support him, or you don't like him, in which case you keep quiet out of politeness. Why make fun of amateur productions of Shakespeare? They bring culture to the masses, dadadada. Why make fun of Civil Defence? It's doing its best in these difficult times, da da. Why mock homosexuals?' And so on. It was a vitriolic review, too, rather than a list of rhetorical questions: 'The four of them are untalented and incapable, it's ill-disciplined, the dreary scenery, bah bah bah bah bah.' We then found that the reviewer in question had been personally affronted by every single sketch insofar as he was gay, he was the local Conservative Party agent, he was involved in Civil Defence and amateur theatricals... There wasn't a sketch that didn't affect him. What was so appalling was the grand old knight of the theatre, Sir Donald Albery—son of

Sir Ronson Albery, you know, services to the theatrical profession and all that balls—could have been so feeble as to pull the show. He said to Willie, 'Well, on your own head be it.' So Willie took it to the Fortune where it was an enormous success, and suddenly Albery had his hand out again for his half of the production takings.

PH: Who out of the Fringe team could you have easily thrashed in a fight?

JB: Ah! [*Laughs*]

PH: Come on, who could you have duffed up?

JB: Absolutely none of them. I was in thrall to all four. I thought Jonathan used to show off by swearing a little unnecessarily. Dudley was practically late for everything, all the time. When I asked him to provide orchestrations for my band I had to tell him the deadline was a week before they were really due—and he was still late delivering the scores! The opening night in Edinburgh was the classic story of Dudley being late. They were all given dressing-rooms way up on the top floor because the main production at the Lyceum was *The Double Dealer* with Ralph Richardson, Maggie Smith and Tom Courteney and they, naturally enough, had the 'star' dressing-rooms and whatnot. So the boys are relegated right to the top. Now, as you know, the opening sketch in Fringe—Steppes In The Right Direction—has Peter, Jon and Alan onstage burbling and fiddling about. Then Dudley comes on and plays *God Save The Queen* on the piano. This was to take the piss out of the fact that in those days all shows had to start with the National Anthem and the audience would stand to attention. But because the anthem was incorporated into the sketch, people wouldn't know whether to stand up or sit down. If you hear a disc of *BTF* you'll notice how confused the audience seem. Dudley was playing a Russian who was extremely patriotic—to this country—and he couldn't play anything but *God Save The Queen*. He played it through once, and the audience stood up, and then he played the first eight bars again which is where the confusion started setting in: 'Do we stand up again? Do we remain seated?' The sketch was supposed to start with the other three talking about this Russian defector, whereupon Dudley would appear and start playing. Only he didn't. Dudley missed his cue so Peter, Alan and Jon began improvising and covering up—'Is that him coming now?'—you know, willing him on. And then we heard the pulling of a lavatory chain, and a door opening and slamming, then this merry I've-got-all-the-time-in-the-world whistling and slowly coming down the stone stairs, dom dom dom dom. Everybody knew he was four floors up and the speed he was taking meant it was going to be a long time before he appeared. That's Dudley's time-keeping.

PH: How long was it, do you think, before Peter and Dudley began forming their comedic partnership?

JB: It wasn't apparent at all in the beginning. Not even after two years in London. Jonathan and Alan were very close. They took their comedy more seriously, if you know what I mean. I'm not saying they're pompous prats at all, but they took the world more seriously, they had similar cultural instincts. They paired off in temperament. Dudley has absolutely no interest in politics and the news of the day. Peter has no interest in music apart from Elvis Presley—and imitating him. But Peter would incorporate the day's news into T.V.P.M., the Macmillan sketch. President John F. Kennedy visited the show in London and normally T.V.P.M. was eight minutes long. I maintain that the night Kennedy visited, the sketch ran for 40 minutes. Whether that's absolutely true or not, I don't know. It was very long and it didn't drag. When Macmillan came it lasted 20 minutes. Because Peter just threw everything in. But Peter had no abiding interest in jazz except as something to dance to, and no interest in classical music. So the personal interests of Peter and Dudley were not complementary and weren't shared and one didn't support the other. I suppose it was really a question of Dudley getting on Peter's wavelength more.

PH: What's this I read about Willie Donaldson taking you all to see a blue film?

JB: Yes. We'd all longed to know of the seamy side of London and Willie was the person to tell us. He had a diary, and the address section contained all his contacts for pornography and the loucher side of life under the letter 'B' for 'Blue'. How he could tell between them, I don't know, because he had 'A. Blue', 'B. Blue' and so on. I think I was a prime mover because I was fascinated—

PH: As you still are!

JB: As I still am. No, no, I'm more naive now... We all met up in a pub near Berkeley Square and were all nervous and giggly because prostitution was very much more illegal then. The brothel was off New Bond Street. Jonathan had brought his wife Rachel, Peter brought his girlfriend Wendy, Fizz [Eleanor Fazan, *BTF*'s London director] I think came along, too. There were about four women and around ten of us in all. We went to the door and Willie rang and, I don't know whether it's still true but, in those days, usually prostitutes had a maid who would be often an elderly prostitute who had gone off the game. And this rather sweet, kindly, fat old bat came down and saw us and took fright at the sight of women, and the numbers, but eventually let us in to a waiting room. There were already one or two gentlemen ahead of us enjoying the film show. We were given magazines of a supposedly salacious nature but, just to show you how innocent it was, the magazines were called *La Vie Parisienne*—i.e. all in French. Well, I know the language of nudity is international but, if I remember rightly, there were no actual photos of nude ladies at all but, instead, little charcoal sketches of nude ladies in black stockings. We thought this was so hysterically funny—it was so naive and innocent—that we were giggling until a complaint came through from the room ahead that we were spoiling their concentration on the deeply moving enactment that was going on within... We quietened down and they, quite obviously, were ushered out through another door because the thing with pornography is that no one can admit to somebody else that they enjoy it. So to catch somebody else's eye when you know they've just done what you're about to do is a sort of psychological mistake... The lady was much surprised by the size of our group and the presence of women. It was a wonderful archetypal prostitute's bedroom insofar as the bed had a quilted headboard covered in transparent talc so that, presumably, the Brylcreemed heads of the punters would not leave their muck behind. We sat down on the bed and near us was a kidney-shaped dressing table with pictures of all her children and golden retrievers and all the other things that these ladies seem to love. There was a very old 16-millimetre cinema projector. The films were black and white and silent, and they'd obviously been made in Egypt some time before the First World War because what few clothes the women had on were definitely from that period: They had stockings that were rolled up at the top—no suspenders—and high-heeled shoes with waists on the heels, which is a pre-First World War thing. The French lady—she was French—gave us a commentary. When a man came onscreen with an enormous erection, she said, 'Now ow ze gentle men in ze owdience will have a inferioriddy gomblex.' When a gentleman lay down and was being pleasured by a large number of ladies: 'Now ow ze gentle men in ze owdience will be jeallouse.' Jonathan and Rachel began giving the medical details, as they're both doctors, and some of the things that were being done were apparently pretty dangerous. Alan dived under the bed because he couldn't stand it any more. Dudley was corpsing. Peter had been a prime mover in this excursion so he was enraptured. As was I. It was just so funny and these films were so old and so scratched and so flickery, with people hitting ladies' bottoms with supposedly red-hot frying pans. It just was marvellous.

PH: You were a member of the Establishment Club.

JB: Yes.

PH: And it's reported that after performing *BTF* they would occasionally go on to perform there as well.

JB: Well, Dudley certainly did—playing the piano down in the dancing area. He'd always turn up...late. Peter, of course, did lots—it being his empire. He was very good at his intros; he liked being the compère at the Establishment. It's quite possible Jonathan may have performed occasionally—but he was pretty domesticated then and wanted to get home to Rachel and the children. Alan, I don't know. He probably went off to his cosy little bed.

PH: I'm wondering whether you could recall any of Peter's performances there.

JB: No, no. They were so 'of the moment', Peter's performances at the Establishment.

PH: Back to the Fringe: Who was this Donald Langdon? Some really old geezer?

JB: No, he was young and, give him his due, he signed up Peter. He'd gone down to the Smokers at Cambridge and seen that Peter was the most talented and so signed him up. You know, that's ace. After Donald, all the agencies went haring down there, snapping up Eleanor Bron or whoever. Eleanor, like Jonathan and others, suffered these conflicts of direction—they were studying for non-theatrical careers, and along come these agents. Peter, on the other hand, never had a conflict about it. He was going to be a writer before he went to Cambridge. So why was he doing a degree? [*Laughs*] I was working for what became the Noel Gay Agency and they asked, 'Who would you get?' And I said Frostikins. David Frost. Noel Gay's entire fortune has been based on Frost. They were virtually bankrupt and doing terribly, terribly, terribly badly, scuffling along the sidewalk before Frost.

PH: Didn't you direct *That Was The Week That Was*?

JB: No. That was Ned Sherrin. Ned was—probably still is—brilliant in manipulating bureaucrats in artistic set-ups, and the BBC then was quite artistic and did have courage in what it was doing—before it was destroyed by shitty old Birt. The old BBC had a bureaucratic layer on top of the whole artistic aesthetic set-up.

PH: Some *Fringe* sketches were performed on *TW3*—Jim's Inn, for one.

JB: Yes, that was Peter's. There was a great deal of thievery.

PH: How did Peter truly feel about David?

JB: Well... I'm not really sure. Imitation is the sincerest form of flattery, they say. I mean, the half-inching of Peter's material ceased very soon because there was a gang of very good writers. One must never forget that Peter was offered the position. When I went on for the pilots there was a spot kept open for Peter but he just couldn't be bothered to turn up.

PH: He wasn't in America at the time?

JB: No, no. Not for the pilots. He was also offered to do sketches from America and send them over, but he refused.

PH: Because he didn't want to be seen to be second fiddle to Frost?

JB: That's partly it, and also the Groucho Marx dictum: 'I'd never join a club that would accept me as a member.' It's difficult to tell. I think Peter was unreasonable but understandable [*Laughs*]. He did have absolutely every chance to be in it. It would've been a waste of him to have him as the link-man for *TW3*, but think of The Two Johns [Bird and Fortune] on Rory Bremner's show nowadays. They stand out, they are special, they're well up to the standard of Rory Bremner yet totally different to him. I don't see why Peter couldn't have done something like that. However, one must respect Peter's feelings when David Frost is performing Peter's material without either a by-your-leave or a royalty, and—in Peter's view—not performing it well and ruining it for him to perform at a later date.

PH: Did this overnight success change Peter into a big-head?

JB: No. Both he and Dudley, but particularly Peter, were immensely warm, caring and generous. There's a story, and it's true: The telephone went at his home in Church Row, and Wendy answers to hear a terribly blurry—she thought drunk or drugged—voice saying, 'Urghh, I can't stand it any more, can't stannit, 'm gonna kill myself.' KACHUNK! Hangs up. She thought, in her sleepy state—she had been woken by the phone ringing—that it was me. I was living 200 yards away, opposite the Everyman Cinema. So she woke Peter up, and Peter got his trousers on and came belting round—with a ladder—and he climbed up and smashed a window, clambered through it and immediately fell all the way down the stairs again because the window was straight over the stairwell. All this noise woke me up. I'm thinking, 'Burglars!' So I came staggering out in my pyjamas to find Peter and Wendy, who he had let in. There he was, a West End star, belting round on a mercy mission. I'm not saying other stars wouldn't do the same, but he did.

PH: Did anyone find out who the would-be suicide caller was?

JB: No. Never found out. But Peter was immensely kind and I found it very sad as he put on weight and got sort of wilder and wilder. I lived in a place above a shop near Hampstead tube station, and it had an enormous window where I could see 'street theatre', and I always saw Peter every morning walking to the newsagents. I would rush down and see him and have giggles and laughs, go to the coffee shop or whatever. And then... you begin to be so sad that you don't want to meet him, really... He was very sad, really.

PH: Why? What had happened?

JB: Well, because he was enormous, he'd put on so much weight and he was shambling about and... The last time I'd heard him was on some chat show that was really beneath his dignity, where he was doing, er, embittered humour at somebody's expense. I just found it very sad. Plus, I'd go round at Christmas time and leave him a card, or write him a letter and drop it through his letterbox, and progressively not get replies. What I'm getting at is that, should we have met by chance we would've had a conversation and so on but as one saw him with all his problems and difficulties, somehow the eagerness to run down and clap him on the shoulder dissipated. Whereas I suppose if one had spoke to him it might've ameliorated the situation.

PH: What do you think his problems were?

JB: I just don't know, I really don't. Some people, of course, talk about a jealousy of Dudley but I don't see that at all. Dudley's stardom... Peter was a star, too... His contributions to *Private Eye* are more than enough for one person; he could have just done that for the rest of his time.

PH: When the *BTF* scripts were published by Methuen in 1987, Dudley, Alan and Peter each contributed new essays for the book. After Peter's death, Dudley said he found Peter's final paragraph— where he claims he hadn't matured, progressed, become deeper, funnier or wiser since *BTF*—had moved him to tears. What do you think of Peter's self-assessment?

JB: Well, in a sense, he never stretched himself because he was already so expansive in his breadth of grasp and vision. It would be hard to think of something that would stretch him any further so therefore, in a way, there was nothing for him to be excited about. Dudley never stretched himself, either. Dudley, musically and dramatically, shouldn't be where he is now. The fascinating thing about Dudley is that he's never been in any really good films—although some have made money—but it's in the truly appalling ones that go out on TV at three in the morning where Dudley acts his best. He acts much better because it is stretching him to overcome a bad script. Dudley's trouble is it all came too easy for him. Finding challenges, y'know... Why didn't Peter write a play? He's not Alan Ayckbourn, he's very different from Ayckbourn, yes of course he is, but don't tell me he couldn't write a full-length perceptive, comic play. I was thinking about Peter last night, oddly enough, at Ronnie Scott's whilst watching Arturo Sandoval. Sandoval plays trumpet like no one else, he can play six, seven, sometimes even eight octaves higher than the acknowledged top note of a trumpet. He's got such total mastery, it's just insanity. Not to go on about this chap too much, but I said to my ex-brother-in-law, 'This is unbelievable. I saw this guy seven years ago playing at this intensity and brilliance. Do you realise he's been playing at this pressure with that sort of command virtually every single night?' Well, in the same way, Peter—who had total and utter command—was doing exactly the same but, for Peter, that wasn't enough. I'm going to see Sandoval again tomorrow, although I know it'll be the same set. I'd love to hear him do other tunes. We'd all have loved to see Peter doing other sketches but for Peter another sketch is still a sketch.

PH: How was his consistency of performances in the Fringe's run? Were there peaks and troughs? Was he erratic?

JB: No, he was absolutely perfect. He never, ever fluctuated or varied in terms of quality of performance as far as I'm aware—and I think I saw some 600 performances, from backstage.

PH: Did they ever vary the set, replacing old sketches for new to stem the onset of boredom?

JB: Not to my knowledge. He had the Macmillan sketch which he could, and would, alter, since he had sole control of it onstage.

PH: And the 'I could have been a judge', the Miner one, of course.

JB: Yes. What's strange about *BTF* is that, the Miner aside, there was very little in the way of Peter's fantasy-fuelled type of comedy.

No swarms of gigantic bees or snakes a million miles long. In fact, nearly every sketch from Peter is concerned with politics and various ridiculous facets of society—even in the Miner one, where he attacks judges.

PH: Prior to *BTF*, the quartet—with the possible exception of Dud—had mostly performed on an amateur basis to small audiences. And Jonathan Miller hadn't been on a stage since 1955-ish. Were there any instances of stage fright?

JB: I never noticed any stage fright from any of them at any point anywhere. It is astounding. I mean, the opening night at Edinburgh, with Duddles in the toilet when he should've been onstage; their handling of a potential crisis was thoroughly overcome. If Duddles had any anxieties it was due to being a Dagenham boy in an Old Etonian-dominated Oxford, but once he'd conquered that, appearing onstage was a piece of cake.

PH: How long did they take to put the show together?

JB: Just under a week which sounds amazing but when you consider each of them had two solo spots—well, that's eight items already—and they all had a backlog of finished material. Especially Peter.

PH: I wonder about the sketches that credit all four of them writing. Did they actually sit down and co-write together as a committee?

JB: No. The Civil Defence one, for example, was originally one of Peter's but it would be amended. Alan added a lot of very good extra material to it. None of the sketches were sacred—no one would mind anyone coming up and suggesting new lines or whatever. It was all very mutual and harmonious, despite the best efforts of the horrendous Donald Langdon.

PH: It's said *BTF* revolutionised British theatre, British revue, comedy and all the rest of it. I'm intrigued by what it made redundant. What was the state of British comedy in theatres by the late '50s?

JB: Well, I think the big change was, prior to *BTF*, no theatrical management could conceive of a sketch where two Oxford dons argue philosophy as being something that had universal appeal. The show's strengths lay in its choice of subject matter.

PH: Yeah, like The Suspense Is Killing Me, where Jonathan is the man waiting to be hanged: It's not something that would instantly spring to mind as being acceptable fun-for-all-the-family fare. Aftermyth Of War, too.[2]

JB: The jokes about *Diary For Timothy* and the Bader film, *Reach For The Sky*—admittedly they were quite tentative about it because World War Two was still quite raw; everyone knew someone who had died in the war. I think the difference *BTF* made was in making jokes about serious topics. It wasn't some frivolous, frothy thing.

PH: No 'I say, I say, I say' and 'I don't wish to know that'.

JB: I've never quite seen the link between *BTF* and The Goons that is forever postulated. Apart from the Miner thing there's no surrealism in the show at all.

PH: The targets are the Royals, patriotism, trendy vicars, capital punishment, and race in Black Equals White.

---

2 Kenneth Griffith, comic actor and serious documentarian, recalls being una-mused by *Beyond The Fringe*:

KG: I taxed Dudley over the [*Beyond The Fringe*] joke sketch about Royal Air Force officers and all the jargon [Aftermyth Of War]. I told him, 'If you lot stop to contemplate for a split second those terrified young men who didn't hesitate to go up and... I'm not sure you should be doing it.' He listened, you know? I didn't push the point any further.

PH: Raw feeling aside, but that sketch was more attacking the legion of glorify-ing-war-films and celluloid heroics rather than actual—

KG: Yes, but I served in the Royal Air Force, you see, and I knew a lot of fellows who went up once and didn't come back again.

JB: Oh, that Black Equals White really is embarrassing now: 'Especially the nine million black idiots who vote for me.'

PH: Lastly, why the title *Beyond The Fringe*?

JB: Robert Ponsonby was implying with the title that the talents of the four and the resources of the Lyceum Theatre were beyond the possibilities of the Festival fringe. In Edinburgh back then, the place was dead after 10.30—pubs and restaurants shut, so the fringe were creaming off vast amounts of people who wanted to spend the night enjoying themselves. This was Robert saying to the fringe, 'Anything you can do, we can do better.'

PH: And you did.

THE BACK PASSAGE

Send us your ravings, your cravings, your pavement slab engravings, be they carefully-considered theses or booze-crazed faeces...

Dear Holy,
    ... Isn't the arithmetic on the first page of the John Bassett interview a little off? If *Beyond The Fringe* played to an audience of 200 on 22nd August 1960, then for the house to have been 32% capacity, wouldn't it have to have approximately 600 seats rather than 1300 or 1400 seats? Pardon the outbreak of pedantry brought on by the fumes of corduroy and tweed I've been inhaling at University. Could you please this solve this problem before my glass of claret evaporates?
    Tally ho!
    JESSE BOPARAI of Canada.

[*Explanatory note: Upon learning of a nascent Soft Machine playing at Cook's Establishment club whilst still in their bumfluffy teens, we thought it worth a stamplick to write to rocky-bottomed old rottenhatted shipbuilder Robert Wyatt for enlightenment...*]

Hallo.

Dudley Moore's trio took a break and we passed a little audition.

Fired after one gig. End of connection, which had in any case been tenuous, with a Nickerless Lewd (? Something simla.) They wanted straight cocktail jazz, we were too experimental* perhaps. (*incompetent.)

P.S. One carried on reading Privet I though, for the Paul Foot bits.

Salut!

Robert (Wyatt)

Dear Eddie Tour,

I think it's great. But that's none of your business or mine. I have great memories of Peter Coke as E.G.Whistle on the David First show T.W.4 but I've forgotten them. This proves that if you can't remember the '60s you probably weren't there.

Yours leglessly,

Lenny Bollox

GOLDEN GRATES

To mark the 1998 release of *Private Eye* magazine's various recordings made over the past million years, we hereby present a hastily slung together pile of unreliable old wankpottery (Shurely "a meticulously-detailed and authoritative document of rare perspicacity"?—Ed.) The recordings are now in three volumes, all under the common title *Golden Satiricals. Volume 1*, subtitled *The Famous Flexies*, housing all the freebie singles given away by *Private Eye* from 1964 to 1980. The independently appointed panel of critics covering the entire spectrum of the comedy rainbow (i.e. me) award it 8 out of 10. Volume 2 (*The Swingeing Sixties*) comprises the 1964 *Blue Record* and the 1967 stage show of *Mrs Wilson's Diary* and together earn a stupendous 7.000000000001 out of 10. *Ho! Ho! Very Satirical*, the third—and entirely Cook-free volume, despite the immortal Neasden and a couple of other chortlers, trails in with only a puny 5 to its name.

INTERESTING FACTS NO.94

Here are the original release dates of the *Eye* flexidiscs slapped together on *Golden Satiricals* Volume One:

His Master's Vass (2/10/64); *I Saw Daddy Kissing Santa Claus* (18/12/64); *The Rites Of Spring* (1/4/65); *The BBC Gnome Service* (23/12/66); *The Abominable Radio Gnome* (8/12/67); *The Loneliness Of The Long Playing Record* (14/2/69); *Dear Sir, Is This A Record?* (5/12/69); *Just For The Record* (4/12/70); *Hullo Sailor* (1/12/72); *Farginson* (21/3/75); *The Sound Of Talbot* (with special guests Pamela Stephenson, Spike Milligan and Larry Adler) (5/12/80). The 'bonus goodie' *Private Eye Sings* EP (by Christopher Booker, Richard Ingrams, Willie Rushton and John Wells, with Christopher Logue reading A True Story) was first issued in November 1962.

PRIVATE EAR: A REVIEW

Peter Cook fans can pop up in the most unlikely places but I think finding one perched on the drummer's stool in Soul Godfather, Mr. Dynamite, James Brown's band has got to be one of themost fantastic locations, hasn't it? In the '60s, Clyde Stubblefield kept on the good foot on cuts like Cold Sweat, I Got The Feelin', Funky Drummer and Say It Loud—I'm Black And I'm Proud and is consequently probably the most sampled drummer of all time. It defies belief than an R & B drummer from Georgia, USA,with a practically non-stop gigging/recording schedule could find the time to seek out the work of Peter and the 'British Satire Boom', doesn't it? And then for him to come out of retirement and send us an unsolicited review of The Famous Flexies is just too much to be true, isn't it? Totally unbefuckinglievable!

THEBESTOFPRIVATEEYE:GOLDENSATIRICALS,VOLUME ONE—THE FAMOUS FLEXIES (MCI GAGDMC085)
(This title ain't long enough—Subtly Ironic Ed.)

During its first decade, the *Private Eye* team consistently produced an annual floppy 7" disc that would be given away free with the magazine. After Cook went to America in 1973 to tour his and Moore's *Good Evening* show, the appearance of subsequent 'flexies' was sporadic at best, and there have been only two since Cook's p*ssing in 1995. C'est la mort.

This double-taper collects all the flexies from 1964 to 1980 (plus the 1962 *Private Eye Sings*, which is exceedingly rare and, unfortunately, exceedingly boring), and since the material is almost exclusively based on the current events and people of the time, one might reasonably surmise that the jokes would now be arcane to the point of brain-crinkling incomprehension. Not so. You don't have to be a stiff to enjoy this stuff. For any memory mangler (Chappaquiddick or Peter O'Toole's disastrous *Macbeth*) there is a wheelbarrow of sketches that still resonate and amuse down the time tunnel, be it the Queen's attempt to be hip ('My bloke and I would like to wish all you cats and chicks a really swinging Christmas and a gear New Year') or voting intentions ('As a trade unionist, people often ask me why I am voting Conservative. The answer is because I am a stupid cunt'). The editing is razor sharp so no sketch outstays its welcome. Harold Wilson, John & Yoko, David Frost, Christian Barnard and Peter Ustinov are amongst the deserved targets for satirical attack or just plain abuse; 'pooves', however, aren't, and the 'Whoops, hello sailor'-isms expose the *Eye*sters to be as reactionary in this respect as the society the *Eye* set itself apart from and against.

For students of comedy ('Ha!-storians') it is interesting to note Peter Cook's subsequent recycling of some of this material for later projects. The Priest's Lesson in ...*Kissing Santa Claus* appears in a reworked form as Cook's closing speech in the 1969 film *The Bed Sitting Room*; Transcendental Mastication (a pisstake of The Beatles' dalliance with all things Eastern) reoccurs in a Dud and Pete Dagenham Dialogue in the 1968 *Goodbye Again* TV series; Enoch Powell's visions (from his 'crystal balls') pops up in Cook's 1970 film *The Rise And Rise Of Michael Rimmer*. (A case can be made for calling Rimmer an *Eye* film in its blunderbus-stylee blasts at politicians of all hues, advertising, the Church, TV, polls, student protests and everything else in its sights.) It also goes the other way: Cook's Idi Amin impression—rather good it is, too—was something he was concurrently performing onstage in *Behind The Fridge*. Peter Cook's presence in these tapes has a fantastic, anarchic energy and bite, but he isn't the sole star. It is a totally integrated team effort and the c*ntributions from Willie Rushton, John Wells, Barry Fantoni and Harry Bumfreeze [Shurely Barry Humphries?] are consistently rib tickling.

The Famous Flexies serves as a skewed, acerbic re-reading of recent socio-political history and poses the question, 'Do we change the times or do the times change us?' But fuck that shit, man! My boss had two axioms. They were 'Make it funky' and 'It is what it is.' Cook & Co made it funny and it still is what it was.

Clyde Stubblefield

YES, I MUST GO OFF AND GET SOME FANTONI

Private Eye *satirist, poet, musician, playwright, artist, Chinese horoscoper and hansom cab lamp fitter Barry Fantoni was twice interviewed for* Publish & Bedazzled. *His debut appearance had John Wallis quizzing him about major generalities, Cookwise. In 1998, the focus was on the origins, motives and recording sessions for* Private Eye's *flexidiscs and albums.*

What amazed the Holy Dragon was that, despite not hearing the Eye tapes for some two decades or more, Barry (who prior to this chat was unaware of the Golden Satirical *reissues) could quote lines from certain sketches with a near total recall, which says a lot about the enduring quality of funniness. (of course, he may have swotted up on the night before...)*

JOHN WALLIS: When did you first meet Peter Cook and become aware of what he was doing?

BARRY FANTONI: When he came back from the U.S., after the Fringe tour. I knew he owned the Establishment Club, and I would see the pictures outside the club of the people performing there. Lenny Bruce, Eleanor Bron, John Fortune, and others who were, or are, still capable of making us laugh. Also Jonathan Miller, the one who looks like David Hockney, and Dudley Moore, who only made us laugh when Peter was around. I'd seen pictures and some film of Peter, but then, in the early '60s, there was very little on TV except *TW3*—which Peter had nothing to do with. I never went in to the Establishment Club, coming from the background I come from I found then, and find now, that I can't stand the sound of middle class voices. especially when they laugh—even more obscene and manic. It was the most undergraduate place.

I was more involved with pop music and pop art. At the time there were a lot of public school boy types. Peter [Asher] and Gordon, and someone else with a turned-up nose. There was a market for people like that. Very aristocratic. I thought that Peter might have a natural talent in that area, and he could develop it. I didn't actually realise he had no talent for pop music whatsoever, although it was something he wanted to do and be associated with.

It is true to say of Peter that of his many talents singing was not one of them. He had no ability to play any musical instrument, but then that didn't get in the way of Mick Jagger or anybody else. The truth is that to be a really fabulous pop star, which Peter wanted to be, you have to be fairly brainless. it is utterly mindless work. Touring, travelling. You are in this 'zero world'. That's why those who had a brain, Ray Davies, Pete Townshend to an extent, found it difficult because a sort of 'real life' appeared in the middle of the 'daydream'.

There was a part of Peter that absolutely hankered after and adored that pop world. I don't think I'd be betraying his confidence, or our friendship, if, I say that he found me 'attractive' because he knew I had access to a part of that world, and I was in a position to walk between the two worlds and belong to neither. A kind of free agent. a 'fifth columnist' in both.

I joined *Private Eye* in January 1963, issue 31. I was working there and learning the trade of a satirist when Peter came to the office. He didn't become involved until he came back from the US, writing Spiggy Topes & The Turds and The Seductive Brethren. Peter became a very important influence, and became involved in the shares side of it. He was quite astute, either by luck or destiny. Gilded. Anyone who knows the truth about Peter knows that he had more than his fair share of everything at one time, and as with all those people who are very clever the price they pay is high. Unless you get rid of it it's too much, and you can't get rid of it, so you become a tragic victim. Tragic is someone who finds themselves in a predicament which is uncontrollable. Tragedy was, and is, a Greek song. It was sung by the satyrs.

JW: Did you share Peter's love of watching sport?

BF: Whereas some of Peter's friends might like football, or they might like boxing, they might not like both. He and I agreed once that what we both enjoyed was a very good heavyweight contest, or a good football match. I am not a Spurs fan, I only really like Italian football, though I support Millwall in the English league because I was born in that part of London. Peter was originally a Torquay United supporter, then took to Spurs when he moved to London. Most people from the provinces do. Their teams are in the 4th division. Football was 90% of Peter's and my conversation. He had very strong views and would stick to them, but one of the things about our friendship was that we never crossed swords. By and large we agreed. Showbiz turns up thousands of people who go to games and they usually have no idea about how the game is played. Peter and I would discuss the minutiae of football. Develop conversations. intellectual cut and thrust, just to check the other guy's 'alive', you know? If you ever care for somebody you have to make sure they're on the case. Make 'em work at it 'cos they will slump.

JW: What did you think of the Derek and Clive albums?

BF: I became *Punch* magazine's (only ever) record reviewer. *Derek and Clive (Live)* came out and I reviewed it. I was un-upset by the language and I regarded it as not unlike a jazz perform- ance when it worked well, and I said so in print. Derek and Clive should have been the beginning of something much, much more interesting. perhaps even a theatrical production. a real theatrical breakthrough, cutting away the dull West End stuff and making it more like Fringe, but livelier.

JW: I have heard that Peter regarded you as his number one fan. is that true? If so, what would have prompted him to say that?

BF: Well, if he did, certainly my appreciation of Derek and Clive, which he had in black and white. a very considered review. Also, I sat next to him on every occasion that he worked at *Private Eye*. The seating arrangements were: behind 'A' desk the editor, Richard Ingrams at one point and, for the last six, and most important years, Ian [Hislop], in front of him Christopher Booker, and to Ian's left Ingrams. facing those three would be Peter and me. Peter always perched on the arm of a chair. He and I would always, always, find ourselves in a minority of two against three, or two versus two in terms of taste and what we knew *Eye* readers would understand.

With Ian it was much easier because he agrees with people when he realises they know something about the world outside that he doesn't. Richard, if he didn't know, would just overlook it, push it to one side, because he was going through a difficult time with his own morality. Yet he would allow some things in, which I found obscene, like gossip, but not straight forward 'fuck' humour which is what Peter and I would very often want. I just found that, very often, Peter and I would think along the same lines. During the last year or two, when Peter turned up and didn't make a major contribution, I would print his viewpoint. I know how his humour operates, and I could never have the brilliance he had, but I would be activated by the same things, because we had so much conversa- tion outside of the office.

JW: Would you say that Peter was a born satirist, or do you think it was something he 'learnt'?

BF: Not only a born satirist, the born satirist. He didn't need the written word, he had the true satirists word, the spoken joke. Everything at *Private Eye* is spoken before it is written, not straight to the page. In my view, it' s a spoken, not written business.

JW: The way in which things are said?

BF: Yes, exactly. you get more out of it. Like 'this man is a proven lawyer', instead of 'proven liar'. He just worked it that way. It takes a long time to learn the role of being a satirist, it took Ian three or four years before he could join in every session.

JW: Barry, any favourite sketches or anecdotes ?

BF: I must confess, I am not anecdotal. My favourite sketch though, would have to come from Derek and Clive. Squatter And The Ant. And Winkie Wanky Woo. 'You're getting fainter!', 'I'm getting Fanta?', 'Yes, I should go off and get some Fanta'. Also the Cancer sketch, breaking all those taboos. I mean, no one ever talked about cancer then. It's very abstract and has a lot going for it.

What makes people laugh is a sense of self recognition, and there is a desire in everyone to have pleasure. For me, laughing is the most intimate form of pleasure you can share with anyone. With a comedian, they are a partner for you to feel really at home. What we cannot answer is why Peter was chosen to be that funny, but what made him funny in practical terms was that he was able to expose so much about the way in which we think about ourselves, in a way that was fresh, new, and a mix of salt and sugar. You had to walk towards the door a bit. He caused me to think differently in terms of humour. Absolutely, undeniably, I could not do the job I do now if it wasn't for Peter.

PAUL HAMILTON: Moving on to those *Private Eye* flexidiscs. Knowing your background in Pop Art and pop music, would I be correct you're the architect of that very early piece of sampling, *Macmillan Sings*, where Harold Macmillan—quoting the song *She Didn't Say No And She Didn't Say Yes* at the Tory Conference in Llandudno—is intercut with manic guitars and teenybop screams?

BF: No, it wouldn't . That might be the work of Christopher Booker, who edited the *Eye* before Richard Ingrams. The EP that track was from was made before I joined the *Eye*.

PH: Tony Rushton at the *Eye* office found a *Daily Mirror* press cutting about that track. Macmillan's wife was asked what she thought of it: 'Lady Dorothy replied, "We haven't heard it. We don't own a gramophone."'

BF: [*Laughs*] Very good. But I've been involved in, I think, all the records they've made since, maybe because Richard thought I was someone who actually understood how records are made. He and I probably formed the backbone and structure for all the flexies. We would have a session together, deciding what to do and who would play the parts. And the great thing to remember, and this is very important, is that if Cook wasn't available we would prefer not to do it. You see, he had this great improvising skill and we could hand him a script and he would work on it. Also, some of us had opted solely for the written satirical path, whereas Peter, Willie and John Wells had taken the performing path too, so they were essential to acting these scripts out. Very often we only had a morning to do a record—and they were intentionally amateur, I think, but not worse than amateur. If it was left to Richard and me to do all the acting, they would've been worse. We were fortunate to have the likes of Eleanor Bron, Pamela Stephenson...

PH: Let's turn to *Private Eye*'s *Blue Record*. That track Lenny Drob; I take it, from the near-anagram of the name, this is a pisstake of Bob Dylan.

BF: Lenny Drob, folksinger, is indeed an attack on Bob Dylan.

PH: And that's Dudley as Drob?

BF: No, it's Peter Cook—interviewed by John Wells.

PH: Really? I'd've risked a brown one on Drob being Dudley.

BF: No, definitely Peter—[*recites Drob's protest song:*] 'Lay down your arms/ Throw your hands in the air/ Love is the thing/ Hate isn't.' That's good. We used to do that in the office for years afterwards—'Love is the thing/ Hate isn't.'

I think the chemistry between Cook and Wells was extremely good. There was a few set-pieces—Humphries' songs were written and then rehearsed with [guitarist Jeremy Taylor], and Willie Rushton's Bum Song had to be done properly too [Stick A Finger Up Yer Bum *should be the Anthem For The Universe!*—Ed.] Joe McGrath, the film director, is on that track. He's in the mob of backing vocalists and when Willie at the end shouts 'Christ, I've ruptured meself,' Joe yells out 'Good old Arthur!'

As for the off-the-cuff aspect of it... Both John and Cook were exceptional improvisers, as we know. I mean, everyone's attested to that. Cook's skill at being interviewed—as opposed to being an interviewer—is unparalleled. John was adept at both but he was a better interviewer; it was better when he was playing the Dudley role. Dudley couldn't do that role. I mean, what's interesting is that throughout the Pete and Dud episodes in their lives, even the Derek and Clive thing, Dudley could never put himself in the position of being the interviewer because he's himself so often been an interviewee, so there was that aspect of their sparring off each other. But John loved that role of subduing himself, with that obsequious, inquisitional voice.

PH: Yes, he uses a Malcolm Muggeridge voice on The Seductive Brethren interview.

BF: Yes, and deliberately so. Some of that sketch was scripted; you can tell it's not comfortably read. But then Peter would deviate from the page—'He died in agony—a lovely part of India'. And,

'He's got very hairy nostrils'; that just comes out of the language.

PH: And they discuss the Riddle of the Sphinx.

BF: Yeah, 'The Riddle of the Sphinx—d'you know that?' [*Laughter*] That's typical Peter. If you knew he was on the session—and John, too—you were made very much happier. I think there was only one flexi that Richard wasn't on—the Farginson one. That was John, myself and Peter. I don't know if Willie came to that one. It wasn't common but all three of us, I think, were going through rather difficult periods, and I think we were all absolutely smashed by 11 o'clock—I know I was—and it went on all day, the performing and editing of it. That was my dubious task, to always edit these things.

PH: The editing is brilliant, actually: it makes the records bear repeated listenings, which you can't do with most comedy records. Someone who may want to get *The Famous Flexies* might have that vague fear of, 'I may not understand what the fuck they're on about'—because the flexies are so of their time—but it's a misguided apprehension 'cos the sketches are pretty rapid. They make their point sharply and then it's on to the next one. If you don't 'get' one item, don't worry, there's another along in a minute, like a 73 bus.

BF: Yes, that's pretty much the intention.

PH: Where did you get the tape of Harold Wilson throwing a wobbler on a TV show that ends up on Farginson?

BF: That was very interesting. Someone at the BBC had leaked these outtakes of Wilson to Peter, I think. Terribly illegal of us to release it because Wilson demanded the tape be destroyed. But we chopped it up and Peter linked it as this painfully weak-voiced interviewer.

PH: In the '60s and '70s there would be at least one flexie a year, but from the mid-'70s they became quite infrequent. Why?

BF: It became something that didn't spring readily to mind to do. They weren't done as some marketing exercise, they were done because it was fun to do. That's the major reason for their existence. We enjoyed doing them because all of us at *Private Eye*—even Booker who is the most cerebral of us all—still enjoy the notion of performing.

The way we arranged the records was to get the best of us who could do it at the time—meaning any of us who could have a stab at playing Heath, for example—because back then there wasn't the artform of voice impressionism. There was Mike Yarwood, who was making a name for himself as an impressionist, but there was no characterization in it, just a voice sound. There'd be no attempt to personalize the individual. Peter Cook had, better than any of us, the ability to characterize and make a caricature of the voice. For example, none of us could 'do' Enoch Powell for a long time. We heard his voice but didn't know how to do it. Then Peter realised Powell was from the Midlands and if you put on a Midlands accent and flattened it down, you would get Enoch Powell. All you needed was a clue, a key to open the door. But anyone could have a fair stab at playing any character. I was Harold Wilson on some flexidiscs and I could do a passable Grocer. I thought my Lennon was pretty faultless [*very good Lennon drawl:*]—'Yer think it's all cock, man.'

PH: And the Lennon one about Transcendental Mastication—?

BF: Yeah, that's Cook.

[*The subject drifts, by way of gurus and football and Swindon, to television watching.*]

BF: I'm just not interested in television at all. People say I should watch this or that but I have absolutely no interest in television.

PH: I can't see how Peter Cook could've watched so much TV without going stark staring mad.

BF: I don't think Peter did watch, really. He didn't watch it as programming, I think he watched it because he was lonely and it was a voice. All his relationships with people were strongest when they were tangential. Our relationship was firmed up through the telephone and he would firm up his other relations with people who were on television making programmes. Like, I'd make a two-minute walk-on on a show called *Happy Birthday, Barry!*—and there'd be eight guys called Barry, of which I'd be one—and he would ring up: 'Terrific, well done!' Incredible! I'd appear on something totally obscure like *Good Evening, Norwich* and he'd know it. He wanted his relationships to develop in a non-tactile fashion. He didn't actually want people to get too close to him. He liked friendship at a distance so he could contain and retain his spatial and territorial preferences.

But all his later problems stem from his success at such a young age. It's too much, too soon and having no time for growth. And it's the same with footballers, pop stars, artists. To be thought of as golden at 23 is actually the worst thing that could happen to you. It's a Faustian pact and just giving a guy his fucking death warrant, man! He's got to get rid of it just so he can live again...

I've reached the Cookian point of my life where I've absolutely no ambition left of any kind. Truthfully, I don't enjoy life much now.

PH: What do you think you need?

BF: Death, basically.

PH: Just like Alphonse Enorme in The Seductive Brethren sketch.

BF: 'I think his interest is in dying.' [*Giggles*] But I'm quite interested by dying. I've seen life –

PH: But death isn't a day-return ticket, Barry.

BF: I wouldn't want one. One must never go back. Just like Lenny Drob—he never goes back: 'I never go back 'cos everywhere's a drag, baby doll'. [*Laughter*] The philosophy of life is contained in a curious way in these tapes. [*Fade out on renewed laughter.*]

FOOTNOTE: COOK-EYED

Richard Ingrams, Christopher Brooker, Barry Fantoni and Ian Hislop as heard on BBC Radio 4's Cooks Tour's

RICHARD INGRAMS: When Peter came into the *Eye* office I just remember him saying 'Good Evening' all the time, which was just ridiculous. And everyone went around saying 'Good Evening', and after a bit you thought 'What a silly thing it is to say "Good Evening"', which was perhaps the intention.

CHRISTOPHER BOOKER: But that was to do with the telly which was, of course, new in everybody's lives. There were all these men coming on saying 'Good Evening.'

BARRY FANTONI: Because it was only on in the evening!

RI: One of the funniest things I ever remember him doing was in the old office at 22 Greek Street. The night before, on the telly, there had been a film of some naked African women dancers—tribal dancers—dancing around. And Cooky rang up the BBC and demanded to speak to the producer. He said he was Sydney Darlow of the Sydney Darlow Dancing Troupe and he had ladies in the Sydney Darlow Dancing Troupe who did exactly the same thing—topless ladies—and could they come on the telly? And this man from the BBC was trying to justify the appearance of topless black dancers and why it wouldn't be all right if they had white ones. And Darlow kept on at them! That was very funny. And he also rang up the Foreign Office saying the Russians were spying on him through his drainpipes.

BF: And he rang up the Director-General of the BBC to complain that there had been a nude scene on the television set at half past ten and his son was already in bed, and he hadn't been told. And he had to wake his son up to show him.

I remember that Cook used to carry a briefcase around with him with a very, very old magazine in. It was a sort of porno mag and it had a woman with her knickers down and a man—that he insisted looked like Edward Heath—spanking her. And since he only came to the office every two years it made this thing even more and more outdated every time he brought it up. I think even after Mrs Thatcher went he still insisted that we carried one of these pictures with a speech-bubble, because this man looked like the Grocer.

IAN HISLOP: Which he didn't.

BF: He didn't look even remotely like him! [*Laughter*]

NOT ONLY "NOT ONLY BUT ALSO" BUT ALSO "BEHIND THE FRIDGE"

*Joe McGrath is one of the televisionary comedy directors, be it for the small screen (*Not Only But Also, *John Cleese's* The Strange Case Of The End Of Civilisation As We Know It, *etc), the monstro screen (films like* The Great McGonagall *and* The Magic Christian*), or the stage (*Behind The Fridge*). This interview took place at his Swiss Cottage home—which isn't a cottage and had little or no Swiss people in it—in December 1996 over a bottle of lovely wine plucked from the McGrath McCellar, some Frenchy-poo cheese, and a bottle of the Holy Dragger's favourite vintage wine—Tesco's '96.*

PAUL HAMILTON: Let's start at a beginning of sorts—*Not Only But Also*. It was originally a TV special for Dudley.

JOE MCGRATH: Yeah. I was under a freelance contract for the BBC, and it was coming to an end in '64. BBC2 was gonna start up and I had done a couple of things for BBC2. Bill Cotton said, 'Do you have any ideas?' And I suggested Dudley Moore. Frank Muir and Denis Norden said that's a good idea, so I asked Dudley to do a TV special. Years before, Dudley had done my Trainee Directors show for ABC Television for free. Bruce Lacey, The Alberts and Sheila Staefel were also in it, and Bob Godfrey had done an animated cartoon for it. None of them were paid for that show but we all had a good dinner. Bob Godfrey drew the food.

Anyway, me and Dudley were to do this show called *The Dudley Moore Show Starring Not Only Dudley Moore But Also*—it was going to be John Lennon. Or Blossom Dearie, y'see? Something like that. With orchestra directed by Henry Rabinowitz. And so, we were working on the show, and Dudley said, 'Why don't I ask Peter as the first guest star with John Lennon?' That's quite a good billing—starring not only John Lennon but also Peter Cook, y'know, that's really good. So Dudley and I went to see Peter and asked him and, Peter being Peter, said, 'Wellllllll, I'll have to think about this very, very carefully I'll do it.' That was his timing—no comma there or anything. So he came along and we did it. He turned up, we switched the tape recorders on, and Dudley'd have an idea, Peter'd have an idea—mostly Peter. Then they would ad-lib into a tape recorder. That would then be transcribed, making sure that nothing was changed because you wanted that sound that you got when they spoke, you didn't want it to be grammatically fixed or changed in any way. And then they'd work on that, reading it together, making changes and stuff like that. Then that would be typed out and that was the routine.

Now, in the first show, the Dud & Pete routine, I suggested the idea that maybe they could have two guys that met in the pub every night and had these fantasies; and they got the fantasies from the films. So they went away and came back with Dud & Pete, and when we rehearsed it it ran four minutes and when we did it to the audience in the first show I think it ran twelve minutes. [*Actually, it's just over seven minutes*—Stopwatching Ed.] It's just wonderful. I mean, Dudley dried during it, into hysteria and so did the audience. My wife is in the audience and I can hear her screaming throughout the whole thing 'cos she'd never heard it before, but she knew them and she knew me... biblically. We couldn't believe it. Afterwards, we just hugged each other. I remember Pete saying, 'God, we've really hit a mine here, we can go on and on with this,' and we knew we could 'cos they were just marvellous characters... That was a very good show. Tom Sloan, who was head of Light Entertainment at the BBC, said, 'If this is light entertainment, I'm in the wrong job!' And Michael Peacock, who was head of BBC2, said, 'I think you are in the wrong job, Tom. I'll have six of these, Joe, any time.'

PH: 'The Ravens' was in the first one, wasn't it?

JM: Yeah, teaching ravens to fly underwater... 'Any success?' 'No, not a bit, no, no, nothing. Just seemed to spiral down into the finny depths.' [Laughter] The finny depths... I can't remember if that's on the tape or not. I mean, as a director and a writer—I wrote the first series with them—but Peter wrote Sir Arthur, but you forget, your mind gets blurred whether what happened in the rehearsal got to the screen. In the first series also there was a *Tour Gastronomique of The Circular du Nord*—a gastronomic tour of the North Circular—do you remember that?

PH: Yeah, yeah!

JM: Barry Humphries is in that as the chef, with those terribly uncooked peas—dubble-lubble-lub!—and he takes his socks out of the oven and then puts them on. And thats absolutely true! 'Cos when I was a student I had a job in a 3-star hotel in Newquay and the chef, every morning, took his vest and socks out of the oven and put them on. [Laughs]... John Bluthal appeared in the first series with Eric Sykes. A sketch about an actor. Oh, Eric is an actor and he turns up to appear in a show with Dud and Pete, and he's very worried about appearing with these young University lads and they said, 'No, no, no need to worry,' and they start the rehearsal. John Bluthal is Eric's minder. And Peter says, 'Could you do a cringe?' [*Cockney:*] 'Oh yes, 'e does a lovely cringe.'—'Is he doing it now?'—'Nah, nah. Would you cringe for the gentleman please?' And Eric does the cringe, and Peter says, 'Yessss, yes, rather good.' Peter plays the director and—have you heard of this?

PH (*laughing sack off*): The Cringe? I've never heard The Cringe.

JM: It's marvellous. They get into this thing about the children. [*Sykes voice:*] 'I like doing pantomime now and again 'cos it's the children, you see,' and Dudley got into this—[*upset Dud voice:*] 'God, these fucking children, I mean, it just brings tears to my eyes!' A complete ad-lib. John Bluthal's in like a shot—'Let me help you, sir!'—wiping his face. Then they did another sketch, about Freemasons.

PH: What happened there? Rolled-up trousers...

JM: Rolled-up trousers and you will be taken out to sea... and thrown overboard... A weight will be placed around your neck... That's been wiped too, I suppose, along with Peter Sellers appearing on *Not Only But Also*. [Sellers played] a boxer who had turned artist and had found his objet trouves during the roadwork. 'Oh yes, how does your day begin?' [*Extremely moronic Cockney:*] 'Well, I'm usually on the canvas by 10 o'clock.' [*Dragger cracks up completely*] 'I got this entry in Who's Who... Who's, Who Who's.' Sellers and I wrote that sketch with Robert Fuest, who made those Dr Phibes films with Vincent Price. Fuest's name appears on the first series of *Not Only But Also* writing additional material... A strange input... So strange, Sellers as a boxer-turned-abstract-painter, so very funny. The marvellous bit is that the seconds—the boxer's assistants—usually hold up a board and you punch it... Dudley held up a palette with colours on it, and Sellers was hitting it then bashing the canvas! That was how he painted. [*Cockney:*] 'Y'see, I get a bit of the Gamboge 'n' a bit o the ol' Burnt Sienna 'n' let 'em 'ave it, yer see.' That was a very good sketch. The other one Sellers was in was *The Gourmets* which was like *The Critics*, where they're blindfolded, given food to eat and they have to guess what it is. This is Pete, Dud, and Sellers. And they give Pete Sellers a spoonful of mussels. He says [*lip-smacking sounds*] 'It's... it's Rosé. It's Rosé d'Anjou. What a lovely girl she was! [*Loud singing*] ROSÉ D'ANJOU, I LOVE YOU! No, its not Rosé. Well it smells, I mean it ta-, I mean—Quick—nurse, the screens!' [*Ripping raspberry*], and he went straight into all that. [*Laughter*] Wonderful stuff! [*Sings:*] 'Rosé d'Anjou, I love you!... I know that [*sniff, sniff*] anywhere!' Its not very PC, is it?

PH: No—

JM: Peter Cook! [*Laughter*] But there you get the link of Peter Sellers and Peter Cook together.[3]

PH: I always thought it a shame Peter Cook never wrote for Sellers. Cook's words and Sellers' delivery and voices...

JM: Well, Sellers at many stages of his career helped many writers on. It would've been interesting for Cook to write for Sellers... See, if you play something with Sellers then he becomes the character, but if you play something with Peter Cook, it's still Peter Cook.

You know I did those commercials for Barclays Bank? Peter Sellers played a character called Monty Casino in them, and then he died. The next thing was, Saatchi and Saatchi came back to me and said, 'We want to do the last one—'cos there was another one that still had to be done—and Peter Cook has agreed to do it and he's be very happy if you do it together.' And I just felt I couldn't do it. I said I really don't want to do it. It wasn't any denigration of Peter's talent, it was because I was involved with Sellers and was supposed to have done four and we only did three; that to bring

---

3. Happily, a recording of this episode of *Not Only But Also* was discovered in The Museum Of Television & Radio, New York City, and was screened at London's National Film Theatre twice in the summer of 2004.

Peter Cook in and do the last one... Emotionally, it would've been quite hurtful. Also, it was an agency thing, it was a real commercial agency thing, saying, 'We need the last one done...' But artistically too, Sellers was Monty Casino—even though you'd look at it and say, 'That's Peter Sellers,' you would accept the character, but when Peter Cook came on, Peter could only be Peter Cook. He wasn't an actor. Sellers was an absolute character actor. The difference is, Cook is a writer. Sellers was never a writer. Sellers could never write anything. You'd never get original pages from Peter—ever. He'd never put an original thing down. He couldn't.

PH: All his original thoughts came from the top of his head.

JM: Well, it's a working class thing. I don't mean this nastily, there's been some great working class writers in TV and film, but the thing with Sellers was basically his background was in variety, circus, the digs, things like that. He wasn't happy with a pen in his hand. He could do funny drawings and a coupla funny lines, but he wasn't a writer. But Cook is a great writer. Great comedy writer, Cook. There's nobody better.

PH: You did only the first series of *Not Only But Also* then?

JM: I did the first series and then fame and fortune beckoned and I went off to do movies. Which I'd always wanted to do. TV was just a means to an end and nothing will get me back into that electronic box, I tell you!

PH: Really?

JM: No, I'll never go back to that fucking electronic box. That's got nothing to do with directing—directing television from a box above a stage. Just madness! The only way you can direct is to be there with them, do it, rehearse it, get it right and shoot it. I mean, to be up in a box shouting, 'Tell 'em to move left a bit, bring it back,' y'know, it's madness and they're still doing it.

PH: So, lets jump ahead a few years to *Behind The Fridge*.

JM: Dudley said, 'We call this *Behind The Fridge* or *The Meaning of Life*. If anybody you care to mention, if you ask them to move their fridge and look what's behind—that's the meaning of life!'

PH: Didn't they do a trial run of *Fridge* in Australia?

JM: Oh yeah. I didn't go to Australia because I was too busy being famous and being fired off numerous feature films. Anyway, they realised it would never be a success without me! [*Laughter*.] So I was telephoned immediately and asked to present myself and start talking about and reading the material, which we did. Then we decided to do film inserts.

PH: Would that be whole sketches on film?

JM: Yes, 'cos I realised as director that when one of them goes offstage we've lost half the cast, and if they both go off we've lost the whole cast, so 'Why don't we write something on film so that both of you can go off, make a change while the film is on?' So we came up with Dud in blackface singing Old Man River whilst taking a shower, ending up white and gradually his voice becoming lyrical, tenor-like and camp. Very funny. And the black make-up going down the plug-hole—that's *Psycho*. There's a point during that where Dudley gives the Black Power salute which takes the curse off being in blackface which shows that, morally, we're on the right side. And there's the Spooch Ompodiment Appeal—very difficult speech to do, and Dudley did it.

PH: Who wrote that?

JM: Mainly Dud. That was really Dud's idea.

PH: Yeah? That's surprising because you'd think—

JM:—that would be Peter. Pete did a very good one on behalf of the Dysentery Sufferers Of Great Britain. Have you ever seen that? Its just an empty desk and a chair and he comes in and says, 'Good Evening. I'd like to talk to you on behalf of the Dysentery Sufferers Of Great Britain. Some us, you know, suffer terribly from this complaint and it's, it, oh, ohh '- and he rushes off! We fade to black with a sign, 'Send Your Donations To –', you know. And there was a very nice one which I always loved, which was Pete as Marlene Dietrich in *The Blue Angel* and Dudley as the Emil Jannings character in the nightclub. I think *Behind The Fridge* played for about eight or nine months or something; the Cambridge Theatre was packed every night. It could've run much longer but then we got the offer to go to the States. So it went to America where it was called *Good Evening* or *God Evening*. It toured Canada and America.

PH: Did you go?

JM: No, but I was getting my royalties, thank you. Coming in every week. One time at the Cambridge—I used to go in every other day. 'cos I liked seeing them, you know—and, of course, in those days it wasn't video, it was film that was shown on the screen. That one night the film broke down, so I ran round to see the projectionist—although you don't worry if the film breaks down because Peter would go onstage and do twenty minutes, no problem. But he came and dragged me onstage saying, 'It's all his fault, you know!' Very funny. And there's the great story—well, the stupid story—that Peter was pissed on the first night.

PH: Why was that?

JM: He was just pissed.

PH: Nerves?

JM: No. What happened was we had a couple of weeks of previews—the show was booked up for a year, we knew it was going to be a success—and then you get the first night with the trendies and the London celebrities and the critics coming. So we knew that whatever happened that night, we were OK. But, unknown to me and Peter, Dudley's agent agreed that Dudley would do *This*

Is Your Life, but Dud didn't know it was a *This Is Your Life*. And neither did I, neither did Peter. Imagine not telling us, the first night in London! Can you imagine? So what (the TV Producers) said was, 'Would, Peter, Dudley and I go for an interview at London Weekend Studios?' And we said, 'Yeah, but it's our first night.' They reasoned that when you've rehearsed and run through it for God knows how long, you know it, surely there's an hour free? So the three of us reluctantly gave in to it. We finished our rehearsal, told the lads to go and have lunch, and a hired car arrived which takes us to the studio—and Oscar Peterson is there for Dudley. We then realise it's Dudley's *This Is Your Life*! Marvellous... They say to Dudley, 'Will you be able to come back next week and do it with an audience?' Because Oscar's here now, we can tape him, and Peter, and use these films in the show next week. So we do it and, of course, Peter got pissed because they were just pouring drink down everybody. And at the end of it he was legless. When we got back to the theatre he was totally out of it. So...

PH: Opening night...

JM: And there's the audience hand-clapping 'Why-Are-We-Waiting?' Dudley and I were on stage with the curtain down between us and the audience, so Dudley took his trousers down and mooned to the audience, singing, 'I'll-Tell-You-Why-You're-Fucking-Waiting, He's-Drunk-The-Cunt-Is-Drunk,' y'know. And Peter was crying. Peter said to me, 'I'm so sorry, I'm so sorry,' and Dudley said, 'He's never fucking said sorry to me!'

What really annoyed Dudley, of course, was that eventually we got Peter up—not sober, but we got him up and standing. And Dudley's going, 'God, we're gonna have to fucking do this!' I looked through the curtain and could see Sean Connery sitting there, and I'm thinking, 'That's all we need! James Bond's gonna punch me head in!' Later on, Sean said to me in the pub, 'Wee bit o' trouble, Joe, eh? Wee bit o' trouble there.' So they go on and Dudley, for the first ten minutes, is prompting Peter 'cos he's forgetting it all.

Eventually Peter recovers and, of course, the next day there's a review saying, 'A strangely nervous Dudley Moore was upstaged by a magisterial performance by the magnificent Peter Cook!' Totally wrong! You got it all fucking wrong! Dudley, the next day, said, 'I'll fucking kill this guy!' It also said, 'What these two need is a martinet of a director who can control them. They're very funny but they're allowed to go on too long.' But the truth was, what he was watching was a terrible performance.

PH: Of the two records of the show, *Good Evening* from the Broadway shows, and *Behind The Fridge*, the English—

JM: (cuts in) The English one's better!

PH: I prefer it, too. It's more freewheeling, there's more of a buzz about it.

JM: That's right. There's more excitement, I do agree. When they went to Broadway they started getting all this, 'Gee, guys, could you change this? They're never gonna understand it!'—'It's English, and also we'd been here before with *Beyond The Fringe*—that's why you asked us back, no other reason. We've always succeeded on our own terms so we're going to do it on our own terms.' But they didn't. They actually compromised a little bit and what you get on that record (*Good Evening*) was a compromise.

PH: Some of the material made for *Fridge* was so strong.

JM: The Mini-Drama! That mini-cab stuff is great. Now, we had been told, after running the show four months, to take it out because it's too black, it's too horrible. I was very glad to see, in the very badly edited—by Michael Hurll—version of the show they did for the BBC, that Pete and Dud stuck by their guns and had that kept in. Because Harold Pinter came backstage and said that was the best thing in the show. What's interesting about the *Behind The Fridge* TV version is that the two film pieces are mine and they stand out like chalk and cheese from the rest of the show because—

PH: It's filmed correctly whereas the performance pieces—

JM:—the camera angles are all wrong and, in editing, Hurll's taken out all the wonderful stuff of Dud [in the On Location sketch] getting up and walking forever to get the tea and bring the tea back, which is just genius. [*Dud voice:*] 'Don't you get up, son! You sit there, son. You're home, son. You're tired. You bin filming in Yugo-bloody-slarva... I didn't know if I was coming or going, I felt like a pea in a biscuit tin.' Another great one (not captured on the *Fridge* TV show or LP) was the Othello where Dudley is the out-of-work actor who turns up as a cleaner. Peter's a high court Judge and he's waiting for a cleaner to arrive to clean his flat while he goes out to hear a murder trial. Dudley arrives—he's playing a very camp, out-of-work actor—and Peter's trying to explain to him, 'Look, just do the lavatory, then the bathroom, there's a kitchen here, and you can hoover the carpet,' and Dudley says, 'D'you mind if I make a phone call before you go?' Peter: 'Well, yes, yes, but I've got to go.' Dudley makes a call to his agent, hangs up, says, 'Oh, fantastic news! I've been offered this part in Othello. Oh yes, I know that play.' And what gradually happens is it changes into a very black thing where Dudley murders Peter.

PH: Weird.

JM: Yeah, its marvellous. What they tended to do was ring the changes and drop sketches they got fed up with. But that was a great sketch—Peter's idea, that, lovely idea. A very camp guy suddenly kills, and he's killing because Peter hated high court judges. 'The Handkerchief, the handkerchief... blood will have blood,' and it suddenly becomes real. And Dud gets him down on the couch and than at the end says, 'Oh My God!... I better phone my agent.' [*Laughter*]

PH: Back to Mini-Drama for a minute. That black glove Peter wears, was that a nod to Dr. Strangelove?

JM: Yes, it was that, yes.

PH: Because one black glove always looks more menacing.

JM: Also he said, 'I'll have a Scots accent.' I said, 'Oh, *don't*. You're terrible at it. Oh, fugginell.' He did it but he's so bad at Scots accents. Peter Sellers couldn't even do a Scots accent. He couldn't bear to see Battle Of The Sexes.

PH: As this interview's coming to an end, I have to ask you—

JM: To sing?

PH: No, we must know whether you smoked?

JM: No, no. Never smoked. It's a thing I don't understand. My wife's very much the same. We don't hate people for smoking, you know what I mean? But we don't understand why they smoke—but then they don't understand why I'm found face down in the gutter! [*General laughter*] But I am a Tory candidate, I tell you! I am an MP!—Much pissed! Are you asking this because of Peter?

PH: Yus, my dear.

JM: Well, Peter could be very annoying, as you'd know if you've ever spoken to Dudley. I mean, if Peter knew you didn't like smoking, he'd blow smoke in your face. He would blow smoke in Dudley's face.

PH: So that *Fridge* sketch where Dudley's the student and Peter's the master—was that deliberately set up so Dudley would have to smoke?

JM: He'd have to smoke yeah.

PH: Was Peter being just malicious and cruel?

JM: I think so... He just used to sit and smoke and drink and bet horses on television. And, at the same time, write sketches. It didn't stop him working. He would still talk into the tape recorder and make notes, so at the end of the day (the work) would be done. He was cybernetic—he could do about six things at one time.

PH: And, er, stupid question really, do you imbibe?

JM: Yes. I thank you for your bottle of cat's piss. Milligan said his idea of Hell would be forever drinking warm sweet wine from a plastic cup. He's been offered it many times at literary do's. The best wine I ever had was the 1961 Cheval Blanc which I drank with Dudley and Peter. [*Dud voice:*] Two fahsand pand a bottle, mate, if there's any still 'ere on the planet.

MAY THE FORBES BE WITH YOU

Bryan Forbes directed The Wrong Box in the summer of '65; a film notable for Peter Cook and Dudley Moore's day-booze for the shilver shcreen, as Sean Connery would have it. The Holy Dragger contacted the man known to Inspector Clouseau as bearded nudie Turk Thrust via ouijagram, asking for an interview about it. Mr Thrust replied in the positive, saying he'd prefer to conduct the chat by e-mail. 'Fair enough,' responded The Dragger, 'but for one problem: I don't have an e-mail machine.'

'No worries,' said Mr Thrust, 'you can use mine.'

This entire interview was conducted at a single typewriter with Messrs Thrust and Dragger taking turns in digit pounding. Not a word was spoken between them during the following exchanges...

PAUL HAMILTON: Your writing and directing credits prior to *The Wrong Box* were for modern dramatic, rather than comedic, films—*King Rat, Whistle Down the Wind*. What attracted you to Victorian period comedy?

BRYAN FORBES: You forget *The League Of Gentlemen, Only Two Can Play* etc—which admittedly I did not direct, but wrote the screenplays. I always liked variety and felt that the films I directed benefited from changing direction. It is true that I have always been drawn to films that explored character in depth and have never been attracted to those that feature blowing up endless cars or destroying whole cities. I could be a very rich man indeed if I had not turned down *Dr. No* and *Where Eagles Dare*—both subjects were mine for the asking, but I felt I would not be good casting. What attracted me to *TWB* was that I thought it was very funny and gave me the chance to work with a number of very talented people.

PH: I've not read Stevenson & Osbourne's novel so forgive my ignorance in asking, but were the cousins Maurice and John Finsury (Peter and Dudley) present in the original work or were they invented especially for the film?

BF: I confess I haven't read Stevenson and Osbourne's original either, so I can't answer this question. Larry Gelbart and Burt Shevelove freely adapted it according to my knowledge and following their efforts I wrote the final shooting script (uncredited) and added some touches of my own.

PH: Were Peter and Dudley the first choices for the roles? If not, who then was originally slated? Was the script substantially altered to accommodate Cook and Moore's personas?

BF: Yes, they were my first choices, and the script was materially altered to accommodate them, although there is one sequence in the woods where I allowed them licence to ad lib and inject some of their own inimitable humour.

PH: Neither Cook or Moore received acting lessons. Did they need any special coaching as regards Big Screen performing? How did they take to being directed?

BF: No, I didn't give them any special coaching. Subsequently I learned (from either an interview or some autobiographical piece) that Dudley found the experience an unhappy one. I can honestly say that I was never aware of his misgivings during the making of the film, which was a supremely happy time. Peter, I felt, was instinctively the better actor and took direction well. My method has always been to allow actors to take their own route to my ultimate destination—i.e. a director has to guide the cast to where he wants to go, otherwise it would all be chaos. You must remember that the majority of their scenes were with Sir Ralph Richardson and Willie Lawson, both masters of the craft—whom they adored—so they were up against stiff competition and acquitted themselves very well the first time out.

PH: Interviewed on the set, Peter seemed in a positive and jokey mood (e.g. 'Do you know who Cecil B. DeMille used for the crowd scenes in Ben Hur? Ants. He'd train ants to race chariots and photograph them and blow them up,' etc). Do you recall any funny exchanges during the shoot?

BF: Both Peter and Dud were in flashing form, especially at the lunches we all shared. When they were on a roll they were hysterical—poor Nanette [Newman, Bryan's wife], who was heavily corseted and had recently given birth to our second daughter, nearly fainted on two occasions, driven to helpless laughter and unable to get a breath. They kept the entire set in a good mood. Pete especially, with his remarkable understanding of the ridiculous, was an enormous asset to me.

PH: Cook had recently lost a fortune with the collapse of *Scene* magazine, a rag he had invested in, and the closure of The Establishment Club. Was he therefore 'careful' with his money, like most comedians are reputed to be?

BF: Careful with money? I wouldn't know. Like Nanette and me he was expecting a child and in fact I let him go early one day when he casually remarked that his wife was in labour. I forced him to leave there and then so that he could be with her. At the time he seemed supremely happily married.

PH: What money were Peter and Dudley on, compared to Michael Caine, for example?

BF: Well, the film cost less that $3,000,000 so nobody walked away with a fortune. I don't have chapter and verse to hand but if memory serves me right I would hazard a guess that they both received something in the region of £20-25,000. Michael Caine would have got something in excess of this.

PH: Moore's opening line—'Funny...'—was also the catchphrase of the cloth-capped Pete and Dud characters from their telly shows. Was that deliberate?

BF: Since 'Funny' was their catchphrase I felt it would be stupid not to use it—audiences love the familiar.

PH: The highlight of *TWB*, for me, is Peter Sellers as Dr Pratt. It's a career apex. Did Sellers see Cook and Moore as rivals—the figureheads of a new wave of comics—and thus employ a threat of competition to pull out all the stops in delivering a performance of giddying comic genius?

BF: Sellers first turned down Dr Pratt, but I finally persuaded him to do it. (It was really the fault of his agent who wanted more money than I had in the budget and in the end I think we settled on a token £25,000 which Peter donated to charity.) There was no professional rivalry that I was aware of and both Pete and Peter got on fine and loved the two sequences—they complemented each other superbly on a set that contained some 60 cats (after a week the smell was horrendous).

PH: Sellers improvised parts of the script, didn't he?

BF: Yes, Peter did ad lib brilliantly. There was one great line he dropped in when he asked Pete whether he liked moggies. Pete replied, 'I prefer eggs, doctor.' The script calls for Peter to reply, 'Oh yes, I like eggs myself.' To which Peter added to the take, 'Oh, I like eggs myself. They don't make good pets, though—you can't get them in at night.' Inspired. To the end of his life Peter always signed letters to me 'Pratt, MD.' I am glad you think this was a career highlight. It personified Peter's comic genius, for during the week we shot the two sequences he never left Pratt.

PH: Peter Cook and his wife Wendy held many dinner parties around this period. Did you and Nanette go to any?

BF: Yes, Nanette and I went to Church Row in Hampstead for dinner on several occasions and equally they came to our home and we also dined out in restaurants. I liked Wendy and Pete was always in good form at the time.

PH: The critical reception to *TWB* was almost schizoid in its being divided so sharply. The American consensus was predominantly effusive and positive, whereas the British overall view was a ripping raspberry and a thumbs-down. Why do you think *TWB* provoked such disparate reactions?

BF: I think it was my turn to be shat upon by the British critics who never failed to build one up before deciding it is time for some correction. I remember that years later Sheridan Morley sent me a screenplay he had written which came with a letter that said I was the only British director who understood comedy. This jogged my memory and I looked up his notice for *TWB* which was a total pan. I sent this script back with a copy of the notice saying, 'I think you sent this to the wrong director.' But you are right, it became a cult film in the US and I would often have strangers come up to me in the street in NY to say they had seen it half a dozen times. Willie Lawson especially was regarded as a classic performance.

PH: What's your opinion of *TWB* nowadays? What moments do you cherish? Are there any parts that set your choppers a-grinding?

BF: I think that if I had my time over again I would probably not include the old fashioned captions, but there is little else I would change. The sets (by the late Ray Sim) were brilliant, especially the train wreck, and the costumes by Julie Harris were in a class of their own. Sir Ralph was marvellous and I was privileged to work with him. It is still a film that evokes many happy memories. Listen, you do the best you can. It ain't easy.

PH: In around 1975 you made a documentary film of Elton John in which, correct me if I'm wrong, Cook and David Frost turned up to play cricket. Am I hallucinating or did that really occur? Do you recall the occasion (the cricket match, not me hallucinating)?

BF: This was a charity match and I think you are right that Pete and Frosty were in the team. Memory a bit hazy on that one.

PH: Were there any other times, by accident or design, when you and Cook met?

BF: Nanette and I stayed in close touch with Pete until he became a recluse. We saw more of Dudley in the later years—often bumping into him in NY. At one time he was married to Tuesday Weld, I cast her in *The Stepford Wives* but for various reasons she had to bow out. Pete and Dud were then on Broadway having a great success. I didn't see much of Pete during this period.

PH: When was the last time you crossed paths with Cook and/or Moore?

BF: It will always be a matter of regret that both of them had such sad ends—Dudley from a physical condition and Pete from self-in-flicted wounds which, I suspect, nobody will ever got to the bottom of. I would have like to have helped him, but he cut himself off from all old friends and I had no inner knowledge of his terminal decline. I wish I had because I flatter myself that Nanette and I might have been able to be of some use. But Dudley was in the States searching for the bluebird of marital happiness and Pete was closeted in a darkened room. I hope they both knew that we loved them in their separate ways. In their day they were uniquely gifted, the nearest thing to a double-act genius that I have ever seen. I was lucky to know them and to have worked with them and I miss them sorely.

PH: Pete's acting has been criticised as being limited in emotional range, shallow, detached, blah blah blah. Did you share that view? What were his shortcomings as an actor, and in which areas did he excel?

BF: Acting can't be defined. Somebody said that an actor is a sculptor who carves in snow. Pete honed his talent to a fine edge and when on form could not be bettered. Obviously he was not and could never have been a classical actor, but he was vastly superior to most of the actors who currently dominate the sitcom screens. He was a political commentator who translated the bigotry of his times into identifiable humour—tilting at windmills, cutting through cant and making statements through humour that most could appreciate. In his own way he was a true master of his art and the fact that the art was on a limited scale does not detract from his worth.

AUF WIEDERSEHEN, PETE

Whilst researching his double-biography of Pete and Dud, Alexander Games popped over to Los Angeles to have a natter with Dick Clement, co-creator (with Ian La Frenais) of TV's The Likely Lads, Porridge *and, most recently, the film* Still Crazy. *Tough life, eh? Dispensing with trivial questions like 'Oh, what happened to you?' and 'Whatever happened to me?' Alex G goes for the jugular with 'What became of those people, Pete and Dudley?'*

ALEXANDER GAMES: How did you come to direct the 1966 series of *Not Only But Also*?

DICK CLEMENT: Frank Muir, who was my boss at the BBC then, gave me the gig. It was the primo job you could get then, because Cook and Moore were so hot. When we did the shows—on Sunday nights—it was a hot ticket to be in the audience.

My first meeting with Peter and Dudley was at the White Tower restaurant in Charlotte Street—now gone, but it used to be a favourite haunt of MI5 during the war. Meeting Peter for the first time I was reasonably nervous because one felt you were in the presence of the most extraordinary comic intelligence you had ever met. The speed of brain—I'm sure when Robin Williams is on it's very similar. Afterwards, I felt deeply stupid—I am not worthy—I can't keep up with him. Dudley laughed a lot more, because he found Peter to be very funny—and indeed it was hard not to. I felt slightly better when I read a quote of Alan Bennett's where he said he felt similarly inhibited by Peter. He said, 'It takes me a week to produce one joke which I unfold in my hands like a butterfly. You sit down with Peter and 20 come out in the first minute.'

AG: How did you set about making the shows?

DC: I had an Assistant Director called Roger and we were brainstorming ideas for the opening titles. Peter said, 'I'd like for us to be playing the piano and then the piano is picked up and dropped into the water and we continue playing the piano.' Roger said 'We can't do that.' Peter, quite fiercely says, 'Why not?' So we thought, right, how to do it. It was the depth of winter when we filmed that sequence. The underwater part was shot in a swimming pool at a Butlins in Bognor.

It was an extraordinary schedule. We'd tape the shows on Sunday night, go out filming on Mondays and Tuesdays, very often with little preparation—there was never a script, usually. We did something called *The Epic That Never Was*, a parody of a TV show about the unfinished film of *I, Claudius*. Peter wanted to play a Josef Von Sternberg character, a German director with jodhpurs and a whip. Dudley was going to be Stanley Moon, the 'tortured' star—a sort of Charles Laughton hunchback type. And they wanted about 13 medieval extras. But there was no script! So we turned up at Bodiam Castle—it was incredibly exciting, actually, because you're flying by the seat of your pants and you only had a short filming day because the light would be gone by four. We'd get down there about eight in the morning, a bit hungover from the night before after we'd shot the show, and they would improvise the most extraordinarily funny stuff. Similarly, with the studio sketches, they would rehearse those into a tape recorder. I quickly discovered that my job was to be a sort of nanny. Because Peter was very prolific, he was apt to want to change things—he got bored very quickly. It was for me to say, 'Peter, that's very funny but what we did yesterday was funnier.' 'Was it? Oh, OK.' Also I had to tighten sketches at times because they tended to be too long. But because I had a writer's eye—or ear—I was quite a good editor, actually. I eventually wrote one sketch, the parody of *Thunderbirds*, which had to be written down because of all the make-up changes. It's quite funny actually. They liked it.

We sat in a little tiny room in Television Centre, just the three of us and a tape recorder, and they would improvise these incredibly funny sketches. The Dud & Pete stuff, you didn't know where that was gonna go, so I just put the cameras on them—two two-shots and two singles—and cut around. I often screwed up the shots because I didn't always know what was going to happen, so I did occasionally miss a shot.

My luckiest bit of shooting ever—and I would love to find this bit of film—was when we went to Felixstowe in February. We were going to shoot Dud & Pete in their deckchairs on the beach, looking out to sea, saying, 'It's wonderful having an out-of-season holiday, isn't it?' and then they get up and trudge through snow. It had snowed overnight. You can't plan that! I was fortunate in working with two people who were smart enough to take advantage of whatever was there. It really was the most intensely creative three months of my life. And every Sunday you'd have the adrenalin rush of a live audience giving you the feedback.

AG: Tell me about their partnership, how it worked.

DC: The chemistry between the two of them ... I always felt, even at the time, that on his own Peter had this intellect but was slightly cold, whereas Dudley had all the warmth but provided a wonderful counterbalance. Dudley was very funny and girls adored him, he was very sexy and enormously non-threatening. That was the sum of their parts.

Peter was the huge driving force behind the sketches but one shouldn't underestimate Dudley's contribution to them. There were the two of them there, bouncing ideas off each other. I can hear Dudley's laugh in my mind's ear now, when he found something really funny. It was an organic process that relied on their bouncing off one another and using the differences in their heights and personalities. It was a very happy relationship at that time. They were really at their peak, everyone wanted to be on the show or in the audience, they were juiced, creative, having a wonderful time, and I don't think there were any signs of discord.

The only moments of tetchiness was when Peter would say 'Why can't we do that?', a steely determination from him not to assume that anything could not be done, which was actually pretty ballsy and worked as a challenge to me to get things done.

AG: Do you recall any non-musical guests on the show? Guest comedians?

DC: No, not really. I think they more or less did it all themselves, actually. We had Henry Cooper and Terry Downes, the two boxers, at Wimbledon Common—unbelievably cold!—where they were the seconds to Peter and Dudley who were doing The Fight Of The Century. Peter was the Torquay Stylist and Dudley the Dagenham Dodger.

AG: Did they perform any of their own songs?

DC: They did *Isn't She A Sweetie*, yes, definitely. [*Sings a bit*]

AG: It's my favourite song of theirs. Dudley sounds so happy on that record. I've never heard him happier. That's what I love about it.

DC: He was happy. I don't think he was ever happier than then. There's no reason not to be, actually. There's always been that worm of angst in Dudley which is why he'd done analysis for years and years. I mean, he was funny, good-looking and, on top of that, he could play the piano. I could only play the piano that good in my dreams! But that's the strangeness of the human psyche in that none of that necessarily matters if there's something else worming at you. But in 1966 we were far too busy having fun and, in fact, far too busy. In many ways, I've never worked harder—even on a movie. I simply never had a day off—maybe a Saturday afternoon but that was it. We'd be taping the show Sunday night, location filming Monday and Tuesday, rehearsing for next Sunday's show Wednesday and Thursday, plus editing the filmed stuff. There was no time off but what the hell, it was only six or seven shows: There was a light at the end of the tunnel.

AG: When did you show the programmes to Frank Muir?

DC: We didn't. The amazing thing was they left you alone. They would come to tapings occasionally for fun but no one ever said 'Show us this week's script'—which was just as well 'cos there was nothing to show them. No interference at all, which is extraordinary. The set designer would ask what sets were required for the next show and I would say, 'A psychiatrist's study.' Then halfway through they would kick that sketch out, replace it with a headmaster sketch. So the designers had to be on their toes. As I said, it was 'flying by the seat of your pants' time but I loved it. I thought it was some of the best fun I've ever had.

JOHN'S TREAT

Long before he directed and produced the Boxing Day 1966 special edition of Not Only But Also, *John Street's career began at MGM studios. He moved from film to television work and became producer for a string of BBC light entertainment comedies, including Michael Bentine's* It's A Square World *(where he was assisted by a young Joe McGrath) and series for Joyce Grenfell and Benny Hill. He retired from the BBC and moved to Cornwall in the early 1970s where our own Peter Gordon tracked him down and listened to his story...*

At the time I met Peter Cook and Dudley Moore they were demi-gods. It was a time when the BBC had people like David Frost and Donald Baverstock [controversial television maker who oversaw the introduction of shows such as *Tonight, That Was The Week That Was* and *Not So Much A Programme, More A Way Of Life*], all those people were just taking over and the establishment were letting them get away with material that was very close to the line. I joined the BBC at a time when if you used the word 'bloody' in Light Entertainment you probably faced the sack. So, these new chaps came along, and they were an unpopular group because they were forming this new type of show that was so near the knuckle that the establishment were really quite worried that they would go too far. They had to be careful. But these people behaved like demigods. If you went to the BBC bar and these people were behind you, Baverstock and the rest of his group of black-coated script writers and over-the-top people, then they would get served before mere mortals like me who made gentle programmes for Benny Hill and Joyce Grenfell. People like Frost and Peter Cook and those script writers were The Untouchables at that time. The only lovely one was Dudley, he'd always have a drink with you, but the others...

Anyway, I'd just been doing one of my shows with Mantovani or Joyce Grenfell, a gentle, musical programme, when I was asked to produce the Christmas *Not Only But Also* show. They'd had a few producers on the show, and I think it was Tom Sloan who asked me. Whoever it was they'd had lined up for it had got sick or been fired or whatever and I was called for. Tom said: 'Would you like to do this programme with Peter Cook and Dudley Moore?' and I said: 'Oh no, that's not my scene at all!' But he said he wanted me and my staff to take over and we did.

The first morning I was introduced to Peter and Dudley. Dudley was a warm, gentle bunny, shook hands with you, almost cuddled you. You were his pal right away. Peter Cook looked down on me from a great intellectual height and thought: 'This is rubbish!' And I looked at him and thought: 'Supercilious so-and-so, I'm not going to get on with him!' [*Laughs*] He always called me Mr. Street for some reason, I never knew why.

I was very worried because I was going from the gentle world of Light Entertainment into this crowd who we disliked as producers at Television Centre and who wouldn't mix with us. They thought we weren't on the same mental plane as them, and we weren't of course. They were paving a new way in television and I was thrown into this.

So, I got the scripts and we started rehearsing. I remember early on we started rehearsing with cameras because I was working out close-up shots, but something seemed to be going wrong—the angles weren't right. My cameraman came up to me and said: 'You're not getting the shots you want because they've got monitors.' Peter and Dudley were looking at their monitors and not bothering about the cameras at all! It had gone all right in rehearsal but all going wrong in the studio.

I went down to the floor-manager and said: 'Get rid of all the monitors on the floor. I don't want artists looking at monitors, it's ridiculous.' So we got rid of them, and at that point they were doing something in the script, I forget what it was but it was very near the knuckle and I knew it wouldn't be allowed. Now, part of what Tom Sloan had put me there for was to keep an eye on this and the powers that be would all be watching the show, along with Mary Whitehouse, and they were always gunning for Light Entertainment shows. So, I went down and Peter said: 'We like to see the monitors, it helps us get the shots right.' I said: 'Well, it doesn't help me. I want big close-ups of you two when you're together and if you look away I can't get the reactions. I don't cut on dialogue, I cut on reaction. And I also want this bit of script cut out!' Well, he got very huffy with me. I went back upstairs to the director's gallery and he said to my floor-manager: 'He's gone up to his cocoon. He's almost sitting on the right hand of his maker up there. He's done his bit down here now, we'll have our monitors back.' And all of this came through into the gallery where I was.

I was furious! I went down those stairs and said: 'How dare you make these remarks about me. I don't give a damn about this show. I don't want to do it and as far as I'm concerned you can stick it! I'm not in your class. You're a brilliant, sophisticated... I can't say it but it begins with b.'

Peter walked off and I went back to my Department. I thought: 'I hate that bastard. I hope he falls down the stairs and breaks his bloody neck.' Tom Sloan said: 'I'll back you up, I know you don't want to do the show.'

Lunchtime came and I went back because the show had to be recorded, and Dudley came up to me and asked if I would go to Peter's dressing room. So I went to Peter and he had a glass of wine and said: 'John, what do you do with prisoners when you've won a battle? You were right and we don't want you to leave. I get so nervous I don't realise what I'm saying.'

'You've got the wit, Peter,' I said, 'but it boils over like a kettle.'

'Ah,' he said, 'Mr. Street, my wit boils over like a kettle, I'll remember that.' And he put his arm around me and from that moment on I found there was a warmth in Peter very few people, I think, knew was there. I didn't realise he was so nervous about working on the set, and he was always watching to see if Dudley was out-shining him, which Dudley could. So I was very careful after that, and from then the shots sometimes favoured Peter a bit more than Dudley, and Peter knew this—he'd say: 'Great shots, lovely, how much do you want for them?' [Laughs]

Peter really was a caring man underneath. One was scared of him because he had a brittle sense of humour—the least thing he could capitalise on and make a joke of it he would.

The opening scene was a sketch in which Dudley had moved out into this high-class society in the country and was on his first hunt. We had the whole of the Hampshire Hunt where we were filming in Aldershot with the full pack of hounds. I introduced Peter and Dudley to the Hunt Master and said how grateful we were, and Peter said [very smooth upper-class voice:] 'Oh yes, we're very grateful.' And they all loved Peter, all gathered around him, and instead of worrying about the cameras Peter was now in a social whirl. He'd met a new gang, a few lords and ladies, the horses chomping away. Peter was acting like Lord Cook [Laughs].

Dudley was saying: 'Look at him and look at me.' Peter had a lovely time and made friends with those people. I loved watching it because it was, to me, a new Peter, he could handle them. He was chatting away, talking about the hounds—he even got down and looked at their teeth at one stage! And the hunt would do what they could for us now they'd met Peter. They'd be saying: 'Oh, do we have to do such-and-such?' and Peter would say: 'Oh yes.' He took over as director really, I was a nobody [*Laughs*]. But it was fine because while he was chatting them up he was breaking them down for me. It was a difficult situation with all those hounds and horses and cameras and he went amongst them and they loved him. They rode up hills, they did re-takes, they'd do anything for him.

The sketch involved Dudley being the fox in this hunt. They got an old fur coat and some ears to dress him up in. Unbeknown to all of us, though, Peter had ordered Props to get real, smelly old bits of meat to hang on hooks around Dudley's coat. We could all smell the stuff, you can see the hunt-members reacting to it in the background on the film. Poor old Dudley stank like nobody's business!

At the end of the sketch Dudley disappears down a foxhole, which we'd had built by the army who were on exercise around Aldershot. It must have been about ten feet deep and they'd covered it with bracken to make it convincing and secured the top. Peter was there on horseback, looking very elegant. But when Dudley went in the foxhole all of a sudden the whole front of it went SPLAT! [*Laughs*] It came down, shutting Dudley in, and Peter started to laugh, which made me think that he must have known something about it. The army were laughing like anything! And out came Dudley covered in dirt. It was the first time I'd seen Dudley Moore not laughing—not amused. And came out and said: 'Funny, who's responsible for that?' And he looked at Peter and he looked at the army and thought, well, I'll take it as a joke, which he did in the end. When we went back for a drink that night Dudley said: 'It was all black, I thought I was done for. Who was it?' I said: 'I don't know.' He said: 'Yes you do, it was that sod Peter.' [*Laughs*] But I said: 'No, no, no, I'm not saying.' Well, I think the army did it, or one of the boys on my team because Dudley was always playing practical jokes—there was always a glass which the bottom fell out of or something. He was a terror!

The Broadwick Street gents scene [Swinging London] is wrapped up in mystery for me. Peter came in with the script and said he had an idea where there would be a commissionaire on the Broadwick Street gents. I said fine, and the script was funny, and Peter said: 'I would like to cast it.' Now, the BBC had a booking department, and a producer could say: 'I would like so-and-so' But no way could a producer intimate how much they would get paid, you weren't allowed to discuss money. You couldn't say to an artist: 'You'll get a couple of hundred if you do this for me.' If the BBC found out you'd be in dire trouble.

So we booked some actor to do it, and we got him dressed and on location in Broadwick Street. My secretary Hettie was very much on edge and I didn't know why. 'Oh, someone's coming,' she said, and up rolled a taxi with Peter and John Lennon. John was marvellously dressed in what I'm sure was a uniform pinched from The Dorchester Hotel. Peter knew the manager of The Dorchester very well—Peter had friends everywhere in those days—and I'm quite convinced he must have taken John to the door-manager at the Dorchester where he was staying. I had a guy dressed in not such a nice uniform and John was resplendent in his.

Hettie started laughing and, well, I hadn't met John Lennon before and he didn't seem to quite know what was going on, but Peter had talked him into doing it and I don't think money had been discussed at all. I said: 'I can't do it. I'm sorry, Mr Lennon, it's more than my job's worth to say "Yes, you'll be in the film."' Then Hettie came up and said: 'Bookings have Okayed it.' Peter had known all this and fixed it! He just thought he'd get me going. And, of course, the final result was a very funny scene but it got me on edge—I can get very agitated on a cold morning in Soho with people walking up and down [Laughs].

Peter did sometimes send me up and try to catch me out by sneaking things into the script that he knew I wouldn't like. But if there was something I wanted taken out of the script he would never query it after our first run-in. He would argue with me, and often his argument overruled me, but then he had a brilliant mind. I had the authority of being the so-called Producer, but when it came to a mental battle about scripts Peter had the edge on all of us. He could take it right to the limit and know it was right. A brilliant man.

It was decided at one of the early production meetings that we should broaden the show and go on location. The brilliance of the two-handed comedy between Peter and Dudley was wonderful, but you could get a bit bored with it, visually. When the fox hunting sketch was proposed I knew it was feasible if we could get the money and I could use my experience in film-making. The same applied to the Pete and Dud sketch with a section on a different planet and the longer documentary item. They were at a stage where they could say anything and it would get laughter. Although he didn't learn a script like Dudley, Peter's timing was so good, and Dudley's, that they could take it anywhere.

Another decision made early on was to cut down on the references to Christmas. Every show around us had The Beverly Sisters and reindeer riding through, and we decided this would be a strictly Peter Cook and Dudley Moore show without any false Christmas ideas. And it was mentioned how nice it was to see a Christmas show without snow falling down. The Fairy Cobbler sketch was a bit pantomime, and worked wonderfully, but that was it. And of course, Peter didn't like Christmas. He didn't like any part of it or any part of any religion very much. I wouldn't say he was an atheist, but he had his own ideas about Christianity and very strong ideas about jingle bells and snowballs on his show.

Relations between Peter and Dudley were normally very good, but I think Peter sometimes used to get a little impatient. He would always push Dudley if he was taking too long over the musical content of the show. Once you got Dudley behind the piano and you got the singer there he was away! But if Dudley took a bit too long on the musical spots while Peter was waiting in the corner to do the sketches he would go up to Dudley, just quietly put the piano lid down and say: 'Come on Dudley, that's marvellous. Now let's get some lyrics together, shall we?'

Dudley would never say a line he didn't like. He never ad-libbed at all, but Peter would, and Dudley would get a bit worried about what was coming next. He learnt a script but Peter just had a rough inkling what the script was about. But they were good pals really. One thing I remember, they didn't mix much. Dudley would be in the bar with me at lunchtime but Peter would disappear somewhere, I don't know where.

I never became a demigod, but I was very satisfied with the show when it was over. I was working with hyper-technical people who were determined to bring this new look to television. It was part of a whole group of writers and performers, all Oxford and Cambridge, and Peter was the shepherd of them all.

THE L.S. BUMBLE BEE

Ronald Bergan states in his 1989 tome *Beyond The Fringe... and Beyond* that '...John Lennon, who had been a guest on their TV show, offered (Pete and Dud) a song of his originally intended for 'Sgt. Pepper's Lonely Hearts Club Band'. It was called L.S.Bumblebee [*sic*], a take-off of a psychedelic song.' Bergan is somewhat out of his depth, rock-wise, here—like Andrew Motion, in his tripartite biography *The Lamberts*, thinking Hendrix's first name was spelt 'Jimmy'. Everyone knows it was Gymi!

So what is *The L.S. Bumble Bee* when it's at hive, and how did it come to be(e)? Well, Lennon was chummy with Cook and Moore, even appearing in the premiere episode of *Not Only But Also* (shown on BBC2 on January 9th,1965), reciting *Deaf Ted, Danoota (And me)*, from his book of verse and prose, *In His Own Write*. Lennon returned for another appearance (as a doorman outside Broadwick Street public lavatories, W.1.) on a show broadcast on Boxing Day 1966, in a long sketch wherein Pete 'n' Dud perform their own (not Lennon's) song, *The L.S. Bumble Bee*, in a (fake) recording studio. The song was taped in November 1966—with no input from The Working Class Walrus—and subsequently issued on Decca

(F 12551, all you catalogue number fans out there) on 27/1/1967. Of chart action there was none, and the single was taken out and shot shortly thereafter, never to resurface on any Cook & Moore LPs. However, it did emerge from the orifice of obscurity in 1982 when it appeared on *Beatlesongs!* (Rhino Records), a U.S.-only LP compiling a myriad of Fab Four soundalike groups and novelty ditties.

'BUT WHAT DOES IT SOUND LIKE?' I hear a strangulated cry. Pretty psychedelic, actually. Sadly, no backwards tapes of Satanic incantations, it's more in the keyboard-heavy pastoral pop mode. In fact, for something made in 1966, it sounds very '1967'—reminiscent of those early, lovely Pink Floyd singles, and The Beatles' *Only A Northern Song*, with a soft touch of *Ogden's Nut Gone Flake* (Small Faces) and a firm smack of The Mothers 0f Invention. The lead vocalist is Dudley:

> I can hear the hum
> Of the lovely L.S. Bum-Bum-Bumble Bee
> Now it's like a fly
> Out of your mind and into the sky.
> I hear with my knees
> Run with my nose
> Smell with my feet
> My heart is a rose—ahhhhh!'

Peter relegates himself to occasional asides ('Freak out, baby, the Bee is coming!' 'This week's bumper Bumble is foor Alf Herbert And His Marijuana Grass and their hit waxing, "Spanish Bee".') and a bit of buzzing here and there.

The L.S. Bumble Bee is a pleasant little musical excursion and the single is rarer than a Howard Hughes World Tour T-Shirt, lipstick for chickens, and fags for fish combined, and should you chance upon a copy at a record fair expect to pay anything from £5 (if the stall-holder doesn't doesn't know its scarcity value) and £40 (if he does).

'Forty quid for an average song about bees? What's the fuss about?'

Well, what really makes this record delectable collectable is *The Bee Side*—a previously unpublished and unreleased elsewhere Dagenham dialogue concerned with the joys of a burgeoning drug culture going overground.

In a recording studio Pete elucidates on 'this peril that lurks in teenage haunts where beat music pulses out into the night, keeping vicars awake and old ladies jumping out of their beds continuously.' To illustrate his case, he proceeds to relate the tale of 'a famous man who shall be nameless'—to which Dud interjects, 'Mr A. Woolley of 31 Wainwright Road, Willesden.'

Pete explains that Mr Woolley (a.k.a. Mr X) was 'a very nice family man', married with 'two beautiful children wot he used to dandle on his knee'. Happy and secure as he was, Mr Woolley one day said, 'Nice though this be I seek yet further kicks,' and motioned 'inexorably' toward a bag of Dolly Mixture (sweeties, in case you didn't know). Mixing some in a glass of cherry brandy, he 'quaffed it down' and was then on 'cloud lucky one-and-a-half, swinging away right up and grooving tremendously'. He became hooked and 'eventually he became so irresponsible he left his lovely wife and kids and home behind and went to Hollywood and lay on a beach all day with a lovely busty starlet with blond hair wot come down to her knees.'

Realising that old Woolley's fate doesn't seem much of a convincing deterrent (in fact, both Cook and—especially—Moore followed in his footsteps to certain degrees), Dud has a bash at telling a worse druggy horror story: 'A one [*sic*] that concerns a brain scientist who used to do interesting experiments on the curdling of milk. One day, when he was pouring milk over a live mouse to see the effect of it on it, he was suddenly consumed by an enormous depression'—more prescience here—'and he flung himself at the medicine cabinet and got an aspirin down his throat.' In true Sunday papers shock-horror-probe fashion, this set the scientist on the slippery slope. Now, Dud reveals, 'he leads his life as a rake—nestling in burnt leaves and compost at the bottom of a garden.' 'The only time he moves,' adds Pete, 'is when somebody treads on him and he jumps up and bangs 'em in the eye. A used gourd,' he concludes, 'a hopeless shard, useless to man, woman or beast.'

Pete then pontificates on the effect mind-altering substances have had on the arts, and cites Samuel T. Coleridge who 'used to cram poppies down his face': 'That's how he wrote that one about "In Xanadu the Aga Khan did an aerodrome decree/ While Alf the Sacred Ramsey ran/ Through caverns specialous to man/ Down to the Zider Sea".'

Dud retorts that, despite the influence drugs have had on Western culture, it cannot be ignored that 'Frankie Vaughan still tops the Palladium on crystallised fruits and weightlifting.'

The Bee Side concludes, much as one would expect, with an anti-drugs commercial ('Beware psychedelic drugs/ Steer clear of LSD/ That type of thing is for the mugs/ Stick to a cup of tea'), but there is a sting in the tail when, after congratulating themselves on their 'wonderful piece of propaganda', they celebrate their good deed by having a cup of tea. Dud asks for six lumps of sugar for his cup and, 'while you're about it, would you dip them in that colourless fluid, Pete?'

THE BACK PASSAGE

Send us your reams of unctuousness, your streams of conscious-ness, your essays, your photos, your videos, loose change, treasured mange, your poor, your sick, you're in need of a holiday...

Dear Soc.Boss,

Back when Danny Baker still did a Sunday show on [BBC Greater London Radio], *L.S. Bumble Bee* was played, bookended by Dan's revelation that Paul McCartney performed on the record. This info was procured from the Beatle's bouche after Baker announced Sir Paul on Channel 4's T.F.I. Friday as Apollo C. Vermouth (Macca's psuedeplume on the Bonzo Dog Band's Urban Spaceman). The Fab One tapped his nose in a conspiratorial manner and said, 'But it's the ones we DIDN'T put any credits on that no one knows about' (obviously enough) and admitted to 'fooling around with' *L.S. Bumble Bee*. That song has appeared on Beatles bootlegs, although some Beatleologists contend that it is The Bee Gees who play on it. I met Peter Cook once—at an exhibition of John Lennon's lithographs at The Design Centre in 1990-something—and asked him if The Beatles played on the song but (perhaps to be expected) he didn't know, suggesting I ask Dudley Moore instead—as if he's a bus ride away.

So what's the truth? Spill the L.S.Bumble beans.

NICHOLAS JACKSON, London.

Dear Paul,

May I contribute my two shillings' worth towards the Beatles/Bumble Bee mass debate that's been simmering furiously away for the past 30 years? Firstly, your correspondent is thinking of an entirely different song (*Have You Heard The Word?* by The Fut) when he writes 'Beatleologists contend that The Bee Gees play on it'. Both songs were useful in the '70s when bootleggers were a bit short of material when compiling their Beatles LPs.

Secondly, and more important, I have *Beatlesongs!*, the 1982 US compilation LP of Beatles-related curios which includes *The L.S. Bumble Bee*. The backsleeve features a letter from Sir Dudley Moore and it goes exactly like this:-

"December 15, 1981.

Dear Mr Bronson,

Many thanks for your letter of the 25th of November. Regarding *The L.S. Bumble Bee*, Peter Cook and I recorded that song about the time when there was so much fuss about LSD, and when everybody thought *Lucy In The Sky With Diamonds* was a reference to drugs. The exciting alternative we offered to the world was LSB!, and I wrote the music to, in some ways, satirize The Beach Boys rather than The Beatles. But I'm grateful if some small part of the world thinks that it may have been them instead of us! The only thing I can remember about the recording session was that Peter Cook had practically lost his voice when we were doing it, and found it very hard to put any tone into it. As you can hear, there is a slight reference to The Supremes' sighing that they used to do on their records. The instrumental line-up was honky-tonk piano, bass guitar, drums, cimbalon, and voices. I did all of the singing voices, including the soprano backup voices. I hope this will be of some use to you.

Best wishes.

Yours sincerely,

Dudley Moore."

Does this help clarify matters?

JOHN POOLE, West Midriff.

HOW GREEN WAS MY FRUNI

And now it's Friday the 17th November 2000. And now it's Peter Cook's 63rd birthday if, if, if. And now it's another noisy restaurant packed with hot, wired lunchtime suits yelling 'You're cracking up!' into mobile phones. And now it's Eleanor Bron and The Holy Dragger charging glasses of wine in memory of wossisname. And now it's time to chat around and about and in and out of Bedazzled, *the film made in the Summer Of Love about someone who pointedly wasn't getting any, free or otherwise.*

PAUL HAMILTON: *Bedazzled* is not like most film comedies in that, to me, it's not simply jokes; there does seem to be layers upon layers of thought bubbling beneath its surface. I wonder what your initial reaction to first seeing the screenplay was.

ELEANOR BRON: I thought there were lots of lovely parts for me to play. Also, I had worked with Stanley Donen before, in *Two For The Road*, and was thrilled to be asked to work for him again. That's how I felt. And the script was so funny.

PH: The rich language of Peter's script reminded me of something

Harold Pinter once said about his own plays; that any one of his lines could be meant in any number of ways. We find that in *Bedazzled* time and again, even with a throwaway line of Margaret's: 'E put so much into those 'amburgers.'

EB (laughs): Yes, that's right, Peter loved that. And I love that scene where the old fellow's stuttering very badly and Peter replies, 'Oh, that's easy for you to say, Lord Dowdy.' The way Peter makes explanations for the very annoying things in life, like finding your new shirt's button's missing and a scratched record that you've never played before—that it's all the work of the devil—is wonderful. I don't know how they deal with those touches in the new version. Have you seen it?

PH: Yes, it's gormless crud.

EB: Oh? Because, surely if Harold Ramis liked the original so much, he would have cared enough to...

PH: Well, the question of religion, of belief, is entirely missing. And the level of wit and originality is moronic. Rather than have Stanley Moon escape a wish by blowing a raspberry, he now has to dial 666 on a telepager to return to wherever the devil is.

EB: Oh, that's too boring.

PH: Quite right, so let's concentrate on the original. Stanley Moon's suicide note is a classic: 'Dear Margaret, This is just to say cheerio.'

EB: Yes, that's lovely. We shot quite a few scenes in this tiny converted church in St. John's Wood, particularly the one where Dudley was a Welshman. The church was used as his flat. It was a most extraordinary apology for a studio, very prone to noise as it was situated in a residential street. Hot studio, too. No air-conditioning.

PH: About the wish where you and Dudley are pseudo-intellectuals talking about touching—'I'm a very tactile person': It's reminiscent of a scene performed by you and John Fortune a few years earlier in The Establishment.

EB: The Date Going Home? Yes. That was the very first sketch we did together, actually.

PH: Did you rake Peter over the coals, accusing him of blatant plagiarism?

EB: No, not at all. It was quite different because it wasn't the same situation and Margaret was a willing victim—if you like, if you see her as a victim. But in The Date Going Home, the couple were much more equal, in a funny way. The Establishment creatures were both more inhibited, if that's possible, than the *Bedazzled* couple.

PH: Was there any indication in Peter's screenplay on how he wanted or preferred Margaret to be played, or indeed any of the 'Wish Margarets'?

EB: I think it was fairly clear in the script. What was interesting was trying to make a difference between the real Margaret and the screaming teenager Margaret in that wonderful pop music sequence. Having done *Help!*, the Beatles' film, two years before, I had seen these over-the-top girls at close quarters. I remember sitting in a dressing room, talking to John Lennon, when suddenly we heard this scrambling at a high window and we looked up to see two girls' screaming faces at this window, and with tears streaming down their faces—'Aaaaaah! John!!' So I used that kind of painful agony for Dudley's song and then I thought, 'How do I top that for Peter's song?' So I decided to not do anything and just be totally mesmerised. I just love that song: 'You fill me with inertia' is a wonderful phrase.

PH: Was there a single person that inspired your characterisation of Margaret Spencer, the waitress? I'm thinking of the ludicrous eye shadow that looked like two church-doors.

EB: Oh, she was an extreme version of what was around at the time. Clare Rendlesham did the costumes for *Two For The Road* and *Bedazzled*, and she was then editor of Vogue and very much into the fashion market. I've never been a great one for fashion so I was left in her capable hands. She collaborated with Jean Muir, who was amazing to watch at work. When I was having [costume] fittings, Jean would be, 'Oh, this'll have to go up half an inch', and her trusted assistant would make the relevant tuck. Tiny, almost infinitesimal alterations that made all the difference. And it did because she cared so much. It was the height of fashion and then made a little more extreme. The eye make-up was probably based on Twiggy.

PH: The voice used for Margaret in the Tastee-Free I thought was reminiscent of E.L. Wisty in its drony lifeless vacancy.

EB: That's it exactly. He wanted something deadening to say something of her whole life, and that comes out in the scene with Michael Bates as the police inspector where she says [*deadpan, emotionless*]: 'Oh, I do 'ope nothing's 'appened to 'im.' I love that flies-on-the-wall scene—'I can't blow raspberries with these stupid fly lips' [*Laughter*].

PH: And the Spiggott fly wearing red socks. But, it must be said, that had to be the world's cheapest animation.

EB: I know, I know. But they decided that it couldn't be done in any other way.

PH: It looks like a couple of kids have been given felt-tip pens and given five minutes to draw flies, preferably with trumpet lips. Tell me about the nuns of St. Beryl.

EB: The nuns. I love that.

PH: Why has Sister Margaret acquired a soft lilting Irish accent?

EB: It seemed to me to be quite natural to me that if she was a nun she would be Irish. They were all Irish nuns in my day. There just seemed to be more nunneries in Ireland than anywhere else, and the nuns would come around door to door to sell their embroidered linen. I remember once, as a little girl, opening the door to see a nun and running to my mother, 'Mummy, mummy, there's a Christian at the door!' [*Laughter*] So that gives you an idea.

PH: I love the imagery of the nuns mopping the lawns and scrubbing the trees.

EB: It's very funny. It's expressing the uselessness of certain kinds of endeavour and worship. I don't know if you noticed but in that last sequence, the Heaven scenes shot in Kew Gardens, if you look carefully you can see Stanley Donen and the film crew reflected in the glass of the greenhouse.

PH: I'm surprised that didn't happen more often since many of the scenes are filmed through transparent barriers. A lot of the action takes place at a strange remove. Was that a deliberation of Peter's script or was it an idea of Stanley's?

EB: That I don't know. I should have brought the script along with me. I'm sure I still have a copy. I still have the Beatles' script, the working title of which was *Eight Arms To Hold You*.

PH: That's a terrible title. It sounds like 'I Married A Teenage Octopus'. When was *Bedazzled* made?

EB: It must have been the summer, because of the scenes in the car where we broke his pipe. Yes, the summer, because I remember we filmed the home scene in Elstree, which is close to where I grew up in a sense.

PH: The 'home' scene?

EB: Where Peter's playing The Model Husband—?

PH:—and you've got that wonderful orange hair.

EB: Oh yes, a terrific wig. And I wish I still had it now.

PH: We'd asked some folks what their favourite bits and pieces of *Bedazzled* were, and one nominated the scene where you and Dudley are blubbering in the car and you cry: 'And we were going to—on his favourite pipe!'

EB [*Laughs*]: 'Favourite pipe.' That's lovely.

PH: And it's not the fact that it's his pipe, it's his favourite pipe. Every line is over-lubricated.

EB: One of my favourite moments, apart from the scratching of the record and the snipping-off of the shirt buttons, I love the moment where they're sitting down to eat Mrs. Wisby's strawberries and Peter pulls out this very long spoon. What's lovely about it is nobody says anything about it, it's not pointed out why. It's like that moment in *It's A Mad Mad Mad Mad World* where Jimmy Durante is lying in the road and he says, "The treasure's in—", and his foot jerks out and kicks a bucket [*Laughter*]. That's such a delight.

PH: Was the script rigidly adhered to?

EB: Yes, I think so, from what I remember.

PH: I thought that, what with your experiences of improvisation in The Establishment days, and Peter and Dudley's occasional abandonment of the script in *Not Only But Also* and winging it, maybe Stanley Donen had to rein you three in a bit to stick to the script.

EB: No. Stanley really loved it, he found Peter and Dudley really engaging and supported them totally. But a lot of the so-called improvisations we did at The Establishment weren't really the same as the ones done by, say, method actors. When we went as The Establishment to Chicago we did an exchange—Peter wasn't part of The Establishment players—with a group called The Second City who, in turn, came over here. Now they did real improvisation—character-based—but when we improvised we were trying to find out where the jokes were. When we did a session with The Second City man who set up their improvisations we were hopeless because we were only thinking "Where are the jokes? Where are the jokes here?" And when there were scriptwriting sessions for The Establishment it was very often a matter of Peter holding forth and we'd feed him tidbits and he'd seize them and elaborate on them. The person who did that wonderfully was Christopher Morris. The Radio 3 series [*Why Bother?*]—magnificent. He has a very wild imagination and whereas we threw Peter crumbs of cheese, Christopher Morris was throwing him meat. Hunks of meat [*Laughter*]. Peter liked to know the area he was working in. He was very professional, [his comedy] wasn't just a mishmash as some people sometimes assume. Improvisation, for Peter, wasn't a be-all and end-all, it was a way of exploring what was in his mind and all the avenues. He was like a spider sitting, spinning wonderful webs.

PH: You had done a couple more films than Peter and Dudley by 1967—*Help!*, *Alfie* and so on—and I wonder whether you gave them any hints regarding screen acting. And what, indeed, you thought of their performances?

EB: I saw *Bedazzled* recently in Los Angeles where they had a screening of '60s films—it was a terrible print, actually—and I thought Dudley was very remarkable. Peter, I thought, always found it difficult to look people in the eye. When I was asked to do *Women In Love*—this sounds like a tangent but it's actually quite germane—there's a description, in D.H. Lawrence's novel that Hermione, my role, always looked at people "along her cheek". And I didn't know what that meant until I realised that that's what Peter did. What Peter needed was a foil—be it Clive Anderson or Christopher Morris—and what he was always doing was watching to see how he was being taken. It wasn't a self-referring thing: he was testing out his material, he wanted to see how it was going. And I think that's an impediment when you're acting. He was never completely in it. But to be playing that particular part, it was suitable.

PH: But then, his apparent lack of acting technique—the way you know it's just Peter in groovy sunglasses to a large extent—makes his performance all the more affecting and vulnerable. His rejection from Heaven, to me at least, is all the more poignant for it. His performance is a success for all the wrong reasons.

EB: Did you see *One Foot In The Algarve*?

PH: Yes.

EB: He was simply wonderful in that and it's also true that he acted on his own. What made his acting particular, if you like, was he wasn't awfully good at relating to other actors.

PH: What I thought notable about Peter in *Algarve* was his transformation from the linguistic dream-weaver and florid comic imagist working in a mainly immobile stance to an exuberant slapsticker giving an almost silent performance. When I first saw the show I thought, "Oh, he's playing Robert Maxwell playing Inspector Clouseau."

You filmed some scenes with Peter for the film of *Black Beauty* not long after *Algarve*. Did you ever take him to one side and say, 'Try emoting'?

EB: No, not at all. In fact, it was a joy doing that film because we hadn't seen each other for about ten years or so. He started speaking in this very strange voice which became a character we were going to base a stage show around. He said [*Italian accent*]: "Dahling, I come from Hampstead, everywhere is no good. The light, all the way, everywhere, the light is green. Is terrible." It was based on the wife of a friend of his. The show was going to be this very impoverished couple who were kind of having to put on a stage show because they were in such financial difficulties. There were all sorts of tasteless ideas that were going to be incarnated.

PH: I remember your contribution to Peter's memorial service. You quoted a writing session with Peter: You turned the tape recorder on and Peter started sighing, 'Oh dear. Oh dear, oh dear,' and you asked, 'Is something wrong?' He replied, 'Oh, nothing. Just thinking aloud.'

EB: He was much mellower, more open. It was lovely because I sort of re-met him.

PH: A lot of our readers may have a fixed image of Peter in his later form of a chainy-smoky chatshow-guesty trivia pursuer and idler. He wasn't like that at the time of *Bedazzled*, was he—a lounging telly addict?

EB: No, not in my recollection, no. He was an enormously charismatic, charming and beguiling person altogether.

PH: How was his off-set appearance? I get the impression of a rakish dandy.

EB: Yes, he was rather. It was a style-conscious time. John Bird used to wear lurex jackets and whatever. It was such a divergence from what went before. It used to be so staid. Nowadays, of course, anything goes. I suppose if you put on a tweed jacket it'd be pretty startling now. Peter loved it, the fashion of it. He was very sophisticated in one way, possibly not so much in another. It may have been partly something to do with public schools but I felt that he—like a lot of men at the time—was not easy around women and didn't know how to behave with them or treat them. I feel that not-knowing leads to a lot of unhappiness. I don't think he was alarmed by women, he just didn't know how to relate to them.

PH: Or writing for women generally?

EB: Writing for women? None of those boys had anything to say for women, actually. When we were at The Establishment and I'd be sitting there at script conferences with Peter and the others, it was very hard work for them to find me anything to do. And that's why John Fortune and I improvised that First Date sketch—because otherwise there would be no reason for my being there. I wasn't politically minded and they were all leaning toward political commentary, whereas I was more interested in social comment. I don't know whether that generation of men saw women as existing except as mothers and girlfriends.

PH: There's a bit in *Bedazzled*'s mortuary scene that jars, particularly nowadays when everyone's careful of what they say, and that's when Inspector Clarke is spouting off about the number of rapes he's got to deal with and blames the women in their summer frocks for leading men on. Margaret, rather than argue, almost shouts, 'I agree.'

EB: That was wonderfully seedy, actually. It makes you wonder what side of the line the policeman was on.

PH: Was it ever discussed, the strange dream-like logic of *Bedazzled*?

EB: Dream logic?

PH: I mean, when Stanley Moon is granted a wish and suddenly he and Margaret are transported to an entirely new environment and lifestyle they have lived all the time, like a parallel universe. Not for a second do either of them question how or why they got there.

EB: Well, it's a common thing of fairytale land that you've got to be very careful what you specify. One of the strongest elements in the film was the flawed wish, the broken dream. You may wish to be fabulously rich but if it came true it might be horrible: You'd never know whether people liked you or your money.

PH: I'm pleased you liken *Bedazzled* to a fairytale, although I have a theory about the film.

EB: Yes?

PH: I see it as a kind of morality tale. When Stanley fails in his suicide bid I think he has a nervous breakdown. George Spiggott and the wishes are hallucinations, scenarios in Moon's head, as he tries to figure out what it's all about, and he comes out of it at the end a different, stronger person.

EB: I think you're absolutely right, because he realises that the only way to achieve anything is under your own steam, however you can do it, and there's no use in relying on wishful thinking. You do feel at the end that he's won. I mean, he's defeated the devil.

PH: He's beaten his inner demons.

EB: Yeah.

PH: How do you feel about *Bedazzled* as a finished film?

EB: I loved it. I've always loved it. It was pretty much slagged-off here as being 'just sketches'. It was more appreciated in America. I think it stands up pretty well today.

BEDAZZLED

MEPHISTOPHELES: Let but the Spirit of all Lies
With works of bedazzling magic blind you;
Then, absolutely mine, I'll have and bind you!-

Faust, Part 1 (Goethe)

A man is kneeling in church praying. He is obviously unused to the act, not sure quite what to say to God amidst the distinctly Romish incense and muttered litanies. But he is at the end of his tether, a man on the verge of suicide, a poet's soul trapped in a burger chef's existence. He pleads with God directly from the heart to show him some sign that He exists, that there is some form of justice in the universe, something that will lend his small, loveless life some meaning. Cut to an interior church wall—a stained glass window clicks open to reveal Satan, coiled like a preying mantis. The devil sees his opportunity and waits for the right time to pounce.

Thus begins one of the funniest, most intelligent films in British comedy, one that covers the fields of love, desire, sexual morality, theology, the notion of free will and a couple of tasty side-swipes at 1960s pop culture while it's about it. The film began with the young Peter Cook, a languages student, seeing a production of Goethe's play *Faust* and fancying his chances of putting on his own production. The idea sat at the back of his mind until, in 1966, the time came for him and Dudley Moore to make their first real pitch for Hollywood and trans-Atlantic success with their own movie. Cook then took it upon himself to script the entire thing himself. Stanley Donen, director of hit musicals such as *Singin' In The Rain*, and considered a big enough name to attract interest, was hired to direct and produce. The film came out in 1967 to a somewhat muted reception, something that has hindered its subsequent reputation. It has since acquired a reputation for being a 'cult' movie, an unfortunate phrase since it implies to most people that it can only be enjoyed by pissed students.

Like Goethe, Cook presents us with a human Satan, one with a personality beyond an evil bogeyman. From Milton's *Paradise Lost* onward the literary treatment of the devil had become progressively more human. Cook's portrayal is perhaps closest to Dostoyevsky's Satan in *The Brothers Karamazov*. In that novel Ivan Karamazov, his mind disintegrating, sees Lucifer in a series of visions in European clothes, a sophisticated aesthete, a cynic who encourages Ivan's atheism and all his doubts, and yet appears to be proof himself of God's existence. He's a likeable old lush who takes great delight in picking apart Ivan's few certainties in life as if picking the legs off a spider.

The extra dimension Cook gives Lucifer is, of course, a comedic one. Cook's Satan, George Spiggott, revels in two things—casual sadism and linguistic paradox. The latter takes the form of typical Cook jokes, telling Moore's Stanley Moon that suicide's "the last thing you should do" or, in the guise of an international arms dealer, worrying about the prospect of a lasting "nuclear peace". He also admits to being caught in a theological paradox himself, acting as an agent of man's free will in a predestined universe, being cast out of heaven for a rebellion that, as it was all part of God's plan, wasn't Spiggott's fault. But he treats these contradictions as just part of life, a nasty job but, well, that's his lot. He's like the traffic warden he dresses up as while telling the story of his fall from Grace, a jobsworth, a petty official who has jobs to do and Jobs to tempt and frustrate. He admits his position is 'pathetic' and is nostalgic for the Old Testament days of fire and brimstone ('I thought up the seven deadly sins in one afternoon. The only thing I thought up recently is advertising.').

The incidents of casual sadism form the funniest scenes in the film, whether general acts of 'routine mischief', such as resetting parking meters or scratching records, or more specific acts such as the Frunigreen Eyewash scene or his continuous frustration of Stanley's wishes. Cook gives such scenes a schoolboyish conspiratorial charm. Stanley laughs along with Spiggott when he breaks the old lady's shopping bag in the same way we laugh with the devil as time after time he frustrates Stanley's wishes.

Stanley Moon cuts an altogether unexpected figure as a latter day Faust. Christopher Marlowe's interpretation (c. 1590) gives us Faust as a wealthy, famed and learned doctor trained in natural philosophy and medicine who lusts after more and more power. Goethe's Faust (1808) is a more academic Doctor, an obscure university lecturer who yearns to swap the dry and dusty world of books for wealth and power. Neither seem that close to a fast food chef in the middle of a nervous breakdown, but a brief look back into the history of the Faust legend might prove useful. Whilst there is some debate on whether Johann Faustus ever existed, stories began to circulate in early 16th century Germany of a traveller who could perform magic, effect medicinal cures and had a veritable treasure trove of money, and that he enlisted the devil to help him. By 1580 the first book on Faust appeared as a collection of folk stories about a learned doctor who sold his soul to the devil. The book was actually a thinly disguised piece of Catholic propaganda. The Vatican was keen to promote the idea that anyone who converted to Protestantism was effectively making a deal with Lucifer and would be damned for all eternity and so Faust became a symbol of all those who fell into the sin of pride and followed the path of Martin Luther. The original story has Faust command the devil to take him to the Vatican where he slaps the Pope in the face, a scene intended to be shocking but which Marlowe turned into a comedy piece.

Another similar story was being dramatised in 16th century theatres across Europe, this time about someone who almost certainly did exist. This story too was Papal propaganda and told the story of Francis Spira, an Italian lawyer who converted to the Protestant church. Eventually he recants and rejoins the Catholic faith, but he is so concerned that his soul has been tainted by the sin of leaving the Roman church that he kills himself. Could this tale be what linked Faust to the themes of despair and suicide in Stanley's character?

Stanley's character is Dud from *The Dagenham Dialogues*. Like Goethe's Faust, he is essentially a rather pathetic figure stuck in a dull life he doesn't want, locked in the dream of wanting a life he believes everyone else is having. Some have complained that Cook sought to belittle Dudley through the script, but in fact the film simply plays to Moore's strengths; Moore is always strongest in films where he plays the innocent idiot stuck in a world he does not fit in with. If one looks at his two great Hollywood successes, *10* and *Arthur*, the first, although it caused a sensation at the time for being a comedy that verged on soft porn, seems a cold affair today. He plays his role effectively enough, but it's against type and Dudley as successful sexual predator simply does not come off. *Arthur*, on the other hand, sees Moore back as innocent victim, albeit a victim of his own alcoholism, a character at odds with the universe—the result is a far warmer film. Although there are sadistic elements in *Bedazzled*'s treatment of Stanley, he retains his own dignity, chastising Spiggott for his pettiness and eventually finding the strength the live his life his own way. There is only one scene, to my mind, where Stanley is abjectly humiliated, in the second wish where he becomes a cuckolded millionaire chasing around after his promiscuous wife with presents. Otherwise his characterisations always carry a strong sense of themselves rather than just being mere victims for Spiggott to play off. Nor should it be forgotten that the script affords Moore far wider scope to showcase his range of characterisations than its author.

The relationship between Spiggot and Stanley is, essentially, the same as that between Pete and Dud, but with an important power shift. Whereas the Dagenham duo are famously an informed idiot and an uninformed idiot, it now becomes the all-powerful Satan, Lord of darkness, all-knowing and omnipotent super-being... and an uninformed idiot. But both seem out of kilter with the world around them. Whilst Stanley is a nobody going nowhere, Spiggott lives in a crumbling mansion peopled by useless sins (including a wonderful cameo by Barry Humphries as Envy which reminds you what a great actor he is). He is also proprietor of the seedy Rendezvous club, a clear satire of Cook's own dead Establishment. For all his power, charm and wit, Spiggott is as much of an outsider as Stanley, although he doesn't seem all that bothered by it. It is Eleanor Bron's Margaret who is the embodiment of '60s London.

Margaret represents the world that Stanley aspires to. She is a part of the new, brash zeitgeist; working class but obviously with enough disposable income to buy the latest clothes, she wears heavy mascara and a mini-skirt, she has boyfriends who pick her up in their bubble cars. Her incarnations in Stanley's various wishes represent many '60s archetypes—the kittenish student who one can imagine poring over *The Bell Jar* and Simone De Beauvior; the promiscuous wife in an open marriage, even if her husband doesn't see it that way; the screaming teenage pop fan. Bron's performance in *Bedazzled* is often overlooked but in many ways it is her role which holds together the film, providing it with the unity it needs to become more than just a series of sketches linked by Pete and Dud dialogues.

The most perfect comment on '60s culture in the film, though, has to be Stanley's pop star wish. Set on a television show with the not-exactly-thickly disguised name *Go Going*, Stanley finds himself surrounded by scantily-clad dancers and screaming fans as he rips into his heartfelt number *Love Me*, a bombastic Scott-Walkerish hymn to yearning ('I'm on my knees, won't you please come and love me/I love you so, please don't go, stay and love me...'). The girls scream his name and, for the first time in the film, Margaret seems to be besotted with him. Then enter Drimbl Wedge And The Vegetations. Wedge (Spiggott in a carpet suit) is somewhere between John Lennon's sneering cynicism and Syd Barrett's other-worldliness, but not exactly like either. It's tempting to see it as a satire of David Bowie if it weren't for the fact that Bowie wouldn't become like that for a good few years. Cook simply talks over the heavily phased, hypnotically monotonous melody of the verses of *Bedazzled*. While the female backing singers implore him with various empty pieces of '60s-speak ('You turn me on... You plug me in... You light me up...'), Wedge stares into the middle distance and dismisses them and the audience as too dull to be bothered with ('You fill me with inertia'). With the final line of the song, 'I'm not available,' the girls, who were wetting their knickers over Stanley, flock to Wedge. In a classic case of 'show not tell' comedy, Cook has given a damning satire of pop culture. Like Andy Warhol, he demonstrates Pop is based not on sincerity or feeling but on attitude. Once again we're in the realm of Cookian paradox—Wedge attracts an audience by telling them they're boring—pop music is full of songs about love and desire but is based purely on fickle consumerism. The scene is not only a devastating piss-take of the music industry but a prediction of how it would go, from Bowie's Ziggy Stardust self-conscious oddity to the spittle-lipped snarl of Punk and the powdered posturing of Steve Strange and onwards.

Cook, as well as wanting to create the funniest film he could make, took the occasion to make a number of very important points about his feelings concerning religion, modern society and Man's place in the world. The fact that it doesn't automatically feel like that's what he's doing is a testament to Cook's art; once again, it's 'show not tell', imparting knowledge without the viewer knowing they're being imparted to. While he never lectures you or attempts to browbeat you with his learning, you leave the film with the 'Cook worldview' firmly implanted in your head. Look at the pillar box scene where Stanley and Spiggott enact Lucifer's fall from Heaven. They do the whole thing in half a minute. John Milton took pages and pages to do that.

We have become accustomed to the figure Cook played for the public on from the 1970s on, that of the wit and cynic who takes nothing too seriously—who never, as he said, matured or got any deeper or wiser from the age of 21. We sometimes forget that he could, when he so chose, write compelling and profound stuff. Look at his play for the *Consequences* album, a very human piece about the pain and misery involved in the legalities of a divorce. The Mini-Drama sketch from *Behind The Fridge* is less of a comedy than a terrific and terrifying portrait of a psychopathic mind. Need more convincing that there's depth to the laughs in *Bedazzled*?

Look at some of the more obscure throwaway jokes and references in it. In the Frunigreen Eyewash scene, when Stanley and Spiggott sit down to eat Mrs. Wisby's raspberries, Spiggott pulls a large wooden spoon from inside his overalls. A reference to the wonderfully medieval proverb 'He that sups with the Devil hath need of a long spoon'? Look at the first scene in the Rendezvous club where Stanley is reading the contract for his soul. On the wall of Spiggot's office behind Stanley you'll see a faded poster for an old British advertising campaign, 'Go To Work On An Egg.' The egg is the symbol of the soul. Just think how many levels that joke works on. The egg as the soul, interestingly, is reference also used by Alan Parker in his film *Angel Heart* (1987), as is the devil as a modern sophisticate and the cage lift for taking souls to Heaven or Hell.

Strangely, no one seems to question the intellectual credentials of a comedy film like *Life Of Brian*, perhaps because the Monty Python crowd wore their cleverness as a badge of pride in a way

Cook never did. But our hero was evidently in a mood to push the horizons of his writing and performing out when he was interviewed by the *Daily Express* shortly before the release of *Bedazzled*. When talking about how doing a film meant temporarily leaving the more regular work of television, he said: 'You can get yourself into a semi-unconscious state of mind and go on forever without extending your brains or your range of comedy at all. It doesn't seem enough to me that people are just willing to sit and watch you do the same old thing... I am a lot more receptive to ideas than I used to be.' (*Daily Express*, Nov 25 1967.)

There's tons more to discover in this film, layer upon layer to unfold. Is Moore's performance as the libidinous Welsh intellectual a reference to Peter Sellers in *Only Two Can Play*? Maybe with a touch of Kenneth Griffith on top (just listen to the way he delivers the word 'virile')? Is the 'Everything I say is a lie' dialogue a description of Bertrand Russell's paradox of classes? Why is so much of the film shot at a remove? The devil appears behind a window, Stanley attempts suicide behind a glass panel in his shower, Lust approaches Stanley behind a gauze curtain, the Drimbl Wedge scene is seen almost entirely on television monitors. A reference to Lewis Carroll's looking-glass world? Is there a reason why St. Beryl's nunnery is described as 'non-denominational'? There are no definite answers here, or in anything I've written so far. I'm not saying the Cook was intimately acquainted with 16th century anti-Luther pamphlets, or that he based his performance as Spiggott on an obscure reference to Russian literature. But what I hope to have done is throw open the doors on what I think is one of the most complex comedies ever made. Perhaps it was the film's failure in the UK and the US that made Cook never again try anything quite so intellectually ambitious.

THE BACK PASSAGE

Just like Jimi Hendrix, we need feedback. What should the PCAS be doing—apart from hard drugs? Grab your quills and scribble some dribble...

Hi!

Perhaps you could start a petition for 20th C*ntury F*x NOT to remake *Bedazzled*? It's surely going to be utter crap.

Cheers,

GEORGE RITCHIE, Glasgow.

Dear Jim Trash,

I am a writer over here (I wrote the screenplay for *Analyze This* and produced and wrote many episodes of *The Larry Sanders Show*) and have just finished a draft, with Harold Ramis, of a remake of *Bedazzled*. I know this is news that no doubt fills you with dread but I do think this version will make for a better movie experience. I love the original but it's very much of its time and Cook is not a great actor, although I think he does a fine job playing the Devil.

I got to talking to my wife tonight at dinner about Cook, and just realised I know almost nothing about his life, just bits and pieces. I checked on Amazon for a biography but the search came up with nothing. Could you suggest any books about Cook that I might read? Has anyone written the definitive bio of Cook? I'm assuming they have, because he seems to be such an important figure in modern British comedy.

Thanks from this side of the pond,

PETER TOLAN, Hollywood, via email.

Dear Dragger,

I have just rewritten the rewriting of *Bedazzled* so it does not incorporate Peter Tolan. I know this is news that no doubt fills you with dread but I do think this version will make for a better movie experience. When I got talking with my wife who, let me tell you, is no expert on one of the jewels of British film comedies, I realised that I knew almost nothing about Peter Tolan other than his name which I have seen on the printed page. Considering this more than equals the sum total of his knowledge regarding Peter Cook, I expect a large development fee from a major motion picture studio forthwith.

I found out more about Peter Tolan in two minutes by going to the Internet Movie Database (www.imdb.com) than he seems to have managed for the man whose vision will be paying to keep Tolan's wife in dinner conversation and his children in therapy which they will need once they find out that their father has not only co-written *My Fellow Americans* but has vandalised a wonderfully-written piece of work that remains a pure joy to watch. 'Could you suggest any books about Cook that I might read?' Why? Does Tolan want to rewrite it, make it a 'better fiction experience', and then laugh all the way to the bank again?

Peter Tolan can fuck off. And you can tell him that from me. 'Oh, I can make that a better swearing experience.' Yeah, yeah. Fuck off, Tolan.

MARC HAYNES, Pinner, Middx.

Dear Clinty,

Looks like Messrs Gelbart and Ramis are destined to be paid the wages of sin for their shameful attempt to rehash Cook's masterpiece. An anagram of their names produces a somewhat apt judgement: 'Grr! Really bad amoral shit.'

Straight to video then. Never mind, chaps.

Yours openmindedly,

SIMON MEACHER, Exeter.

THE ZSA ZSA MAN

Peter says that Zsa Zsa Gabor has never forgiven him for what he did to her on Eamonn Andrews' show, 'She flounced in with a little dog [*sic*] under her arm to say how much she loved animals, darlink. But, far from loving her little pet, the dog was clearly uncomfortable under the bright lights. So I was rude to her, I'm afraid. But then she flew out to Los Angeles and started giving press conferences about me. I'm sure when I go, people in the States will see the headline "Zsa Zsa Man Dies".' Says Peter.

The Sun, 16th November 1990.

We ghastly minnows at Wisty Towers, ever wildly driven by crazed curiosity (tempered only by abject apathy), want to know more of this celebrated stand off. Therefore our resident historian, Professor Smuggleigh Harrogant, the lecturer in Applied Bandages at the University of West Zambia, was hurled into the vaults to dig up any press reports of the time. He emerged, slightly smouldering and missing both arms, three months later with this clipping clenched between his gums.

ZSA ZSA TO PETER COOK: YOU'RE THE RUDEST
By Victor Davis

A furious row broke out between Zsa Zsa Gabor and satirist Peter Cook on television last night—a few hours before Zsa Zsa leaves England after a stormy two-months stay.

Eamonn Andrews unwittingly fuelled the fire when he invited Cook to give his opinion of the 45 year old Hungarian-American actress. The languid Cook puffed on his cigarette and said crisply that she was vain, had no talent, and was altogether 'a non-event'. If the show had been in colour I think it would have revealed Eamonn Andrews with a Dublin green face.'Why do you say these things? You are the rudest young man I have met for many years.' Snapped Zsa Zsa.

Retorted Cook: 'I was asked to speak the truth.'

Zsa Zsa: 'How dare you say I have no talent? I get 150,000 dollars a picture'

Cook (to a round of applause): 'That is not necessarily talent.'

Zsa Zsa to Eamonn: 'I don't even know what he does. I don't know his name, and I don't want to know his name.'

When Zsa Zsa appeared as the last guest of Eamonn's late night ITV programme she described herself as 'prudish and kind to animals.' With her she had her fluffy white cat, Madame Pompadour.

Said Peter Cook coldly: 'If you really cared about animals you would not bring that cat under these hot television lights.'

Forcing a grin, Eamonn swiftly brought his programme to a close. The Zsa Zsa versus Cook controversy was left to continue behind the scenes at the Royal Lancaster Hotel, Bayswater, where the programme was being televised. Said Cook: 'I hope you're not going to throw your cat at me.'

Zsa Zsa's last word: 'She is too good for you.'

The Daily Sketch, 10th Jan. 1969.

For an eye-witness account, we now wheel in the eye (and the rest) of Steve Grant, former executive editor of *Time Out* magazine.

"I'm happy to help you with the Zsa Zsa Gabor incident. Intriguingly, it happened at a time when, as a post-graduate student in Manchester, I was spending most of my time in pubs and bars and snooker halls rather than watching TV or working. I was round at a friend's house, the worse for wear, when the programme was switched on. As Peter Cook was a guest we watched and couldn't believe it when, after going round a couple of boring wally fellow guests with the same question, Andrews asked innocently, 'What do you think is the real Zsa Zsa?' Cookie then proceeded to tell the viewers and the studio audience what he really thought, saying that she went round the world drumming up publicity to hide her lack of talent. She then said she didn't know who he was, and he said he wrote a bit and acted a bit, very laid back, fag in hand, not giving a flying fuck. She told him to get his hair cut as he looked like a woman, and PC replied with, 'Well, it doesn't matter because I'm a raving poof anyway', which got a great laugh. Then some obscure worthy tried to calm things down by saying something like 'I'd remind Mr.Cook that none of us is perfect', or some such bollocks. I know that he remembered this incident well as he once said he was terrified that he'd be remembered as the man who was once rude to Zsa Zsa Gabor on TV. I must have been pissed though because I don't recall the animal at all. But I'll never forget the look on Shamus Android's face."

A PIPE AND FLIPPERS MAN

A Juney day in 2000 found The Holy Dragger skipping like an asthmatic chicken to Eel Pie Island on the River Thames to have his lugs bent by Trevor Baylis. A champion swimmist in his youth, Baylis later utilised his talent for breath holding in an underwater escapology act. Recent times have seen Mr B justly celebrated for inventing the clockwork radio and for dedicating his out-of-water existence to the noble pipe. His aqua-snout for deep-sea chain-smokers is still in development.

Typical of the enquiring mind, it was Trevor who asked the first question.

TREVOR BAYLIS: How old would Peter have been now?

PAUL HAMILTON: Sixty-two. Sixty-three in November.

TB: Right, 'cos I've just turned 63 in May so we're contemporaries and we would have shared that whole experience of listening to the radio; *Dick Barton—Special Agent*, and Spike Milligan and *The Goon Show*, of course, which you couldn't escape from. *The Goon Show* type of humour isn't that dissimilar from Peter's. Like,

The Goons had an upside-down lighthouse for submarines. Bizarre stuff. Brilliant things.

PH: Aside from radio, what sort of humour was there in the '40s and '50s?

TB: We were brought up with Heath Robinson and Walter Emmett. Heath Robinson drew wild machines, insane gadgets, dream stuff. I see Peter as a continuation of Heath Robinson's imagination, in a way.

PH: Like James Last, you've had this fascination with water.

TB: When I was at school I suppose I would have been regarded as ESN—educationally subnormal—but I was very good at swimming. I was swimming for my country by age fifteen. So water's played a big part in my life. I'm surrounded by water to this day!

PH: And water connects you to Peter and Dudley.

TB: Of course. I did a water escape act, as it were, with Peter and Dudley in a car. We did this in Borehamwood in, I think, 1969. Peter had one of those goatee beards on—he was playing Herr Lacquer or someone. What happened was I had been on a Dave Allen show the week before, helping out this Swedish hot-shot who was explaining that it was possible for you to survive if you drove your car into the river. Provided you have the patience and courage, you let the car fill up with water, surviving on the air that's trapped in the ceiling of the car, and then you carefully open the door and you swim to the surface. It all sounds very good, so this bloke was demonstrating it in an enormous water tank, and I was acting as the health and safety man. Peter had seen the show and had been amused by this very boring man, so he called up to say that he and Dudley wanted to do a satire of him on their one-hour ATV show *Goodbye Again*. I was there to make sure Peter and Dudley didn't come to grief. The sketch was very funny because Peter was much taller than Dudley and they'd be strapped into this car which would be filling up with water and Peter would be saying, [*Swedish accent:*] "So you see, you can survive on zee air." Meanwhile, Dudley's totally submerged underwater, going cross-eyed and all that. Definitely drowning. My job was to stop him from actually drowning. I would be hidden on the backseat of the car, regularly supplying him with oxygen from an aqualung. I was doing my best not to make any bubbles myself—or that would have given me away.

PH: Did Peter and Dudley arrive with a prepared script?

TB: No. They had this extraordinary way of putting together gags. The three of us were going in for make-up and, as I was sitting there, they started talking to each other. And it's all gobbledegook. I couldn't understand what the fucking hell's going on. It was all rhyming slang, riddles, different words, different shapes of words—I dunno, it was all hieroglyphic stuff. Every now and again they'd whip out something that was amusing which they would jot down. They had a strange way of ricocheting off one another which I guess was how they got their punchlines to their sketches. They shared some wild card, do-your-own-dream, try-and-mix-it-with-my-dream type of scenario. It was very strange, that way of working. I'd never come across anything like it before.

PH: A private language?

TB: Yeah, they'd obviously developed over the years a strange way of talking to one another. But I tell you what—it was a technique that certainly worked. They would drop into the vernacular, try different accents, play with words, laugh a lot. Dudley was a rascal, very impish. And Peter had this amazing ability, once the camera was on, to become extremely serious and knowledgeable, talking with grave authority about crap or something so stupid. He could do those "I say, look here", lord of the manor voices and, back then, class was determined by accent. If someone had a "QUAR-QUAR" accent, you know, people had to "know their place". This whole class divide started with the 11-Plus at school. If you failed your 11-Plus you were on the voyage of the damned. You failed that and you're A.B.—Arsehole Brigade. You had to serve those that passed the 11-Plus for the rest of your life. One of the pleasures in life was ribbing the affectations of those that passed and went on to Grammar School, and I think taking the piss out of them was part of Peter and Dudley's comedy. I think Peter used to knock the system for what it was. They were both great ones for knocking authority and tradition. The Sixties was the time of sex'n'drugs'n'rock'n'roll. It was the time for these things to be discussed. A liberalising time—although, you know, it was really nothing new. Go back to the Roaring Twenties and the 1930s and there's Josephine Baker dancing with nothing on but a belt made of bananas and Billie Holiday singing "Cocaine all around my brain"...

But anyway, they did the water escape sketch and then they filmed a second sketch. It went like this: Peter Cook turned up as a brigadier, I think, with red epaulettes, in a scout car. Standing there, like Montgomery. He arrives on the square and delivers this speech about new Army regulations and how important it is that we are aware of when it is going to rain. He says that there is new procedure for determining the presence of rain. Then the Sergeant Major—who might've been Dudley Moore—takes over. After a lot of "LEFT! RIGHT! LEFT! RIGHT!" it ends up with these soldiers in their best BD laying down on the ground with their hands on their chests, palms facing the sky. And when there's the presence of rain you hear [*high-pitched soldier's voice:*] "Feelin' the speckles, SAH!" Then they all start shouting, "Feelin' the speckles, SAH!" And Peter goes, "Rightio, Sarn't Major, I think we've got a spot of rain." It was a silly, what-could-happen-on-an-army-base-on-a-boring-day type sketch. A lovely, lovely piece.

NOT ONLY DOCKETED BUT ALSO RONEO'D

James Gilbert has done very many things. One thing was to produce the 1970 series of Not Only But Also. *Another thing was to talk about it thirty years later into the ear trumpet of The Holy Dragger. This is wot he said...*

I'd gotten a call from the Head Of Light Entertainment saying Peter and Dudley wanted to do another series so I zipped round to meet them at Dudley's house. He lived in Hampstead then with his wife, Judy—no, not Judy. Who was his current wife? Suzy! That's right, Suzy Kendall. How many wives did Dudley have? There was Tuesday Weld, er, Tuesday, Wednesday. Anyway, this was November 1969 and we started filming in mid-January 1970. There's no way you can produce a series from scratch at such short notice. All you can do is be grateful for the material you've got and get on with it—because there's no time to re-write it, like you could if you had all the scripts done twelve weeks before you began shooting. The situation we were in, we couldn't afford to toss out substandard material. For instance, The Con Man sketch that was in, I think, show 6. I didn't like that one at all but eventually, obviously, by Episode 6 there was a great big gaping wound to be filled. It'd been filmed quite early on and they knew my opinion of it. They probably felt the same since they didn't put up much of a fight when I kept on postponing it from the show and pleading, 'Please write something else.'

There were so many time problems: How to fill 45 minutes, for instance. This is why we brought in this very pretty singer called Nanette to do a song every week and she sank without trace afterwards. Then we also had people that Peter really liked—Joe Cocker, Yes; you know, the top contemporary groups. And [preparation] time was lessened by Dudley being in a play on the West End, giving eight performances a week in *Play It Again, Sam*. I don't know why Dudley agreed to all this. I know they had had a thin period doing those four hour-long specials for ATV [*Goodbye Again*], which had some good things in it, I think, but I didn't like the presentation much. I can't fathom the reason why it was all so rushed. Maybe Peter needed the money, I dunno.

Sunday was the only day Dudley had off from the play and they couldn't write on matinee days. So Saturday was right out, as was the Wednesday or Thursday when Dudley had to perform matinee shows. They could only write on two or three days a week. Luckily, Dudley didn't have to rehearse with his band. They would generally decide on the day what to play, so there was no pressure there. But location shoots could only be done at weekends because Dudley had to be back in the theatre by the evening, and some of the film sequences were overnight shoots—like The Glidd Of Glood which was shot at Bodiam Castle, and the Ark Royal footage.

The only thing that was written in advance of our first day of rehearsal was the first show's script which they spent two weeks or more in writing. I had thought there were other items prepared but there weren't. They would come in and I would put them in a room down the corridor with a tape recorder, and my secretary would be sitting there, fingers poised, and as the tapes came in she would type it. I had no control over it because it was such last-minute stuff. After it was typed up we'd all look at it and decide whether this could be strengthened or that could be cut, whatever, but in the meantime they would have to be writing something else.

It was fortunate that the series was being shown fortnightly, because for the filmed sketches they usually didn't have the script until the day of shooting. They had a deadline to meet as regards what location was required, what props and costumes were necessary and so on, but the actual content of the script was often an unknown quantity until the day. Dudley's Beethoven piece, for instance, was technically demanding, being shot on video and in the studio, but we didn't get the music—the Ludwigged Tom Jones medley—until the actual day.

We also had the Poets Cornered spot which proved to be a great bonus in the running order because that was elastic: If we were running short of the 45 minute mark we could extend the item, if we were over then I could cut it short because I had my finger on the button. Poets Cornered—or The Gunge, as we called it—was Peter's idea. Basically, Peter and Dudley, plus a guest, would improvise a poem. Spike Milligan was on one show, and we had Ronnie Barker, Willie Rushton, Barry Humphries, Frank Muir, Denis Norden and Alan Bennett. Yes, Alan wasn't too keen on The Gunge but he did it and was marvellous. The set-up was a huge tank and, above it, three seats—Peter always sat in the middle one—and it was a bit like the gallows, really, because I'd press a lever up in the control room and a seat would go down and propel the sitter into the tank of green gunge. My supposed role was to penalise the contestants for dithering and whatnot but I used to cheat like mad. If we were going over the allotted time I'd press any button and send whoever into the gunge. They'd be fulminating in the tank—'How dare you!'—but I was watching the clock more than anything else, really. Of course, there were no technical winners since they all ended up in the gunge eventually. What was great was having the last one perched on his seat trying to carry on improvising couplets, eyes panic-struck like a startled rabbit, wondering when he's going to be fired into the tank.

It's said that some of the Pete and Dud dialogues weren't up to previous standards, but the first one was because we actually had time to rehearse. That was Dud Dreams, Dudley being re-born in the bedroom wardrobe. I suggested a bit of 'business'—Dud skulking in the bottom of the wardrobe, sucking his thumb at the end of the sketch. But the rest of the time there was little opportunity to work on the material. I don't think Peter and Dudley cared that much for rehearsing. They made pretty certain that they'd left it so late that I was never able to rehearse like the first show again!

They never actually wrote as such. They would improvise into a tape recorder. The improvisations would be typed up and that would be the script. That was our Bible, if you like, for marking all the camera angles and shots so that if they digressed from the script, or got the giggles, the cameras would be there to catch it. The crew had to know what was going on—or supposed to be going on, anyway. Their attitude to script writing wasn't far removed from Mike Leigh and his plays, in that although it originates from improvisation it ends up as a very hard script.

It'd be rare that I would get more than two run-throughs of the show before the actual shooting, but by the end of the second run—dress rehearsal—on the Sunday they were pretty word-perfect. Didn't need autocue or idiot boards. With Peter and Dudley, I wouldn't say they were One-Take Wonders, but I would try to avoid saying: 'Could you do that again?' for whatever reason. It's understandable if there was a technical hitch and everything ground to a halt, or if Peter has asked for something to be re-done, but as a policy—I mean, imagine re-doing a Pete and Dud sketch: Some of them lasted for 15 minutes. There'd be no time for anything else.

By a fortuitous quirk of fate in our favour, somehow in our timetable of making the shows and their being transmitted, we found we had almost a month in which to write and rehearse and shoot loads of material. The Ark Royal stuff, Good Vs Evil [cricket match], The Making Of A Movie, Ludwig—all that would have been done in that four week period—partly because there was nothing else to do!

Glidd came about because Peter had decided to write a book of poems, primarily for his own children, I guess, and this was a brilliant children's poem. But, you know, this was a fable, a fairy tale, not comedy, and having to shoot it in mid-winter—when it was freezing cold—on location in a ruined castle on the south coast. Peter, at one time, was so cold—he was dressed in only a brown paper parcel—he was perishing. I was pouring brandy down his throat to keep him warm.

For all its good and bad points—the lowest being The Con Man, of course—it wasn't fair that almost all the series has been lost to posterity, and if I could have a word with The Man Upstairs to ask for one sketch to be saved I'd have to say Lengths. Without a doubt. Lengths came about from Peter being in the office and watching all the chaos—which he, in effect, was responsible for—of secretaries typing and retyping scripts, booking acts, locations, editing the previous show, planning meetings, all this continuous madness. I hadn't realised that Peter had been observing this and the fact that my secretary and I had the same telephone extension. She had a strip of red Sellotape round the receiver to her telephone, and I had green on mine, and the Production Assistant had blue, and the other secretary had yellow. He was silently watching us going 'Yes, I'm on yellow, I'll put you through to Jimmy on green', and later he said, 'I'm going to do a thing on dockets.' I remember saying, 'God, that doesn't sound very funny.'—'I think you'll find it funny.' He was right because it was brilliant. He didn't write it alone, of course. He would've explained the set-up to Dudley and they would improvise the thing together because he probably didn't have the self-discipline, I don't think, to have done it on his own. He said his big sadness was in going around London to dinner parties and God-knows-what and knowing he's coming out with things but if only he could remember them the next day to write them down, store them, or have a Boswell tag along after him, like Boswell did for Johnson. Instead it all vanished, especially if he'd had a few, because then nobody remembers anything the next day. Dudley caught Peter well, I thought, when he said Peter was a confident performer but an un-confident person and he had to boost himself with booze, endless fags and all the rest of it, you know.

Anyway! Since the film of Lengths has been destroyed, I'll explain that it takes place in an office. Peter was behind one desk, Dudley was at an angle at another one, and each desk had about four or five phones. I thought the tag-line to each phone-call was brilliant—'I can't talk to you now 'cos he's here... I love you, too.'

Of the snatches of the surviving film, though, I don't know if the Ludwig Van Beethoven material makes much sense on the *Comedy Greats* compilation video since the linking sketches shot in the studio, vital pieces, are lost. But in the Good Vs. Evil Cricket Match we had the most extraordinary piece of luck when, as they were doing a rain dance, it began to snow. Hollywood couldn't have got that for two million dollars. Peter re-wrote the script immediately because, initially, I was thinking 'Oh no, it's ruined,' but he said, 'No, it's wonderful.' And turned the rain dance into a snow dance. I remember the extra who had to do that dance: This poor African chap dressed only in a loincloth in freezing February having to get out and do this silly dance again in the snow.

When the series was repeated I cut out Nanette and all the groups, just concentrating on them, and they made absolutely terrific half-hour shows. The series was shown on ABC in Australia in that format and I can't figure out why ABC haven't got the shows in their archives. When the BBC were restoring and re-issuing the old *Hancock's Half-Hour* shows they had to go to ABC who had lovingly kept them. Maybe ABC wiped the *Not Only But Also* tapes themselves, or they had sent them back to London, I dunno.

The film footage was kept in a box in a warehouse in Ealing and I was told it would be destroyed unless someone paid a storage fee.

It was only £60 so I stumped up for it and later edited the footage together for a half-hour compilation that went out on Christmas Eve 1974, BBC2, with some new bits that I filmed with Peter and Dudley in New York. They were doing their *Good Evening* show on Broadway at the time. I told Peter that I had this stuff [i.e. the filmed sketches] and would he write a half-hour incorporating this material. He came up with this crazy idea of Pete and Dud getting on the Isle of Wight ferry and the ferry goes into this fog. When the fog cleared, there's Pete and Dud going slowly up the East River on a barge, with a piano. And we had to film on the river because the American unions wouldn't allow a BBC film crew to work in New York, on land. So we had to rent a boat and do everything aboard that, including Dudley playing the piano, sailing round and round Manhattan Island. It was such a ridiculous premise that it didn't really work, but it was an attempt to salvage the remains.

Whilst I was in New York I arranged to go to see their revue. I must say that, personally speaking, I thought there was a drop in the writing quality there, compared to what they had done before on the telly and *Beyond The Fringe*.

Some may wonder why, when they seemed to thrive artistically on invention and disliked repetition, did they carry on with this two-man show for four years. I suppose it must have been the money. They both had families and lifestyles and bank managers, you know. You can imagine how much they would have been earning, just the two of them on Broadway. Despite some misgivings about the material, I did enjoy it as an event: Pete and Dud on Broadway. Even when Peter walked on stage to look for me: "Where's Jimmy? Jimmy? There you are. Is Fiona there?" I thought that was a touch odd. I found out afterwards that he had had a few before the show. Had quite a lot, actually. Mind you, I would never have guessed it from his performance. But I'm sidetracking...

Not Only But Also had gained a bit of a reputation for its outlandish opening sequences. One time they played cavemen who had carved 'Not Only... But Also...' out of a chalkhill, they played the piano underwater, and we felt obliged to carry on the tradition. The best opening we did in the third series was the Ark Royal one. The Ark Royal was such an extraordinary facility to be offered and it all came about from my P.A. on the series, a famous fixer called Tony James. On the first day I said: 'We've got to get some marvellous opening sequences,' and he piped up: 'Would you like the Ark Royal?'—'How do you mean?'—'Well, I can fix that if you want. Look, I've got a private telephone number.' He then proceeded to ring the captain of the Ark Royal on the bridge—Tony had a private line to the ship itself—and he got a verbal interest from the captain which was eventually firmed-up.

We went down to the army base in Somerset and were flown by helicopter—Pete, Dud, me, Tony, my P.A.—to the ship and the deal was fixed. A condition of the captain's was that "Fly Navy" was written on the piano—it was in fact his idea to catapult the piano into the sea. He told us that when they were in the Far East that was how they would get rid of their old cars: They'd buy old bangers over there and then just junk 'em, catapult them into the sea. The other condition was that, since the ratings would all be chipping in, painting a huge NOT ONLY BUT ALSO on the deck, Pete and Dud would oblige them with a concert, which they agreed to do, although they were a tad reluctant—frightened, really—to perform before a full ship's company, steaming down the Channel.

Well, we went down there—the crew had done their job, a marvellous effort—and we filmed the opening and closing sequences, catapulted the piano off over the bows. Later that day one of their jets crashed and the two-man crew was killed. It was caused by the fact that there was no horizon and, if you lose your sense of balance and perspective you might think your plane's upside-down, even though your instruments are saying 'straight and level'. If you don't have sufficient belief in your instruments, you will—like they did, because all they could see was haze—turn your plane upside-down and fly straight into the sea. And so that night, because we stayed over, the crew drank the pilots' health in the mess hall, and the drinks were put on the dead pilots' mess bill. That was the tradition. But, obviously, the concert was cancelled.

Reading the scripts again, I realise that the Pete and Dud conversation about Racial Prejudice is about the only sketch one couldn't do nowadays. The times are very different now. Maybe it was done the way it was because of the racial tensions at the time—you know, Enoch Powell's 'Rivers Of Blood' speech was made not long before the series. Perhaps it was the same feeling that made Spike Milligan do *The Melting Pot*, a series that was never screened. The theory behind *Melting Pot* was that if you have a go at everybody then you point out the absolute absurdity of racial prejudice. That was Spike's theory, but when you actually saw it as a programme it didn't come over like that. It wasn't well written, to be blunt, and when you're treading that razor's edge, you couldn't be on dodgier ground. The pilot show was very funny but the series was just totally offensive. If we'd shown it, it would have closed the BBC down. But the idea was worth a go, and I think Pete and Dud—who were not even fractionally racist; the exact opposite, in fact—would have thought the same. But there was something about the bongo-bongos and missionaries being eaten—all the old clichés which they, of course, would think was just being satirical, not being taken seriously and showing how absurd it was. But some people might not see it at that level but at just face value like they would Alf Garnett. I don't, however, recall any complaints from the viewers—and, although we were on BBC2, *Not Only But Also* did garner a large, wide audience. I think that Racial Prejudice sketch, at the time, probably wouldn't have been regarded as politically incorrect because they wouldn't have the mindset of 'Let's make fun of the blacks.' Obviously, it would be totally unacceptable now. It was a noble idea but dodgily executed. I mean, Dudley blacked up for that sketch and if I thought there was any ugly racism in there I would have cut it out. I was embarrassed by *The Black And White Minstrel Show* and when I got into a strong enough position in the BBC I had that show cancelled—in 1977, when I took over Light Entertainment from Bill Cotton.

Talking of changes in acceptability over the last thirty years I noticed that in The Scriptwriter, the Johnny Speight lampoon, my typist had censored the word 'tits' and typed 't*ts' instead. She was very prim, very disapproving of that sort of thing, and probably couldn't bring herself to type the word. The Scriptwriter is my other favourite of the entire series, along with Lengths. 'I'll swap you ten bloodies for one bum.' That was based on a meeting with Frank Muir haggling over the number of swearwords permissible.

The Garbo film—Peter as Emma Bargo—was excellent, too, and Peter just loved doing it, especially going through the streets of Ealing with a loudhailer, atop an armoured car, shouting "I Wornt To Be Alorn!"

Peter and Dudley worked very well together and very hard—in their fashion—on the series, and a very cheerful staff ably supported them. They were a likeable pair, Peter and Dudley, and they would always have a party after each show up in a restaurant—Fagin's Restaurant, near Hampstead tube station. The last party they had was after they did The Making Of A Movie film, and we'd all had quite a bit of wine when they bounced up on their chairs with Dudley in one corner of the restaurant and Peter in another, with rather astonished diners in the middle while they did all this cod-Shakespeare. They were very much into the pomposity, as they saw it, of the Great Actors and theatrical knights.

One could never accuse them of being reluctant performers. They really loved performing. What they were both reluctant about was actually starting work. They liked leaving everything to the last minute—the whole writing aspect, putting it all together. Peter, I think, felt he had to play it off the seat of his pants. I was talking with him a year after Not Only But Also and asked him what he's up to. 'Oh, I'm doing a chat show [Where Do I Sit?].' I said, 'Oh, and when's that?'—'Next Friday.'—'What's it going to be like?'—'Oh, I dunno.' He didn't seem to be particularly worried about it but I think he had a terrible shock when it turned into a complete disaster.

However, the great joy of working with the both of them was the feeling of spontaneity between the two, and Peter was in control more. I mean, he would spend the entire session in front of an audience as the cameras were rolling and try to get Dudley to corpse. And succeeding, too, occasionally. You could see it in Dudley's eyes: 'Uh-oh, he's got him!' And on one or two proud occasions Dudley got Peter—especially with In The Club. He went completely during that one—'What's my line?' God, that was funny.

Peter was a delightful person to work for—once you got used to the fact that you were on a razor's edge of having to do a show in two weeks and 'Wait a minute, folks—what are we gonna do? Where's the script?'—and you've got filming and editing and music and casting and guest stars and whatnot [going on]. Once you've got used to that, it would appear sometimes not of as-quite-a-high-a-standard if they'd had more time to do it, but considering how little time they did it in the standard of some of the stuff was absolutely brilliant.

THE BACK PASSAGE

We welcome your maunderings and musings, be they botty-slurping or abusing. This is your Back Passage—SEIZE IT!

Dear Clintistorit,

May I bore your readers with a memory of the 1970 *Not Only But Also* series, stirred up by James Gilbert's excellent and amusing article? [*Oh, go on then*—Ed.] When he mentioned his prim secretary's censoring of the word 'tits' when typing up the Scriptwriter sketch, it reminded me that said offending word was itself censored by Peter and Dudley when they performed it, meaning that instead of saying 'tits' they said 't*ts' (pronounced 'teh-tiss'). Whether that was their original intention or their reaction to seeing their scripts censored, I don't really know. I do know it was very funny to see, especially because Dudley gave his Cockney scriptwriter character a stutter.

I hope this letter is worthy of publication as it would be a proud day to see my name in your fine fagazine.

Yours sincerely and Good Evening,

[UNSIGNED]

THE GLIDD OF GLOOD

One of the remaining fragments of the 1970 series of Not Only But Also *is the filmed dramatisation of Peter Cook's poem The Glidd Of Glood. Peter stated in a press interview that The Glidd Of Glood was probably his most self-revealing work. Seeing as it takes a thief to catch a thief, we gave the text of the poem to actual real-life poet Clare Pollard for analysis. This is her interpretation.*

The Glidd Of Glood is a subtle, complex work of art that works simultaneously on two levels. On the first hand, it is an updating of Coleridge's *Lyrical Ballads*, both reinventing the quatrains of the folk form, and participating in a process of mythmaking reminiscent of *The Ancient Mariner* or *Kubla Khan*. In such a reading, we can concentrate on Cook's sensuous feel for language: the sinuous alliteration of the title; the subtle half-rhyme of 'castle' and 'parcel'; the rich connotations of the names, with Glidd suggesting 'gilded,' and the jester 'Sparquin' signalling in 'spar-' that he will ultimately do battle with his superior. On another level, however, it becomes clear that the poem plays out a Freudian nightmare. The first stanza begins with the Glidd wandering 'nude' except for his 'huge brown paper parcel'—clearly a symbolic penis. We soon discover that the 'parcel' is:

> Tied to his wrist with bits of string.
> He never put it down.

The Glidd is a compulsive masturbator, with the 'bits of string' representing his ejaculations. His parcel is 'cuddled' perpetually. Unfortunately, it is his 'only pleasure'—the masturbation has become the main symptom of an over-arching self-involvement, which means he is unable to communicate with other people. Instead, he uses them only as fodder for his sexual depravity—we are told that the Glidd feeds his courtiers his 'wood,' along with 'grains of rice' that evoke sperm. On Sundays they receive his 'boiled mice'—a wonderful and startling metaphor for the Glidd's bollocks. Within this context, the theft of his jewels by a moustached figure in a 'nightie' becomes a scene of castration: of the vagina dentata or dominant mother stripping him of his precious parcel, leaving the sheets 'soaking wet' with blood. It is no coincidence that Sparquin goes 'South.' And, as a man whose life is based on a foundation of power and wanking, death for Glidd inevitably follows. The moral of this phallic 'tale' is in fact: don't let anyone take your knob off you.

I LOVE A MAN WITH NO CONVICTIONS

If any one film has ever deserved the description 'curate's egg', *The Rise And Rise Of Michael Rimmer* is it. By and large ignored or given the briefest of passing mention in any Cook article, there is actually much worth savouring within. It contains flaws—my God, it's got massive flaws: there aren't enough jokes, it goes on far too long with too many scenes piddling around for an eternity and failing to go anywhere, and Cook's portrayal of the central character is unengaging—but at its heart is a fascinating story.

The film's genesis is a strange one in itself. David Frost claims to have had the original idea after witnessing the Hull North by-election where one party's 8% lead at the exit polls in the morning had turned into 12% by the evening as the losing party's supporters lost heart. Opinion polls were no longer just reflecting the mood of the electorate, they were beginning to have an effect on the election results themselves.

John Cleese and Graham Chapman were commissioned to write the script circa 1967/1968. At the time both artists were tied to

Frost's Paradine Productions company which offered it to Cook, who agreed to use it for his first solo starring feature film. He did some work of his own on Cleese and Chapman's script along with the film's director Kevin Billington, and it was made with an 'all-star British comedy' cast, i.e. all the usual suspects. Then, in a spirit of pure belligerence it was refused distribution by its own studio until long after the 1970 General Election because of its comments on the Election process and its rather obvious satire on Harold Wilson. Protests that it was precisely George A. Cooper's portrayal of Prime Minister Blackett as Wilson and the timing of the film's release just before the election that gave the movie its potent satirical punch fell on deaf ears, and by the time the film came out Ted Heath was firmly ensconced at Number 10 Downing Street and *Rimmer* seemed out-of-date and limp, doing little business at the British box office and failing to even get a theatrical release in America. A pity, but I think it's high time the film was rediscovered by a new generation, particularly as the film's plot—the story of the rise to Prime Minister of a young fresh-faced chap with no background, no personality and, more importantly, no political ideology other than the accumulation of power by smiling and giving people what they think they want—seems more relevant today than ever before. If E.L. Wisty is reminiscent of John Major, Michael Rimmer is strikingly like Tony Blair.

A quick summary of the plot: We start in Fairburn Opinion Polls, a small-time market research company. The offices are rundown and ramshackle. The manager Mr. Ferret (Arthur Lowe) spends the majority of his working day watching cricket on the telly and wooing his secretary Tanya (Valerie Leon). The rest of Ferret's staff are similarly distracted spending most of their time on the toilet reading their paper, studying horseracing form or, in the case of Mr. Pumer (John Cleese), practising their ballroom dancing. Into this world walks Michael Rimmer (Peter Cook), a time-and-motion efficiency man who shakes everyone up.

Here is where the element of mystery starts to creep in that gives this film its edge. When they begin to ask themselves where Rimmer has come from no one can remember any warning he was coming. When Rimmer goes to report his findings to company chairman Lord Fairburn (Dennis Price), his lordship can't remember having met Rimmer before, let alone hiring him, but seems to accept his presence after Rimmer presents him with a report detailing FOP's sloth and inefficiency. Ferret is demoted and Rimmer installed as manager, the offices updated to the latest in expansive '60s minimalism and the staff turned into a lean, mean market-researching team.

Rimmer's tactic for the company is to raise their profile, firstly by making what is quite frankly the filthiest advert for humbugs ever made and publishing a headline-grabbing sex survey, and secondly by nobbling their main opposition, International Opinion Polls. Having headhunted IOP's main man, Peter Niss (Denholm Elliot), Rimmer has heard that IOP are due to take a survey in Nuneaton about people's religious leanings. Rimmer sends all his employees to Nuneaton and makes sure that they are the only people the IOP man (Ronnie Corbett) speaks to, each one claiming to be a Buddhist. When IOP publish their findings, that 42% of people in Nuneaton are Buddhists and 9% worshippers of The Great White Ram, there is a national outcry and Rimmer is invited on to a chat show to defend market research companies. On the programme, hosted by Steven Hench (Harold Pinter), Rimmer claims he will predict the outcome of the next by-election to within 1%, which he then proceeds to do by polling every household in the constituency.

Having found a measure of television fame, Rimmer then becomes PR consultant for both the Conservative Party (privately) and Labour Party (publicly) during the Election, helping to bring Tory leader Tom Hutchinson (Ronald Fraser) into Number 10 to replace Labour's Blackett. Hutchinson becomes completely reliant on Rimmer and offers him a chance to stand for MP in the safe seat of Budleigh Moor (ho ho). Rimmer enters the House of Commons and marries a woman who he's never met but who opinion polls tell him is the most popular girl in the country, horseshow jumper Patricia Cartwright (Vanessa Howard). When appointed Chancellor Of The Exchequer, Rimmer comes up with the novel plan of shoring up the UK's gold reserves by stealing Switzerland's bullion. Rimmer works his way into Hutchinson's affections until, at a photo opportunity with the press on an oil rig, Rimmer pushes Hutchinson into the North Sea and, as no one seems able to believe he has just committed murder, Rimmer is made Prime Minister.

This is followed by another set-piece where Rimmer introduces, some 30 years ahead of its time, interactive television. Instead of decisions going through Parliament, people at home are given a chance to vote, via their television, on every piece of government legislation. At first everyone is delighted to be given this chance to make decisions but eventually tire of the whole thing and it is decided that Rimmer should be made dictator of the country so that nobody else ever has to make a decision again. The end.

If all that makes the film's plot seem rather awkward and cumbersome, that's because it is. I don't want to dwell on Rimmer's shortcomings too much here, but this is a big one. Although *Bedazzled* is often criticised for being sketch-like, it is actually one of that film's strengths that the whole thing revolves around a very simple idea with a small number of main characters throughout the movie (Spiggot, Stanley and Margaret). In Rimmer, however, vast numbers of characters come in and drop out again before you've had a chance to get to know them or be particularly bothered about whether or not they're funny. The plot itself meanders from subplot to subplot in a stilted, rather mechanical way which serves to stifle most of the film's jokes rather than bring them to the surface. It is a film in desperate need of paring down.

One of the most intriguing and frustrating elements in the film is the character of Rimmer himself. It is sometimes cited as one of Cook's worst ever screen appearances. Actually, Cook's performance is exactly right for the role. Rimmer is a blank, a nobody—no one can remember ever having hired him or even meeting him before the film starts. All he ever tells his wife about his background is that he was 'found in the bulrushes'. Rimmer walks through the film with a bland smile on his face, gently using anyone he can to gain more and more power and steering any enemies to disaster. He is not dissimilar to Michael Dobbs' creation, the scheming politician Francis Urquhart from the *House Of Cards* novel and TV series—but without Urquhart's ability to address the audience directly and confide his innermost thoughts, Rimmer becomes inhuman, a calculating Machiavellian monster. One aspect of Cook's Rimmer that is often overlooked is his absolute confidence. Nothing can faze him, he always behaves as if he is exactly where he belongs no matter how bizarre the situation.

It is also this spooky otherworldliness that attracts me to Rimmer and gives the film its power. His lack of background, the way he appears to have a magical hold over people to the extent that no one accuses him of murdering Hutchinson even though he is clearly filmed doing so, gives the character a supernatural air.

There is something undeniably disturbing about Rimmer. In one scene, just after he has been made Prime Minister, Rimmer announces that he is going to make Niss his Minister for Opinion Polls. Behind Rimmer's head we see some footage of Niss taken from an earlier scene in the film, part of a subplot where Niss tries to seduce Rimmer's wife. It's distinctly chilling. Has Rimmer been filming Niss? Why choose that clip then? The scene has a feel of Patrick McGoohan's *The Prisoner* about it. It's a glimpse of things to come—CCTV, Big Brother fly-on-the-wall television.

It might be a tenuous link, but could Rimmer be George Spiggott, Satan from *Bedazzled*? Consider: At the end of *Bedazzled* Spiggott, rejected from Heaven and spurned by Stanley Moon, walks off towards Piccadilly/Soho, shouting at the skies and promising God that he is going to ruin the world. Now go to the start of Rimmer: Rimmer/Spiggot turns up in a market research agency, the centre of the market research and advertising industry in London being Soho/Piccadilly. From this humble start, and with remarkable speed, Rimmer manipulates those around him until, as Dictator, he has an almost hypnotic hold on Britain. In the final shot of the film Rimmer/Spiggot looks directly into the camera and smiles a smile which is distinctly diabolical and genuinely chilling.

Whatever, *The Rise And Rise Of Michael Rimmer* is certainly the political counterpart to the theological elements in *Bedazzled*. Although Cook's double act with Denholm Elliot lacks the charm of the Spiggott/Moon partnership, the effect is the same—one man demonstrating to another how, with a mixture of overwhelming charm and extreme cynicism, it is possible to expose and bypass the hypocrisies of convention. Like Spiggott, Rimmer succeeds by telling people what they want to hear, promising quick and easy solutions to life's problems, all the time seeming to sort things out for other people when, in fact, he is merely furthering his own ends. The moral of both films is exactly the same: Beware wolves in sheep's clothing. The only difference is that by the end of *Bedazzled* the audience do feel some genuine warmth for Spiggott and sympathy for his plight, while Rimmer is about as warm and likeable as a dose of the clap.

A number of other mysteries remain attached to the film—how far was Rimmer a satire of the film's producer and originator David Frost? Was it really an 'accident', as Cook claimed it was, that the set designer, when asked to create Rimmer's flat, produced an exact copy of Frost's own living room? More importantly, how much of the script is Cleese and Chapman's original concept and how much did Cook write, change and develop?

On the former question, Rimmer's lack of background might be equated with Frost's Grammar School education, along with his lack of political ideology (Frost famously claims that he has never voted in an election). Chapman certainly wrote disdainfully about Frost in his excellent *A Liar's Autobiography*, and Cook did a scathing satire on the son of the preacher man in the Not So Much A Programme More A Shower Of Shit sketch from a 1965 *Private Eye* flexidisc. Added to this John Fortune's story about Cook's reaction to Frost being offered a safe Liberal seat in the '60s and there can be no doubt that there are large elements of Frost (or the satirists' view of Frost) in Rimmer: The ambitious boy from nowhere with a smile for everyone. But then there are also traits of Frost present in the rather more obvious figure of Pinter's beautifully played Steven Hench, a template for the hypocritical political interviewer, best mates with the politicians behind the scenes while pretending neutrality on camera. Pinter gives Hench a wonderfully unctuous quality, not unlike Robert Kilroy-Silk—and who invented Kilroy-style 'trial by television' audience manipulation if it wasn't Frost in his 1967 interview with insurance fraudster Emil Savbundra? The acronymous result of the title of Hench's chat show, *Steven Hench Is Talking To You*, seems a wonderfully Cookie-esque dig.

The latter question, how much of the film's vision is Cook's and how much Cleese and Chapman's, is less easy to answer. Some of the lines have a lovely Cook feel to them: When Rimmer gives Niss a piece of paper explaining the reasons why Niss should leave his company and join Fairburn, Niss says: 'Yes, very well put. I particularly like the noughts.' Other scenes obviously came straight from Cleese and Chapman, especially the satire of television coverage of General Elections which bears a distinct resemblance to the *Election Night Special* sketch from Monty Python, although *Private Eye* satirised the same thing in their pages.

Rimmer came at the end of Peter Cook's great productive phase during the 1960s. It was his only solo lead role in a film and its failure must have been a great personal blow to him. But I feel that, although the laughter rate may not be on a par with *Bedazzled*, there is still much for the dedicated Peterphile to savour here.

FOOTNOTE: RIMMER RIMMER UBER ALLES

When Michael Rimmer first enters the office of the Fairburn Opinion Polls offices he claims to be working on behalf of their Coordination department. 'Coordination' was also a term employed in Nazi Germany to refer to the method of turning the democratic institutions of the Weimar Republic into a totalitarian state. Reporting anonymously on this in 1937 in the opposition journal *Deutschland-Berichte der SOPADE*, one journalist compared the Nazi 'coordination' of Germany to the re-building of a railway bridge. You can't knock the bridge down because that would mean travelling by train would be impossible. So you do it piece by piece, replacing one girder or rail at a time. Those passengers who didn't pay attention to what was going on around them wouldn't realise until too late that they were travelling on a completely new bridge. A more perfect description of Rimmer's rise to power one could not ask for.

Rimmer's story also bears comparison to Bertolt Brecht's 1941 play *The Resistable Rise Of Arturo Ui*. There is more than a titular resemblance between the two. In the play Brecht retells the story of Hitler's rise to power, but sets the story in Depression-era America with Hitler as the gangster of the play's title. Ui is a mobster boss who, by stealth, cunning and violence, eventually monopolizes the Chicago vegetable trade after taking over The Cauliflower Trust. The stories of the film, the play and the rise of Nazi Germany have many features in common. All concern a loner from outside the Establishment (Rimmer, Ui, Hitler) entering a corrupt, rundown and complacent system (Fairburn's, The Cauliflower Trust, the Weimar Republic). They combine the methods of the schemer and the thug to establish their own powerbase. Also, all are adept at gaining the confidence of those who are already in power (Tom Hutchinson, Dogsborough, Hindenburg) before disposing of their patrons when they have outlived their use.

THE DAWN OF ENTROPY

In these days of the po-faced dirge that is rock and roll, Robyn Hitchcock, with his gift of melody and startling imagery, is a national treasure. Coupled with his psychedelic musical sensibilities, Hitchcock's use of the surreal turn of phrase in both his lyrics and his between-song banter at gigs demonstrate a fine sense of comedy. With this in mind, Clinty tracked Mr. Hitchcock down to a West End caff and asked him if he had any thoughts on Cook he'd like to share. The answer, as it turned out, was yes, rather a lot of them.

As we join them, Robyn is flicking through the last issue of Pub & Bed and having a quick scan of the article on The Rise And Rise Of Michael Rimmer.

ROBYN HITCHCOCK: When was *Rimmer* made?

PETER GORDON: 1970.

RH: Ah 1970—the cusp. As it was all tipping. That was when the momentum kind of stopped for so many people. They seemed to run out of steam. My theory is that people actually ran out of steam in possibly January 1968. There seems to have been some incredible momentum—I was around at the time but I was negotiating puberty so quite how good my antennae were at decoding the outside world I don't know—but there was this terrific momentum from 1962 to 1967. Certainly in the rock world everybody just seemed to drain away, some very drastically and some more discreetly, but by the time we're talking about, 1970, most of the great work had been done and some of them were incapable of doing anything. If you read that Harry Thompson book, I think he refers to Peter Cook having a kind of coiled-up spring which just unwound, it began to unwind quite drastically about 1970, having had an incredibly prolific '60s.

PG: Do you see Cook's decline after the '60s as part of a more general cultural... thing?

RH: Mmm, yeah, very much. I think, like a lot of them, he had nowhere to go. It was almost as if some element had been taken out of the air that they couldn't feed on anymore, so they became drunks. For a lot of people there's been a hangover since 1970. In the '60s people just got higher and higher until they popped or had nowhere to go, so you take refuge in Mother Alcohol, the great tranquilliser. So, as one of the most vivid, receptive minds of that era, I would say he's pretty much the same, y'know? Bob Dylan's been a drunk and a drug addict pretty much since then—he doesn't parade it, but it seems fairly clear he's suffered similarly. What's another word for when things run out of momentum? There's probably some term in physics. The pendulum has gone completely one way and it's just about to start going the other way.

PG: Entropy?

RH: Maybe it's entropy, yeah. Maybe the beginning of the entropy was 1968 and the end of it was 1974, when a lot of the so-called Permissive Society was gaining ground and ordinary people were allowed to wander round in long hair and floppy lapels. It was becoming acceptable to sleep with someone you weren't married to and you could start showing breasts on telly. 1974 was a bit of a desert, really. It was very clear to me—I was 21—that the revolution had got as far as it was going, it had been absorbed into the culture. Banks were saying, 'Whatever turns you on'. The 'Us' and 'Them' had dissipated to a large extent. But, in fact, behind that a larger 'Them' was looming—Margaret Thatcher became leader of the Conservative Party the next year, and in fact the Blue Meanies were getting ready to counter attack, as foreseen in both *Yellow Submarine* and *Dougal And The Blue Cat*. Both those films have these blue forces waiting to come back and clobber freedom—the collective unconscious was really firing when they wrote those two. By 1974 the lid had been taken off, there wasn't any atmospheric pressure.

In comedy, people like Python and Cook had run out of people to rubbish. The establishment was no longer there in the way that it had been. What were they [Cook and the Pythons] there for after that? Once they'd tried to attack further taboos they just became obnoxious. The Pythons did their best stuff before they were allowed to swear and the same goes for Cook and Moore. Once Cook is reduced to saying 'Kick the cunt' it's over. For me, Cook was like a very intense, condensed spirit of what the Pythons were about. He could be very silly or he could be as acute as the other six of them were—it's not a contest. Just as... what was John Lennon in '74 going to do except write miserable records about being split up with Yoko? What's Dylan going to do except write miserable records about being split up with his wife? McCartney wrote *Jet*, er, which was pretty good, but he was never one of the obvious leader figures of the '60s, he was a nice songwriter. Syd Barrett was taken into a studio and he tried to bite the guy who handed him the guitar 'cos he thought it was an invoice or something. Brian Wilson was gone. Captain Beefheart made a wretched album.

Then the angst came back, the right wing came in. In '73 there was still the three day week, and it looked at the time like the Conservatives would never get back in power. It looked like we were going to have a permanent watery socialism running things and the unions wouldn't permit the Tories to come back. But uh-oh, they did. Then Punk came in and the angst came back, the antagonism, the sense of something happening. Later in life you might remember the big divorces and the epic pinnacles of sex or whatever, but most of your life is spent just screwing up bits of paper and throwing them into a bin, or opening the fridge. Sometimes you go to the fridge, open it, then sit down and wonder if you've opened it or not. That's how banal our life is. It's there despite its banality.

PG: So, Derek and Clive fits in with your theory, then?

RH: Well, I didn't really listen to it. The first one was quite funny but I couldn't really take it after that. Anger's good if it kicks you up the arse to the point where you're actually propelled through the hedge or wherever you're meant to be going, but not if it propels you into being more and more obnoxious. Obnoxious people just make life difficult for themselves and then they wonder why no one wants to be around them, and then they get more obnoxious. I also just turn off when I hear bad language being used to get a laugh. I don't mind swearing, if it's there to make a point. I thought it was pitiful when Python started to be allowed to say 'fuck', because that was the easy way out. You need certain restrictions for humour to function, because subversion is a big part of it. Once you're just saying, 'I hate this fucking shit' it's not being subversive—you're just waiting for someone to come and slap you down and say, 'You're a naughty boy, go home and clean up. Five years inside for you,' or whatever. Peter Cook kicked against the barriers and when there were no barriers left he kicked himself, which he did copiously and expensively... with some nice vintages.

PG: Moving into, um, a more celebratory mode: When you think of Peter Cook, what's the first image that comes to mind?

RH [*Laughs*]: I'm not sure it's even an image. It's sort of a nose, the way he talked through the bottom of his nose. He was obviously really delighted by it [performing], when it was good, and there was good late things as well. *A Life In Pieces* is just delightful. I think of his nose and his voice more than anything.You could see it was tragic for him that he couldn't sing, he was so close to being a rock star. He was the first sort of comedian-as-rock-star. There's been a few since, like Eric Idle—good looking, could play music, hung out with rock stars—but Cook was the first.

PG: He had the instincts of a rock star.

RH: Yeah, and the life. I think he and The Beatles were the biggest single modifiers of the British class system. They didn't destroy it but they inverted it. The Beatles made their way up from being effectively working class—historians will argue for decades about whether The Fabs actually were working class, but they were effectively working class—whereas Cook obviously came from the upper echelons and made his way down. Listen to his accent in 1962 and he's still more or less [*Posh voice:*] speaking like this because one did very much. [*Normal:*] So he was, essentially, a sort of Streeb-Greebling figure. By the time it's 1974 and he sounds more... Cockney, almost. His aspirations and his voice went directly downwards and The Beatles went upwards.

Cook prefigured what happened. Look at *Steptoe & Son* in the mid-'60s: Harold is meant to be funny because we're laughing at the aspirations of a rag and bone man who wants to see Fellini films. He wants to better himself. Now that's gone, you're not supposed to better yourself. If anything, upper class people are meant to trash themselves out. Aspiration not in terms of money—people are greedier than ever and Thatcher certainly fed that snake and watered those gerbils—but aspiring upwards to better yourself, to get that education: That's gone. What you have now is a national celebration of football and dumb culture, and Peter Cook, although very bright, kind of spearheaded that. He was very happy to seek out the lowest common denominator, which is probably what made him a universal thing—he wasn't an elitist. He came from an elite and he did his best to get out of it. He knew how to rubbish it from the inside. He was in the first lot to really take the piss out of the establishment. Milligan did it in a quite poetic way, more childlike, whereas Cook was more analytical. There are probably laws of comedy physics that Cook and the Fringers obeyed when they were doing it. They numbered the establishment and they took it down. They were part of the process that's both liberalised and coarsened out our society. I would pick Cook and The Fabs as instant symbols of the way Britain changed from '62 to '68—the dawn of entropy [*Laughs*].

PG: What do you think Cook had that no one else did?

RH: He had a lot of things. He was very good looking, which sadly went the way of the bottle. He had a very quick mind. It's a combination of looks, wit and imagination, and a terrific lack of faith in anything. His nihilism was really almost a conviction. He had no respect for platitudes or clichés. I always felt the same. I don't want to project, but a way in which I identify with him is his real lack of conviction about anything—not in a watery way but a passionate, fiery lack of faith. It's an incandescent nihilism. It's almost the nihilism of a preacher, and therefore it's got a lot of life in it. I mean, it's a known fact that he was left by his parents when he was six months old and bought up by some bees in Torquay, and he became obsessed by bees and insects and when he was drunk and had to do speeches at dinners he'd talk about them. I think it is a known fact that he was bought up by two insects who were a bit older than him and he always identified with them. Probably had sexual issues because of that. He was quite sexually driven as well, but I don't think he was very good with women. When you have that degree of success your relationships are being constantly undermined by temptation. I think he was probably quite insecure. He reached 1970 on the same wings that had borne everyone else there, and he suddenly saw his family disintegrate and he thought 'Oh shit, what am I going to do?'

PG: But I think he was quite old-fashioned, in a way that, say, Dudley Moore wasn't. Dudley seemed to me to have a much more 'modern' view on marriage and divorce, that they were just things that happen. But Cook still had something in him that wanted it to be permanent and perfect and roses round the door—

RH: So he was more upset? He could handle the reality less well?

PG: Yeah, the real implications of screwing around, which is that your wife leaves you.

RH: Mmm. But it didn't stop him.

PG: Er, no.

RH: Also, if you're a big drinker that tends to be your primary relationship. It's not easy for someone else to get into bed with that. Or a drug habit, something where you're physically and psychologically dependent on things.

PG: So, returning to a theme, do you think there's something inevitable in the process you've described—to have the liberation you've got to have the collapse?

RH: What, you mean decline and fall? Well, maybe it enhances the myth, but it seems to be the case. All the interesting ones go wrong, they get clobbered. It's like Icarus. The guys who play it safe—Bowie, McCartney and Mick Jagger and doubtless Michael Palin will get a Knighthood; Sir John Cleese, y'know—will live on into their mid-eighties with the occasional glass of sherry. Whereas the ones who take more risks are more likely to do something interesting but also more likely to get hit, especially if they start young. There's the odd exception—Iggy survived, Lou Reed, Dylan survived, so they're not all casualties. But comedians—well, Milligan lasted until he was 83, which was amazing, but Arthur Lowe died in his dressing room, Tommy Cooper died on stage, Eric Morecambe just after he came off stage. In some ways Cook lasting to his mid-fifties wasn't bad really, he could have burst his liver ten years before that.

PG: Yeah, I think there was inevitability about Cook's alcoholism, probably connected, as you said, with his evangelical atheism.

RH: I read somewhere that he went to Alcoholic's Anonymous but he didn't like the fact that AA had this stuff where they hold hands and talk to God at the end of it. He wanted to see if you could have one without God in it. [*Laughs*] He didn't look hard enough.

But I always think he didn't have much to comfort him. There's a lack of consolation in heavy drinking. I mean, the whole thing about how the ruling classes are emotionally crippled and then sent out to rule the country—most little lads are supposed to be knocking around their mummy and daddy's until they're six and a half and then they're sent off. You can imagine there was this extra big hole in him to fill that was very hard on him.

Another thing Cook had was a real nose for bullshit, which is so essential. It's very important for people to do that because it's only by cutting through the crap that you find out what your genuine beliefs are, and what moral glue, if any, holds the universe together. It's just sometimes you can be so corrosive, like Cook was and I think Bob Dylan is too, that nothing satisfies them, that you end up swallowing your own tail, or if not swallowing it then corroding it. No relationship, no way of working, nothing is beyond challenge.

PG: How do you view the use of comedy in your music? Was Cook an influence?

RH: Yeah. I mean, I like The Goons, Cook and Moore, Python and The Marx Brothers. I also like other rock performers who were funny. Bob Dylan and Lennon could be hysterically funny at times. I've never liked art that didn't have humour. I mean, Peter Cook—we're both tall degenerate public schoolboys who tried to get as far away from our origins as possible.

I did a gig at Cambridge about five years ago and this young chap came up afterwards and said 'You're a cross between Syd Barrett and Peter Cook.' I'd had Syd Barrett before, but I thought, 'Peter Cook, of course, the missing link'. [*Laughs*]

PG: And all of you Cambridge men.

RH: Yeah. Well, my parents met there and I went back there long enough to pick up The Soft Boys [*RH's band of the late '70s, recently reformed*] When I started The Soft Boys I hated cliches in words, people saying 'you pays your money and you takes your choice' and 'swings and roundabouts'. Using a cliché is a closed mind reading from a dead book. It's the ultimate mental laziness. When we're reduced to saying 'horses for courses' and 'at the end of the day' then anyone who talks in those terms is mentally lazy, they're not finding their own way to express themselves. And I think you can see in Cook a contempt for that way of thinking and a delight in playing with phrases. There's that bit when he says 'if you do they tend to take against you'. [*Laughs*] And [*from* A Life In Pieces: *part 11*] where he's talking about goats or the great line about the self-confessed player of the pink oboe. It's making your own mock-cliches.

PG: One of the things I've always loved about Cook is that he never made his point of view explicit in the way that say a Jim Davidson or a Mark Thomas does. You never knew quite what Cook was coming from or what he believed in.

RH: Well, I don't think he did believe in anything in life. I could be wrong, but... you could say that he didn't accept anything or that he questioned everything, either way. I always like to think that humane people are basically left wing, but I don't think he honestly cared much, really. Everything was there to be rubbished or to be used. I don't think he had a political or moral agenda to come from, apart from, presumably, some degree of faith in his own perception. He must have believed in that, in the way he saw things.

NOT ONLY BUT AUSSIE

Once upon a time there was a Goons-obsessed television director from Melbourne who wanted to make comedy programmes. Alas he could find no real openings for this in his home country so he set sail for England, where he was hired by Frank Muir to work for London Weekend Television. While at LWT he directed many new comedy programmes such as Hark At Barker *(with Ronnie Barker),* Doctor In The House *and* The Complete And Utter History Of Britain, *starring a pre-Python Michael Palin and Terry Jones. He returned home in 1970 and produced two seminal shows in Australian comedy,* Auntie Jack *and* The Norman Gunston Show. *His first job on returning to Australia, however, was to direct two* Not Only But Also In Australia *shows (hereto referred to as* NOBAIA). *He still produces comedy down under and has also made his first film, 15 Amore, which he came to Britain to promote. Peter Gordon met up with him in the Royal Festival Hall on 10 April 2001.*

PETER GORDON: How did *NOBAIA* come about?

MAURICE MURPHY: I arrived back in Australia in 1970 and it was almost the first thing I had to do, I think. The promoter came to ABC [Australian Broadcasting Corporation] and said he was bringing Dudley Moore and his Trio to do a couple of concerts and would ABC be interested in doing a show with Peter and Dudley? 'Would we?' I screamed and we negotiated from there. So it was organised that we would do two specials pretty much around the same themes that Jimmy Gilbert had done at the BBC—*Not Only But Also In Australia*—which is what we did. And out they came and I had one the best months of my life organising and directing these wonderfully talented people who were as funny as you get.

PG: When in 1970?

MM: I must have got off the plane in 1970, December, and walked straight into it.

PG: Were Peter and Dudley big in Australia?

MM: Oh, absolutely. *NOBA* had been run and repeated a hundred and fifty times, like they do in Australia.

PG: The sketches with the cricket team—was that designed purposely around the Ashes cricket tour that year?

MM: Not at all. They were just there so we rang them up and just organised it. It was very easy to organise anything with Pete and Dud. You'd just ring someone up and say, 'We're coming to film,'—not 'Can we?'—and they'd say 'Oh yes,' and bang. So we joined the cricket team just for the morning, just for a practise session, and the England team were thrilled to be doing it. The same with the sequence on the beach: Normally you have to have some life-savers around, and we had a whole beach full of life-savers looking after us in case they drowned trying to surf in their full-length coats and stuff.

PG: That wasn't them surfing, was it?

MM: Yeah.

PG: No!

MM: Well, it wasn't Peter, but Dudley had a go. We intercut them with a guy who could do it really well, but Dudley had a go.

PG: Why two shows?

MM: I think that was just Australian greed, you know. [*Laughs*] 'My God, we've got them here, let's get—' well, not so much two for the price of one, but I think it was organised by the promoter who was bringing out the concert, and he convinced ABC that, you know, if they got twice the money then that would be better. It was possibly to do with how much we had to pay Peter and Dudley. In order to pay this fee that was vast in Australian terms, we'd have to get two shows out of them to justify it. I don't think performers and promoters tell each other much and Pete and Dud were a bit surprised they had to do two shows when they got there. There wasn't any drama, we just did it. And we also had the Trio playing in it a bit to fill things out, and it was fine.

PG: Had you worked with Peter and Dudley before?

MM: No. The first time I met them was at the airport in Sydney and, being the good director I am, the first thing I said was 'Hello, lovely to meet you, have you got a script?' And, of course, they'd enjoyed themselves on the plane and elsewhere and hadn't put one pen to one bit of paper at all. [*Laughter*]

PG: No script at all?

MM: No.

PG: So they wrote the whole thing—

MM: While rehearsing it, basically. Fascinating. I'd never worked with people who could do that before. It was just wonderful. They could just do Pete and Dud and the sketch about the spiders in Australia. They really could come into a rehearsal room and just say [*Pete voice:*] 'Well, what do you think, Dud, of Australia?' and just do it and we'd have a sketch together after a very short time.

PG: So you got the script from the improvisation?

MM: Yes. My P.A. would be scribbling it down, I don't think we even had a recorder with us. But they could remember what they'd said anyway. This didn't apply to everything we did, but certainly to the characters they knew well. And then we'd improve it in rehearsal. There were a couple of sketches with characters that were not their normal ones, and that was more like a normal process where you write it, rehearse it and get it ready for the studio.

PG: What kind of schedule were you working to?

MM: We did the pre-filmed stuff over three days, I think. One day at the airport with Barry Humphries as the customs guy, those really cruel customs officials that he played particularly well. Then the beach another day and the cricket. We didn't have to hurry and, anyway, Dudley... you know... there were girlfriends that had to be accommodated in all of this. Peter was out there with Judy Huxtable, his girlfriend at the time, and I can't remember if Dudley was out there with anyone, but to this day I've only ever heard that Peter Sellers had more charisma that Dudley. Dudley was the greatest chick-magnet of any human being I've ever met, seen, known or read about in my life. It was remarkable. Without asking for it, I mean just walking down the street, honestly, women would throw themselves at him. He's got what we all want. And also so charming. Might have been his size but he was incredibly sexually charismatic. I've always wondered how much Peter was amused by it—or bemused by it even—'I'm the bloke with all the brains but he pulls the chicks.' Anyway, the studio stuff was done within a week of all this, maybe even less. I must have had two days to do it in, one for each show. Peter did one of those things that always surprises people about comedians—I was doing this, not so much a warm-up, but introducing everybody to the studio audience and Peter was saying thanks at the end doing this impersonation of me that was scarily precise. He did it in my Australian accent, the way

I stand, he just had me down to a tee. People who know me were saying 'It was remarkable, he knew how you stood,' and so on.

PG: And he also did his Elvis impersonation, didn't he?

MM [*Laughing*]: Yes.

PG: Not quite so successful.

MM: Well, he was good at getting the attitude. Far more of a physical comedian than people think. He was very good at picking up how characters were physically like and how they sat and stuff. And he didn't talk about it. If you're working with an actor-comedian like, say, Ronnie Barker you talk about that stuff all the time, what sort of shoes you're going to wear and what kind of attitude to do. But Peter didn't talk about it, he just did it. You would discuss clothes 'cos you've got to order those, but you wouldn't discuss the way he would sit in a chair and he just had the ability to seeing visual attitudes that would make the character believable, besides what the voice was like.

PG: Maybe talking would have spoiled the initial insight for him? Maybe Peter knew that for him the first instinct was always the right one?

MM: I can't imagine Peter Cook talking about humour really. He sort of just did it. I don't know, he may have written buckets of stuff about comedy. Did he?

PG: Er, no, not really.

MM: No, he just did it. And I don't think he thought it was a very intellectual exercise anyway. I'm guessing because, well, because he didn't talk about it.

PG: The sketches used were a mixture of old and new stuff.

MM: Well, I think that was because they hadn't written a script. [*Laughs*] I said, 'I think we should do something new, guys. I mean, can we do Tarzan again?' It was just that there were many parties in Sydney and, you know, they'd be 'Are we finished now?' and then whoosh, out the door. So we got the original stuff, which was pretty much Pete and Dud stuff and then the old things. I think the Australian audience really enjoyed the old stuff too. People love seeing some of the traditional stuff. Otherwise it's a bit like a singer coming on and not singing their greatest hit. I mean, everybody loves the Tarzan sketch. Well, poor old Dudley's knee didn't.

PG: So there was no resentment from them about having to go over old ground?

MM: No, no.

PG: Did they plunge themselves into Australian culture looking for references to use?

MM: In a way they sort of knew that by the time they were off the plane. Getting through Customs in Australia used to be such a bizarre thing, 'cos they'd spray you with insecticide—

PG: What? That wasn't just a joke for the sketch?

MM: No, no, that's what used to happen. They used to spray you. And they're doing it again because of this foot and mouth disease. I'm going back next week and they'll make me walk through sheep dip, they'll take my shoes out and make me clean 'em.

PG: What are they spraying for? Insects?

MM: So that we don't get bugs or other diseases because we've got our own animals and plants who've got their own bugs and diseases but not European or Asian ones. So by the time Peter and Dudley were off the plane they'd been effectively insulted at Customs, and they knew it had to go into the show.

PG: And there's lots of little references for the Australian audience, like Dud picking up a prostitute in the Kings Cross region of Sydney.

MM: Well, that's where they were living and rehearsing. And it was there that Dudley got into lots and lots of trouble, I think. Well, I don't think he would have called it trouble, [*Laughs*] he thought it was joyous. Again, the women were so generous and kind to him.

PG: That's funny when you think of the cricket sketch where Pete's giving Dud advice in case he finds women in his bed. Was Peter having a dig at Dudley there?

MM [*Laughing*]: Absolutely. 'In case' he found women there! In case he didn't find women there, that's what he needed advice for. He didn't talk about it, but he kind of indicated that it wasn't really his fault. What could he do? They were in his bed, what could he do? Australia really thought of them as big stars, it was like The Beatles of comedy arriving—people who were the funniest people on Earth. And they probably were, in the English speaking world—I don't know what the Poles were doing. ABC had never had ratings like it before in its life because the whole country watched it.

PG: Was Barry Humphries involved from the beginning?

MM: Not from Day One maybe, but it would have been Day Two. I'd seen Barry recently, dunno where—I got back on December 20th 1970—so I'd seen him and said hello and then Peter and Dudley decided to do this Customs stuff and I said 'What about Barry?' He seemed obvious once you were going to have a horrible person from Australia. [*Laughter*]

PG: His Customs Official is wonderfully seedy with the lank hair and the croaky voice and the dirty book he's reading at the start.

MM: Oh yeah. Because at that stage Australia was still impounding, you know... *Noddy In Toyland* was impounded there because one of the character's names could mean 'a penis'. It might even have been Noddy. So that was the famous impounding by Customs to keep the moral fibre of Australia hard. There's a move in some parts of Australia to ban Harry Potter books because it's about magic and it's giving a wrong religious message. [*Waving his arm dismissively*] Oh, go away, you know. So Barry was making fun of our Customs people who have for some reason got this power.

PG: Were there any complaints about, you know, the material about prostitutes and such?

MM: No, no. We're a strange sort of society that will ban Noddy but at the same time the News always has bare breasts on it. Well, not always, but they usually try to, you know...

PG: Squeeze them in?

MM: Yeah. But you'd be hard pressed in a comedy show to have to have an actress walk around with no top on, but in the News it's perfectly acceptable.

PG: One of the sketches, Pseudelon, seems a bit of a departure for them. It's quite a cold sketch. Brilliant, but—

MM: It's not all that funny though.

PG: Not funny, but there's a darkness to it, and an element to satirizing slapstick humour.

MM: I don't think, when you make something like that, you make those kind of assessments in your head. You're not trying to be 'edgy', you just go 'Let's do a restaurant sketch'. And you do it and it ends up how it ends up. It's not trying to be dark or edgy, it probably just didn't come out quite as well as it should've. Like, it wasn't as funny as it should've been so one starts adding adjectives about 'edginess' and 'darkness' and 'depth', all of which is just another way of saying 'not funny' [*Laughter*].

   In more practical terms of having to turn it out, you know, Peter wrote more of that than Dudley did. In the Dagenham Dialogue sketches Dudley could do that thing of going 'Yeah, yeah, go on' and waiting for Pete to come out with something that they could make funny. But when it was a written sketch that they couldn't muck around with—I think I'd put it more in that context than whether or not they were trying to be different—once they had a written sketch where you did those words and you weren't extemporizing around it, then it feels a bit more dramatic because they weren't using any of those skills they normally do. Dudley, as Dud, could pull a laugh by not saying anything.

PG: Would Dudley have been worried that Pseudelon was set up just to humiliate him?

MM: No, I don't think so. I don't know what their relationship was like through their careers, but for their time in Australia everyone was having a very social time, lots of fun, but we had to do the shows fairly quickly and I think Dudley was very happy that the sketch was written and he didn't have to have any input, he could just act in that one, in the same way that Peter didn't have to give a hoot about what the Trio were doing.

PG: The Funnel Web Spider sketch with Sir Arthur Streeb-Greebling. Magnificent.

MM: Yeah, it's great.

PG: Do you recall Peter doing his scissor-kick leg crossing throughout the sketch?

MM: Yeah. My guess is that he used that sort of stuff to think of the next line. As well as coming up with a character, it also gives you a pause. It worked for Streeb, he just seemed to be like a spider in that sketch. He could've done it for a long time and still got laughs with it. Don't you wish you could do that? Cross your legs and get laughs?

PG: And it also served to make Dudley giggle.

MM: Well, it's one of the things comedians like to do with each other, beside cracking each other up, is to get their respect, and the respect is laughter. It doesn't matter how well you know somebody, if someone comes up with a line that really makes you laugh then that's the respect.

PG: During the *Goodbyee* song at the end of the first show, Peter says 'And our special thanks to the Duke Of Edinburgh for not being here.'

MM [*Laughs*]: Yeah, meant nothing, it just fell into his head at the time.

PG: Were they a handful to control in front of the camera?

MM: No, not in front of the cameras. Handful to control at rehearsals 'cos they didn't want to be there and handful to control to get a script out of them, but once they were in front of the camera they were just great. Not many re-takes or anything. The handful comes from the fact that once comedians have worked for a bit they realise their best work is not too rehearsed, but directors like to know how it's going to be done so they can get the best shots. So we're pushing them to over-rehearse it and they're going 'Oh God, haven't we done this enough?' The reason being that it's funnier to them if they haven't done it lots of times. Now I'm a bit older I never ask comedians to do anything too often. Probably by then I knew not to do it.

PG: Were there any problems with sketches over-running?

MM: I don't think we would've cared if it went on for three hours! I didn't have the problem of producers saying, you know, 'This must be fifty-one minutes and twenty-three seconds.'

PG: How were relations between Peter and Dudley?

MM: Well, the only thing I remember was this mystification from Peter about why Dudley had these women hanging off him all the time. I wouldn't call it disagreement, but the only bit of, er, abrasion was that Dudley was so attractive to people.

PG: Any particular instances of this magnetism manifesting itself?

MM: Mostly we'd be going down the street to lunch or we'd be walking somewhere and there'd suddenly be four women hanging off Dudley like apples on a tree. And Peter would be there with Judy and whoever else from the production crew and we all just had to wait for Dudley. I think it annoyed Peter a little. And Peter was a good-looking guy, it wasn't as if he wasn't. If it was, say, Morecambe and Wise then you'd expect them to go for one more than the other, but with Peter and Dudley you'd think they would be equally lauded. But Peter was stuck with eggheads coming up to him telling him how clever he was—unattractive young males saying 'God, we love you,' and Dudley would get the gorgeous women. [*Laughter*] Somehow it wasn't just any women, they were all incredibly desirable. It fascinated me.

PG: With no effort of Dudley's part at all?

MM: No. I don't know, I've never read anything about it and I wish somebody would write about it, 'cos I believe, as I said earlier, that Sellers had it as well. My wife makes documentaries and when I was working for LWT she was working for the BBC in what I think was the first all-women crew they'd put together. There was a producer, a director, er, five women anyway, and their first documentary was about Bryan Forbes, the director. One day they had to go and film Sellers because he'd worked with Forbes and they were friends. And I always remember the night they came back from the shoot. Myself and the partners of the other women, one or two of them were lesbians and the others' boyfriends, or husband in my case, we were all waiting in one of their flats to have dinner together. The women came home and they were not just besotted by Sellers, they were totally in love with him. It was fascinating to watch. My wife says I exaggerate about this, but I know they would have gone off with him. They were twittering like women transported, it was lovely to hear. Remarkable. And other people have told me he could do this. So the only friction I can remember is that Dudley was such a pants man, and Peter—I'm guessing, we didn't have a conversation about it—Peter imagined he wasn't a bad pants man himself and why was Dudley doing so well?

PG: How did find directing someone like Ronnie Barker, a trained actor, as opposed to Peter and Dudley's more 'turn up and do it' approach?

MM: With Ronnie you could ask him to pause at the door if you've got a good reason, because of camera shot, and then he'll know how to turn that into something that will work, and it'll help him be funnier. But for someone who's more of a sketch comedian than an actor that would just get in the way. They don't want to have to think about that stuff. The hardest thing with a Peter Cook-type person is to stop them performing in rehearsals—'No, no, don't do it for me here, I don't want to see it here. I can cope with whatever you do in front of the audience.' I mean, you sort out where they're going to be, how tall, that he's going to cross his legs, say, with those high kicks so that he can be wired to do that. But most untrained people will want to be funny straight off the top, they want the crew to laugh, but by the time you block that out with cameras quite often the first time in rehearsals is the funniest one you'll get, so you have to dowse them down. So you'll say 'Yeah, we won't do the rest of the words now, we know you sit there and you're going to be there for so long and you'll stand up then.' You try not to do the rehearsal as a performance, 'cos the spark can go away too quickly.

PG: Was there any reason for shooting in black and white?

MM: We had no choice, we didn't have colour until 1975. This is Australia we're talking about! [Laughs] We had colour late. I started filming in colour in 1972, but we were still going out in black and white. But in 1971 I don't think we even thought colour was going to come to Australia, we thought it was gonna be a black and white world.

Tell me, do they run Peter's film over here? The send-up of Frost?

PG: *The Rise And Rise Of Michael Rimmer*? Not much. It's been on television once in the last couple of years, buried somewhere in the late-night schedules.

MM: That should be on at the National Film Theatre once a year forever more! Completely unique bit of filmmaking. I keep saying to television stations 'I think you're mad for just showing old comedy shows. You should try to give the audience a context.' If someone could talk about Rimmer, about Frost going crazy when he realised that it was him, you would enjoy the film a lot more. I know they don't state it in the film, but the knowledge about it makes it so enjoyable. Imagine someone having the courage to do a satire on the person who's financing the film. [*Laughter*] Frost's company, Paradine Productions, owned Ronnie Barker, Ronnie Corbett and John Cleese, so he had rights to some of the shows I did at LWT. Frost wasn't calling himself executive producer, but he had an exclusivity on the performers, and quite a few of the meetings about *Rimmer* were held in his offices so I got to hear all this gossip about Frost going ballistic about it. Well, you would get angry. But he still allowed it to be made, so he couldn't have gone too ballistic, not like the Grades over *Life Of Brian*.

ZSA ZSA MAN DIES ON HIS ARSE

OK, it's 1971, you're Peter Cook. Everything you touch seems to turn to gold.

You've been in a West End revue that's a smash and gone to Broadway. You've had three BBC series with Dudley Moore which have been hailed as some of the greatest comedy shows ever made. You're one of the shining wits of the chat show circuit. Your film career hasn't really taken off, but all in all you're not doing badly at all.

Now's the time for your first solo TV series, a mixture of comedy sketches and chat show interviews. You've got the likes of Spike Milligan, Johnny Speight and Ned Sherrin coming along. Doesn't it sound great? Three weeks later you've got a disaster on your hands, a 12-part series cancelled after just three shows. The only people tuning in are those fascinated by just how big the disaster is. How could such a thing happen? Surely it can't have been any worse than *Skinner And Baddiel Unplanned*? Well, maybe not, but then in those days there was none of this ironic Laddism that lets you get away with being knowingly bad and pretending that's part of the joke.

Though the BBC tapes for *Where Do I Sit?* have long since been wiped, we can get some kind of idea how the show looked and felt by going through contemporary newspaper reports about the show. So that's what we did.

PRELUDE

SUSPENSE STORY FOR PETER COOK
Comedian Peter Cook swapped Dudley Moore for Ilkley Moor yesterday. His girlfriend, Judy Huxtable, went along to see sketches being shot for his next TV series. Peter imitates pop stars, including Johnny Cash, in the BBC series *Where Do I Sit?* One of his songs, '25 Minutes To Go', is about an execution. So after the last minute has gone, Johnny—that is Peter—is hanged!

[*Daily Mail* 28.1.71]

SHOW ONE

Where Do I Sit? (BBC2): Review by Chris Dunkley
THE FIRST EPISODE of Peter Cook's new show was, sadly, all too much like a televised version of an early copy of *Private Eye*. That magazine took, and takes, great glee not only in satirizing politicians but also in poking fun at the medium of which the magazine itself is a part. In the case of *Private Eye* this involves parodies of newspapers and magazines, and small jokes about the professional habits of the trade, presented in a hardly exemplary professional form. In the case of *Where Do I Sit?* it involved endless weak jokes about the trivial technicalities of television production: again and again Mr. Cook asked 'Am I on my mark?' (meaning was he in the right position for the cameras). Again and again we cut to shots of Ian Macnaughton,

the producer, behind his glass screen, to hear him tell Peter
Cook, live on air, what was to happen next. Funny just once,
perhaps, but like schoolboy jokes this sort of thing palls fast.
Unfortunately even the "Ho, ho, very satirical" screen captions,
such as "In Smashing Colour" or "Another Simulation", looked
precisely what they were; a poor copy of an idea borrowed from
Monty Python, of which Mr. MacNaughton is the producer.

The whole thing reeked of an old boys' get together: there sat
Dudley Moore in the front row of the dutifully laughing studio
audience, and Auberon Waugh, Ralph Steadman and Christopher Logue all featured on the show—and all three contribute
to *Private Eye*, with which Mr. Cook retains strong connexions
[...]

Peter Cooks [*sic*], seemingly, will persist in the belief that his ad
lib material is better than the rehearsed sections. Unfortunately
the precise opposite is true, though there are rare exceptions.
His filmed dramatization of an S.J. Perelman piece was profi-
cient, but his live interview with Perelman himself was truly
pathetic (through no fault of Perelman's), as was a short skit
with Stanley Unwin, whose gobbledygook patter was long ago
surpassed by Kenneth Williams' nonsense songs on *Round The
Horne*. A sad disappointment.

[*The Times* 20.2.71]

SHOW TWO

WHAT WILL PETER COOK DO NEXT?

Peter Cook's new live show [...] seemed a little disjointed when
it began last week, and the BBC cautiously admits that it had 'a
few teething problems'. His guests in tonight's programme[...]
are ex-Goons Spike Milligan and Ray Ellington—but Peter is
not sure what will be happening.

He said, 'I had too many sketches last week. This week I intend
to leave the chat up to Spike, although I don't know what we'll

talk about.' However, on the cards for tonight's show (BBC2 9.20) is a pre-filmed sketch with Peter and Spike, a musical number by Spike and Ray, and some Elvis numbers sung by Peter.

[*The Sun* 26.2.71]

PETER COOK TV SKETCH ROW
MRS. MARY Whitehouse, the clean-up-TV campaigner, today labelled the BBC2 comedy show starring Peter Cook 'blasphemous'. After watching the show [...] last night, during which the comedian claimed to be God, Mrs. Mary Whitehouse claims he deliberately taunted viewers. [...] The sketch involved 'two trampish looking fellows,' she said. 'Peter Cook said: "I'm Gawd" and his companion [Spike Milligan] said, "Oh Christ. Oh dear, I'm sorry, he's your son isn't he?"'
Peter Cook said today: 'I think God has a better sense of humour than Mrs. Mary Whitehouse.'

[*Evening Standard* 27.2.71]

SHOW THREE: THE AXE FALLS

BBC DROPS COOK SHOW: by Richard Last, TV staff
The BBC2 comedy series *Where Do I Sit?* starring Peter Cook has been axed after three programmes. It was scheduled for 12 weeks and should have been screened again [next] Friday. The BBC announced last night: 'After a great deal of consideration we have decided that the programme was not doing the job it set out to do.'
The show, which was broadcast live, featured Cook and 'guests' in sketches and informal 'chat'. The comedy side, particularly Cook's virtuoso imitations of pop singers, was acclaimed. The live talk part of the show remained well below the acceptable standard [...]
The programme had also attracted unfavourable notice because

of the amount of self-indulgence allowed to Cook. In one programme, after a sketch in which he had appeared as God, he
asked the studio audience if anyone had found it offensive. A
young man who replied that he did was treated rudely.

[*Daily Telegraph* 10.3.71]

WHAT DO I DO? PETER COOK ASKS AS HIS TV SHOW IS
AXED: by Keith Deves

Satirist Peter Cook's new TV show *Where Do I Sit?* was axed
by the BBC last night [...]

Cook said he and [...] Ian McNaughton [*sic*] were called to
the office of Bill Cotton, BBC head of Light Entertainment,
on Monday and given 24 hours to accept a new formula. "We
told them that it was unlikely we would accept the idea," he
said. Cook said: "What I want to know is if any BBC show has
ever been chopped like this before, without giving it a chance
to develop." He said the BBC threatened to axe the show after
only the second programme when he had to quickly inject an
interview with playwright Johnny Speight because Spike Milligan was ill. "Yet they actually asked me to do the series. And
when I said there would be six or seven, they came back and
asked me for twelve shows, so it could develop," he said.

[*Evening Standard* 10.3.71]

MR COOK REGRETS—HE WON'T BE KILLING NETTLES
TONIGHT: by Leslie Watkins

Peter Cook should have been supervising a massacre yesterday afternoon. He ought to have been slaughtering his hated
enemy—an army of giant nettles—with a Sten gun. Instead he
pottered sadly round a North London pond feeding ducks with
bread and cake [...]

So the death agonies of the stinging nettles, which were to have
featured tonight, will now never be seen. Nor will Mr. Cook's
efforts to sail round the world in a blotting paper boat. 'A terri-

ble shame,' he said. 'I'm certain it would have been the funniest
show yet in the series [...]

'Being an interviewer on TV was a completely new experience
for me and I found it nerve-racking, particularly as the interviews were done live, and I'm quite aware of the fact that I
made mistakes. But I'd love to have gone on.'

Puzzled? 'Who wouldn't be? They gave me no reason for axing
the series.'

But, in his bewilderment, there is one fact of which Mr. Cook
is confident. His downfall was not connected with Mrs. Mary
Whitehouse's recent 'blasphemy complaint' about him... 'How
could anybody have taken that sketch seriously? There was I
wearing tatty old shorts and a steel helmet—an obvious idiot if
ever there was one—claiming to be God. Her objections were
too farcical for words...'

[Newspaper unknown 12.3.71]

AFTERMYTH

PETE'S DUD WAS TOO YOUNG TO DIE:
Kenneth Eastaugh looks in.

Three weeks. That's all the BBC gave Peter Cook to prove himself in the new role of knockabout chat man in his series *Where
Do I Sit?* And it's worrying.

My fear, in this impatient age of instant coffee, instant sex
and instant death, is that the ratings-conscious TV bosses are
beginning to delude themselves that a series which does not
work immediately is not worth doing. But to limit television
programmes to those which are an instant success is to limit
television's growth. [...]

The critics were right to pan Cook's show. Some of it was
childish. A lot was sheer self-indulgence. But Cook is also right
when he says that the BBC should have given him more time. It
is futile to give a top performer like Cook a new type of series,

to attempt to stretch him, then snatch the opportunity from him when he had hardly begun! [...]

The BBC has taken off a show which, given a longer run and more thought, I believe would have proved itself a refreshing two-finger gesture at everything in TV and in life which is safe, dull and pretentious.

[*The Sun* 13.3.71]

HOW TO COOK YOUR OWN GOOSE

[author uncredited]

NO-ONE AT the BBC is pleased that after only three editions the answer to Peter Cook's *Where Do I Sit?* should have turned out to be 'Nowhere.' Sniffing behind the scenes of this famous collapse, Mandrake's man found more sorrow than self-justification.

The trouble was that Peter Cook, adept as he may be as a comedian, mimic and writer, simply could not handle the chatty, live side of the programme. 'There are certain basic requirements when you're interviewing someone on the air,' said one veteran light entertainment hand, heavily. 'I mean, you've got to listen to his answers, help him say what he wants to say. Peter seemed to have closed his mind in advance. Did you see that bit when after a send-up of God he asked the audience if anyone found the sketch to be in bad taste and the usual sycophants yelled "No" and one brave bloke said "Yes"? Peter swatted him like a fly. He couldn't even manage the mechanics of a chat show. I mean, we've got past the days of saying, "I'm sorry, I'm getting the wind-up signal from the producer." In the old days prospective interviewers used to get a terrible dressing-down from someone like Donald Baverstock after every show. Even Simon Dee was put through the mill until he could handle things efficiently, whatever else you might say about him.'

Mandrake's man mentioned the point made by TV critic Philip Purser [...] about Cook sometimes seeming to put on a dead common voice, as if seeking to identify with such favoured guests as Johnny Speight. The old hand said, 'To tell the truth, only on the first try-out did Peter ever seem to be himself. Ever afterwards he was always playing some sort of part. We're not sure he's capable of being himself.'

Anyway, what happened was that after the third edition of *Where Do I Sit?* Bill Cotton proposed to Cook that he should rest the show for a couple of weeks and then bring it back purely as a comedy programme. Cook, for whom the experiment marked his debut as a co-producer, as well as performer, declined.

What now? Cotton remains an admirer of Cook's comedy. It's said he regards the savage parody of his own recent star Rod McKuen as one of the funniest take-offs he has ever seen. Certainly the doors of the Television Centre are wide open to Peter any time he cares to return. But it may well be that our hero is even now crying thoughtfully all the way to The Other Channel.

[*Sunday Times* 14.3.71]

HELP, I'M A PRISONER IN A COMEDY FACTORY

John Antrobus has been a stalwart of the comedy writing scene since the 1950s. Most famous, perhaps, for his collaborations with people like Spike Milligan and Ray Galton as well as his work on such series as The Army Game *and* The Marty Feldman Comedy Machine, *he has also made quite a name for himself as a leading British absurdist playwright with plays like* An Apple A Day, *as well as a popular children's author. Thus it was that Clinty Of Wintistering tracked him down for an interview in a delightful café on the King's Road in London's fashionable London.*

PETER GORDON: How well did you get to know Peter Cook through the projects you both worked on?

JOHN ANTROBUS: I'm afraid to say not very well at all. My two encounters with him professionally were with the film of *The Bed Sitting Room* and the play for television *An Apple A Day*. While *The Bed Sitting Room* was being filmed I became ill, unwell in the way that Jeffrey Bernard was unwell. It meant I never visited the set at all. When *An Apple A Day* came along some years later I was still rather withdrawn though well into recovery. I went to a few rehearsals for the latter, but we only really exchanged pleasantries. In fact, I'm not sure how you're going to get an interview out of this [*Laughs*].

I did meet him later on, however, when he was trying to get over his own alcoholism. We went to the same self-help group and talked on the phone sometimes. He did manage to stay sober for some time as well. But certainly at the times our paths crossed professionally I can't say I got to know him all that well.

PG: How did the original play of *The Bed Sitting Room* come about?

JA: Well, I'd had this idea about a man who turns into a bedsitting room, and the doctor treating him moves in with his well-known fiancee. I'd told this idea to Spike Milligan and Spike told the story at an after dinner speech. He added the stuff about it happening after a nuclear war and this man being Lord Fortnum of Alamein and the other chap being Captain Pontius Kak. Anyway, he had the whole room roaring with laughter. When a group called Tomorrow's Audience asked Spike for a play, he asked me and we decided to write it up together. I remember Spike was playing Ben Gunn in *Treasure Island* at the time we were writing it. I'd go to Spike's dressing room, which was decorated as a grotto for the kids to come and meet Gunn after the show, and he never came out of character, and we'd write it there, so I had to write with this mad toothless idiot.

It was first performed as a one-act play at The Marlow Theatre in Canterbury, with Willie Rushton in it. It all went very well and then Kenneth Tynan, the *Observer* critic, told us he was coming down to see it. Spike sent a telegram: 'Don't come. It's an experimental piece. Work in progress, not a finished thing!' Well, thank God, he didn't take any notice of Spike, and in the next issue of *The Observer* Tynan dedicated his whole page to our play, saying how wonderful it was, how it was a brilliant piece of theatre and so on.

PG: So, how did the film come about?

JA: Richard Lester's company wanted to make it, so I was commissioned to write a screenplay. I added quite a lot of stuff from my other plays: I knew I wanted to have a family in it who rode around on a tube train underneath ruined London, the one played by Arthur Lowe, Rita Tushingham and Mona Washbourne, so I used the family from my play *Why Bournemouth?* and then took the medical scenes, the ones with Marty Feldman as the nurse, from a play I'd written called *You'll Come To Love Your Sperm Test*.

PG: Were the ballooning policemen written with Peter and Dudley in mind?

JA: No, I don't think I wrote any of it with anyone in particular in mind apart from Spike in the 'Mate' role.

PG: Peter's speech at the end of the play, the one about 'the goat shall give suckle to the bee', has a very Cookish flavour to it. Did you write that or would he have made it up?

JA: Well, I didn't write it. There was a last script re-write which I didn't do, that was by Charles Wood, so it might have come up in that, but yes, Peter might well have come up with it himself. Well, thank you Peter, wherever you are, it's a lovely little speech.

PG: What did you think of Peter and Dudley's performances in the film?

JA: Yeah, very good. Those policemen bossing everyone around— 'Keep moving, keep moving!' Peter and Dudley were perfect petty officials. Anything that stayed still might present a target for another nuclear attack.

PG: What do you think of the film now?

JA: I find I like it more and more as time goes on. It didn't do very well at the time, I don't think anyone really knew how to promote it, but it certainly seems to have picked up quite a cult following—I met a girl who told me she's seen it 27 times. One's first reaction to something is not always the best one, you're too close to it and I was not so keen on it then, but now I find I like it a lot and it does seem to have become very popular.

PG: Was there any hidden meaning behind all that stuff at the end of the film, where Peter becomes the messenger of God and Dudley turns into a dog?

JA: No, not really. It was just absurdist, when you're writing like that you're not thinking about meaning.

PG: So the meaning gets added on later by people like me who think about these things too much?

J.A. [*Laughs*]: Yes, I suppose so.

PG: Moving on to *An Apple A Day* in 1971, how did that come about?

JA: I'd read an article in a newspaper about this chap who made notes from newspaper reports of women who'd been run over and he then went around their houses claiming to be a doctor from the council and he'd come to 'measure their liabilities' and he... well, he had sex with quite a lot of them. [*Laughs*] I sold the play to the BBC some years before it got made. They paid me half of my fee and then backed out of making it. A couple of years later Peter Sellers read the play and starting raving to me about how he must make it and the BBC became interested again and it was re-commissioned. Then Peter's enthusiasm went, as it was wont to do, so the BBC said that they'd got Peter Cook and Dudley Moore to do it instead.

PG: What part was Sellers supposed to have played?

JA: The son.

PG: So it wasn't written with Peter or Dudley in mind?

JA: Not at all, no.

PG: It's just that there's some wonderful dialogue between the two of them that seems almost perfectly suited for their comic sensibilities. There's a lovely joke in the opening scene where Dudley says 'You might respect my principles,' to which Peter replies, 'Oh I *do* respect your principles. I ignore them but I certainly respect them.' It's a beautifully Cookish inversion of a cliché that's not just a joke, it also tells you a great deal about the relationship between father and son. There's another line when Cook and Milligan's characters are discussing Dudley, and Spike says, 'There's something not quite right about your boy... it's not that one leg's longer than the other or anything like that.' Was that just a synchronicity?

JA [*A tad shocked*]: I never thought of it like that. Well, I couldn't have had him in mind, so yes, it was just a synchronicity. God, I hope he wasn't offended by it!

PG: You were saying you didn't get to know Peter and Dudley during the filming?

JA: No. I knew Dudley slightly better than Peter because I'd approached him before and we'd had lunch at Wheeler's and discussed working together. This was quite some time before *An Apple A Day*. But Peter, no. It's a great pity because when I saw the play I thought Peter was playing it in too sketch-like a fashion. Dudley was better because he was playing the younger man so he only had to play himself, but Peter played it up too much, which if I'd had a hand in directing it I could have sorted out. When you're in an absurdist play the acting has to be more grounded, that way the absurd nature of the characters becomes more apparent. If you're playing it up you can lose that. You go for Ibsen, against the grain. Not Peter's fault, and if it was to happen today I'd roll my sleeves up and make sure it was done better.

It's such a shame, a real shame that the BBC wiped that tape along with so much else. You think of that cast—Peter, Dudley,

Spike, Ken Griffith—all together in a play, all lost. I would like the chance to do it again.

PG: Do you think that you can see any reflection of Peter's alcoholism in his work, such as the nihilism and cruelty in *Derek and Clive*?

JA: Yes, I heard some *Derek and Clive* once and I can see that in there. I can't say I liked it that much. You see, when we all started off as satirists we had the things we wanted to attack, the things we were against in life. But as you get on in life you find out that that's not enough, to simply be against things is ultimately destructive. I picked up on a quote you made in your interview with Stephen Fry, the one from Rilke—'If you take my demons away you might also take my angels'—related to Peter's drinking. I can only really speak for myself, but that really does seem tied in with this romantic idea about alcoholism that drinking was somehow related to creativity, and it's not. I believed it myself once, the whole Brendan Behan myth, but it's something we've really got to move on from. Alcoholism just takes everything away, your enjoyment of everything, your life, all of it. It takes away your enjoyment of your angels along with the rest of it. I don't really know Peter's later work that well, but that's how it seems to me.

GOOD EVENING BEHIND THE FRIDGE

Here's a rundown of all the sketches from Behind The Fridge, *(Australian and UK runs) and* Good Evening *in the States, and a quick summary of what they were about, along with comments from Joe McGrath, who directed all the filmed sketches and the London run of the show.*

Behind The Fridge (Australia): Hello/ Foreign Office/ Dudley Moore/ On Location/ An Appeal/ Chanson/ Come In/ A Conservative/ Moody/ Peter Cook/ Blow The Wind Southerly/ Resting/ The Gospel Truth/ Dudley Moore/ So Much Toulouse/ Conservative/ Not An Asp/ Boy Joy/ Prestissimo/ Lambeth Walk/ Tea For Two/ Goodbyee

Behind The Fridge (London): Hello/ On Location/ Eine Kleine Brechtmusik/ Come In/ Chanson/ A Conservative/ Moody/ Old Man River/ Resting/ The Gospel Truth/ Dudley Moore/ Kampala/ An Appeal/ Mini Drama/ Boy Joy/ Tea For Two/ Goodbyee

Good Evening (US): Hello/ On Location/ Madrigal/ Crime & Pun-
ishment/ Die Flabbergast/ Down The Mine/ *'One Leg Too Few'*/
Soap Opera/ The Gospel Truth/ The Kwai Sonata/ Mini Drama/
The Frog & Peach/ An Appeal/ Tea For Two/ Goodbyee

AN APPEAL
New sketch, filmed, with Dudley talking on behalf of The Spooch
Impodiment Society.

BLOW THE WIND SOUTHERLY
New sketch, filmed.
JOE McGRATH: 'Dudley's dragged up as Kathleen Ferrier on a
bandstand singing *Blow The Wind Southerly* and, of course, the
wind blows stronger and stronger. We used a Spitfire engine to act
as a wind machine. We filmed this at Barnes Common. Dudley's
dress is attached to wires and my wife Peta is yanking them off him
as the wind increases.'

BOY JOY
New sketch.
McGRATH: 'Boy Joy was like a five second commercial. Boy
Joy is this stuff for pooves to spray each others' bums with. Peter
said it was the smell of smoked salmon. They would chase each
other around the stage with these Boy Joy canisters, spraying each
other's bums, and then Dudley would sing a jingle—'Boyyyy
Joooyyyy'—in that castrato choirboy voice.'

CHANSON
Song written by Richard Ingrams and John Wells in French.
RICHARD INGRAMS: 'This was a party piece by John Wells and
myself. JW was a Maurice Chevalier type singing about a 'little
phrase' he picked up on his travels in England, the phrase being
'Pissoff.'

COME IN

New sketch.

A lecturer (Cook) invites a student (Moore) to his room for a pointless tutorial.

CONSERVATIVE, A CONSERVATIVE

Two Cook solo filmed pieces, a) where he gives a speech after losing his seat in an election, b) where he delivers a TV election broadcast and attempts to hypnotise the viewers to vote Conservative. These monologues were originally written and filmed, although never screened, for the BBC's coverage of the 1964 General Election.

McGRATH: [*on (b)*] 'This is a marvellous idea. He's actually stoned, isn't he? It's a great performance. He looks like a wax-work.'

CRIME AND PUNISHMENT

a.k.a. *Six Of The Best* from the second series of *Not Only But Also*. 'I'm much bigger than you.'

DIE FLABBERGAST

Dudley's parody of the Wagnerian aria of *Fringe* vintage.

DOWN THE MINE

Cook's old Sitting On The Bench routine.

EINE KLEINE BRECHTMUSIK

New sketch. Filmed.

McGRATH: 'That was a silent film, based on *The Blue Angel* with Brecht-type music and singing by Dudley. A very beautiful film with Peter as Marlene Dietrich—you know, "Falling In Love Again, What Am I To Do..."—and Dudley as the Emil Jennings character, the schoolteacher madly in love with Dietrich the cabaret singer. Peter liked dressing up as Marlene and got into top hat and the tights—shaved his legs. When we were shooting it, we broke for lunch, and Peter being Peter—not an actor—he went out for lunch in full Dietrich drag rather than take it off. We're sitting in this restaurant, and there's people going "Who the fuck is this?" at this vision of Peter in a silver top hat, legs crossed, smoking a cigarette. No comedian would do that, no actor would do that—they'd be more, "Oh, I'll have lunch in the dressing room rather than get changed." I don't know whether it was complete naivety on his part or whether he did it to cause a stir and show off.'

FOREIGN OFFICE

New sketch about the Foreign Minister, a coded message and an annoying git.

McGRATH: 'Superb acting. Notice how Dudley's got padding under his raincoat to suggest he's hunchbacked or deformed. With the braying voice and obsequious manner he's a truly pathetic character, in the original sense of the word. Peter counterbalances Dudley's freakishness with his urbane middleclass type. Foreign Office is a marvellous concept, isn't it?; that the Foreign Office is run and peopled by these ill-educated berks. The upper classes don't know the first thing about it and all these comprehensive school idiots are running the country.'

THE FROG AND PEACH

From the second series of *Not Only But Also*, Sir Arthur Streeb-Greebling discusses his failed restaurant.

GOODBYEE

From *Not Only But Also*, the old farewell song.

THE GOSPEL TRUTH

New sketch with five brief filmed scenes in which a Biblical Jerusalem journalist (Moore) tracks down witnesses to the life of Jesus, including Arthur Shepherd (Cook).

McGRATH: 'That Jimmy Christ thing about "You save the world

and I'll deal with the built-in cupboards"—that's a steal from Mel Brooks' *2000 Year Old Man* when he's talking about Joan Of Arc: "You save France, I'll wash up."'

'Dudley's hair and makeup for Mrs. McMyer was based on Golda Meir. His Scots accent is good—his Dad was Scottish. When you see Dudley doing this kind of thing it hits you how fucking good he was. Peter's doing a David Frost here—his reaction shots are wonderful. "Tickle your arse with a feather."—"I beg your pardon?"—"I said *particularly nasty weather*." That's a terrible joke. These outside, meaning 'nonstudio', sketches were filmed in Wimbledon, Putney, that area. The walking on the water scene was shot at Black Rock, near Pinewood. It's so funny, Peter as Jesus testing the water with his toe—good detail there.'

HELLO

New sketch. Two men who don't know each other discuss mutual acquaintances they haven't got.

KAMPALA

New interview sketch, where Dudley questions Peter as African dictator Idi Amin.

A snippet is preserved on the 1972 *Private Eye* flexidisc *Hello Sailor*:

Q: What first gave you the idea of expelling the Ugandan Asians?

AMIN: Well, I tell you, my friend; it came to me in the bath. *Lots* of things are coming to me in the bath, including my six wives—Lord bless their big bottoms and huge black wobbly titties.

Q: A lot of people in Britain have suggested cutting off your aid.

AMIN: ARGHHH! Nobody goes round chopping off people's aids except me! I'm doing it all the time...

THE KWAI SONATA

a.k.a. And The Same To You. Dudley's ancient party piece of Colonel Bogey via Beethoven.

LAMBETH WALK

Unidentified.

MADRIGAL

Another of Dudley's musical parodies from the *Fringe* era, this time of medieval music.

MINI-DRAMA

New sketch. Psychotic taxi driver takes a fare to the House Of Lords in a sketch about twenty five years ahead of its time.

MOODY

New sketch. Husband (Cook) and wife (Moore) have a tense conversation while their thoughts are played out on a filmscreen behind their heads.

McGRATH: 'So they could be sure they were in sync with the film Peter and Dudley had a mirror in the footlights and one on the TV set. The mirror was a big help. Dudley was always spot-on for timing, just from being a musician, he could do it mentally. Peter at first was all over the place but he got just as a good as Dudley.

'The editing of the film was very difficult. I put it together according to the script and then they came in to the cutting room and sat down at the Moviola and ran the film and ran the film and they read it, read it again, and would say, "Ah, we need another second or two of this," or "We'll have to shorten that," until they were pretty comfortable. And they always got it right on stage. And Peter's attitude to things... Dudley was saying "Suppose we get it all wrong one night?" and Peter said, "Well it'll be twice as funny then." Dudley, of course, was, "Will it fuck!"

'These scenes were shot in Isleworth Studios, a small film studio. We also shot Old Man River there, Gospel Truth and the *Blue Angel* film [Eine Kliene Brechtmusick], everything over three or four days. They had an impressive energy about them, getting so much done, and done well, in a very limited time.'

NOT AN ASP

From all the way back to Cook's undergraduate days as a writer for Kenneth Williams, Arthur Grole waxes on to a stranger about the contents of his box.

OLD MAN RIVER

From the second series of *Not Only But Also*: A blacked-up Dudley goes into a shower and turns from Paul Robeson into Bertie Wooster.

ONE LEG TOO FEW

Another from Cook's Cambridge days. The Tarzan audition sketch.

ON LOCATION

New sketch. An actor (Cook) goes to the home of his father (Moore) having missed his mother's funeral.

PRESTISSIMO

New sketch. An excuse for puns based around musical terminology as Dudley is arrested for being drunk in charge of a piano.

RESTING

New sketch. Dudley plays a camp, out-of-work actor turned cleaner who persuades his stuffy employer (Cook) to help him rehearse for Othello.

McGRATH: 'What was funny about this one was when we did it in London we put Dudley on these Elton John stack heel shoes. He was the same height as Peter and every time he stopped mincing around, Peter had to hold him up.

'Interestingly, one wonders how this sketch, thirty years later, would be received, because Dudley is so gay. It might be construed today as very offensive. But, knowing Dudley, it wasn't meant offensively.'

SOAP OPERA

Another title for Resting.

SO MUCH TOULOUSE

New sketch, kind of. Actually it's the old Balloon Pregnancy Test sketch from the Establishment Club Players, but, for no readily apparent reason other than sheer bloodymindedness, transported to the studio of Toulouse-Lautrec and spoken entirely in French. Peter is Henri T-L, crawling about with shoes attached to his kneecaps (just like Sellers' subsequent impression of the artist in *The Pink Panther Strikes Again*). Dudley plays the balloon-infected female. Odd.

McGRATH: 'They never used that one in London. I wonder why... It takes a great courage to a whole sketch in French and still make it very funny.'

TEA FOR TWO

New sketch. Replete in macs and cloth caps, Pete and Dud discuss the Women's Movement.

MCGRATH: 'The thing about Dudley and Peter which is never mentioned is that the sketches are all about different characters. Everyone just remembers "Dud and Pete", y'know? But the sketches are incredibly well-written—mainly by Peter—and the characters are very developed. They're not just putting on funny voices, there's pathos too.

'They did another "father and son" sketch, didn't they, for *Not Only But Also*, but that was very different in tone to On Location.

This one is quite sad when you realise it's based on Dudley's father dying. They built a very funny sketch on an authentic death. There's no real jokes as such in things like On Location, Mini-Drama and Soap Opera, the humour's all coming out of the characters. It's almost a disservice calling these works "sketches"—they're more than that, they're tales with a beginning, a middle and an end.

'What makes them so much better than other double acts is the authority with which they performed—and complete confidence because they've written it. Nobody's come and said "You can't do this, you must do that." They're totally in charge. They were amazing together. Monty Python aren't in the same league. A lot of it's down to Dudley's character playing and also to Peter's willingness to let Dudley do those performances. Peter was a self-conscious performer—you can see it in his body language, the way he caresses himself in Hello—but they used that to benefit him as the son in On Location where he's contrite for not being at his mother's side when she was dying. But then he's so great as the Foreign Office bureaucrat in that Chinese riddle thing—that came naturally to him.

'They were more than professional. What is astounding is that, for On Location, Dudley has not sat in a makeup chair for three hours like Peter Sellers would have. He's not wearing a wig, he's not got lines drawn on his face. He's just adopted a stoop and wears NHS glasses and a cardigan and yet you accept him as an old man, and when Peter arrives—"Hello father"—you accept Peter as his son. It's brilliant.'

WILL SELF DESTRUCTS

WILL SELF: All the people I view as cultural icons, I sort of purposefully don't find out too much about them. For example, I haven't read Harry Thompson's book about Cook. I could have met Cook when he was alive—I knew people who knew him—but I didn't want to. So I don't know very much about the creative partnership or what's been written or what's been said by either of them. The main question, as a satirist, of viewing them as a double act was that Dudley was absolutely unimportant, and indeed that is the essence of being the straight man—being a martyr.

Anyway, *Not Only But Also*; my brother and I did comedy double acts throughout our childhood, we were obsessed with them and we had sickening parents who brought us up without a telly. We depended on *Round The Horne*—'Hello, I'm Julian and this is my friend Sandy...'—but at some point I saw *Not Only But Also* and I realised that this was the real fucking McCoy, This was pure satiric comedy and timeless. Mumsy took us to see *Behind The Fridge* when I was ten; that made a big impression and, in fact, I virtually memorised that show. They did a lot with a large screen which (showed) their thoughts. That was pretty revolutionary. I can't remember the sketches now but I certainly remember that Dudley was not the funny one.

ALEX GAMES: Do you regard Dudley Moore as a musician first and a comic second?

WS: It's a classic thing with English vaudevillians where you do another turn, you play the piano or do comic dancing, I recall hearing him play and thinking he was a white Oscar Peterson, that school of white jazz. (But I'm a real jazz snob.) Then you have things like *10* and it being the most bogus twaddle imaginable—and upsetting. It was just sort of so sad. Even at the time, you thought, 'You poor, unhappy, short man who's got a complex about fucking beautiful women'. God, how sad, how sad.

I suppose the Pete and Dud act, when you look back on it now, with the long plastic macs and the knotted scarves and the soft caps, has dated much more and show up and undermine the purity of Cook's vision with an acute class consciousness that he couldn't quite shake off, could he? It certainly emerges in Pete and Dud, and the latent homophobia as well, they're obviously supposed to be a gay couple in a perverse way. Or an impotent gay couple. Hence the plastic macs. I mean, they are low rent but venal. I'm sure he was homophobic—I'd lay a bet on it.

AG: It seems to me there was a kind of love between them that dare not speak its name—more so on Cook's side.

WS: When [Harry Thompson's biography of Peter Cook] came out there did seem to be a strong indication... You'd need someone who was there, who saw them interact when they were young, because this sort of thing is clearly going to be an Oxford affair, which does happen. I mean a lot of impressionable young men go up each others' arses in Oxford and never forget it. You'd want someone who had preferably seen his engorged turgid member actually disappear into the tiny man's rear end...

The other big bite of intense influence was *Derek and Clive* which is—now let's see if I can get this exactly right—1974-5? 'Cos I was in Class 3R at Christ's College, Finchley, and the class heavies were Ian Gordon and Joss Pym. One day they brought this tape in, put it on and this voice went, 'You fucking cunt, cunt'. I thought they had gone and made a tape of themselves and it took me five or ten minutes to work out that this was not a tape of the class hard boys trying to be funny and, when I realised, it was an enormous epiphany. For quite a while I was genuinely shocked by *Derek and Clive*. The one that totally got me was the cancer sketch. Cancer was such a big thing in my family life; my grandfather had died of it, my mother was well on the way of dying of it. Almost every day she'd get up and say, 'I'm going to die of cancer...' That sketch just did it for me, it was Nothing Was Taboo. And the range of *Derek and Clive* as well; there's almost every comic mode, from burlesque, the very traditional comic ditty 'We are miserable sin- ners, filthy fuckers'—all that stuff, to the surreal lobsters and Jayne Mansfield's bum. It's a sort of reprise through a glass darkly of their entire relationship... It existed as a one-off, as an epiphanic realisation of what the potential of satire was in that way. And again, Dudley—no impression on me at all. None. I always got the impression that he was trying to be Cook, that was how the partnership existed. He was trying to be up to the beat and trying to do what Cook is doing effortlessly, he's straining for. He exists as a straight man—as a strain man, really.

About two and a half years ago, I was doing a long drive up to Orkney and I bought a Cook and Moore tape, one of those tapes you can get in a garage. It had two sides of E.L. Wisty monologues [which] took me over absolutely, and I started talking like him. There's a long piece about C.P. Snow's view of the world: 'In the future, people won't have relationships and they won't kiss; they will all be like robots with horrible long spindly legs. Can you imagine it, a cinema full of robots with their horribly long spindly legs and all clacking their metal faces together? Horrible.' And I got this voice stuck in my head like a fucking record for about four months. I was Peter Cook for four months and I'd interpret every situation in Cookese. It really does take me over, and I don't just mean the level of the voice, I mean at the level of the satiric vision and the timing...

AG: Would you say Cook influenced your writing?

WS: Not at all, it's a different thing, no, no. Except possibly a kind of inverted Stevie Smith suburban bleakness, a kind of love affair that the English satirist has with—it's like the Morrissey song *Every Day Is Like Sunday*: 'This is the seaside town they forgot to bomb/Come, come nuclear Bomb'—that kind of attitude which, I think, formed some of his attitude in his work and was there for me to draw on in my affections of suburban mundanity which is the mise-en-scene of a lot of my novels... It's a personal thing for me, Cooky, it's a personal attitude. It's more related to my journalism, I'd say, and being a London boulevardier and being in *Private Eye*'s Pseud's Corner—you know, being in the thick of that ongoing satire of being a thorn in the establishment's side and to do with my public gestural anarchism. Cook, for me, relates to taking the piss out of the governing class. The English have such a reliable appetite for hearing what wankers they are, there's such a steady demand for it, it's like some dominatrix advert in a phone booth.

AG: Is it a problem for a satirist to become adopted by the establishment?

WS: Definitely, definitely, and maybe that's what happened to him. He realised he'd been muted and he decided, 'I'd rather fucking go to seed'. Cook would never have taken a public honour or gone to Number 10 to shake hands with Tony Blair, and that's really important, what you're saying about being co-opted by the English establishment. To me it's incredibly important not to lick the State's arsehole.

AG: I like the idea that you can be a fan of Peter Cook and yet feature in the Pseud's Corner column of *Private Eye*.

WS: I was once Pseud Of The Year and justifiably so. I'm pissed off I'm no longer Pseud Of The Year. But Cook didn't take much interest in the day-to-day running of the *Eye*. It was always Richard Ingrams' vehicle, and this is where it comes back to class. Ingrams is, in a sense, totally unreconstructed English bourgeois. I think maybe Cook couldn't see a way out, and people like Ingrams and Moore showed him that there was even less of a way out because of the compromises they made... Cook had a sense of honour, that's why he killed himself.

AG: Why do you think he killed himself?

WS: Because he knew his talent didn't go any further. He was right about himself. To extemporise purely is to be atemporal which is, in a sense, to have an in-built death wish—which is the epitaph of an emotion, as Wilde said—and Cook's whole life was an epitaph of his own emotion. Which is why he became such a banal wreck. There's a pathos about things that that guy wrote... Cook was destined to die in a Hampstead mews smoking too much shitty Moroccan and drinking carry-out Vladivars. I mean, at least if you're going to fucking blow out like that, blow out in style.

ELECTRIC LADY LANDLORD

The accepted tale of how Derek and Clive came to be goes something like this... New York, late 1973, and Peter Cook and Dudley Moore, in an attempt to stave off the boredom and creative stagnation of performing their *Good Evening* show at the Plymouth Theatre on Broadway, book themselves into Jimi Hendrix's old studio Electric Lady for an evening of improvisation and scatology. Tapes of the session find their way into the drug-crazed paws of various hair-and-flare wearing rock'n'rolly boogie ditty musicians and proliferate until, almost three years later and recognising their commercial potential, Peter and Dudley make a deal with Island Records and issue the recordings as the *Derek & Clive (Live)* album in the summer of 1976.

However, if their recording session was a spur-of-the-moment, morale-lifting moment of whimsy, why did Cook and Moore then perform a second set of rudery at Greenwich Village's Bottom Line club, excerpts of which are included in the album? (The existence of a 'live' take of Winkie Wanky Woo, under the title Sex Crime, on the B-side of the Squatter And The Ant promo single suggests that the sketches performed at Electric Lady were enacted at the club too.) Plus, if the Derek and Clive characters were purely a private pleasure of Cook and Moore's, why did they hire a top-of-the-range fancyshanks recording studio rather than capture their outpourings with an El Cheapo tape recorder like the ones they improvised their *Not Only But Also* sketches into?

Unable to sleep at night for these questions twirling in the spin-drier of his mind, the Holy Dragger telephoned Eddie Kramer, the engineer of *Derek & Clive (Live)*, to set the record straight. Because the Derek and Clive sessions occurred some 27 years ago and a lot of bridges have since fallen into the water, there was an element of fuzziness about his memories as Kramer was then concurrently producing the album of Peter and Dudley's Broadway show. The *Good Evening* LP was issued in America on Chris Blackwell's Island label. It is Eddie's understanding of the situation that Cook and Moore had a two-album deal with Blackwell, the Derek and Clive material from Electric Lady and The Bottom Line making up the contracted second album. It transpired that *Good Evening* was not in fact taped live on Broadway—the info on the LP sleeve is spare and ambiguous—but at two special performances at The Bottom Line before an invited audience ('In my mind I still see Dudley hopping around The Bottom Line on one leg,' Kramer recalls.) A close study of the two albums—for similarities in the sound of the audience, the venue's acoustics etc—make it implausible that *Good Evening* and the live sketches on *Derek & Clive (Live)* were all taped on the same day.

During the phone call, Eddie Kramer asked the astounding question, 'So, where's all the stuff they recorded in England?' *What?* He elaborated that the Derek and Clive dialogues he recorded were re-makes of sketches originally taped a year or so previously at Olympic Studios in London. Those recordings were the ones that fell into the bewarted mitts of yer actual rock stars. And what's happened to that tape, I hear a pitiful shriek.

Thanks to the fine efforts of our line-dancing buddies Pink Floyd, we traced Keith Grant who for aeons was the cove responsible for giving musicians more top in their cans at Olympic. He says that, as far as he can recall, Cook and Moore did not make a specific booking for a session. The likelihood is that Peter visited a Dudley Moore Trio recording date (perhaps an overdubbing session for their live *Today* LP that was issued in 1972) and stayed to tape some dialogues with Ol' Twinklefingers afterwards. In 1985 Olympic was bought by Virgin Records who lovingly dumped all the studio's master tapes—'Unreleased stuff by The Who, Rod Stewart, the Stones, everyone; a whole alternative history of British rock'n'roll,' according to Grant—into a builder's skip. Keith Grant believes the master reel of the Derek and Clive blueprint would have been amongst the jettisoned tapes.

PAUL HAMILTON: How did these original tapes [i.e. the ones recorded in London] circulate?

EDDIE KRAMER: How do tapes circulate? [*Laughter*] Somebody, an engineer maybe, at the studio must have made a dub [i.e. copy] of it for himself and then subsequently made dubs for whoever. I mean, every bloody rock band would be saying, 'Here, have you heard this Peter Cook tape?' It was like the staple diet, if you will, for the bands travelling on their buses. The Faces, Traffic—any English band that came over to the States in the '70s had that tape. That's what started it all.

PH: So Chris Blackwell knew of the *Derek and Clive* bootleg doing the rounds and wanted an official release on Island Records?

EK: Right. There was a little bit of resentment from Peter and Dudley that they had to do it all over again for Chris Blackwell. But once they were performing it again they were away. Every time they did it—they had the same material—but each time they did it, it was different. They were like jazz musicians. They could take a theme and just go anywhere with it, if they were in the mood. They were up.

PH: Were the Electric Lady recordings done over a matter of

days?

EK: No, it was a one-evening thing and totally hysterical and ludicrous. I was under the desk crying with laughter. That thing with the baby and the handbag—Bo Dudley—that was brilliant man. Dudley had it all down.

PH: What was the American perception of Cook and Moore in 1973?

EK: They were seen as a very eclectic 'in' thing; very good in New York City but I don't know whether it translated much beyond New York. I'm not sure what the rest of the country—even L.A.—would have made of Peter Cook and Dudley Moore. Probably just a pair of kooky English comedians.

Eddie then descended into the lower bowels of his basement where, he remembered, he stored typed transcripts of *Derek and Clive* material, plus production notes and proposed running-orders by Kramer, Moore and Cook regarding *Good Evening* and *Derek & Clive (Live)*. Why was it deemed necessary to type up the tapes? Perhaps because this was back in the days before digital editing technology, Cook and Moore could edit the scripts whilst they were on tour and send their amendments back to Kramer in NYC, who would then cut the tapes accordingly. 'I'll send these to you,' quoth the flowin' Eddie, 'you'll get a kick out of this.'

Stuff a mattress in your pants, gentle reader, you're about to receive the kicking of your life.The scripts for *Derek and Clive (Live)*—the Electric Lady studio sessions only; Eddie didn't have, or couldn't find, a transcript of the Bottom Line performance—is revelatory in its comprehensive demolishing of the myth of the genesis of *Derek and Clive* as propounded by Cook and Moore, in that there are multiple takes of The Worst Job I've Ever Had and The Worst Job He Ever Had. If this session was just a lark, with no consideration of commercial possibilities, why then did they feel the need to make three attempts apiece in discussing Derek's experiences of snot gathering for Winston Churchill and Clive's retrieval of lobsters from the barking spider of Jayne Mansfield?

The first batch of typed pages, entitled, "FIRST TAKE—'Worst Jobs'" has plenty of false starts, resulting in Cook and Moore getting tangled up as regards who is Derek and who is Clive. There is a good deal of expositionary waffle about their being long-term unemployed but there are nonetheless a couple of nuggets of pure gold. Of lobster felching, Cook relates, 'That was a bad job and in the end I says to Jayne, "You know, Jayne, enough's enough." And, being the star she was, she said, "Fuck off, cunt." And I left on that note.' And, in the Churchill's Titanic bogie reminiscence, Moore reveals that 'The regular bogie does not float. You know how you test if a substance is a bogie? You put a bogie in a glass of beer. If it floats, it is not a bogie. If it goes down to the bottom, it is a bogie. Well, I mean, I think it's cruel, but there you are.'

The second clutch of pages ("SECOND TAKE—'WORST JOB'"), shows Cook and Moore vamping the Mansfield and Churchill material again, this time minus a lot of its flabbiness. The material is becoming more cohesive and naturalistic. This time Cook explains that the bottom-encased lobsters were comatose because 'they were overcome by the fame of it all.' Although a demeaning occupation, it did have its perks: 'In the fashionable bistro scene in Hollywood in those days, you know, if you could walk in to a restaurant with a brown forearm—they knew where that had come from. You could pick up a few birds, I'll tell you that.'

Transcript 3 is where they hit the n. on the h. They start with the released version of The Worst Job I Ever Had, leading seamlessly on to an unreleased version of The Worst Job He Ever Had where Derek recalls his time spent getting snails out of Kirk Douglas' nose, which rather swiftly degenerates (or elevates) into a Clive curse-out of Kirk ('You cunt, Kirk! You fucking midget you—you don't know anything, do you? With your blue eyes, just because you appeared in *The Vikings*—think you can go around, swanning around the world, don't you? Well, you fucking can't, cunt. Fuck off!').

From there, Cook and Moore go immediately into This Bloke Came Up To Me, the take released on *Derek and Clive (Live)*. This is followed by another unissued Worst Job—Clive/Cook's sojourn as General Eisenhower's dandruff flake counter. (Moore is still on a high from the previous sketch's swear-for-all and so punctuates almost all of Cook's lines with 'Oh fucking hell!) Without seemingly taking a break, they then tear in to The Worst Job He Ever Had, the released version (with a few small cuts).

Winkie Wanky Woo was the next item taped, with a minor excision falling between Peter's 'Come back and see me and we'll see if we can sort things out' and Dudley's 'You're very kind', a poor digression where Cook attempts sexual congress with a tap.

The last sketch from Transcript 3 is Squatter And The Ant, with an extraordinary section concerning Squatter's problem of, in Cook's words, 'un-poko constipado'. A few minutes are given to ruminating on 'sixty-five years of pent-up fury' in Squatter's bum. There is a fascinating coda to this unreleased half of Squatter And The Ant as Cook and Moore come out of character, where it is revealed that Peter's enthusiasm for scatology is markedly not as boundless as Dudley's:

PETER: That's a fuck-up.
DUDLEY: No, it is wonderful. That's beautiful.

None of the pieces that comprise the final set of transcripts (labelled 'Tape 2') have gained official release. The first sketch, A Million Pounds, is not a *Derek and Clive* dialogue at all, but a husband-and-wife scenario with Peter playing the woman (a rare occurrence). She is having an hysterical fit, angrily crying about being 'treated by people as some kind of object... some kind of whore' when all she wants in life is 'a million pounds. I always wanted a million pounds, and nobody has given me a million pounds and I'm so miserable.'

Next is a loose and rambly take of Top Rank, unissued in preference to the taut, superior live version from The Bottom Line.

The final dialogue, Vietnam, begins as a D&C vamp on sustaining various war wounds but, by dint of Derek/Moore's persistent requests for a 'suck', meanders into recollections of the great and good that *Derek and Clive* have fellated. Churchill, Prince Philip, General Montgomery, Sir Francis Chichester, Anthony Eden and Harold Wilson are all alleged recipients. Hilarious as it is, the worry of resultant libel cases that would have been brought against Cook, Moore and Island Records should it have been sanctioned for public consumption has meant Vietnam being consigned to tape vault ignominy.

Notable in its absolute absence from both the scripts and album production notes (where we discover the original LP title was *The World's Gone Mad*) is any mention of In The Lav, the only other studio sketch on *Derek & Clive (Live)*. Taking this into account, plus the noticeably rougher recording quality and Peter and Dudley's employment of deeply monged voices, it seems likely that this cut was culled from the Olympic Studio session that produced the original *Derek and Clive* bootleg tape, and added to the tracklist to make up an acceptable playing time (44 minutes) for the album.

SADISTIC WIT

Jerry Sadowitz—comical magician, magical comedian, first-rate hate man who railed against everything in his path and in his garden (and still does)—spoke to John Hind about *Derek and Clive*.

JOHN HIND: Did humour play a large part in your youth?

JERRY SADOWITZ: I adored *Monty Python*. That, and card-tricks, got me through schools and hospitals. It gave me a respite from being a miserable bastard. I went over to America at one point, but my Dad chucked me back on the next plane. I had a breakdown—I didn't know what was going on. My Mum was now in London, trying to set up home, so I went there—I was seventeen. I got a job at Selfridges (the shop) and the council put my family into separate bed and breakfast accommodation. At one point the three of us were put in one tiny room, for three months, three beds cramped up together. It was a very unhappy time of my life—I had nothing to look forward to. But I bought a crappy record-player and then I chanced upon a *Derek and Clive* album. And not only did I find that funnier than Python but they became my companions, at a time when I had no friends. I knew nobody, had no social life, but *Derek and Clive* were in my head—as friends almost. They were a safety blanket.

I just think they're the poetry of comedy. It's like beautiful music really, like Lennon and McCartney in tandem—Peter Cook plays rhythm and Dudley Moore harmonises, adds melodies. They were beautiful—absolute poetry. They knew how to use swear-words. 'Shit', 'wanker', 'fuck off'—they're all great words, with wonderful consonants. 'Cunt' and 'fuck' combined is poetry, pure attack. The point is, how come I can listen to *Derek and Clive*, which is racist and sexist, laugh at it and know they don't really mean it, and yet people can't accept what I do? When I was in Glasgow, playing cards with a friend, if one of us won the other would say 'You big-nosed Jewish bastard' and it was perfectly acceptable. Just a bit of banter between friends. You've got to be able to laugh."

STEPHEN FRY ON *DEREK AND CLIVE*

One of the greatest pleasures I ever had was reciting *Derek and Clive* to Peter who howled with laughter as if hearing them for the first time. He always laughed most at Dudley's bits. I'll never forget his reaction to the nun (as in, 'so naturally I stooped to rape her')—when I got to the bit where Dudley says 'Well haven't you got the message then, hasn't it got through?' Peter was completely helpless. After all, these pieces were mostly ad-libbed under the influence of grass. Peter wasn't so vain as to listen back to them more than once, probably. Whereas fans like me heard them over and over again.

THE BACK PASSAGE

Is there something you need to get out in the open? You'd be better advised to stick it in The Back Passage...

Dear Clinty,

I wish I could still laugh as much as I used to around 1976 when we would play *Derek & Clive (Live)* after a night at the pub. It was so funny it hurt. We'd be crawling around on the floor with tears streaming down our faces.

An uncanny thing occurred about three years later. I was arrested on Waterloo Station for swearing at two police officers and, as was then the custom, spent the night in a cell at a nearby police station. [...]

I don't know if you've ever seen the inside of one of those huge vans that take prisoners to court. They have a central corridor lined with doors to locked cubicles so to prevent passengers having any contact with each other. When police officers led me to my seat, they allowed me to pause so that I could poke my last cigarette through the wire mesh of one of the doors and a kindly criminal could give me a light.

As the vehicle left the courtyard of the police station I distinctly heard one of my unknown colleagues begin to sing, 'As I was walking down the street one day, I saw a house on fi-ire...' So, of course, I joined in with, 'There was a man screaming and shout-ing from an upstairs window, for he was sore afraid...' and so on. Before we got to the end of the song we were getting some big laughs from the other passengers. So I followed Jump by asking my unseen companion, 'What's the worst job you ever had?' And on we went word for word through 'Winston's Bogie' and maybe one or two other Derek & Clive sketches. This was many years ago, you understand, and I had the mother of all hangovers.

By the time we debussed in the secure courtyard of Horseferry Road Magistrates Court, our morale was high and we might have been a group of friends on a charabanc trip organised by the local pub. For all I knew, my companions may have been rapists and robbers. To my embarrassment, one of them even confessed as much to me in my cell later on. But there was a sense that we were indestructible and, even though we were powerless in the hands of authority, none of us would allow that to spoil our day. It just goes to show one of the Godlike ways that Peter Cook's genius shone a little comedy into some very dark places.

MICHAEL C. BURGESS, San Diego, USA.

Dear Sir/Madam,

I am a real fan of Dudley Moore and Peter Cook. Please send me a photo of Dudley Moore in 1975.

J.R.STONE, Letchworth.

[*I'm afraid you're over a quarter of a century late*—Ed.]

ROCK'N'DROLL

In 1976 Britain had ground to a virtual standstill as it faced total economic and social collapse. Inflation peaked at 25%, unemployment hit the million mark the first time since the 1930s, the Labour government jettisoned any pretence at socialism by kowtowing to the monetarist demands of the IMF and Saudi oil barons, and the unions—realising turncoat Labour's intentions of robbing the poor to appease the rich—embarked on a course of debilitating strikes. [*This is jolly, ribald stuff. More!*—Ed.]

Hindsight reveals that inflammatory shock tactics by a disaffected youth culture were not only inevitable but also reasonable. Hence the explosion of Punk Rock spearheaded by the Sex Pistols. The sense of a long repressed rage against conformity was also expressed through Carl Andre's notorious brick installation at the Tate Gallery and the release of *Derek and Clive (Live)*. We should also bear in mind the rise of the neo-Nazi National Front which went overground and attracted mass working-class support directly following the release of Paul Nicholas' *Reggae Like It Used To Be*.

By February 1977, the Pistols, after one single, were kicked off

EMI Records following intense media overkill of various real and imagined outrages and their total lack of self-control. Banned from playing live in Britain and without a record deal they may have been finished but that didn't stop their manager, Situationist Anarchist Half-Pissed modern day pirate Malcolm McLaren from trying to set up a film—tentatively called *Rock Around the Contract*—starring the Sex Pistols.

7 FEB 1977
... Malcolm is in a bit of a weird mood. Thinking too much about record companies. I continued slugging through the petty cash while he sat and made desultory phone calls—one useful one to Peter Cook...

10 FEB 1977
... The tension grows. John & Malcolm go off to meet Peter Cook—good luck to them!
                                    —from the diary of SOPHIE RICHMOND,
                                    Secretary and Office Manager to
                                    Malcolm McLaren and The Sex Pistols.

"When we were putting together *The Great Rock'n'Roll Swindle* with the Sex Pistols, I wanted Peter Cook as one of the people involved. And when we went round his house he was so deeply insane and taking the piss out of the whole idea that it never got off the ground with him... As we walked in the door, he had a big basket full of sweeties and you'd put your hand in, and there was all these syringes underneath. And he went, 'Oooh yes, we're all into heroin in this house.' Absolutely threw Malcolm for six!"
                                    —JOHN LYDON (formerly Johnny Rotten), from the
                                    BBC Radio 4 series *Cook's Tours*, 1995.

Wanting to know more about this would-be tantalising collaboration, your Dragger asked Malcolm McLaren to elucidate. Malcolm was more than willing to be interviewed—in fact he was begging on bended knees at the solid gold gates of Wisty Towers for four days—but the Dragger was far too busy for all of that so he left Talcy Malcy a list of questions to answer.

The questions were:

1. Why did you choose Peter Cook to script the Sex Pistols' film? How did the meeting go ?
2. Do you recall finding syringes in a sweetie bowl?
3. Why did the Cook/Pistols collaboration fail to take off?

The mercurial Malcolm's answers were:

1. We thought at the time that Peter Cook was irreverent enough and subversive enough to take on what was then a punk rebellious anti-establishment viewpoint. We met him in Hampstead—he was terrified that Johnny Rotten would steal his cutlery and followed us everywhere around his house and wouldn't leave us alone for one second. He seemed rather terrified of the prospect of working with the Sex Pistols and didn't hit it off with the then extremely arrogant Johnny Rotten.

2. I can't remember the syringes but it is possible. He was trying to get an angle on Rotten and myself.

3. We were meeting various writers (including Johnny Speight and Graham Chapman) but we had to decide on a director and the director we chose was Russ Meyer who wanted to use his own writer. It's normal in the film world that the director, if he is somewhat of a auteur, would work with his own team. So Roger Ebert—Meyer's collaborator on *Beyond The Valley of the Dolls*, etc—was chosen.

THEY CAN'T GET CHARLES HAWTREY

An extract from Kenneth Williams' Diaries

1977

Thursday, 2 June. Peter Eade [KW's agent] at 10.30. He's been sent a film script for me [*The Hound Of The Baskervilles*], written by Peter Cook and Dudley Moore, offering me the part of Sir Henry. It made me laugh out loud: some of it is v. funny.

Monday, 20 June. Eade telephoned and said 'They want you to play Sir Henry after all, they can't get [Charles] Hawtrey. Will you leave me to do the deal? They are trying it on at the moment with *Carry On* salaries. I think we should try to get them to fix transport.' I said a fervent yes to that.

Sunday, 26 June. Walked to the Paris [Theatre] in the evening to do *Quote Unquote* [BBC radio show] for John Lloyd. The team was Peter Cook, Irene Handl, Richard Ingrams and me... Peter Cook on the way to the pub: 'I was frightened of you during the revue days!

Let's face it, I still am.' Goodness knows why anyone should think me formidable!

Monday, 4 July. Script conference with Peter C., Dudley M., Irene Handl, Max Wall, and Paul Morrissey. Peter Cook reiterated: 'Sir Henry must be very mild and vulnerable... Careful you don't get that edge into your voice...' It's ludicrous the way he and Dudley talk about truth in characterisation the whole time, 'cos the script contains a mass of inconsistencies. They object to 'law enforcement' and 'twit' because 'it's not right for the period' but they've written a line 'Good evening & welcome & piss off' which isn't right for Baskerville Hall either. The seriousness with which everyone sits around discussing the merit of this word or that word for inclusion in this hotch-potch o' rubbish is the sort of thing Cook would have ridiculed in his undergraduate days.

Wednesday, 13 July. I was suprised watching the rushes today. I looked very good, the light blue summer suit photographed well, the lighting was excellent, and the projection room looked very good. The whole thing looked stylish and smart. Of course the dialogue is lousy a lot of the time, but the look and the manner are OK. Critics will say 'tired, laboured, unfunny' etc. but it don't matter, and I do need the money.

Monday, 18 July. Car at 9 o'c. And we were at Bray in 40 minutes. It is a rambling & derelict house with dirt, decay & cobwebs everywhere. I talked with Paul Morrissey & John Goldstone [film producer] & then Peter & Dudley came up. Peter cried 'Hello, you camp Ada!' which completely threw me, but I repeated it gaily adding 'Yes!'

Tuesday, 19 July. We picked up Irene Handl at 7 o'c. She chattered away to me and to Beulah the chihuahua all the time. Boundless energy. We started off with the scene where Mrs Barrymore shows us into the attic room. Irene was rather halting & her work didn't have great flow—as I'd expected—& Paul went again and again.

I find Dudley's Welsh accent hilarious & I'm doing it myself!! all the time. I must stop it 'cos it can be v. irritating for him. Don't care for Peter's voice—curiously muted Jewish—don't know why he's saddled himself with such a rotten sound.

Thursday, 21 July. Peter Cook said on the phone: 'John Goldstone & Dudley & I agree that Paul has made you do things which are over the top & bogus & we must put it right... I want this picture to be really good... Dudley & I have had a row with Paul about it... but he was the only one at the rushes who was laughing at your stuff...' He certainly threw me for six.

Friday, 22 July. All of it seemed to go well, Talked with Peter most of the day... At the end of the day Peter asked me to rushes. I saw myself for the first time. The character looks other than me. It's a good wig and the alopecia is convincing. The moments when I stay in character are good... the odd bits (snorting etc.) when I don't, are bogus. The whole film looks lavish & expensive. P.C. gave me drinks & brought me home in his car. His conversation is infectiously good-humoured & enthusiastic. Lovely fellow.

Monday, 25 July. I talked to Peter a lot in the morning & he was funny about the Sitwells—'That was all they could do: sit well. That Sir Several told Edith to stay stationary. They used her for stationery. They actually wrote on her... wonderful woman... she could rhyme anything! When they gave her "Sitting here upon my bottom" she straightaway replied with "Always wondering how I got 'em" & she brought the house down. They left her in the rubble. She couldn't get out. She was stationary you see...'

Tuesday, 26 July. None of it was quick work. Max Wall put in 'fish & chips' instead of 'fried potatoes' & we had to go all over again. Dudley came on & did his Mrs Holmes & was v. funny indeed. He suddenly bashed me with his handbag & said 'I saw you looking at my breasts!' & I could hardly keep a straight face.

Tuesday, 2 August. I talked to P.C. most of the time. 'Edith Sitwell became an enormous cult. The papers built her up. She wasn't aware of the size of her cult 'cos she was absorbed by her Art. She didn't notice the cult at all. It was the same with Sir Several Sitwell. He was a huge cult' etc. etc About 10.10 the telephone rang: 'This is John Goldstone, we are not shooting tomorrow because Paul Morrissey has got hepatitis and he must rest for a few days...'

Friday, 5 August. To Audley Square, where everyone gathered to watch 63 minutes of what has been shot so far on *Hound Of The Baskervilles*. It was all rather depressing. Again & again in this script, I've thought, 'That is hilarious' yet the fact remains, there is nothing hilarious in any of the stuff I saw in the cinema today. It looked as if cues weren't being taken up with enough expertise & there were certain bits (the sex-talk between Holmes & Watson, and the one-legged man) which don't really belong to the story at all.

Monday, 12 September. I talked with P.C. & he was hilarious as a French director with an appalling accent discussing the filming. O! he makes me laugh. Apropos Dudley Moore living in California, he said 'It's the space you see... he loves the space... Californians have a lot of space... most of it's between their ears' and I fell about.

Friday, 23 September. P.C. said stay for lunch at The Crown in Bray. I had far too much to drink & we drove back to the Old House and suddenly P.C. started 'You're wanted on the set for another shot of you & the dog' stuff, and he & Charles Knode pushed me into some stables & pulled my clothes off. It was like some daft sort of public schoolboy cruelty and had a curiously sinister undertone. I was shoved in front of the camera and Paul kept giving me directions about kissing the dog, but it was all rather perfunctory & I could see a lot of people giggling expectantly & I suddenly realised they were hoping I would make a drunken exhibition of myself.

1978

Thursday, 2 November. Walked to Alan Bennett['s house], past the lady tramp who was undressing in her van & smiling invitingly! I rang the bell pretending not to notice. Peter Cook came—'I'll just have a tonic water'—& sat smoking fags & gleefully relating the worst notices he'd read for *Baskervilles*. [*Compare this behaviour with Cook's ambitions for this film, noted by K.W. in the 21/7/77 entry*—Ed.] ...Peter was v. funny about [Robert Boothby's autobiog, *Boothby: Recollections Of A Rebel*] saying Churchill had a 'cruel streak' & started endless fantasies: 'It's been revealed in these hitherto unknown letters that Hitler had a cruel streak.' Then it was Princess Margaret: 'It's been revealed she has a cruel streak...' Alan didn't offer much: he made it obvious that we should go, by pointedly collecting all the crockery and glasses into the kitchen sink at about 11.15.

THE HOUND OF THE BASKERVILLES

Harry Thompson, in his Peter Cook biography, hailed *The Hound of the Baskervilles* as one of the greatest turkeys of all time. It bombed at the box office and every critic who got near it hated it. Is it really that shit?

On re-viewing the film in the newly released, re-edited form, you're forced to admit that there is actually quite a lot of decent material lurking beneath the surface. The film's spiral into critical disaster is well chronicled in Thompson's book; the woeful decision on director Paul Morrissey's part to make a *Carry On* film, the huge script changes to Cook and Moore's original ideas, Morrissey's bout of hepatitis in the middle of shooting causing a delay. Perhaps the most glaring fault of the film is Morrissey's attempts to turn the comedy up to eleven by making everyone SHOUT THEIR LINES ALL THE TIME, which grates very quickly. There are some absurd attempts of shoe-horn incredibly old and inappropriate material from the Cook and Moore back catalogue which blatantly doesn't belong here, including One Leg

Too Few and The Great Train Robbery from *Beyond The Fringe*.

And it's not just Cook and Moore who recycle old jokes. There's plenty to spot for the comedy anorak. Kenneth Williams, as Henry Baskerville, revives material from his old Julian And Sandy days, as well as revisiting the caravan scene from the more recent *Carry On Behind*; Roy Kinnear gives us a brief rendition of his muttering idiot from *The Bed Sitting Room*; Milligan is, well, Milligan; and Irene Handl gives the same Cockney-trying-to-speak-posh she gave on the *Songs For Swinging* Sellers album and had been doing on-and-off ever since. In fact, it's Handl who comes away from this film with the best performance, wonderfully bustling through and malapropping like a good 'un. In addition, Penelope Keith gives an unexpected and surprisingly sexy cameo as a brothel madam.

There are also a number of quite decent gags in it. Milligan's moustache joke, Denholm Elliot's incontinent dog, the 'flocking blind beggars' line. Also worthy of mention, although not actually funny, is the sheer what-the-hell bizzaritude of the scene where Joan Greenwood tries to seduce Moore's Watson, *Exorcist*-style. Cook and Moore themselves have some nice bits to do; Cook with this pipe and cigarette joke, Moore asking Handl to show him to the clues. Some gags are odd little bizarre ones—Moore running into his look-a-like; the fog in the house—with a distinctly Milliganesque aroma.

But we're watching this film to see what Cook can do, and, with the best will in the world, he does bugger all. His Holmes, who for some reason is saddled with a harsh cod-Jewish voice, is unsympathetic, confusing and, worst of all, never given anything particularly funny to do. Aside from the recycled material, Cook hardly gets one joke to himself in the whole film and the shouting-is-funny school of comedy employed by Morrissey spoils most of the other performances.

Let's take a moment to look at the rendition of the classic One Leg Too Few sketch given in *Baskervilles*. At the risk of going all Dr. Miller, cast your mind back to the original and look at it afresh. A one-legged man called Mr. Spiggott auditions for the role of Tarzan. It's easy to forget what a breathtakingly audacious idea this is. And the theatrical agent, faced with the unidexter's bounding idiot-optimism, how does he play it? With an almost loving tact and diplomacy. The beauty of the sketch is in the tortuous lengths Cook has to go through to let Spiggott down gently, never once losing his temper, and even, at the end, doing his best to keep Spiggott's hopes alive that he may still stand a chance of getting the part. The agent is easily one of Cook's most instantly likeable and sympathetic creations, a million miles from the cosmic stillness of a Wisty or a Streeb-Greebling. And it is this character's endless resources of tact that give the power to the famous build-up to the 'Neither have you' punchline.

You would expect that, given that the Cook and Moore had performed the same sketch countless times on stage and with this chance to put a definitive version on film, it would be masterly. In fact, it falls flat. The first problem is the change in nature of the audition. Now, instead of auditioning for Tarzan, Spiggott wants to be a runner of the moors. What on Earth is a runner on the moors? With someone auditioning for Tarzan, you have an automatic common frame of reference with the audience, which *Baskervilles* loses. But, sad to say, most of the fault with the scene lies with Cook's performance. All the gentle tact that had been so important to the original sketch is either gone or unconvincing. We have already had a number of scenes in the film where Cook's Holmes is rude, sarcastic and decidedly unsympathetic; not necessarily a bad thing in itself, but it destroys the whole dynamic for this sketch. We are supposed to believe that this Holmes, who we have seen being generally impatient and angry with everyone, would take time out of his day to interview a man who is plainly unsuited for the job he is applying for. The magic of the sketch crumbles away, the pauses are just empty, and the jokes no longer work as they should.

Elsewhere, Cook's Holmes is confusing. He begins the film as a joke Holmes, an ignorant ogre of a character. He then all but disappears for a large section of the film, which is true to the original book, I suppose, but would seem to be a bit of a waste of someone who's meant to be one of the film's stars. He does re-appear for a brothel scene (where he is rather bizarrely accused of being fat by Rita Webb, when in fact he is as thin as a rake) and another with Moore as his mother, but neither really gives him any scope to perform. He then re-appears at the end of the film, for some reason, as a proper Holmes, accent aside, who quickly solves the case and ties up all the loose ends. It just doesn't work, the conflict between the former and the later Holmes is too great, and it is a major weakness right at the heart of the film.

If you compare it to *Bedazzled*, Moore has the greater variety of roles than Cook. In both films Moore is on the screen for considerably longer than Cook. But *Bedazzled* is certainly a Cook and Moore film with, if anything, Cook's sardonic but sympathetic Satan in the ascendance. In *Baskervilles* though, Cook's hardly there at all, doesn't really seem to want to turn in a decent performance and allows Moore to steal every scene that they're in together.

Consider where the two stars had been in the lead-up to this film. Since the finish of the *Good Evening* US tour in 1975 they had gone their separate ways. Peter bided his time in England, settling into the pattern of boozing, chat shows and occasional stabs at a career that was to feature heavily in the coming years. Dudley, meanwhile, had been trying to make a go of it in Hollywood, tinkling away on the piano and waiting for the phone to ring, which it conspicuously failed to do. And I think you can see the change in attitude throughout this film. While Peter looks for all the world as if he's thinking 'God, this is a shit film' and rarely bothering to try to put on a good show, Dudley has learnt the lesson of Tinsel Town; being in a shit film doesn't matter, being in a film does, and turning in a good performance in anything, even a giant turkey, might, just might, get you noticed for a bigger film, a better role and a chance to grope Bo Derek. Over the previous years Moore had, piece by piece, been severing his ties with Cook; in *Baskervilles* he barely acknowledges Cook's presence.

But, even allowing for good performances here and there, the whole film has a desultory and flat feel. If Morrissey was attempting to re-create the feel of the classic *Carry On* films, he failed. You can say what you like about the *Carry On*s, but at least Peter Rogers and Gerald Thomas knew how to make this type of comedy, and on almost non-existent budgets. It requires tight cutting and quick-fire jokes—establish the scene, set up premise, go to joke, go to reaction, go to next joke. It's easy to forget how much skill went in to make a *Carry On*, even if they eventually became formulaic. By comparison, Morrissey's direction is dire, including such basic gaffes as, at the opening of the second big scene, keeping the camera on Williams for ages while everyone else is talking and he's obviously just idly waiting for his cue. Perhaps some of the jokes would have worked given the *Carry On* treatment, but Morrissey's camera hangs still on every scene, leaving the paucity of decent material laid bare.

The Hound Of The Baskervilles is an interesting historical document about where Pete and Dud were in their working relationship at the time. It's OK in places. If you want a decent Holmes spoof, though, try Billy Wilder's *The Private Life Of Sherlock Holmes* or perhaps *Without A Clue*, a 1988 film with a neat cameo from one Peter Cook.

In 2002 a DVD of *The Hound Of The Baskervilles* was let loose, including both the original 1978 cinema version with Moore's improvised silent movie-type piano accompaniment, and the re-edited video version of 2000 that replaced Moore's inspired keyboard cavortings with jarring and inappropriate synthesizer doodlings. The new producer's cut is so catastrophically dreadful it achieves a small miracle in making one begin to reconsider the original a lost and misunderstood masterpiece of comic subtlety and understatement.

THE BACK PASSAGE

...where buttocks talk and wisdom walks. Shriek to me, thou puke varlets!

Dear Clinty,

Leafing through the summer 2000 issue of *The Idler* I noticed an article by Nicholas Blincoe about Sherlock Holmes. A few phrases sprang out at me, seeming to relate to Peter Cook just as much as Holmes. I quote:

'He is a freelance in control of his life. He works when he is interested, at other times he chills—or occasionally slips into an ennui that is relieved through a little casual drug taking.'

Again:-

'... he is an ascetic who idles for months without a flicker of guilt. In short, Holmes is the Uber Petit Bourgeois: a concept so impossible that it requires two European languages and an oxymoron even to conceive of existing.'

Perhaps this was the attraction of *Hound Of The Baskervilles* for Peter, bearing in mind what he said to John Lloyd about all his stuff being to some degree autobiographical.

MARY HARTY, Limehouse, London.

REVOLTER

Let me roll back the foreskin of time to reveal the bell-end of 1995. Chief Rammer John Wallis a.k.a. Reg Futtock-Armitage, founder of the PCAS, is rambling down the phone to me...

'I was having a few jars in Camden with Knox (of The Vibrators rockin'combo) and Dave Treganna (ex-Sham 69), and when I left The Dublin Castle, fuck me, I only bumps into Hugh Cornwell'

'As in Huge Cornball, late of The Stranglers?'

'Thazzim. Naturally, I button'ole him and execute my duty and ask him if he knew Peter Cook.'

'And?'

'He goes—real sniffy—"Peter Cook? Oh yeah—the dead man. Well, that's what you get for insulting The Stranglers."'

'Was this some joke?'

'No, he meant it. I says, "When did he insult you, then?" He said it was on *Revolver*...'

Ah, *Revolver*. For Pop fans of a certain vintage *Revolver* is The Beatles LP that either marked the end of an Age of Innocence or the heralding of the Dawn of Experience, depending on which stereo speaker you're sitting. However, if you were more tweeter than woofer in the late '70s, that word is synonymous with one of the great rock'n'roll assaults on TV. Preceding *Revolver* there was the predictable false euphoria of *Top Of The Pops*, the mellow *Old Grey Withered Tits* with its fine array of tasteful beard designs, the pre-teen *Blow Off With Ayshea* presented by a young woman whose eyelashes were subliminally dyed with the legend 'Vote Tory And It'll Be Alright', and there was *So It Goes* from Granada TV. Made at the height of the Punk explosion of 1976-7, *So It Goes* captured a revolution in Pop as it happened and is therefore of much cultural and historical import, from the 1976 explosion of Sex Pistols to the 1979 implosion of Joy Division (who just happened to be signed to *SIG*'s presenter Tony Wilson's Factory Records). Tony Wilson, then an earnest young chap crouched under a bail of hair, was enthusiastically championing the new and therefore, mostly reviled groups.

Peter Cook, hosting *Revolver*, dispensed with such generosity of spirit, playing the misinformed, knuckle-dragging, gutterpress-believing card, thus giving the show its vital charge. Cook, in his laidback way, is the spirit of the show, *Revolver*'s trigger if you like, firing off a volley of well-aimed insults. (I mean, seventeen years after the fact and big, tough, hard man Hugh Cornwell is still upset about what Peter Cook said about The Stranglers? Diddums!)

Sarcasm, it's said, is the lowest form of wit and Cook sinks to the challenge admirably. But it's not just the jokes that makes Cook so essential to *Revolver*, it's the whole psychological baggage that he brings to the role of unwilling host. Look at him in his office full of ashtrays, bottles and bad memories, not caring less, slumped in his chair, cigarette in hand, jaded eyes mentally daring the audience to rise up and attack him—*Come on, burn me at a stake, he seems to be thinking; Do something, if you got any guts. I don't give a fuck*. And he's such a nihilist that, even whilst ablaze, he would accuse them of setting fire to him in a totally boring manner: *You can't even think of an interesting way to burn me alive...*

Looking for some kind of conceptual continuity in Peter Cook's work, one wonders about the ballroom manager he portrays in *Revolver*. Maybe he's learnt the lesson of his disastrous 1971 BBC TV chat show *Where Do I Sit?*, where he found out he had no interest in the guests he was supposed to interview. Maybe *Revolver* is a subtle revenge where, rather than exchange pleasantries with Pop stars (which he always rather fancied being), he could just mock them—and their fans too. Cook uses the 'Clive' voice from the *Derek & Clive* records—and *Revolver* was made between *Come Again* and *Ad Nauseam*.

Surprisingly, out of almost six hours of transmitted footage, Peter is onscreen for barely thirty minutes. In a way, he's like Orson Welles in *The Third Man*: Welles' Harry Lime character makes a fifteen minute appearance almost three-quarters into the film, yet he permeates the whole movie. Similarly, Peter's appearances influence entirely the tone and style of *Revolver*.

Chris Tookey, the director, understood that probably the most fascinating aspect of Pop is the audience itself and there's footage a-plenty of spotty oiks dressed in Punk regalia (pink mohair jumpers, clothes pegs worn in the hair, lurid sunglasses). Some kids look like they've come straight from school (enormo tie knots). We also see the dances of the day—the Pogo, the Skank, the Meccanik ('robot'dancing), air guitar posing, and for one delicious moment, to the theme tune of ATV's daily soap opera Crossroads, the entire audience do the Dead Fly (lay on your back and kick your legs and wave your arms in the air).

By deft editing—and extending the meaning of the show's title beyond explosive hits and turntables—each show begins with the headline act playing the final bars of the song that will eventually close that particular programme. So the first show starts as the Tom Robinson Band finish *Up Against The Wall*, whereupon Peter, on a video screen to the left of the stage, says to us, 'You're late. You've Just missed the first and best act.'

The music, though heavily favoured toward white male rock as one would expect, takes in such pigeonhole terms as reggae, disco,

MOR balladry and, in Patrick Fitzgerald, the never-popular hybrid of folk-Punk. We get the brilliant powerpoppery of Buzzcocks with Pete Shelley singing their gender-nonspecific love songs in his head-tilted camper-than-Butlins Mancunian whine. We get XTC coming on like BSE-infected Wurzels on amyl nitrate—delirious! There's Nick Lowe backed by Dave Edmunds, (The Other) Billy Bremner and Terry Williams—together, one of the Great Forgotten R'n'R Bands, Rockpile. And we have The Motors, incredibly ancient coves who transform BBC TV's hoary old Grandstand theme into the lovely *Forget About You*. The Jam play their horrid Gumby cover of The Kinks *David Watts*.

The wildest, freest singing comes from X-Ray Spex's Poly Styrene, a sound as liberating as a Coltrane solo. A maverick, a visionary, a truly original Pop poetess, our Poly. In the style wars of the '70s The Rich Kids were reviled for their supposed 'irrelevance'. Today, they sound fine and dandy, just like Supergrass or any other loud Pop group. With a wizard set of Terry-Thomas choppers and a Mullet Almighty, malicious observer Elvis Costello, backed by his Attractions, is pure fucking dynamite. Stunt motorbike daredevil Eddie Kidd crashes in on his fame with one of the worst Heavy Metal songs ever (sample lyric: 'Wild woman! I'm gonna tame yer!') which provides the unintentional comic highlight. Ian Dury & The Blockheads are a transcendent joy, one of Britain's funkiest bands. (Blockheads drummer, the late, great Charlie Charles is a doppelganger for Joan Armatrading.)

The Tom Robinson Band's 'agit-pop'songs would be the ones you'd expect to be most dated. It took the late-90s nail-bombings in Brixton, Brick Lane and Soho to remind us of TRB's continued social relevance: Britain remains intolerant, philistine, a 'Gestapo Khazi'. Dire Straits, in one of their first TV gigs, perform 'Sultans Of Swing' and the crowd pogo like mad—until it dawns on them that this is not Punk at all, but West Coast (via the North East) AOR boogie, and they resort to meek shuffling. Suzi Quatro falls flat: After a turgid lump of white reggae rubbish, she introduces her hit song with a scream of 'DO YA WANNA GO DOWN TO DEVIL GATE DRIIIVE???' to an exceedingly muted response. She yells the question again and a disinterested punter clearly mouths, 'Oh fuck off.' And so on.

Peter Cook isn't the sole host. Chris Hill, pioneering funk DJ, expertly orchestrates the crowd and—in leading their heckling of Cook and telling them the City Council want to close down the club—fuels the teen spirit of Us vs. Them. And there's Les Ross trying to serve hamburgers to kids intent on helping themselves ('Get your hands off my gherkin!') whilst introducing little-known acts. The best of these unsigned bands is probably Brent Ford & The Nylons who wear ladies' hosiery on their heads (to evade identification by the dole office?) and give us an ecstatic *19th Nervous Breakdown*.

In May and June 1999 the Dragger tracked down some of the show's performers for mind-plundering purposes. Let Peter himself introduce them to you...

'All right. Ladies and Gentlemen, a band I very much love—[*Audience, curious, shuts up*]—and I mean that in the truest sense of the word. A band that have brought jollity... happiness... a certain amount of gaiety to the world, people who can pluck their strings—and yours! Ladies and gentlemen, The Tom Robinson Band! [*Audience cheers*] You better clap or else you'll get it!'

TOM ROBINSON: Seeing *Revolver* again, I was surprised how bad we all were. Hearing the intro to *Glad To Be Gay*, I thought 'Hmm, it—might've been a good idea to tune up the bass guitar before doing a national television broadcast'. Obviously it hadn't occurred to me at the time. It wasn't very 'Punk' to tune your guitars. Even XTC, who went on to make fantastically sophisticated albums, sounded rough as old boots. And parachuting into the middle of all this you get Kate Bush!... It wasn't the worst sound balance I've ever heard on a TV show—but it was fucking close! The weird thing about *Revolver* was the notion of having Peter Cook removed from the audience, in a completely separate room, and having him deliberately antagonizing them. It was like a rowdy, even more undisciplined version of *The Word*. Ineffectual as Terry Christian was as a host, he at least was there physically. With Peter, he was this tinny, haranguing voice pouring out of the speakers and this mob going 'Off! Off! Off! Off!' and all of Peter's witticisms going zoom! over their heads. They were a generation who maybe didn't know, or didn't care, who he was—and the feeling of Punk was that everything that went before is shite—regardless—and must be consigned to the dustbin. It was a strange concept and I don't think it did Peter justice.

He was at his best when people were with him and would go with him on his flights of fancy. There was a bit too much of that 'Oh yes he is', 'Oh no he isn't' pantomime stuff with him and the audience. Having him making mildly offensive remarks about the bands wasn't a good enough basis for a show.

I was kind of touched to see him introduce us by saying he actually did like us, which is interesting because he doesn't say that about anybody else, except Ian Dury. But you didn't know what he really thought of the bands—you didn't know if he was slagging somebody off because he really didn't like them. It seemed to me a classic misuse of his talent.

Peter has been accused of unfulfilled promise, of loafing, of a producing a lot of rubbish, but so what? Prince chucks out a prodigious amount—two or three double CDs a year, sometimes—of which 60% is dross. But the other 40% is so fucking good, it's fresh-minted every time he does it. It's right on the money because he refuses to be fettered by the demands of being commercially acceptable and working to the record company script. That is what makes him so great—the fact he's got this antic spirit so this creative insanity just bursts out of the top of his head. It's unchecked, there's no Quality Control, but that's how you get the really, truly, inspirationally, insanely great stuff. You can forgive him the lapses and the lamenesses. And the same applies to Peter. He did enough in his lifetime, including the wild phone-ins to the local radio station, that justifies any amount of slobbing around or just getting pissed and unproductivity. To hell with it! He achieved such peaks that the rest doesn't matter. He wasn't like anybody else—The Goons or whoever—before or since. He was a true original.

PETER COOK: I'd just like to ask you all a question which is very simple, really, and I was asked it years ago: If three men with two buckets containing eight potatoes walked for three miles, discarding one potato every four inches, how long would it take them to get back? The answer is, of course, quite simple and my task now is to introduce The Buzzcock Tombs... The Boomtown Cocks... The Buzz Rat Things... Am I getting close? OK, The Buzzcocks, here they are.

PETER SHELLEY (of BUZZCOCKS): *Revolver* was quite good—there was certainly nothing else like it at the time. No one else would have us! The show was taped on a Sunday and I remember we drove all the way to Birmingham to do our four minute set. We never saw Peter to talk to as we were doing—well, whatever groups do in dressing rooms. He appeared on this vast screen to the side of the stage to bait everybody but, in actual fact, he was sitting on the other side of the studio, facing the stage. As we were waiting to go on, Peter and I caught each other's gaze across the studio, and he winked at me. A saucy wink. I thought, 'Ohh, what does *he* know?' Doing that was perfectly natural for him. Suffice it to say, our relationship blossomed, withered and died then and there. Gone in the wink of an eye.

PETER COOK: 'Ere! You like, er, Elvis Costello? [*Audience: 'YEAH!'*] You like the band that plays with him? [*'YEAH!'*] You like to see him and them play together? [*'YEAH!'*] Well you can't. [*'BOO!'*] First of all, first of all you have to sing something very simple—a lovely little tune called 'Peter Is The Greatest'. Can we hear that? (warbles) 'Peter is the greatest, Peter is the greatest—[*Audience:'PETER IS A RAPIST! PETER IS A RAPIST! PETER IS A RAPIST!' Peter, trying to shout over them:*] PETER IS THE GREATEST!'... Well, you nearly got it right so here he is—Elvis Costello!'

ELVIS COSTELLO: Back in 1978, The Attractions and I were very much on an assault course of gigs, TV, recording sessions, very little rest, and people giving us free booze wherever we went. We would stagger off some plane, bundled into a car, whisked to the Pebble Mill studios or whatever, led to the 'green room', handed more booze so you're pissed by 1pm, played one song at breakneck speed into a TV camera, then off to another car and another show. Saying all that, I do remember *Revolver*, principally because of Peter Cook.

We were in the 'green room' drinking, as was our wont, and Peter Cook was there, too. He was a bit pissed, maybe, and wearing his nightclub manager clothes—a seedy-looking tuxedo. I was rather snotty in those days, being all of 23. I said, 'What are you doing here?' Because when you're that age, you find it incredible that someone who was on the television when you were a kid could still be alive. When you're 23 you can't even begin to imagine reaching the age of 30, you know?

My dad was a singer and in 1964 he was singing in the clubs in Hamburg. He told me that whilst he was there he was known by the other musicians there as The Beat Grandfather, he having reached the grand old age of 31. I was reminded of that phrase when I saw Peter Cook backstage: The Beat Grandfather. I couldn't fathom a reason for his being there. What was odd about the show—I don't know Mickie Most's strategy—but with other Pop shows you would have pleasant if fairly unexceptional hosts introducing ex-citing—hopefully—and new bands. *So It Goes*, *The Tube* and *The*

Word operated on that kind of policy. But, casting my mind back, it'd seem as if a reverse plan was in operation with *Revolver*. I think Peter Cook got more genuine reaction from the audience than any of the bands. It was a bizarre career decision of his—which might be the very reason he did it.

Revolver was made in Birmingham which is useless because, unlike London, you don't know where to go and what to do before and after your gig. The studio had a revolving stage for the bands, didn't it? In theory, one act plays their latest hit whilst behind the screen the next band can be setting up their gear. I recall the revolving stage breaking down a few times which kind of made a mockery of the show's title. I thought at the time that the show was a totally inappropriate use of Cook's talent. But what was notable about *Revolver* was the bands all played live—none of that *Top Of The Pops* miming nonsense—which lent it some edge. Plus, Peter could say anything he liked, it seemed. Insulting both bands and audience was pretty novel at the time. I suppose it's pretty much the norm now, but Peter Cook was rude in a funny way. I imagine *Revolver* would look pretty quaint in 1999 but it's probably a fair picture of the state of late '70s British Pop music.

I saw Peter Cook again, years later, in Hampstead. I think he was buying some cigarettes, but I didn't go up and talk to him because I can't, or won't, do that sort of thing. It's his life; why should I impose on it?

His performance [as singing sensation Drimbl Wedge] in *Bedazzled* was excellent. When I saw it again recently I thought, 'Why hasn't Neil Tennant of the Pet Shop Boys covered this?' He reminded me of Neil Tennant so much—the flat but appealing singing, the campness, the impassivity, the clothes! Totally Tennant.

PETER COOK: For all you Judy Garland freaks, Poly Styrene and X-Ray Spex, available on the National Health label.

MARIAN ELLIOTT (A.K.A. POLY STYRENE, FOR IT IS SHE):
I was about 17 or 18 when I appeared on *Revolver*. I wasn't attempting to sing in the traditional manner, like a nice crooning voice. My
basic training was in the operatic style at Wigmore Studios, so I
had that power but I wanted to make it wild. You can't croon *Oh
Bondage, Up Yours!*

Peter Cook was a fab celebrity comedian. Everyone really liked
him, a popular, cool, funny man. They were pretty trendy, him and
Dudley Moore, they had a trendy image—unlike, say, Morecambe
and Wise.

I never saw him at the *Revolver* studios because we were wheeled
on and off very quickly. X-Ray Spex had such a tight schedule; you
go on, do your thing, get off and on to the next thing, so you never
really know what's going on.

In 1979 or '80 I wanted to lose a bit of weight and get healthy
so I went to Champney's, the health farm in Tring, for a month.
It was a great, fantastic place. You get exercises, treatments,
massages every day, eat very little, do yoga and then you can go
country-walking and horse-riding, whatever you like. Peter Cook
was there, drying out. He was a bit of a drinker, wasn't he? Also
there was the Shah of Iran's son, a very handsome young man that
all the ladies wanted to bed. They all wanted to bed Peter Cook as
well. He was quite popular there. Everyone was abuzz that he was
there. The ladies were at Champney's to either lose weight or find
a rich husband!... He was a bit of a smoker. He was never without
a cigarette and since I didn't smoke I never went, but there was a
room called The Sin Bin, which was the refuge for smokers, so
he would be a frequent user of The Sin Bin...I never saw Peter
in the swimming pool or doing yoga, but I did occasionally see
him going up to his room with a few ladies. [*Laughter.*] That was
probably his way of losing weight... The drinking, I guess, was
how he handled the pressure. In essence, there are two choices; you
can carry on being a creative and risky artist or you can continue
doing whatever first made you famous and successful. That's great

if you only want to make millions of pounds—and your managers would prefer you did that—but if you have any imagination you feel like you're stuck in some boring job. [*Laughter.*] I can't get my music released because it's not the same as the records I'm known for. Record companies would like me trapped in some 1977 timewarp...

MY FAVOURITE EARACHE

Chris Hill—club DJ, record producer and trainee giant—recounts his days as The King Of The Kids in the smoking chambers of Revolver...

CHRIS HILL: You ever see that Peter O'Toole movie, *My Favourite Year*?

PAUL HAMILTON: Oh yeah!

CH: That's exactly what my three months with Peter Cook was like. It was my version of *My Favourite Year*. I was told to keep him sober; keep him amused; keep him out of trouble; keep him in the hotel or in the studio and not let him wander off anywhere; stop him from getting fucked by groupies and things. Because there were some very peculiar women that used to hang out at the hotel. They weren't kids, they were, like, strange middle-aged women hanging about.

PH: For him?

CH: No, not just for him. They were obsessives because—well, it was Birmingham, the World's Most Dour Place. I don't think we ventured beyond the hotel or the studio in the three months we were there. I thought of Birmingham, especially then, the same way people think of Eastern Europe. You know—horrible, dour, ugly place full of ugly people. But the punters on the show were funny because they were real. They hadn't written in for tickets, Mickie Most's people had actually gone out and found them. They acted like an authentic audience in the studio. They had fights; we caught one couple shagging backstage; someone had gone and had a crap behind the stage because he couldn't be bothered to find the toilets. They were mad, fucking mad! I was running clubs so I was used to it but it did get scary for the TV crew. A fight broke out once and I jumped off the stage to break it up, and I'm in there flaying about, whacking people. After, I said to the cameramen, 'Did you get all that?'—'No.'—'You cunts! I threw myself in there and you didn't film it? You silly fuckers!' I said, 'Next time there's a fight, fucking film it! Don't just watch it.'

PH: What did you think of the bands on the show?

CH: I was running Ensign Records at the time and I was the biggest club DJ, so nothing fazed me. They were all cunts as far as I was concerned, the bands were all full of cunts. They were all nobodies then. Like, it was the first time Siouxsie Sioux had ever been on TV, The Eurythmics—who were then called The Tourists—hadn't been on TV before. It was the first time for lots of these bands, and I managed to blag The Boomtown Rats on to *Revolver* because I ran their label. The only one who kind of fitted with me and Peter was Ian Dury because he was as funny as we were when it came to fucking about. Everyone else was a bit well-behaved because it was their Big Shot. The only band who didn't behave themselves was Eddie & The Hot Rods who wrecked their dressing room and were thrown out. And Peter was always professional. Once the cameras were rolling, he was a total professional—but he had incredible mood swings. He could be so very funny but at night sometimes he would be incredibly depressed. He was very upset about his wife,

Judy. He sat for hours with my then girlfriend, saying he'd fucked
the marriage up. And he would always be ringing Judy at funny
times all day and night...

We spent lots of time sitting in the bar or the swimming-pool area
of this Holiday Inn. It was like being on a rock 'n' roll tour going
round the world—although we were in Birmingham every night,
but it was like being in a different hotel every night. He would get
very maudlin and then, the next day, he'd be as funny as fuck. He
used to go into these strange characters, these peculiar roles, that
would last all day... One of Peter's finest things was the Judge in
the Jeremy Thorpe trial, and all these revelations of hit squads were
coming out at the time we did *Revolver*. He was regularly coming
up with verbals about Thorpe... He was a very 'Old Theatre' person
rather than a TV or Pop personality, you know? A real old thespian.
It was like being with Sir John Gielgud sometimes—and yet he
wasn't that old. He wasn't that much older than me. I was closer
to his age than I was to the punters, and yet I was playing a punter.
That's probably why Mickie wanted me to look after him and keep
him sober—which wasn't easy 'cos he was fucking off his head
sometimes. I've never seen anyone drink vodka like he did. He'd
have an empty vodka bottle in his hand at 11 in the morning. That's
why it was like *My Favourite Year* because I'd be like, 'Oh Fuck,
What Now?' Other times he'd be fine. He was just as good performing pissed, maybe better. But these characters we played in the
show I mean, offscreen we got on like a house on fire. It was like
I'd known him for years, which was very odd. We totally 'clicked'
in being irreverent towards the bands and everything else. But the
minute we got to do the show, he'd become the character and he'd
be vicious. He'd go to me, 'What's your name?'—'Hill.'—'You're
over it. Fuck off!' Nothing was scripted at all, not a fucking thing,
which is a pity, really, because I'm sure if they let him script things
it would be more of a comedy thing than a music show. Everything
he said was straight off the top of his head.

PH: The strange thing about *Revolver* is why Peter was on a video screen rather than onstage.

CH: Yeah. He was supposed to be in his office. That was one of Mickie's ideas—quite good ideas at the time, actually. I mean, *Revolver* is the forerunner of *The Tube*. *The Tube* nicked every idea from *Revolver* and tarted them up. And they had Paula [Yates] and Jools [Holland], another couple of herbert characters instead of the old, staid, Radio One DJ. I suppose *Revolver* set the trend for having completely untrained, unlikely presenters.

PH: How did you get the *Revolver* job?

CH: I got a call saying, 'Do you want to be on a TV series? They want some complete herbert.' So when I met Mickie, he mentioned *Ready Steady Go* and I told him I had been a dancer on that show for God-knows-how-many editions. He said, 'Right, you've got the gig, because that's the show I want to make.' I got involved in the picking of bands, because he knew I was running a label. Mickie was very astute in picking the right acts because the hit rate on that show was far better than most rock shows have been since.

PH: When VH1 repeated it this year the shows were only 30 minutes long. I seem to recall them originally being longer.

CH: Yeah, I think it was nearer 45 minutes.

PH: On the show with Suzi Quatro—one of Mickie Most's stars— we just hear Peter shout 'Suzi Quatro!' which suggests his intro was cut.

CH: Yeah, he probably took the piss. He took the piss out of a lot of them—particularly the black bands. He used to say things like, 'They're black! I won't have black people in my club!', and I'd be rucking with him, going, 'This is the band I want!' I had actually persuaded them to have an all-black show with Kandidate, Hi-Tension, Heatwave—and it was very cool to have Heatwave 'cos they were just starting out—and the reggae bands Steel Pulse and Matumbi. I brought all the kids up from The Lacy Lady in Ilford and The Goldmine in Canvey Island—punters who could dance to that shit. It was a completely different show, but Mickie said, 'I like that show so much I'm going to put bits of it in all the other shows because it fits better.' Basically, he sussed ATV would hate an all-black show. But at least we managed to get black groups on TV although, when you look at the audience, it didn't make sense because firstly there's lots of black people dancing and then there isn't. You think, 'What?' But Peter, because he's playing the bigoted National Front fucking herbert, made lots of racialist—but very funny—remarks. I'm sure nowadays it wouldn't be allowed because everyone's so sensitive, but then he would be ranting and the audience'd be cracking up. The best line he ever came up with—and I've used it a million times since—is the Sid Vicious one: 'At a recent Pistols gig a member of the audience smashed Sid Vicious round the face. This was a rare case of the fan hitting the shit.' He made that one up on the spur of the moment.

PH: Was Peter the first-choice as host?

CH: No idea. He was already in the frame when I was hired. I was told, 'It's you and Peter Cook and this Les Ross who'll be the hamburger salesman. All the way you gotta keep this banter up—you hate him, he hates you, you got the kids behind you and you wanna take the club over.' It was a funny idea but it was never developed enough. We were busking it.

PH: I wonder whether Peter's character was inspired by that awful, sniffy square who co-hosted *Ready Steady Go*.

CH: Keith Fordyce.

PH: Yeah.

CH: No, I don't think he had anyone special in mind. No, he definitely became that that seedy old club owner who would much rather have Bingo instead of all these Punk bands and herberts and black people. And that screen—he was on the screen all the way through the performances, and he was doing funny shit before, during and after the bands. A lot was cut because it was a music show, not a comedy. I think Peter was brought in as a way to sell the series. He brought a lot of attitude, cynical attitude, to the show. Instead of the usual, cheesy, simpering 'Isn't this wunnerful?' he was 'This is SHITE!' The bands couldn't handle that; some of them really took it personally.

PH: Yes, he knew their Achilles' heels—how seriously they took their art, their vanity, their ages.

CH: Some bands just didn't get half the fucking jokes—he was too quick for them. And he attacked the right ones, too.

PH: Did he ever go onstage and face the audience in person?

CH: Yeah, he did that a number of times, to shut us up and to have me thrown out of the club. And, as I say, the punters were quite volatile and I'm sure a lot of them thought he was for real, you know: 'Who is this old cunt?' They were just kids, some of them, they didn't know who he was! 'Who the fuck's this? Fuck off!' So they were shouting back, which is just what he wanted.

PH: How long would a shoot take for each programme?

CH: It'd take a whole bloody weekend—Friday, Saturday, Sunday—so you can imagine the tons of footage cut out. If filming dragged, I would get out my records and play them to keep the kids entertained 'cos they easily got restless. But, because the shows were all re-edited, the continuity's all over the place. Some shows were unbalanced, musically...

After the series was finished, I never saw Peter again, either socially or by chance, which was really strange considering the togetherness we had.

PH: How did Peter get along with Mickie?

CH: Very well. Mickie's a good, entertaining character, with great stories. They were roughly the same age.

PH: Did Peter rib Mickie about his being the 'Elvis Presley of South Africa'? [*Interesting fact: Prior to becoming record producer for The Animals, Donovan etc., Most exploited non-availability of US music in SA and scored 11 consecutive No.1 singles, covering the likes of Chuck Berry.*]

CH: No. There was a huge jump between Peter's onscreen character where he's vicious and scathing, and off screen where he was an absolute gentleman, very charming, very warm. There were moments when he was very quiet and down, and you knew he wanted his space. Often, I'd see him walking about with a huge pile of newspapers. Really, he was like one of those old theatrical geezers who liked their drink but... y'know, he wasn't always pissed. Also, he wore an awful lot of make-up.

PH: Off screen?

CH: No, on TV, but I wasn't expecting that. He was heavily made-up. I couldn't see the point for a show like that. It came as a shock 'cos I expected him just to stroll on and do the character. I suppose that's the kind of theatrical tradition he came from. But, I mean, he spent a lot of time having his hair done meticulously and everything—even though he looked like a sack of shit.

THE BACK PASSAGE

Let the inhabitants of Planet Cook share your thoughts like mind-spliffs.

Dear fat face,

Free beers for tracking down Chris Hill for the *Revolver* issue. I attended many a Hill gig in my funkateering daze of the '70s and I recall he once introduced *One Nation Under A Groove* by Funkadelic with, 'If Jeremy Thorpe won the General Election we'd be one nation under a poove.'

Yours on the good foot (the other one's got gout),

ALBIE THE BOPPIN' WOODLOUSE, Castle Saburac.

HOW'S THAT FOR SOUND, HUGH?

Hugh Padgham has engineered and produced more records than you can shake a stylus at. XTC, David Bowie, Sting, The Human League, Joan Armatrading, Brian Wilson and Paul McCartney are but a few of the horde of the drug-haired, long-crazed layabouts he's whipped into shape to make with the finger-twitchin', hip-clickin' sound. However, it was as a beardie of 23 that the saucy HP recorded the final Derek & Clive magnum o'pus, Ad Nauseam, *which was also captured on filmy substances as* Derek & Clive Get The Horn. *This is his story...*

As you no doubt know, the original *Derek and Clive* tape circulated as a bootleg, one of many such tapes that went around studios and music circles. A famous one was The Troggs Tape—'we need a bit of fairy dust on the bastard!'—but there was also a rude tape of a posh young woman on a train talking to somebody and she starts, well, playing with herself, basically. To me then—I mean, at the time pubic hair had only just started appearing in *Playboy*—I'd never heard pornography on tape before, so I suppose I was quite shocked. Now, of course, we're all older and hardened to it but even so, young children of today have a period where they don't know about naughty things. I was rudely awakened to the seedier side of the music biz with the first recording session I ever worked on. It was with Mott The Hoople, and members of The Grease Band—Joe Cocker's old backing group—were there too. I went into the loo to find two black girls in there holding two of The Grease Band guys' willies while they were peeing into the urinal. There was quite a lot of debauchery that went on in music then—there still is now. But a lot more then, before AIDS.

However, back then, Peter singing 'I'm a nigger and I've fucked a white chick' was totally out of control and not on. It was so outrageous you couldn't help but laugh—but sometimes you laugh not out of amusement but out of nervousness. But most of that stuff is funny; it's so off the wall no one else can have thought of that stuff.

What happened with *Ad Nauseam* was I had just started working for Virgin Records at their Townhouse Studios on the Goldhawk Road. The studio had only been open for a few months. Or a few weeks even. It might have been a few days. But that was one of the first sessions at that studio. I was just told, 'You're doing this', being a dogsbody, more or less, but when I found out it was Pete and Dud I thought, 'Oh, great!'

The sessions would start in the afternoon and we'd go through until around 11 at night. I can't remember exactly now, but I think they recorded for two or three days. Probably just two days. Subsequently, I went to Virgin's other studio, The Manor, near Oxford, with Peter and all the tapes. We were there to edit some 20 hours of tape down to an album's length. Everything they said was caught on tape. Peter and I spent two and a half weeks sifting and editing. Dudley had no part in that process, so his credit as co-producer is a bit 'cosmetic' since all the decisions were Peter's.

If you play the *Ad Nauseam* album and then watch the *Derek and Clive Get The Horn* video you'll notice different versions of the same material. *Labels*, for instance, has the same premise but they're different versions. That's because they would busk the material, trying it various ways, like a band would experiment with alternative arrangements for a song. You know, honing it, getting it right. If you see them performing *Get The Horn* on the video, Peter asks me at the end how long they've been going. I reply, 'about an hour'. So both the film and album versions of *Get The Horn* are edited differently. This wasn't some contract-filler or sloppily-slung-together-at-the-last-minute job. Peter and I worked hard in sequencing that sketch, cutting the superfluous waffle and rearranging sections to make it play better.

Of the two, Peter was the most prepared with ideas. Apart from the Durex Handicap horseracing thing, nothing was in a finished script form. He had lots of scribbled notes and words on sheets of paper, which would remind him of some comic idea they could ad-lib and extemporise on.

It was very interesting because Dud was just beginning to make his career in Hollywood and Pete was—not jealous, that's not the right word—somehow disapproving in a way. Dud, I think, came from Hollywood back to London the night before the first day at the Townhouse. Peter, I feel, was very much leading the show; Dudley was hardly contributing much more than an 'oh yeah?' and 'right'. In some ways it's really a Peter Cook solo album since 75-80% of the impetus is his. Dudley may have been jet-lagged or just unprepared for the job.

If I'm remembering this right, Peter had not long come out of a drying-out clinic and he was on the wagon. He was sober and pretty straight for the first day, but at the end of the evening he started to crack under the pressure of carrying the whole show. There was minimal effort on Dudley's part. And at the end of the first day or beginning of the second day he had to get pissed to be funny or just relax. I don't recall Dud getting into the drink: his vices were cough linctus and French figs. But whatever kind of internal strife or friction was going on between them, I've never met or worked with anyone as funny as Peter Cook. He was classic. So good.

In the film there's a fake drug bust in the studio. That was Richard Branson's prank. I was informed but under strict instructions from Richard not to let on. I think Russell Mulcahy, the director, knew as well. My God, Dudley was extremely pissed off! Scared. But Peter was going, 'That's the last time I ever do a Policeman's Ball!' I think Richard got the idea from the first day's session—the filming was done on the second day—because, during breaks in recording, Peter would be saying, 'Hugh—roll us a joint, will you?' He had a little bit of hash in some aluminium foil, and Richard thought, 'Right, I'll get you and your Jazz Woodbines'.

I only recently saw the *Get The Horn* video and, firstly, I was quite amazed at how young Peter and Dudley looked. Secondly, and more amazingly, is the difference between the film and the album. The album, being obviously an aural experience, enables you to imagine *Derek & Clive*, the characters, in whatever you imagine them to dress in, however you imagine them to look. The film's a somewhat different proposition, where we have Pete and Dud, best of friends and best of enemies, on their stools in the studio, needling each other. You'll notice in the film Pete and Dud, when performing, always face the control room. We would be their focal point; they needed to feel like they were playing to an audience. The great thing about them was it was all so mad. You're either into that humour or you're not. But, for me, even the larking around between takes is priceless in its way because it's not ever going to happen again.

Personally, I prefer the more scripted, prepared stuff—*Behind The Fridge* and so on—because there's more substance to it, not so reliant on effing and blinding. The *Derek & Clive* albums deserve their place 'cos no one but Pete and Dud had the balls to do it and I suppose it broke down barriers for the next wave of comedians. Some *Derek & Clive* skits are very funny, others marginally so, but seeing the film again brought home to me the fact Pete and Dud as a collaboration were past their best. The first *Derek & Clive* was the most spontaneous; the other two were formulaic. Their *Derek & Clive* alter egos became sort of restrictive. I record and produce bands and the trouble with musicians is that by the third album they can get lazy, rest on their laurels, and become repetitive. They constantly need kicking up the arse to get them to be as inspired and responsive as when they began, fresh and hungry. Peter and Dudley had the same trouble with *Ad Nauseam*. Rather than working with each other as they used to, they were working *against* each other. A lot of their comedic vocabulary narrowed and they went for easier laughs through general laziness. Bits of the film are great but a lot more, for me in hindsight, is tinged with sadness. One upsetting incident was the stripper episode, when Peter has his hands round her neck. You can see she's shitting herself. Absolutely mortified. He had this mad look in his eyes that was unnerving. I think Peter got peeved about her telling him he's horrible and going off to talk with Dudley at the piano. While Dud's flirtily chatting with her you realise there's not another sound in the room. Peter's there, but he's silent, perched on his chair. He's probably thinking, how can I get one up on him? That's maybe why he launched himself onto her. He gave her a hug after, but she was frightened there. The old myth about comedians being miserable sods may be true, and you wonder whether Peter was a bit of a woman-hater. It's hard to tell when comedians are being themselves or when they're putting on an act, deliberately acting contrary, and that Line Of Snot skit, the Guinness Book Of World Records skit, is a case in point. This begins as a really cool sketch, going on about the ten-yard trail of snot looping, and then it suddenly degenerated into this 'I kicked and kicked for half an hour!' Jekyll and Hyde time.

The whole experience of watching the film is an odd one. The film is very dark—they didn't use any of the lights film sets generally employ—which gives it that forbidding atmosphere. It looks like they're down a mineshaft or in a cell. Uneasy viewing. It's the end of a long and close relationship, and it's ugly in places. A shame, but there it is. The record is much funnier, more entertaining. With the film, you're left wondering about the state of Peter's mind. Pete and Dud are caught in the twilight of their career together; not only does Dud seem unable to make much of a contribution to the session, he also seems to be unwilling. Saying all that, though, there are moments when Peter cracks Dud up hilariously. That's when the bitchiness stops and you see the friendship. Those instances are warm and touching. Then they go and call each other 'cunt!' again.

After the second night we all went off to some party and got horribly drunk. I can't recall much of it since I got pretty drunk myself, although I vaguely remember Dudley trying to say some mad drunken speech. After that, Peter and I went to The Manor, which is a huge, vast place with four or five live-in staff. We had two and a half staff each. Peter would get up very early, about five or six, and I'd wake up at ten to start work at eleven. He'd already had most of a bottle of wine by then. He was all right. His judgements weren't impaired, but he carried on drinking through the day. We had a good time and we got the work done. We listened to all the tapes and did lots of editing. We tightened up the material by 'losing' fluffs, stammers, pauses and giggles, and occasionally by splicing one take of a sketch to another. Endangered Species is a particular favourite of mine.

Peter would toddle off to bed by about ten or eleven at night. He would be fairly sozzled by then because, other than working on your record, there was absolutely nothing to do at the Manor. There was a snooker table and that was about it for entertainment. If you didn't relish long strolls in wintry countryside then you had pretty much had it.

He'd wake so early because that's generally what happens when you have a skinful the night before. He may have been an insomniac, I dunno. But he was always pleasant. There was none of the verbal violence and obnoxiousness one saw in the studio. So, because of his sleep habits—or lack of them—we worked quite

early in the morning. Early for me anyway—we rock and rollers
don't usually emerge from our beds till midday! We'd work through
the afternoon, supper, then perhaps an hour or so after that. It was
a lot of work dredging through the tapes. Marking the good bits,
cutting. Nowadays, with digital editing, it would take a fraction of
the time. After a day's work I'd go and play snooker with the staff
and Peter went off to his room. He didn't socialise particularly, but
he was never rude or brusque with anyone. He smoked the entire
time we were there and still liked his joints. I saw on the credits to
the video—'Herbal cigarettes by Haile Selassie'.

As for the shocking content of those *Derek & Clive* records, I
suppose Peter just didn't care about what anyone else thought. But
I think he probably needed a drink inside him to conjure up some of
those statements. He didn't act like a raving nutcase when he was
sober. He was perfectly nice to everybody. That part of him, to me,
was him showing off when the microphone was on and him being
pissed. You know, 'Right, I'll shock the fuckers!' I think there was
a side of Peter that never grew up, the naughty schoolboy aspect.

THE SECRET POLICEMAN'S DEBRIEFING

Martin Lewis has an incredible memory. 'It's frightening,' he admits; 'I have total recall of the 1970s. I didn't do drugs, you see. I'm the only one who remembers the '60s! My drug of choice was pastrami and I remember vividly every pastrami sandwich I ever ate.'

Starting out as a freelance journalist for Disc *and* NME *in the early '70s, Lewis drifted to Warner Bros Records. Since then he had a stint managing Alexei Sayle, produced numerous TV and film projects, executive-produced The Rutles' excellent* Archaeology *CD, blah blah blah. He appears on American TV and stages as a satirical commentator and indulges his acute Beatlemania with his involvement in conventions honouring the wacky scallies. Does this man ever sleep?*

The ensuing conversation happened in The Holly Bush garglehouse in London NW3, Tuesday 4th of May 1999. I expressed some doubt that his replies might end up buried on the tape beneath the noise of sundry foam-headed revellers. 'Don't worry,' said Martin,

*'I'll shout.' And shout he did for the next four amazing hours. And
before you ask—yes, he does occasionally speak in parentheses.*

PAUL HAMILTON: You were involved with the first Amnesty
International gala concert, *A Poke In The Eye (With A Sharp Stick)*,
in 1976 at the tender age of 22. How did that come about?

MARTIN LEWIS: What happened was, in 1975, I was Head Of
Special Projects (impressive title! It was Derek Taylor's job title
at Warners and I nicked it) at Transatlantic Records, a really indie
label—folky stuff, leftfield quirkiness like medieval rock band
Gryphon, Billy Connolly, all these mad, leftfield acts—Joshua
Rifkin, The Pasadena Roof Orchestra, The Portsmouth Sinfonia.
Then that dear man John Bird came to us with the idea of making an album of Punch magazine's Idi Amin columns, written by
Alan Coren. I got closely involved with John on *The Collected
Broadcasts Of Idi Amin* LP, and did a whole bunch of promotional
things. We had him outside the Royal Albert Hall with the Field
Marshall uniform on, his face blacked-up—before Political Correctness—and playing a guitar. I stayed in touch with John who, a
while later, was telling me about three benefit shows he was doing
for Amnesty International (it was their fifteenth anniversary). He
said it'd be an idea to sell the *Idi* LP in the foyer and give the profits
to Amnesty. But my mind was immediately saying, 'Who else is
in this show? What, Python? The Goodies? *Beyond The Fringe*?
My God, this we have to tape!' It was John Cleese's idea to do the
show. He was originally approached by Amnesty for help, and the
show was the result. It was me who went to Amnesty to say there
should be an album and a film. We got a very talented documentary
maker to do the film: Roger Graef. However, talented as he was at
making documentaries about the British steel industry and London
transport, he should be commended as a man spectacularly devoid
of any sense of humour imaginable. He came up with the film's
title, saying [*Canadian accent:*] 'Well, uh, since it took place at

Her Majesty's Theatre and it's about prisoners, let's call it *Pleasure At Her Majesty's*. D'ya geddit, Mordin? It's some kinda pun, I gather.'

A Poke In The Eye was performed on the 1st, 2nd and 3rd of April 1976 and its original title was a Cleese suggestion: *An Evening Without David Frost*, because it had all the Footlights veterans bar him. The Sunday 8th of May 1977 show we called *An Evening Without Sir Bernard Miles*, remembering the original title of the '76 show and because we were at The Mermaid, Bernard Miles' theatre in Puddledock. Finally the TV show and LP were called *The Mermaid Frolics*. We skipped '78 but in '79 I was at Cleese's house and we were kicking around titles for the next show. 'Who can we have *An Evening Without...* this time?' Because it's about human rights, Cleese said, 'An Evening Without The Secret Police,' and I just went, '*The Secret Policeman's Ball*!' He said, 'That's it, that's the title.'

PH: Back to *A Poke In The Eye* for a sec. Jonathan Miller directed the actual stage show, didn't he?

ML: He did indeed and there's a wonderful moment in the rehearsal footage of the film: He was concurrently directing Chekhov at one of the Royal theatres and in the middle of a run-through he says, "I have to go now; I have to go and do *Three Sisters*".

I had met Peter a few times. I first met Peter when I was a school-boy at University College School in Frognal, near Hampstead. We all knew he lived in Church Row and one day I got one of those charity collecting tins—like in *Bedazzled*—and put on it a label: 'Save The British Virgin Fund'. So I went—11 years old but looking all of 8 in my school uniform—waving this tin and knocked on his door, totally petrified. He opened the door, saw the label and went into a kind of Wisty thing about 'I can't be expected to save your virgins, I've got my own virgins to consider', which pleased and thrilled me beyond belief.

PH: Why wasn't Dudley Moore at the '76 show? Was it something to do with attaining US citizenship and therefore not being able to return to Britain, or wot?

ML: He wasn't due to be on the show, he might've had other commitments, although we did later get him to provide a brief narration for the film. We had Terry Jones depping for Dudley in So That's The Way You Like It, from *Beyond The Fringe*, and then Peter became an honorary Python by stepping into Eric Idle's shoes in the Monty Python Court Room sketch. Eric Idle was far away in St John's Wood, over a mile and a half away from the theatre, way too far for him to go if he wasn't being paid. And although Eric was a very talented performer in his day, I happen to think Peter was far superior in the role. Extraordinarily funny, and ad-libbed his way wonderfully through it. Mainly 'cos he was drunk, but he performed brilliantly.

PH: Was he pissed during the performances?

ML: Not very, no, no. But he did address Terry Jones onstage as 'Michael'. [*Terry Jones voice:*] 'Don't call me Michael in court!'

Peter had decided to do a couple of things for the show. One was the Miner who could've been a judge but never had the Latin—and he changed it every night. It was a constantly evolving piece. I mean, the genius aspect of Peter was that he would take a script and elaborate, embroider and bring new things to it. He also did Asp—'I've got an asp in this box, it's not a viper'—which he performed with John Fortune. He did the Shakespeare thing and the Python sketch.

PH: Were there any others?

ML: I don't think so. But he was exhilarating for me. He was a childhood hero and to be producing him—I mean, I didn't get to know him too well at that point 'cos it was a large ensemble cast, but we made a sort of connection. What I remember most was how much he was revered by the others, especially the Pythons. For

them it was like dealing with God. Pure reverence and appreciation. Peter would watch their stuff but they really paid attention to
him... Monty Python in 1976 were seen as the kingpins but Peter
was Peter Cook. He knew the hierarchy but he didn't lord it in any
way, shape or form. He was just like one of the lads and very at
ease.

PH: I'd like to know something of the interpersonal relationships
between Bennett, Miller and Cook. It'd been twelve years since
their last stage performances together. Did they regard each other
warily? Were they critical of each others' subsequent directions?

ML: It was a little odd. It really felt like a reunion. Miller was
very much in control as director, articulate as one would expect,
never at a loss for a word or an idea. Peter was slightly—amiably—ramshackle. This is pre-*Revolver*, but Peter had a pleasantly
ramshackle quality. He shuffles along—not Old Man Shuffle but
more Absent-Minded Professor Shuffle—and he was slightly diffused in focus. Alan was very tense. I didn't observe that much
inner group dynamic other than they were wildly different in their
comfort zones. Cook was totally comfy and relaxed with everything, Miller was permanently exploding with energy, Bennett was
just like a caricature of himself, all bunched up.

When it came to the 1977 show, we wanted it a bit different, just
the one night instead of three. I was even more hands-on involved.
Terry Jones volunteered to direct it. John Cleese did Bookshop with
Connie Booth and Words... And Things with Miller. Peter Ustinov
told a couple of tales. And Peter... Well, the *original* plan was to
have Dudley in it with Peter, he was gonna fly back especially for
the gig, but he cancelled right at the last minute. At the rehearsal
Peter was running through this sketch about The Bishop Of The
World—are you familiar with it?

PH: Never heard of this one before. Was he in costume?

ML: No, just a suit. During the afternoon he had press-ganged Jones into playing the interviewer. There was a part where the bishop lists various types of sinner, including [*Peter Cook's drunken, angry 'Clive' voice:*] 'Diminished British people 'oo go to 'Ollywood finkin' they're stars an' don't turn up for fuckin' charity shows they're supposed to be performing at—if you know what I mean.' He wove in some caustic remarks about Dudley whom he had been expecting to be there with him. Dudley never gave an excuse for his no-show. Peter, for *The Mermaid Frolics*, was definitely looser. That day, he did drink quite a bit. I don't know if he was just in the mood to drink, whatever, but he was irritated that Dudley wasn't there. He did do some fabulous work, though, that night. The Bishop Of The World sketch is standard issue TV interview set-up. Peter is asked how one gets to Heaven: 'Well, you *can't* get to Heaven. Heaven is full up. Plus, of course, if you touch Heaven—*if you touch it*—you go straight to Hell.' 'What about praying to God?' 'No use praying to God. The man's a cunt!' The audience just collapsed. It's very funny, quite surreal.

PH: Why didn't that sketch appear on the LP of the show?

ML: Well, the album was 60 minutes—a really long player—with 20 minutes of music and 40 minutes comedy. I think there was some anxiety—partially to do with the language but mostly to do with the actual concept of that sketch. The anxiety was shared by both Amnesty and Polydor, who I was now working for and who released the LP. Peter wasn't hung up about it at all. He didn't mind if Bishop was on the LP or not. I put Miner from the '76 show on instead because it was a more iconic performance. The E.L.Wisty—From Beyond The Veil thing was inspired. He wanted a Question and Answer session with the audience and didn't want 'plants'—you know, pre-written questions. He just wanted to go out and completely do it. You can hear how drunk he was on the tape, because he stumbles on the word 'budgerigar' which came out as 'bugger-jah-ree-jarrr'. But he plays on it in the way that only Cook was brilliant enough to do. All that 'In the wrong cage with the wrong chap' stuff—I mean, he's slightly rambling but turning it into a funny thing. Then some American woman yells out—and the Equal Rights Amendment was a big issue at the time—'Whaddabout the Equal Rights Amendment?' And Peter's timing was so exquisite. He just holds it for a beat and then says, softly, 'Fuck 'em.' It was the pause, the stoic face, and then the succinct delivery. 'Fuck 'em.' It was just perfection. He was drunk and he was on top of his form.

I see Peter quite a bit in '78 and we start to socialise. And the great thing about Peter was he treated everybody as an equal unless they gave him cause not to. His departure point was not 'I'm a fucking major star and you're a nothing unless you prove to me that you are something'. His attitude was 'Until you prove to me you're a complete twat I'm going to treat you as an equal.' And that was *rare... exceptional... gracious... special*. It made you—if you were young—feel like a million dollars because he treated you with respect.

PH: What sort of things did you and he talk about?

ML: Sixties Pop music and remembering all the obscure artists of that time. A favourite of his was *Come Away, Melinda* by Tim Rose. We'd talk about The Honeycombs, The Applejacks...

PH: So, 1979: *The Secret Policeman's Ball*.

ML: Peter was much sharper here than he'd been in '77. He wanted to do Interesting Facts, partly because he wanted to work with John Cleese, which he hadn't, except in the group sense in the *Court Room Sketch* in '76. He did Pregnancy Test with Eleanor Bron—'It's a balloon, Penelope!'—and End Of The World.

In '76, Palin and Cleese were trying to corpse one another in The Parrot Sketch, each trying to crack the other up laughing. Cook had seen this and he must've thought, 'Right, I'm not going to lose it and corpse, but I'm going to get Cleese to laugh.' I saw them doing this over the four nights. The dates were—don't tell me!—27th,

28th, 29th and 30th of June. During those sketches, Cleese's head would disappear under his newspaper and he's biting his cheeks, his tongue, he's trying his utmost not to crack up. Cook remains deadpan throughout.

PH: I've just remembered something I maybe should've asked earlier: When Peter performed Miner he didn't blink at all. It amazes me how he could concentrate on giving a nine minute or so monologue without hardly blinking once in that time. I think of Malcolm McDowell's pinned-back eyelids in *A Clockwork Orange*. How could Peter achieve this?

ML: The received wisdom is 'Peter wasn't a great actor' and maybe he couldn't have sustained a character throughout the length of a feature film. I actually think in those moments that he did go deeply into character, he really did hold that persona. Now maybe that's not quite the same as being a great movie actor but the fact remains, he became Wisty, he became the miner. I feel this 'Peter's not an actor' thing is rather unfair criticism.

The first night, Cook opened a book—you know, betting on how long the show would last, because these shows always overran. The first show was scheduled to last two and a half hours and Cook bet it would be four hours fifteen minutes, and he was the closest. He won the pool of money.

PH: Would he deliberately extemporise a sketch just to make sure the show went over time, nearer to his bet?

ML: No, he was gambling—very wisely—on my inefficiency as a producer! But that first night was way too long. I persuaded Pete Townshend to come along and do *Pinball Wizard* and *Drowned*, and he was supposed to come back with classical guitarist John Williams for a finale of *Won't Get Fooled Again*. After Pete did his first set I said, 'You may as well go upstairs and have a rest, it'll be about an hour before your next spot,' and he asked for a glass of brandy. Because he was good enough to do this for free, I wanted to take care of him and so gave him a bottle of five star brandy, not knowing what A Drinking Problem was... Three hours later, I went to collect him for the finale and he was completely smashed. He managed to get onstage but halfway through *Won't Get Fooled Again* he falls asleep with his hands still playing. John Williams is panicking: 'Where are we in this song? I'm lost!'

Because the shows didn't start till eleven at night, obviously we didn't get any reviews until the morning of the third show, Friday 29th June 1979. *The Daily Telegraph* said, 'Oh, it's pretty good but everybody's doing their old turns, their tried and tested party pieces'—which was true, it's like a summer festival; you don't want some group doing just their brand new album, you want to hear all the old favourites. But this review said, 'Where's the satire?' Cook had seen that review and was on the phone to me very early in the morning, before 8 o'clock. Cook was steaming, angry: 'Who the fuck does he think he is—"Where's the satire?" I'll show 'im the fucking satire! Look, here's what I want you to do. Can you get me a judge's wig, a lectern, a judge robe, a gavel, all that kind of stuff?' I said, 'Oh, what are you going to do?' 'Just get me that stuff, don't worry about what I'm going to do.' So I'm getting these props and wracking my brains, 'Was there a judge sketch from *Not Only But Also* or something?' At the theatre that evening Peter barely spoke to anybody. He was subdued and very, very focused. I tried to have a word with him but he was, 'No, I'm sorry, I'm working on this script.' He had pages and pages of notes and scribbles. He spoke to Billy Connolly before going onstage to ask him for a euphemism for masturbator and Connolly said, 'A player of the pink oboe.'

PH: You're talking about *Entirely A Matter For You*, Peter's take on Judge Cantley's summing-up of the Jeremy Thorpe trial.

ML: I can't recall the actual date of the judge's summation. I think it was the Thursday or Friday of the week previous to *Policeman's Ball*, I'm not sure. [*It was a two-day summation, 18th and 19th June*—Ed.]

PH: Did Peter co-write *Entirely A Matter For You* with Christopher Booker and Richard Ingrams from *Private Eye*?

ML: No, no, no. It was pure Peter. He may have phoned them up to kick ideas around but the end result was just Peter. He got up there and I knew it was going to be something special because he wouldn't share it with anyone, what he was going to do. Peter had caught the zeitgeist. There had been that feeling throughout the country the moment after hearing the verdict of the Thorpe trial. Peter had captured the moment. I remember being struck by it—I'm here, up against the wall, here's the stalls, and Peter's there. I felt like, 'Shit! This must've been what the first night of *Beyond The Fringe* was like.' I felt like I was in the presence of history, in the presence of something that really matters. And we all knew it. They weren't reacting to something they'd read in the *Daily Telegraph*, they just knew that Peter had captured A Moment. The audience were with him from the first second and were wondering how far will he go, and he raised the bar constantly, lifting it higher and higher, and he delivered on every line. After the last line, a huge roar went up from the audience. I rushed backstage to hug Peter and everyone was congratulating him. They had all been watching him from the wings. The only thing comparable was the first time people heard The Beatles' *Sgt Pepper* LP. Even the *Fringe*—I mean, that was topical but it wasn't that topical. This was plucked straight from the headlines and he captured the mood of the nation. It was un-fucking-believable. The first performance of it was the best and the second was very good. What do you think?

PH: Well, the version in the film is different to the one on the LP. They're both beyond superlatives and I find very little difference between them. One thing: He starts with a muttered 'I hope you've brought a toothbrush.' What's that about?

ML: Glad you reminded me. Yes, that's from the court case where the judge threatened to hold a journalist in contempt and said that line, meaning, 'I'm going to have you kept in the cells overnight.' Peter was so into the minutiae of the trial and his attention to detail—I mean, a day doesn't go by when I don't think of Peter: when the Clinton scandal, Monica Lewinsky and all that, was raging, I was on American TV doing satirical commentary. I thought, 'My God, what if Peter were here right now? What would he have made of the richness of detail!' He revelled in the minutiae of the Thorpe trial. I hereby declare that I really think Peter Cook played the English language like Menuhin played the Stradivarius. I don't believe there was anybody that was better than Cook at mining the richness of our language. His ability to juxtapose words and phrases and make them so apposite and capture the prejudice of the man—'pagan limbo dancing', for example. He knew what he was doing. He took a joy in language. He was a genius, like P.G. Wodehouse. Peter, of course, would shrug these salutations off...

But anyway, the energy and drive of that first performance was just remarkable. Oh, and the name of Thorpe's doctor! Dr Gleadle. The name just struck Cook so much. In the film, where he says, 'The excellent Dr Gleadle... And The Gleadletones'—it's straight out of nowhere! That was the genius of Peter Cook. To him it's just a throwaway line, an aside, but to me, I'd like to spend an hour discussing The Gleadletones and who would be in them.

PH: And why would an eminent physician front a rock band?

ML: Yeah, stuff like that.

PH: So Peter was stung that badly by that *Telegraph* review?

ML: Totally, totally. 'I'll show 'im the fucking satire!' It's a great thing that review happened. I said to Cook that night, 'We've got to do something, we can't possibly wait. The album's not due out till the end of the year to coincide with the film, da-da-da-da.'

PH: Hence the *Here Comes The Judge* mini-album.

ML: Yeah. My mind was on an immediate release for *Entirely A*

Matter For You, so on the Monday after the shows I saw Peter at Perrins Walk to discuss a special record of it. I had it cleared with the Amnesty people—'Yeah, fine, do whatever you like'—and, although the deal was with Island Records to release the two *Secret Policeman's Ball* LPs, Peter had an allegiance with Richard Branson as Virgin had issued the *Come Again* and *Ad Nauseam* LPs. We knew it wouldn't be a billion-seller because it was neither an album nor a single.

PH: Yes, it was priced halfway between the cost of an LP and the cost of a single. 'Do not pay more than £2.99 for this record.'

ML: Did you see the poster for the record? 'If you are charged more than £2.99 at a Virgin store, shoot the person at the till.'

PH: As if only professional hitmen shop at Virgin.

ML: Peter and I met Richard Branson and Simon Draper, the then Managing Director of Virgin, and they gave me carte blanche to do anything I felt necessary regarding the record. The first thing I said was, 'We've got to have some other sketches to go with it, we can't just have a one-sided record, there's got to be something on Side Two.' Peter suggested, 'Can't we have a "dub" version?'

PH [*Laughing*]: A "dub" version of a monologue! That's fantastic!

ML: "Dub" instrumental versions of A-sides of singles were pretty common then. Nowadays it'd be a special DJ remix thing. A brilliant idea of Cook's but, y'know, I really wanted some other material. He was pretty reticent: 'I don't wanna do any more bloody work. Do an instrumental version or something.' But I was insistent and—

PH:—so you went to Berwick Street Studios—

ML: Yeah, and I called a mate of mine, John Lloyd, to accompany us. The studio sketches were basically improvised. Peter had written a few ideas down. If memory serves, we did Well Hung Jury, because the original jury had been sequestered for the decision-making. Thanksgiving sprang from the news item that the priest in Thorpe's local church had organised a huge service of thanksgiving in honour of Thorpe getting off the charge. Only in Peter's version, the priest is honouring the Yorkshire Ripper.

PH: Who was still at large at the time. And, of course, the last track, one of my favourites, Rad Job.

ML: Oh, Rad Job! Yes, that was the first one we recorded. Oh, I got my knuckles rapped for that.

PH: Who by?

ML: Peter, because it was taking ages to get the effect of two people talking on the phone. Berwick Street Studios wasn't a brilliantly-equipped studio and it was a major problem trying to achieve this effect. We even considered Peter and John using actual telephones and miking them up. This is when I got my first taste of Peter at his most withering: 'We're in a studio—an audio studio—a studio presumably capable of making some kind of effect with audio—and I'm not asking for a sophisticated sound. All I want is the sound of two people talking on the telephone. Not, you would think, to be something very difficult for an audio studio to arrange. Yet here we are, two hours later, and we still haven't got the sound of a telephone!' Oh dear... We finally got it by using lots of 'Compression' on the mixing desk. As I say, it was totally improvised. Peter discussed it with John for a few minutes and erected a number of tent poles—

PH: Tent poles?

ML: Er, they're like markers, points, that you want to hit in the performance: 'I want to talk about this, and then we go on to this ...' Totally improvised, first take, done! Rad Job was totally inspired. Peter was intrigued by all the code language and terminology used by hitmen and other villains...

Thanksgiving was pretty much written out beforehand. The Well Hung Jury one—

PH: Who did all the snoring on that one?

ML: All of us—me, Peter, John, the engineer—did this bed [backing track] of snoring. We were the jury sleeping overnight in some hotel. It was amazing to see Peter at work because he's thinking, 'We've got to do something about the jury. The jury, the jury, the jury!' So we did this track of snoring then Peter led John through this conversation between two jurors about homosexuality. The whole session took one afternoon to record. I remember feeling that, since Peter treated me as an equal, I really had to rise to the occasion as producer. Peter's idea was to get Gerald Scarfe to do the record cover, so he called Gerald who delivered a wonderful cover. My expertise was in marketing and publicity and after a get-together with the Virgin people—who weren't too bright, they didn't really understand what we were doing—I organised a launch where we showed the film extract Graef had been working on at The Bijoux, a viewing theatre, on Dean or Wardour Street. We then went to an outer room where we served Chinese food. (There was also a cake in the shape of a pink oboe.) We renamed the Chinese food in honour of the trial. Peter and I had sat down and made a list of funny food. Like, because Norman Scott, in the trial, had said Jeremy Thorpe had nodules on his back, our menu therefore had Crispy Fried Nodules. The reception went exceptionally well; the Press came along and were ecstatic about the film clip.

PH: How well did *Here Comes The Judge* sell?

ML: As well as you would expect a comedy 12-inch EP to sell in 1979. It was such an unusual configuration, it was never gonna sell that well. Albums sold, singles didn't sell, and 12-inch EPs were neither fish nor fowl. I hope it's a collectors' item now because it's so special, but I'd never expect it to be reissued.

PH: That'd be a shame. I think it definitely needs to be out again. The points made in *Entirely A Matter For You* about the Establishment closing ranks and protecting its own are still pertinent.

ML: It's a combination, that sketch, of being the most time-sensitive and timeless in the same breath. 'Timeless' in the sense of it being Great Comedy—this is Molière, this is Shakespeare, and I really don't exaggerate when I say that. When Peter Cook said, 'The trouble with being a miner is as soon as you're too old and tired and sick and stupid to do the job properly, you have to go. Well, the very opposite applies to judges,' he never captured it better than that. In *Entirely A Matter For You* he caught the essence of what England was about in the late '70s, and the wit within it is utterly timeless. I personally believe it was Cook's finest work in some senses. I was just there as an enabler, fortunate enough to be helping, blah-blah-blah, but the genius is pure Cook. There was nobody else who created that other than Peter Cook, which is why I revere him to this day for the genius he had within him.

I had immense pride in doing *Here Comes The Judge* but the greatest joy was yet to come: The TV showing of a 52-minute version of *The Secret Policeman's Ball* [*The full-length film came out in 1980*—Ed.] was tied-in with Island's releasing of the respective Music and Comedy albums of the shows in December '79. I wanted a big launch for the TV show and the LPs so I met Peter and we had a few drinks, tossing ideas around, when suddenly I thought, 'Let's hold it at the National Liberal Club!' I knew it wasn't technically attached to the Liberal Party any longer. You could rent it for functions, special occasions. Cook was going, 'Yeah, yeah, go for it, go for it!'

I booked the Club for December the 8th or 9th where we showed the TV version to the Press and then had a photo call with the cast. Afterwards, I'd arranged a lunch for the cast in the library of the Club. We're all sitting at this long table—I'm sitting next to Cook—lots of different conversations going on. Cook's going, 'What's with all these books?'—'We're in the library.' On a whim, I pulled one of the books off a shelf and it was *International Who's Who*, 1935. I took it over to Peter—'Look at this, man, look at this: *Who's Who*.' Peter started going through it and started improvising and to this day I don't think I've heard anything funnier. He looked through it and found an entry for Adolf Hitler, with a phone number—Reichstag 1234 or something. I presume it was the official government telephone number but it was listed as if it were Hitler's private number. And Peter went into this surreal LBC Radio hook-up between Adolf Hitler and this sweet little old lady phoning in: 'Oh hi, Mr Hitler, I've just seen your policies and I'd like to enquire whether—', you know. I can't recall the detail now but I remember all the 20 or so conversations hushed so everyone could hear this magical improvisation.

I remember once I had to go and meet him at the [Private] Eye office and I was late—I was always running late in those days—and I arrived about 15 minutes late. Peter says, 'Where were you?' 'Um, caught in heavy traffic.' 'Traffic? On a Friday lunchtime? In the West End of London? How could you have anticipated that? It must have come as a complete shock to you to find traffic, a large number of cars, in the West End of London!' And he really ragged me about it, kept harping on about it to such an extent that I could never, ever, ever, ever offer any excuse ever again.

Another memory that sticks out like a shard: He was editing the Derek and Clive Get The Horn movie with Russell Mulcahy, and he invited me to go and hang with him. They show me some footage and Peter says, 'Martin, what do you think?' The sequence is with the world's longest bogey that's all around the room, where his wife comes in and breaks the line of snot and he kicks her and stomps her. And I am literally on the floor, howling with laughter, when Peter asks me—and I don't think he was trying to be funny—'Do you think that goes a bit too far?' That line just set me off, I couldn't stop laughing. That sketch had gone beyond all notions of decency and boundaries of what can be funny, and he asks if it's gone a bit too far! A priceless moment...

The Secret Policeman's Ball film came out in May, June 1980 and did fantastically well.

PH: I must admit to mixed feelings about the film. There's some funny stuff going on but the film is so dark, it's like it's been lit by a solitary Zippo. And the audience shots where you see people in absolute hysterics that bear no relation to what's going on on-stage—they're reaction shots to different sketches—are intensely irritating.

ML: Well, that's how impoverished Roger Graef was as a serious film maker. Great documentarian, yes, but we didn't know any bet-ter at the time, which is why for the September 1981 show [*The Secret Policeman's Other Ball*] I hired Julien Temple, who had a more filmic flair.

PH: Peter was absent from *Other Ball*. Why was that?

ML: He was in the States doing *The Two Of Us* TV series. I des-perately wanted him in it but he was filming and couldn't get back till about January, February 1982. When he came back he was seriously bloated, about 25-30 lbs heavier. Peter had been piling it on. He was unhappy out there so he ate more. Comfort eating. I approached him to do a couple of things. One was a cinema ad for the film, and the other was some radio commercials. Again, what happened was I'd give him the concept and he would write all the words. The cinema trailer was a set of excerpts that would be a bit boring on its own so it was linked by Peter's voice-over as a man in the audience: 'Ooh, what's this? *The Secret Policeman's Other Ball*. Oh look, there's John Cleese in his underpants. That's Jeff Beck, innit?... Oh yeah, there's String...' I also got him to do the voice-over for the opening credits of the film: 'Ladies and gentle-men, *The Secret Policeman's Other Ball*.' I wrote those words—the only words I could write. For the radio ads I wanted something more than 'Come and see this wonderful film.' I told Peter that Capital Radio had these ads saying if you liked such-and-such a film, then you'll really like this one. That's all it took to set him off: 'If you liked *The Sound Of Music* and *The Texas Chainsaw Mas-*

sacre, you will love *The Secret Policeman's Other Ball*... If you liked *On Golden Pond* and *The Village Of The Damned*...' Mad, bizarre juxtapositions he made.

PH: He did all these for free?

ML: Oh yeah, no money. For the launch of the film I thought of doing a spoof on the BAFTA Awards ceremony, to be held the day before the actual BAFTA Awards and, rather naughtily, in BAFTA's own theatre. Four days beforehand, BAFTA got wind of it, freaked, and cancelled our booking, saying it was disrespectful. Instead, we held The Other Awards at a Universal theatre on Regent Street for an 11 o'clock premiere. Peter agreed to be the Oscars night MC host.

PH: He quite liked being an MC, didn't he? In addition to The Establishment Club and *Revolver*, he hosted the Melody Maker Readers' Poll Awards a couple of times.

ML: Thanks for reminding me because he came out with a great line at one Melody Maker Awards 'do'. I think it was the '76 one. Thin Lizzy had won the award for Best Group or Best Album. Phil Lynott [leader of Thin Lizzy] comes up to the microphone [*stoned voice:*], "Duhh... I wanna shay, uhh...'sgreat, y'know, uhhh... An', uh, y'know... 'Sgreat, yeah." He leaves the stage and he's halfway back to his seat when Peter says, "You can tell he writes the lyrics." Seven words, devastating.

Back to The Other Awards. We had all these award nominations that related to the *Other Ball* film, like 'Best Striptease By John Cleese And Pamela Stephenson Award', which John collected, saying, 'I'm sorry I can't be here tonight but I'd like to thank myself for receiving this award in my place.' With every award nomination, the envelopes would get progressively bigger. And Peter would be ad-libbing like crazy. Big old hippy I am, I booked Donovan to play at the Awards, and he was magic. Do you know of him?

PH: Yeah. 'First there is a mountain, then there is no mountain, then there is.'

ML: Right. To my eternal shame I succumbed to '80s cynicism and wrote for his introduction, 'The Award For Reminding Us How Silly We All Were In The '60s—Donovan'. However, Peter—bless him—rewrote it as, 'The Award For Reminding Us How Sensible We Were In The '60s'. It wasn't a funny change, it was Peter saying, 'Why should we apologise for the '60s? They were fucking great!' I loved that. It was a fun, silly night and Cook was on great form. In 1982 I relocated to Los Angeles

PH: —Where you promptly sold your soul?

ML: Sold my soul? It's not that easy. I've been trying for years! I managed to get someone to take out an option on my integrity... I would try and catch Peter whenever I came back to London and we'd have lunch, talk Pop trivia, whatever. I would periodically call him from LA: 'Look, it's great here. Why not come over, do a TV show?'—but he just got stuck in his boots and didn't feel that America was the place to do anything.

I remember this date exactly: July the 24th, 1987. (Well, it's my birthday so I should know it.) I'm on the phone to Peter, begging him to do something and he's standfast, 'No, they don't understand me,' dah-dah-dah. I said, 'Well, if you have any ideas –' 'No, I haven't got any ideas.' Then I said, 'Next year's the Presidential elections. Why don't you run for President?' And there was this silence. And it was a good silence. He wasn't saying no. Then he said, 'Well, I couldn't run for President but'—and this name came out almost immediately—"Morton P. Fergleberger could." We started running with this idea of a ficticious candidate for an hour on the phone. I was only five minutes walk away from his house but I knew if I hung up and raced round, the spell would be broken. I said, 'You could do an offbeat, leftfield TV Special about him,' and Peter replied, 'No, it must be an on-beat, right-field TV Special.'

Later, I went round and we discussed it at great length. He was going to be a nutty multimillionaire industrialist running as a third party candidate. This was long before Ross Perot—we'd never heard of Perot then. Morton P. Fergleberger of Al Ladd.- the Aluminium Ladder Company—was the original Perot. I gave Peter a book on Gerald Ford's 1976 election campaign and he was struck by Ford's constantly going on about his golf clubs and by Jimmy Carter having hallucinations. I pitched the idea to Stu Smiley, the Head of Comedy at HBO. The guy bought it in three seconds! HBO in LA said, 'Bring Peter over', and sent him and David Wilkinson, Peter's agent, two first-class tickets on Concorde. (These guys ain't cheap.) We had a meeting to die for. Everything we said, they loved. Magic! Peter, in the meeting, told them that, at some point, Fergleberger would get a titanium rod stuck up his bum. HBO: 'Wow, yeah, right, cool.' After, I asked Peter what that was all about. He said, 'I wanted to see how far I could push it.'

We got the commission to do the show but Peter was slow on the writing of it.

PH: Why was that?

ML: He hadn't done anything like this for a long time. He could talk and invent stuff but writing it down was hard. We both got sidetracked easily. The working title was *The Dark Horse From The Grass Roots* but we came up with something better when I suggested we needed a campaign song. American politicians like to use rock songs in their electoral campaigns—Bruce Springsteen's *Born In The USA*, Fleetwood Mac's *Don't Stop*. We needed a song for our candidate to reflect his manifesto. What would his slogan be? I assume it was Peter who suggested the Status Quo song *Whatever You Want*. Whenever one of us said 'Whatever you want' we'd go straight into that head-butting, head-banging thing, [*sings:*] 'WOTEVER YOU WANT, DUH-DUM DUH-DUM, WOTEVER YOU LIKE, DUH-DUM DUH-DUM!' Peter said, 'That's our campaign song.' So, er, what's your policy on Afghanistan? [*Smarmy American voice:*] 'Whadever yew want.' [*sings:*] 'WOTEVER YOU WANT, DUH-DUM DUH-DUM!' 'Mr Fergleberger, what about taxes?' 'Whadever yew want.' 'WOTEVER YOU WANT, DUHDUM DUH-DUM!'

We split the duties. Peter would write it and I would deal with the marketing. The plan was to premiere the film in Washington at a mock Presidential candidate's launch. We'd invite all the media—telling them it was a surprise mystery candidate who was going to announce himself. Then we'd show the film and Peter would come out as Fergleberger. Another idea was to do a music video, like *We Are The World*, of *Whatever You Want* with an all-star cast. I had David Bowie and Sting lined up to do it. Then we were going to do a spoof fund-raiser in LA with Robin Williams and Steve Martin.

I went back to London, got in at 11 o'clock at night, phoned Peter and he said, 'Let's record the theme song now! Ronnie Wood's in town. Call Ronnie. Keith Richards is in town. Call them up and let's do it now!' I said, 'You're crazy! How am I going to find an open studio at this time of night?' It was a Sisyphean task.

PH: Did you record it?

ML: No!... As I said, we'd had lots of brainstorming sessions, lots of inventive discussion on the phone, but Peter was pretty slow in writing it. I'm getting anxious now because we had a deadline date of early November. It's now October so he brought in John Lloyd to help out, and I'm really pleased he did 'cos Lloyd actually focused Peter into finishing it. The script came in and I howled and howled and howled. It was wonderful, beyond my wildest dreams.

I sent this first draft script to Stu Smiley at HBO. He calls me: 'It's great, I'm very excited, we've got to see Peter.' (Stu's in New York, Peter's in London, I'm in LA.) 'We totally love this.'

Quite separate to all this is the second annual US Comic Relief show which Robin Williams, Billy Crystal and Whoopi Goldberg had helped set up to raise money for the homeless. I broached it with Peter very, very, very cautiously—about him appearing on Comic

Relief with Dudley Moore—because I never raised Dudley's name to him. Except once: I was going, 'Come on, admit it. Aren't you a bit jealous of all that fame he's got?' 'Martin, there's two kinds of fame. There's fame like Charles Manson's and there's fame like Dudley's. There has to be something between the two.'

I knew the producer, Bob Zmuda, and he knew I was working with Peter. He asked, 'Do you think they'd reunite for Comic Relief?' I said, 'Naah! No way,' but then I thought, 'Well, why not ask anyway?' I didn't know of Peter and Dudley's dynamic. I'm saying to Peter, 'They've got this charity thing here, blah blah, Robin Williams, blah blah, and would you'—gulp!—'would you be open to doing it with Dudley?' I'm almost burying the words 'cos I'm expecting him to go, '*How fucking stupid are you?*' Instead, he seemed open about it. HBO, who were broadcasting the show, had to bring Peter and David Wilkinson to LA anyway so there was a possibility. Peter phoned Dudley about it and Dudley was willing to do it, too.

PH: They did a pretty ragged One Leg Too Few.

ML: It was loose, yes. Very loose. They rehearsed for an hour at Dud's house.

Flash forward. Peter, David and I met Stu Smiley for breakfast at the Westwood Marquee and Stu said, quote, 'This is the funniest script I've ever read,' unquote. 'We really wanna do this, it may need a bit more work.' They were due to give us their final decision in late November, but Smiley asks if we can give them a little more time. We said, 'Yeah, sure, whatever,' you know, we're pretty confident, he loves it, we're quids in. Gary Weis was to direct it—he did The Rutles film.

PH: So what happened?

ML: They asked us to wait till January to make up their minds. We knew HBO wanted to do something in Election Year and we were starting to get worried because we hadn't heard anything and time's getting on. We were supposed to have gotten the go-ahead in November and now it's January.

John Lloyd in London picks up *The Guardian* one day early January and reads of a big announcement: Channel 4 are doing an Election spoof with HBO called *Tanner '88*, written by Garry Trudeau, directed by Robert Altman. I can understand why they went with it—it was a series whereas ours was a one-off Special—but they should have come to us and told us, 'Hey guys, I'm sorry, we've got other irons in the fire,' so we could've then gone to another channel. They intentionally didn't tell us because they didn't want us to go with a rival channel. Their timing was such that had we gone to another channel they'd have turned round to us with, 'Oh, you're just copying *Tanner '88*.' David was extremely angry, Peter was totally depressed. He said, 'I told you they'd fuck us.' I felt miserable beyond words 'cos I'd promised Peter I'd protect him as best I could but, you know, the HBO guys played dirty pool. I tried to get Showtime interested but Peter was just, 'Ah fuck it, I just don't want to do it anymore.' Peter never held it against me; he knew we'd been fucked by Smiley. So we just let it go. *Tanner '88* transpired to be not that good. I mean, I like Trudeau, I like Altman, but that series was whimsical, not funny. Peter was really crushed by the whole experience, really hurt.

PH: The 1980s was the most frustrating decade for Peter Cook, wasn't it? He'd make films that were either artistic or box office failures. One film remains unreleased. His two TV series were disasters of Streeb-Greebling proportions. He had scripts rejected, plugs pulled on projects. He reminds me of Terry Southern who in the '60s produced marvellous, original books and film scripts—*Dr Strangelove*, *Barbarella*, *Blue Movie*, *Magic Christian*, *Easy Rider*—and then was scarcely heard of again. People may assume, 'Oh, he's stuck under a syringe or inside a bottle', but the fact is he spent some twenty years writing movies that, for some reason or another, never got made. Peter disappeared from public view for large chunks of the '80s, didn't he?

ML: Yes, and this was to be his big entrance back into the arena. The view that Peter lost his gift in later life is not one I subscribe to. He was just as funny as he always was and that *Clive Anderson Talks Back* Special bears that out. He just worked to a different timetable.

PH: Did you remain in touch with Peter after the Fergleberger fiasco?

ML: Yeah. Up until 1993 I kept a place in Hampstead and would come over once a year to see family and friends. I had a party there and, as we all know, Peter loved a wager and I don't know how we got on to it but he said, 'Boxers or briefs?'—meaning, what type of underwear am I wearing. He put fifty quid on briefs. I had to take my fucking trousers down to prove I was actually wearing very enchanting black boxers. He said it was the best fifty quid he had ever spent, seeing how ridiculous I looked without my trousers on.

PH: What was he wearing?

ML: God, I never asked. A bad bet, wasn't it, in that sense. But he didn't regret the bet at all and paid up.

I saw him when he very occasionally visited LA and I saw him becoming—reclusive isn't the word—more self-contained. We'd chat on the phone but it wasn't for as long, but... The day he died, I was so devastated, I was really... [*Lewis sighs heavily, lost for words.*]

PH: Did you think, 'This was coming'?

ML: No. I was looking forward to a long, long friendship continuing down the years where we'd be talking about rock stars and *Come Away, Melinda* and things in the news—when I told him Elizabeth Dole, wife of Republican senator Bob Dole, was described as 'The world's highest-paid charity worker', it floored him, he loved that. I expected another 20 years seeing Peter and sharing jokes, ideas, memories. I never, I just never... I had no idea...

I was invited to the memorial service in Hampstead and it meant a lot for me to go. I think Dudley and I were the only two from the States. It was very emotional seeing Barry Fantoni and all these people I knew. After the service, a lot of us went for some food at La Sorpresa, the Italian restaurant. I spent a lot of time with Dudley and Suzy and I thought it so sweet that, after their divorce, more than 20 years on, they were still fond of one another, still close. No one wanted to leave the restaurant because it felt like Peter was there, and if anyone got up and left, it'd be over. Peter was alive whilst we were there. When you left, you knew he was dead.

FOOTNOTE ONE: THE TRIAL OF THE CENTURY

(A brief, if exhaustive, re-zoom of the Jeremy Thorpe and Norman Scott affair which, in turn, led to one of Peter Cook's most brilliant performances.)

John Jeremy Thorpe was a product of the Establishment—father a Conservative MP, schooled at Eton and thence to Oxford University to study Law. Thorpe graduated from Oxford in 1952 and became the successful Liberal Party candidate for the North Devon constituency soon after, retaining the seat for 27 years. As Jeremy Thorpe, MP, he was known as a very friendly, charismatic, persuasive, political showman, once described as the 'JFK of the UK'. Fellow Liberal MP Cyril Smith, however, said Thorpe was 'a Jekyll and Hyde character, always ready to go for the jugular' if it meant increased popularity for himself and the Liberals. When the then PM Harold Macmillan sacked half of his cabinet, Thorpe on the backbenches said, 'Greater love hath no man like this, that he would lay down his friends for his life.' (These words would return to haunt Thorpe when his private life became public...)

Norman Scott, meanwhile, worked as a groom at a horse stables at Squirrel Cottage, Kingham, Oxfordshire when Thorpe visited there in 1960. They chatted about horses although, to Scott, Thorpe had no interest in matters horsey. Scott: 'He said that if anything should ever happen, I should get in touch with him.'

When Scott left his job he visited Thorpe at Westminster. That same day their relationship became sexual when Thorpe seduced Scott. They shared a London flat but Thorpe had made a mistake in pairing with Scott, a mercurial character with a history of mental instability. As their relationship cooled, tempers became frayed when Thorpe, for reasons unknown, refused to hand Scott back his National Insurance card. (Without it, Scott could not get a job.)

Liberal MP Peter Bessell (immortalised by Peter Cook in *Entirely A Matter For You* as Bex Bissell, a make of carpet sweeper) knew of Thorpe's secret life and was asked by Thorpe to 'deal with Scott'. Bessell tried to buy Scott's silence with a series of Thorpe-funded payments.

The cover-up worked. In 1967, Thorpe became leader of the Liberal Party and he got married. His wife Caroline died in a car crash two years later. Thorpe was consumed with grief but when he recovered, in 1971, he faced a new shock: The Liberal Party had learnt of The Affair. Word had reached them that Scott, now in Wales, would tell anyone who would listen that Thorpe and he had been lovers. Scott was called to a Liberal investigation, led by Lord Byers, who did Thorpe no favours by immediately accusing Scott of being 'a common blackmailer'.

Marian Harwood became the second Mrs Thorpe in 1973 and in the first General Election of 1974 the Liberals scored their highest share of the vote in 50 years. Thorpe was offered a coalition government with Edward Heath but the Liberals refused to back such a move. The Liberals' success was in no small part due to Thorpe's vigorous and popular campaigning.

Bessell moved to America in 1974 and David Holmes (Lib. Party treasurer) took on the job of keeping Scott shtum, paying him £2,500 for incriminating 'love letters' from Thorpe which were then burnt. Thorpe confided to Holmes, 'I will never be safe whilst Scott is around'. It was then that Holmes set about trying to get rid of Scott once and for all. He contacted carpet dealer John Le Mesurier about The Problem and Le Mesurier in turn, through an intermediary, hired one Andrew Newton to kill Scott. (Newton would be paid out of Liberal Party donations made by Jack Hayward, a Bahamas-based businessman who knew nothing of Scott. These donations, ostensibly 'election expenses', were paid by Hayward, at Thorpe's urging, to another businessman, Nadir Dinshaw, thus bypassing scrutiny of Liberal Party accountants.)

In October 1975, Scott, who was now living in Barnstaple, North Devon, was beaten up by two unidentified men. Incriminating pay-off notes were stolen by a man posing as a journalist soon after.

Newton met Scott at a hotel, saying he was there to protect him and suggested they drive to Porlock, via desolate Exmoor. On a dark, rainy night Scott got into Newton's car with his dog, a Great Dane that Scott called Rinka. On the road to Exmoor it was decided that Scott take over the driving for a while. Newton stopped the car and they got out to change seats. It was then that Newton shot Scott's dog dead. Newton said to Scott, 'Now it's your turn,' but the gun had jammed. Scott ran off, luckily finding an AA man on patrol in the area. Newton panicked and drove off. However, in March '76 Newton was convicted of attempted murder and gaoled.

On 10th May '76 Jeremy Thorpe resigned as Liberal leader but not as MP for North Devon.

In April '77 Newton was released. He went to South Wales to collect £5,000, the first instalment of his pay-off. He cashed in further by selling his story to the Press (and taping phone calls to Holmes and Le Mesurier along the way).

On 2nd August 1978 Thorpe, Le Mesurier and club owner George Deakin, the intermediary, were charged with incitement and conspiracy to murder Norman Scott. One by one, Thorpe's colleagues deserted him to appear instead as prosecution witnesses. The trial—called at the time Britain's Watergate and The Trial Of The Century—was postponed until after the May 1979 General Election. Due to the overwhelming press coverage it was no surprise that Thorpe lost his North Devon seat to the Tories.

At the trial in June '79, Bessell stated that Thorpe had suggested murdering Scott as long ago as 1968, but Bessell's character was held up for ridicule for his sexual and financial shenanigans and his evidence was further undermined by the fact he was paid for his story by *The Daily Telegraph*. Norman Scott was similarly demolished by the defence as a 'blackmailer'. And Newton, during his cross-examination by the prosecution, 'made a fool of himself, deliberately made a farce of the trial' (John Le Mesurier). Thorpe, Holmes and Le Mesurier never took the witness stand.

The judge, Mr Justice Cantley, respectful to the last of Thorpe as pillar of the Establishment, etc, etc, in his summing-up called Scott 'a crook, a sponger and a parasite', Bessell 'a humbug', and Newton 'no more than a perjuror'. With these characters thoroughly assassinated and discredited in court, the Jury acquitted Thorpe, Deakin and Le Mesurier of all charges.

Jeremy Thorpe made a total withdrawal from politics and public life, his reputation destroyed. In the 1980s he was diagnosed as suffering from Parkinson's Disease.

FOOTNOTE TWO: THE SUMMER OF '79

TOM ROBINSON: Peter Cook walked *The Secret Policeman's Ball* in majesty. It was a very interesting and surprising night, a great treat to be able to watch that show, and to take part in it. The two big surprises were Rowan Atkinson—from nowhere—doing The School Master which just brought the house down. Completely unknown comic delivering this stuff, and it just made him. The other surprise was Peter, who just showed these young things where to get off—you know, 'This is how it's done. This is class. Just remember, this is the elder statesman'. He did his Most Boring Man

In The World—with his Interesting Facts—right at top level, and then the Judge—so brilliantly written. The keynote about *Entirely A Matter For You*, and about me doing *Glad To Be Gay*, was that the issue at stake was Amnesty and whether they were going to support gay prisoners, people who were imprisoned simply for being homosexual. Up till then, Amnesty had always said, 'We're for prisoners of conscience only. That's our brief, that's what we do. These people are very sad, I'm sure, but it's nothing to do with us.' For all that, I gave a more-than-usually-pissed-off performance of *Glad To Be Gay* during *Policeman's Ball*. But with Peter raising the spectre of the topic there, and the event becoming a film, so the whole of Amnesty International—its top brass and its supporters—would get to see it... I don't know if it had any effect or not, but the fact is Amnesty now is an organization of human rights, rather than purely prisoners of conscience, so it's much broader. If people's basic human rights are being fucked with, then Amnesty steps in.

FOOTNOTE THREE: "I SHOT NORMAN SCOTT"— PAUL COX CONFESSES

I had just left college, twenty years old, and started working for London Features, and because I was the photographer for *The Secret Policeman's Ball*, Martin Lewis sent me and Peter Cook down to see Norman Scott and get a lot of shots of Norman and Peter in his Judge gear as publicity for the *Here Comes The Judge* album. Martin was the man behind it all—a total powerhouse of energy, absolutely full on, all the time.

Norman lived on some farm place in Tavistock, I think, in Devon, so me and Peter got the train down there. That was a bit of a mad journey because, obviously, Peter goes rabbiting off, just talk, talk, talk, talk, y'know. The whole journey was just him cracking jokes, and the people sitting opposite—and anyone within earshot—were just totally into his banter. He was really funny; a real character, Peter.

It was a totally bonkers idea and Norman wasn't totally into it to start with, because he was a bit worried about all the implications of his involvement. When we turned up at his place we had trouble getting in, because someone—obviously a supporter of Jeremy Thorpe—had gone and poisoned all of Scott's animals. Cats, dogs, everything, all dead. So, justifiably, Scott was rather paranoid and had locked himself indoors. Peter took the record down with us so he could play it to Norman and convince him that, rather than vilifying him, like a lot of the press were, it was the Judge that Peter was attacking. We feared he was going to be totally uncooperative, but Peter was really charming and persuasive and pretty soon Norman was being pushed around the place in a wheelbarrow by Peter and generally having a merry old time. We got some lovely, mad pictures that day—some weird scenarios—like Norman giving the Judge a piggy-back. It was a brilliant, bizarre photo session.

We had taken lots of pictures in the day and then went off to the pub in the evening. Drinky, drinky, drinky. We were supposed to get the train back to London that evening—I had some job the next day—but Norman started going, 'Stay the night, stay down here, it'll be great'. I got this uncomfortable feeling that something was going to go off. I was rather nervous, being a kid fresh out of college, a whole new world, so I made my excuses and caught the train home.

Peter stayed, though.

PETER COOK AND CO-WRITER

Born in 1944 and a graduate of the Royal Scottish Academy Of Music and Drama, Bernard McKenna was taken under Frank Muir's wing, when the Patron Saint of Bow-Ties was the Big Chicken at London Weekend Television, to write and script-edit for their stable of comedy shows. His innumerable writing and producing credits include Hark At Barker, *the* Doctor... *series (co-written with Graham Chapman),* Robin's Nest, Shelley, The New Statesman, The Top Secret Life Of Edgar Briggs *(starring David Jason—remember that one? It was brilliant!) and* The Odd Job *TV playlet (subsequently stretched to film length and starring Chapman and Jason). His most famous acting role is that of the Centurion—'Shut up, you Jewish turd!'—in* Monty Python's Life Of Brian. *From 1980 to 1986 he was a script collaborator with Peter Cook on various TV, stage and film projects. To find out a mite more, Paul Hamilton set out on his penny-farthing one July day in 1998 and trundled fifty miles down cobbled roads to Mr. McKenna's modest country castle for convivial conversation and essential genital bandaging.*

PAUL HAMILTON: How did you become involved with Peter Cook and his TV Special *Peter Cook & Co.*?

BERNARD MCKENNA: Someone—probably Humphrey Barclay, the head of comedy at London Weekend Television—had come up with the idea of a TV Special, and because Peter had not been with Dudley, he was maybe going to have a problem in doing a show involving lots of sketches and dialogues. I was brought in because of my experience in editing scripts and—being a writer—having sympathy for the writing. I had met Peter beforehand at one of Graham Chapman's parties—we had all lived nearby, Peter in Hampstead, I was in Swiss Cottage, Graham in Highgate. Maybe it was one of Graham's Coming Out (Yet Again) parties. You don't really talk to Peter, you improvise with him, and if you can improvise with him, you become part of his accepted surroundings. I'm not saying I gave as good as I got but I joined in in a manner he enjoyed. This is possibly why he thought I was acceptable to do *Peter Cook & Co.* with him. I wanted to call it *Cook For 45 Minutes* but Michael Grade, then the Head of Entertainment at LWT, said it sounded like a food programme. I was overruled.

PH: Your official title in the programme's credits—

BM: 'Script Associate', yes. It means you will probably write bits but you're not going to co-write, which is an interesting division. A co-writer has a much stronger position. But I didn't care. I was happy, I was a fan of Peter's and to work with him was payment enough—almost.

My job was to keep Peter on the right track because he had this wonderful tendency to meander off for hours in all sorts of odd directions. I had to pull in the strands. Basically, Peter would write bits of sketches and ideas and send them to me. I would make notes and discuss it with him on the phone or go and see him. There was no remit as to what it was to include other than 'room for guests'. This is part of the Humphrey Barclay-slightly- old-maidish-I-don't-think-we-can-watch-Peter-for-an-hour attitude. Now some of us could watch him for an hour, but this sort of 'ITV Entertainment Thinking' required there would be a let-up from Peter because he isn't everybody's cup of tea.

PH: Why else would they be watching the show?

BM: Exactly. But we had to fit that Light Entertainment framework. Maybe it would've been better as a half-hour show. But the trouble is, there's no set Peter Cook length to a sketch. It's not like anybody else's. He's closer to Milligan in that way you must follow it through to its logical, or illogical, conclusion. Having not seen it for ages, I was amazed at The Bee Plumber sketch. I'd forgotten where it went until I saw it again the other day. What started as a sketch about a blocked toilet—'How did this blockage occur?', *real* lavatory humour—ended with world domination by Bee People. Peter had a say in who he'd like on the show and he wanted Beryl Reid. In the middle of nowhere he said, 'I see Beryl dressed as a bee'. Humphrey Barclay would ring up occasionally—and you always get this with careful producers like Humphrey, they don't ring to push you because they know they'll get nowhere, they ring up to ask how it's going and you can throw certain things at him that will excite him. So saying 'Beryl Reid as a bee' will have him laughing so long he forgets to ask, 'How many sketches have you actually written?' The truthful answer would've been half a sketch about vegetables...

PH: So how much had Peter actually written before you entered the frame?

BM: Just notes and ideas. What was in the show? Err...The New York cabbie who linked the show. He always loved New York and New York cabbies so he thought it'd be fun to play one. I think he blatantly had a view to the American market. Tales Of The Much As We Expected was one that just arrived. Just a very obvious one of Roald Dahl catching fire. Peter was very good at impersonating somebody like Dahl who had this very pallid, lugubrious look. Father And Son was the idea of a father giving advice to his son, except the son isn't 13 years old, he's 44. These sketches are all pretty short. Peter was very good at starting sketches but most of the writing would come out of improvising. He'd say, 'I've got this thing about Professor Globnik and ze ants', and he tested it by going, 'So here ve are!' I'd say, 'Professor Globnik, you are an expert on ants'. Peter: 'I am zer numero uno!' He loved putting those kinds of phrases into an old German's mouth. I would act as the straight man and try and lead Peter into directions where he would be at his best. You'd have skeletons of sketches. I think only the Roald Dahl one was complete. Later, he added to it by saying his real name was Ronald Dahl but he changed it in order to become more mysterious.

PH: 'And if Ronald Biggs had been Roald Biggs...'

BM:—Yes, and there you'd have to stop him otherwise he'd be on to Roald Reagan or Roald McDonald. The writing sessions were always funny meetings.

PH: At Perrin's Walk, was it?

BM: Mostly. We didn't use tape recorders. I would write it all down. When we had just about completed the script, we had a secretary come up to type up all our handwritten bits and pieces. Then we three went out for a nice, jolly lunch. Peter said he had to go back home to make a few phone calls, and told us to come back in half an hour. When we left, the secretary spotted John Cleese and Graham Chapman leaving a rival—and more expensive—restaurant. But Peter had an account with the restaurant we had been in—all the Italian waiters would call him 'Mister Peter'. Anyway, Graham and John were doing this big thing hiding behind lamp posts and spotting me with a strange woman in Hampstead. Eventually they asked what I was up to. I said I'm working with Peter and why don't you come back to his house for a coffee. When we got in,

Peter was upstairs so I shouted, 'Oh Peter, some of the waiters were wondering what your house is like, so I've brought them along.' Peter's startled voice: 'WHAT?' Graham and John were doing excitable Italian accents and Peter came shooting down his spiral staircase at a million miles an hour to be greeted by John and Graham. Then we hung out, having our coffees, and Cleese is strutting around in his typical manner, leafing through the scripts, going, 'Well, what sort of stuff are you having in this show, hm? What have you got here?' And we told him we'd just finished one about Neville Chamberlain returning from Munich with the 'peace in our time' letter. Cleese read it and said, 'I'd love to play Chamberlain'. So we promptly rang Humphrey and said, 'We've been casting and we've got John Cleese'. Chamberlain is a distant relation of Humphrey Barclay's—if that means anything. It seems like perfect casting since Cleese does resemble Chamberlain.

PH: Yes, he captured the awkwardness very well.

BM: And, from that, we managed to get John to do the other filmed sketch, the Father And Son. Whilst we were doing it, there were thoughts that if it was a success and we could do one or two Specials a year, that there should be regular features, one of which would've been Out-Takes Of History—like Chamberlain—and another would be Father And Son.

PH: Peter's characterisation of the son in Father And Son is very touching and not dissimilar to Harry Enfield's Tim Nice-But-Dim.

BM: Yes, a very naive innocent. Peter loved the idea of this upper-class family where Mummy was jugging hare and plucking pheasant all day, and that life was very happy for this person. When we wrote the second—unmade—Special we went one further with Father suggesting suicide to his son. The Father And Son set-up had a lot of mileage in it.

There was a conscious attempt by Peter to get away from the Dudley Moore stuff he had done, although he always loved that.

He resented Dudley's popularity because he felt it was on a shallow basis—a dreadful film like *10*. It wasn't jealousy—and I don't want to malign Peter—but he did think that what Dudley was doing was wrong because he considered Dudley a very talented comedian and was selling himself short for stardom. But Peter, rather blindly, didn't realise that Dudley's comedic talent was very much linked to Peter's. It was like Morecambe and Wise—'Were they ever without each other?' Well, Peter was definitely still Peter without Dudley, but Dudley in terms of comedy...? Peter had a large affection for Dudley and very much wanted him to be in the follow up to *Peter Cook & Co*. That wasn't a ploy to sell the show to America where Dudley was riding the wave of success, but to say to Dudley, 'Look, you can still do very funny things. Why *don't* you? And do them with *me*?'

PH: Dudley's films invariably have a sentimental streak a mile wide, which must've gotten Peter's back up.

BM: Peter also resented anyone making money out of such dross. Even so, Peter wasn't averse to doing the same thing. He vowed he would never do a commercial but then went and did one for Barclays Bank. He would never talk about it. He was greatly embarrassed having done it because he needed money at the time—it's the old story. Because it limited his comic persona and I think that's always a problem. That's what I wanted to make sure I was never going to do when I was script-associating with him, to limit his scope. I was always on the lookout for when the tangent he was going off into was more valuable than the original premise; then we'd go with the tangent and rewrite the beginning. The Bee Plumber was developed in that sort of way. I remember the Vegetable one, Peter had—

PH: Er, the Vegetable one?

BM: The Vegetable sketch?

PH [*totally flummoxed*]: ... Vegetables...?

BM: The sketch in the shop?

PH: OHHH! Oh right! The village shop with Paula Wilcox as the doctor's wife on holiday and Rowan Atkinson as the sinister Cornish shopkeeper. Very creepy scene.

BM: Yes, Peter and I called it *Vegetables*. Originally it started with Peter going [*Cornish accent:*] 'Some noice... *potatoes*... And 'ow are you off for... *carrots*?' That came about because—I don't think he had a house in the country, did he?—but he would sometimes venture out there to see his legion of wives. He didn't like the country much. He was like Woody Allen. He'd go out and tolerate it but he hated it and found everyone in the countryside mysterious. He thought the way people would say something as innocuous as 'Good morning' was absolutely *loaded* with mysteriousness or murderous intent or bestiality or something untoward...

PH: So Peter would've played the shopkeeper?

BM: Yes, but for Humphrey Barclay's insistence on guests, and Rowan was up-and-coming with *Not The Nine O'Clock News* and so on. But it wasn't just Humphrey, it was to do with Peter's acting being somewhat limited. He's great at Mad Major parts and so on, and he probably realised his limitations. But he was happy to let other people take centre stage, so long as he had the choicest roles. He was meant to play the man in the Railway Carriage sketch but that ended up going to Terry Jones.

PH: That's weird, because, if you see it, a strange, droning man sitting opposite a city gent and going on about 'Are you gay?', it'd be naturally assumed Peter would play the stranger. I mean, Rowan Atkinson plays that character as a kind of Son Of E.L. Wisty.

BM: Yes he does and that's why Peter didn't want to do it, because it would've turned into Wisty. But, er, we had a sketch that wasn't broadcast, called Publisher. Terry Jones plays a book publisher and

Peter is Streeb-Greebling. Terry Jones was very bad in it. [*Laughter*] As Terry is in quite a lot of things! Anyway, Streeb-Greebling's in his deer-stalker hat, moustache and tweeds, and he comes to see a publisher about a book. He had this idea for a book. It was all about a man's very pathetic attempt to sell a book about nothing. He says, 'Some of it will take place in Europe, I don't know *where* in Europe, er, maybe somewhere like Bruges. I've never actually been to Bruges but that doesn't matter; the wife's got a book on the Bruges tapestries so that'll be handy for the background research... I'll throw in a bit of sex. A chap says, "Hello, I fancy you, I'll go to bed with you", that sort of thing.'

PH: How was Terry Jones so bad?

BM: He was over-acting. Mugging. He'd be like [*screeching Terry Jones impression:*] 'WELL, WHAT'S THIS BOOK GOING TO BE *ABOUT*?' It was like Mandy from *Life Of Brian*, you know? Peter'd go, 'It's got a murder in it.'—'Ooh, a *murder*?'—'Well, it *needn't* have a murder in it. He might die naturally.' So it was all about a man trying to sell a book that he hadn't given any real thought to at all, had no idea what it was going to be about, but was *terribly keen* to get an advance. [*Laughter*] I haven't got a video of that but I do have the handwritten sketch we did whilst drinking four bottles of Frascati. It's about an alien who pops out of one of those Space Invader machines they used to have in pubs. He comes from the planet Gluton... where they marry slugs. It's about seventeen pages long and not really very good and it should've only been three minutes long. Seventeen pages of script would equal about twenty minutes or more. Therefore it was totally unusable.

PH: *Peter Cook & Co* was Peter's first collection of new scripted sketches since 1971. After the sketches were written, did Peter have any doubts about the quality of the material or his ability to perform it?

BM: No, he actually queried *after* we made it. Typical of Peter. But no worries whilst doing it. He was happy and into learning his lines. In fact, I've just delved into my 1980 diary and saw an entry about the early rehearsals: 'Nobody knows their lines except Peter.' Which isn't what people might expect of Peter. People may get the impression that he didn't know his lines but *he would* because he'd always be looking for a better line. He was worried about the New York cabbie scenes when we shot it. It took two days, and he was very bad-tempered, which was rare. You'd seen him bad-tempered about politicians and idiots. Normally, he's wonderful with everybody around him but I think he was wearing difficult make-up—cropped hair, buzzcut wig—and was worried about losing his accent. His New York accent was great. But he was concerned about his accent. Plus his acting alone. He's always at his best when he's interacting with someone. I would get as close to him as possible without getting into shot so as he had someone to act to.

We did the cabbie stuff straight after the other filmed sketches—we hadn't yet taped the TV studio stuff—but he was nervous knowing that in a week's time he was going to bear a huge weight on his shoulders. Every comedy writer and performer goes through the same scenario, wanting to back out and cancel, thinking it's all rubbish. It's the fear that all the writing and improvisation sessions, hilarious though they may be in private, may just not make good television viewing. And Peter was constantly refining, rewriting, looking for a better phrase or going off on curves because of something he read in the papers that morning.

He always knew precisely what was in the papers and on TV and who said what, and a lot of his references—unless you had read a lot of papers, too—you just wouldn't know. But he knew that enough people out there would pick up his obscure references. Peter wanted to appeal to everyone, not just to Oxbridge graduates... I think he was happy when we went in to the editing. But comedic speed is not the same as what you film, and Peter had a few doubts about the director's ability to get the right comedic pace. He feared the director was taking it too slow.

PH: Is that how you feel about the show now? Too slow?

BM: Yeah. Too slow *now*, but maybe then it seemed OK. I mean, I always liked the Neville Chamberlain Out-Takes Of History but, seeing it again, I found it went on too long. John Cleese put in a bit of extemporisation which slowed the flow. Father And Son also went on just a little bit. We were under pressure from Humphrey to come up with endings for sketches, and so that sketch is a leisurely, silly piece with an ending *imposed* on it which I don't think Peter was happy with. I think he cared more about the content in what happened before. Having the sketch end with a bikini-clad girl being thrown into a river is very Dick Emery-type territory. Milligan and the Pythons could get away without conclusions but ITV Entertainment demanded a beginning, middle and resolved end to the sketches. Some of the sketches do seem to be overlong but, apart from the passage of time, one is affected by how fast everything is on TV now. Even when Peter did one of his last stints, that famous *Clive Anderson Talks Back* thing, those interviews were kept to a decent length—

PH: Six or seven minutes each.

BM: Yeah, a reasonable length, whereas years ago you'd be allowed to ramble on a bit more.

PH: *Peter Cook & Co*'s big finale was the glitzy rendition of *Lovely Lady Of The Roses*.

BM: Personally, I was not keen to see E.L.Wisty in a pink coat and hat, but Peter didn't mind. It was his character, but I objected on the grounds that Wisty was a grubby little man in grubby clothes, and having him dance around in pink clothes kind of broke the spell. It meant, 'Would you ever see this man again?' He was one of Peter's stock characters who could always appear at any stage.

PH: Hmm, that's right, 'cos all those Wisty monologues in the '60s had his endless fantasising about being adored and pursued by millions of nude ladies. The big Las Vegas number of *Lovely Lady* with the dancers in wet blouses seemed as though E.L.'s wish fulfilment finally happened.

BM: It was also wish fulfillment by the New York cabbie: 'Who wants to hear a guy tokkin' 'bout vegetables? *Bring on the gals in duh wet blouses!*'

PH: I was going to say, for all its faults—and there are a few—I'd like to see *Peter Cook & Co* released, if only to counter the general view that all Peter did was turn up on chat shows. There was more to him than that, a lot more vitality and versatility.

BM: Yeah, he was always more comfortable in bits of costume where he could assume a character. When he did things like that Joan Rivers show and be himself, he hated it because when you were with him socially he would always go into these voices. He didn't have that kind of freedom in chat shows. It is a pity not to have people see these things...

PH: Do you think *Peter Cook & Co.* was his bid for wider acceptance? Because before that there were the *Derek & Clive* albums which definitely brought in a new breed of fans but also definitely alienated a lot of older fans.

BM: No, I don't think so. He just wanted to work and do a show. The BBC didn't ask him; nobody in the BBC thought, 'Let's get Cook in'—because they presumed that, as he'd split with Dudley, there wouldn't be any more *Not Only But Also*s. He wasn't looking for wider acceptance. He loved to write and perform, and when LWT said, 'Do you wanna do a show?' he said, 'Yes'. There was no conscious bid on his part to be widely accepted because he was going to be himself come-what-may. It may have been in the minds of LWT which may explain the *Lovely Lady* finale. It was Peter's idea to do a song-and-dance Busby Berkeley thing, and Paul Smith—the director—wanted to, too. It was intended to be more spoof-ish but it ended up looking like a very tedious Black And White Minstrels routine...Were there any other sketches?

PH: Errr... The Amnesiac*s*.

BM: Oh, The Amnesiacs!

PH: You'd forgotten it.

BM: Totally skipped my brain, that. The lovely thing about The Amnesiacs, which was Peter slumped in front of the telly and never looking at his wife, Beryl Reid, at the ironing board, and behind them there's their son, Robert Longden, getting more and more irritated by them getting everything wrong. Peter had this idea of a family who can't remember much and wanted them to get all confused. I told him about when I was in a pub one day when these two blokes started up: 'Oh, I saw George the other day'—'Oh yeah? What, in Finchley?'—'George don't live in Finchley, he lives down in Camden Town'—'Oh yeah, right, with his Greek wife'—'He ain't got a Greek wife, he's with that Irish girl'. And this kept going on and I was going to say, 'Have you two ever met?' I recall telling Peter about this and I thought they would conclude with, 'Who are you, then?'—'I've no idea'. When we started writing, Peter would say, 'Oh, who was that man in that series?', and I'd be, 'Was that the, er...?' Then Peter says, 'Wait a minute! Are you acting or do you not know?' I'd say, 'Er, I don't know', and he'd say, 'Neither do I'. 'Oh, you weren't acting!' What we had to do was raise our pencil if we actually didn't know what we were talking about, as opposed to if we were acting that we didn't know. Then we'd keep our pencils down. But we fell about when he did that bit about John Mills as the mad goblin in *Ryan's Daughter*: 'He got an Oscar for his goblin'. We threw that in thinking we'd never get away with it. But we had to mention John Mills' portrayal of a village idiot because it was so over-the-top and appalling.

The other name that comes up is Dom Mintoff, who was Prime

Minister of Malta, because I was married to his daughter and I told Peter I was once introduced to someone as, 'This is Bernard, he's married to the President of Gibraltar'. Peter put that in because he loved to have a reference that would mean something to me, and he loved the name Dom Mintoff. And the Amnesiacs getting little John Mills mixed up with Freddie Mills. Freddie Mills was a boxer who'd turn up on *6.5 Special*—

PH: A sort of Frank Bruno celebrity boxer for your generation?

BM: Yeah, he was a white Frank Bruno. [*American Deep South negro accent:*] 'Unlike Blind Willy Lemon! Blind Willy Lemon wasn't black, he wasn't no colour! He wasn't black, white, grey, didn't care what colour he was. That's how cool he was!' Peter used to do Blind Willy Lemon for his daughters, apparently. 'Used ta drive fo' Ray Charles!' Going back to that recorded episode, a Blind Willy Lemon was taped but, very unfortunately, it couldn't be used. The make-up was brilliant apart from a tiny little bit round the neck which was still white and you could see it. Therefore it was deemed unacceptable for transmission. Peter was supposed to be black. Now we have the technology to fix that, but not then. We didn't have the Paintbox facility to doctor it so it was cheaper to just leave it out. Peter was furious. In the sketch, he put this Coke bottle to his face and stuck the straw up his nose and snorted. Something I've seen lesser comedians do since. He was sitting on a veranda in the Deep South but was actually on the river where we filmed Father And Son; there were these houses on stilts which, filmed from the right angle, looked like the Deep South. He used to go into Blind Willy quite a bit...

Peter Cook & Co received pretty positive reviews—and we enjoyed doing it—and that's why we were then asked eventually to do another one.

PH: The first draft script of which is dated February 1984.

BM: Yes, and it includes a sketch we had written a year before for a charity show for Humphrey Barclay's, er...I have to go a circuitous route to get to this: Who wrote *Salad Days*?

PH: Julian Slade.

BM: Right. Julian Slade is Humphrey's cousin. Julian's brother is Adrian Slade. Adrian Slade was a prospective Liberal candidate for somewhere in South London, and was found by the Conservatives to have misappropriated something like two shillings and six-pence—he hadn't added his election expenses figures up right. I've forgotten the legalese but he was taken to court for putting in false financial returns. He tried to defend himself but it cost £40,000 which he didn't have. So Humphrey produced and directed a fund-raiser in Drury Lane, called *An Evening In Court*. I was assistant producer/director and we got Peter and Cleese to do a wonderful sketch Peter and I wrote called Inalienable Rights. It was Peter going on about the Queen tucking into a nice bit of swan and 'the Queen owns all the swans... and vice-versa'. I remember rehears-ing it with Peter and with Cleese, when Cleese wasn't hobnobbing with [Liberal Party leader] David Steel.

PH: Was it televised?

BM: No. They wanted to film it but Cleese felt he'd been ripped off with *The Secret Policeman's Ball* and so wouldn't allow it.

PH: But that was a charity gig! You're not supposed to profit... But, anyway, let's talk about the projected follow-up to *Peter Cook & Co*.

BM: Barclay spoke to HBO in America—they showed classy British dramas and the Python shows. HBO broke the Pythons in the US by showing the BBC shows. Humphrey said to them, 'We can do a show with Peter', and showed them *Peter Cook & Co*. They said, 'Yeah, we'd love to do Peter's view of England or America'—I can't remember which. They wanted a quirky view of one of the countries, so we were asked to write that and we said yes. But, discussing it, we thought it wasn't a rich area. Too old-fashioned. It's such a terrible, clinging title—'And now my view of the tourist industry' or 'Now my view of Parliament'. It seemed too tired and too pat.

So we told Humphrey we didn't want to do that, we'd rather just do another show but this time tighter and with more reprises, links, giving it a more cohesive flow. We wrote another Father And Son and a sketch about Ancient Britons when the Romans left after 300 years. I'd read how the Ancient Brits had just gone and taken the Roman buildings with their heating systems and baths and pulled them down. They didn't think of moving in to them. They'd destroy them in a 'So there! We've shown them!' spirit. Then it's, 'Come on, lads, back to the mud hut!'...We learned from the 1980 show to sharpen the material more.

PH: Reading through this draft script to *Cook For One Hour*, I think the sketches are more concise, much stronger and funnier.

BM: I thought that as we worked on it. Funnily enough, Peter wasn't in good nick when we wrote it. He was going through marital problems with Judy. Judy was sometimes in the country and sometimes at Perrin's Walk when I went round there to work. I'd come in and say 'Good morning' to her and she'd nod and go off, and Peter'd say, ''E fuckin' said Good Morning to you! You can fuckin' say Good Morning back!' And I'm thinking, 'I don't want to be part of this...'

So we started to work at my place and in the end I realised he couldn't avoid the vodka, because that's how he was feeling. He wanted to have large slugs of vodka. And he would frequently stop working on a sketch and say, 'I can't go on, I've really got all these problems,' which didn't make for easy writing sessions. This explains why there are gaps in the draft script where, instead of a finished scene, there'd be a short note saying what the scene will be about. We had to get the script delivered on schedule and you can get away with short explanatory notes. So there were difficulties trying to get Peter to—not to work, he was very keen to work, but the marriage situation kept seeping in.

PH: The problem was in keeping Peter comedically focused?

BM: When you're writing it always begins with sitting and thinking, and when you're sitting, staring into space and you're thinking, 'What's my wife up to?', it just clouds it. It's easier if you're acting, then you've got lines to learn and so on, but to be creative... When we delivered the script to HBO they said, 'This isn't what your brief was! Where's our *View Of England*?' They didn't appreciate it for what it was. The same thing happened to Tracey Ullman—'Tracey's View Of America'. That thinking still exists. They can't let her do what she likes, she has to fit that generic, overall view that is her in America; American shops, American airlines, American family... Well, we didn't want to do that because Peter's thinking can't be tied down to those narrow strictures. There's not much more to say other than we wrote it and we didn't make it! We didn't try to get it made by another channel...We both drifted. I went off to other things, Peter did other things, so that was that.

PH: What was writing with Peter like when he was on the sauce? He wasn't incoherent, was he?

BM: No, no, never incoherent. The one time he was, we were both incoherent. He was never drunk during work. I like wine with food but am not prepared to drink large vodkas in the morning. For Peter, that was to do with the marriage breakdown. Very often at the end of a working day we'd crack open a bottle or go to the pub. Sometimes he'd be totally off drinking and, coming to my place, I didn't have any hard stuff, only wine. He had a desire to not fully concentrate. He wasn't very good at concentrating for very long periods, you know. You really had to get in there to get a sketch going. But he'd be telling you what was on the telly the night before.

He was an insomniac as well. He was up all night phoning radio stations back in those days. After the script was finished and rejected we would meet socially—he would ring up when he felt happier, and say, 'Shall we have a meaningless lunch?' and we'd meet and talk. People have often said, 'Oh, if only you had taped those! They were works of genius', because you could just pick a news item and he could free-associate, and we'd assume characters. But I would never have wanted to tape those because they were Meaningless Lunches. If it was taped, it would have meaning. But they were funny and very warm and I think I enjoyed them more than trying to extract work out of him.

He loved the fun but he didn't like the graft. I didn't much like it either but if the work wasn't done, no one was going to pay us.

PH: So, let's talk about the script to the unmade show.

BM: I loved doing the Globnik sketch which linked the whole show.

PH: Yes, Professor Globnik—previously the world's numero uno on ants is now the leading authority on humour, saying every joke in the world was originally made up by the German duo Fritz and Boris.[4]

BM: Yes, very good: Germans have the greatest sense of humour. And I really like Art, with the two old ladies whining on about dead artists, and the Ancient Britons one.

---

4 He actually performed some of it on Clive James' show—*Saturday Night Clive*—in 1990. He said, 'Ve haff in Dusseldorf ze Museum Das Europeane-scherhahamachengeschidstadt where we study what makes things funny. Like the man vandering along the street and he slips on a banana skin—falls over—Ka-put!—bang bang. What iss so funny about zat? Is it funnier if two men walk along and zere are two banana skins? Is zat twice as funny or half as funny? What if ten people vander down ze street? Is that mass ha-ha-machen? And, what is ze banana skin doing on zer street in ze first place? In Germany we put banana skins in a lidder basket. So zer joke in Germany is: A man vanders along zer street, jumps in to ze lidder basket. And zat is a good joke, you see?'

PH: And there's a Hawaii 5-0 sketch where Peter plays Jack Lord as Steve McGarrett. It's kind of reminiscent of the Neville Chamberlain Out-Takes Of History thing where Neville continually flunks his speech. Here, though, Jack Lord keeps screwing up his 'Book 'em, Danno' line. Was that a deliberate move to write something that would be easily accessible to American viewers?

BM: It was. We couldn't use a figure like Chamberlain in a US show because Americans don't even know their own politicians. There were two reasons for choosing Jack Lord. One, and probably the stronger reason, was Peter always wanted to play Jack Lord. The secondary reason was Americans understand Jack Lord and know who he is.

PH: It's such a shame we never got to see Peter as Jack Lord with his leather hair.

BM: He could do that Jack Lord stare, too... Actors, when they forget lines, will always blame it on someone making a noise outside. You know there's no one outside making a noise, it's 'cos they can't recall their lines, but you don't tell them that. You say 'I'll go and shut them up,' and hope they remember their lines in the meantime. Actors are notorious for this. So what we did with this sketch is take it further. It starts with Jack Lord blaming a wasp for his forgetting to say 'Book 'em, Danno', and escalates to blaming political upheaval in Chad. It was a reflection on Americans, who would be willing to invade Chad just so Jack Lord can get his line right. Jack Lord was an icon and gave completely wooden performances, so you can always presume he never knew quite what he was doing. It wasn't Jack Lord getting it wrong that's the humour of it, it's the route—the reasons—for getting it wrong. Talking of TV 'tecs, Peter had an idea which we discussed... You remember Raymond Burr, who played Perry Mason?

PH: Yeah. Vast bloke.

BM: Right. Perry Mason didn't move around much, did he? He

was very static. Then Raymond Burr played *A Man Called Ironside* where he's in a wheelchair. Peter reasoned it was because Burr was obviously too fat to move. Peter's idea was the next logical step—A Man Called Bedside, a detective so huge that he couldn't get out of bed. He would solve cases, interrogate suspects, give evidence in court without ever getting out of bed. Chase scenes would have Bedside driving his bed through piles of cardboard boxes—like Starsky & Hutch. We discussed the possibilities of Bedside but I don't think we even wrote it up... What else was in for *Cook For An Hour*?

PH: The Art sketch with two old ladies. Northern ladies mithering. That could be an Alan Bennett scene.

BM: I like the language in that one, where they're complaining of 'being forced around the National Gallery'. *Forced*. The idea was wonderful. It starts off moaning about dead artists and then dead actors, dead composers, and it all culminates in a film with a dead actor playing a dead artist with a dead composer's music playing under it: '*Oh, it's so morbid!*' It seems careless of us not to have pursued trying to get the show made, but that's life. If Project A has stalled and someone takes an interest in Project B, then that's what you go with, and you put all your energy into that.

PH: Well, it must've been Project D or something when you two got together again for the Channel 4 show *Saturday Live* in 1986, which I recall as being one of the funniest things Peter had ever done. His Lord Stockton—Harold Macmillan, as was—was peerless.

BM: Well, he did him in *Beyond The Fringe*—TVPM—and he wanted to reprise him. With pretty minimal make-up, he looked like him. And there was also the Kubla Khan sketch which was two workmen talking about this awful job and reading off a list: 'Stately pleasure dome...' 'Ow big is stately?' Samuel Taylor Coleridge's Kubla Khan poem was the builders' work-list. One idea I came up with was Peter as James Last.

PH: That was brilliant! Peter in a big white wig atop a bus.

BM: Yeah. We were sitting in his place one day thinking, 'Whose view of England would be really odd?' We were told we had so many days filming for a filmed sketch. I suggested James Last and Peter fell off his chair laughing, saying, 'That's it!' It appealed to Peter because James Last is German with this terrible made-up name and rotten orchestra, which ruin everything they touch. So that meant this man's philosophy, like the clothes he wore, must be appalling. We rang the director, Paul Jackson, and told him we were going to do James Last and can they send us some albums—*James Last Murders The Beatles*. We got pissed and listened to this awfulness—*Lara's Theme* from Dr Zhivago—all at full blast with the windows open... We did some filming in Piccadilly with a bus with 'JAMES LAST AND HIS ORCHESTRA' plastered on the side. We were parked in a side street waiting for the cameras to be set up, and Peter was fully made-up sitting in the bus with me when these old ladies went by. They saw him and went, 'Ooh, look...' and Peter started up [*exaggerated German accent:*] 'Hello fanz! Vunderful to be in your country again!'

The great thing was these people totally accepted it was James Last. We also did some filming at Luton airport were we see a piano going round the baggage carousel—and James Last appears on the carousel, like he travels with his instruments. I recall Peter and I went to see a recording of an earlier *Saturday Live* just to see what the set-up was. He didn't like Ben Elton at all... You know how you start a rumour to see how long it takes to get back to you?

PH: Right.

BM: We decided to spread a rumour that Ben Elton was Max Bygraves' son. [*Laughter*] This came from Peter saying, 'Oh, he's just a Jewish-looking lad who thinks a lot of himself,' and his body language was all 'I wanna tell you a story,' like Max Bygraves. It was Ben Elton's early days, but it was Peter spotting that. He was very much looking forward to doing *Saturday Live*, but it terrified him slightly—the live aspect—and also the fact that he was treated as an icon. There was Stephen Fry, Hugh Laurie, et cetera, all going, 'Ahh, here comes Peter Cook—*the god!*' He was terribly worried—

PH:—that he wouldn't live up to their expectations?

BM: Yeah. They weren't *that* well known. They'd done a few things but they hadn't *really* found their feet. Peter, however, had his reputation at stake. But it worked very well and people were very happy and pleased with him.

PH: And you co-wrote Peter's five sketches?

BM: Yeah.

PH: How long does it take to write that amount of material with Peter? Was it all in one concentrated burst or was it in sporadic moments?

BM: Writing for *Saturday Live* took about three weeks. It should've been faster but both of us would ring up and cancel—'Something else has come up'—or you're hungover, whatever. In those days you'd go to meetings with producers and then go to lunch and drink vast quantities of wine. That doesn't happen now. I was at a meeting with writers last year and we were laughing, saying, 'Look, we're all drinking *mineral water*!' We had realised there's no point otherwise—the afternoon would be wiped out. And if Peter was around today, even he wouldn't be trying to work like we did in the '80s.

PH: You believe he could have made the change?

BM: I've known Peter when he's decided to stay off the booze and drugs. He was very much like that when he had to act.

PH: Was *Saturday Live* the last time you worked together?

BM: Yeah.

PH: Why did you stop? Because you moved out of London?

BM: No, I was still in London, er—oh no, that's it: I went to live in America.

PH: You must've forgotten about that.

BM: I went to live there for a whole afternoon! Er, when was *Saturday Live*?

PH: 1986.

BM: Oh, I went to live in America in 1980! [*Laughter*] Yes, that's when Graham Chapman and I wrote the original *Yellowbeard* script.

PH: So, after the writing partnership, did you two stay in touch?

BM: I saw Peter for a few Meaningless Lunches but Carla [Zanetti, BM's partner] and I moved to Portugal to live. A friend of Carla's had arranged a surprise farewell party for me. Peter and Lin were there, and Peter gave me a bright orange extra extra large shirt that he got from High & Mighty. Lin said he went in saying, 'I want the most 'orrible shirt.' They said, 'We don't have horrible shirts.' And he pointed and said, 'What about *that*? That's fuckin' 'orrible! I'll have that!' He got it for me to wear because I was going to be in a foreign country. Peter never knew this but every time someone visited us I took a photograph of them wearing this shirt, so I have lots of photos of people wearing orange shirts for no reason other than I never wore it because it was too hideous. I dyed it and even that didn't work; you could still see it was orange...

LOVELY LADDIE OF THE ROSES

Paul Smith on directing Peter Cook & Co

Peter Cook & Co wasn't the original title. That was foisted on us by Michael Grade. Peter Cook and I both wanted to name it after a reference to *Lovely Lady Of The Roses,* the big production number in the show. Peter played an American cab driver who would pop up throughout the show and demand to see 'chicks in wet blouses'; they eventually do appear during that song. So the title would've been something about wet blouses—*Peter Cook And Chums In Wet Blouses*, maybe—but Michael said, 'No, totally inappropriate for a family audience', so we were stuck with the hardly imaginative *Peter Cook & Co.*

It was a no-expense-spared production. An example: the *Lovely Lady Of The Roses* number was shot in Studio 1 or Studio 2 of London Weekend, which were the two biggest studios. In modern costing terms, each of those studios would cost £35,000 per day. Add to that the dancers, the orchestra, all the other palaver—top hats—plus Beryl Reid in her bee costume swinging about on a wire. All that would have been budgeted at around £75,000 in today's terms for a full day's filming to produce a three minute number. The money spent on that show was absolutely mammoth! The New York cab driver scenes had background shots especially made by a New York camera crew. Lavish resources also paid for such a wonderful cast. Peter didn't appear in a couple of sketches and in a couple of others he let the likes of John Cleese and Beryl Reid take centre stage. I think that decision was partially made out of Peter's generosity: 'We have all these marvellous performers and it'd be a waste not to give them an opportunity to shine'. Peter's primary role was as writer.

About his writing style: The odd thing about the Train Carriage sketch was, when I first read it, I thought, 'This is just not very funny'. However, when we rehearsed it, it suddenly came alive and was very vital. Peter's comedy had to be heard more than read to really work.

The two items filmed on location with Peter and John Cleese were both done on the same day. John Cleese is a master of comedy and so generous in terms of input. The sketch where he plays Neville Chamberlain making his 'Peace In Our Time' speech is a splendid instance. What happens is Chamberlain is proving to be inept at talking and moving at the same time—he's mangling his speech up and losing the infamous paper—and Peter's playing the director telling him to go for another take again and again. Eventually, Chamberlain gets through the speech but, at the culmination, where he holds the piece of paper aloft—'I hold here this piece of'—and it flies out of his grasp—'SHIT!' Then they cut and Chamberlain's saying, 'I think I said shit', but Peter's saying, 'Don't worry, Neville, it'll be OK when it's edited together'. Cue the newsreel which is a montage of Chamberlain shot from all angles, one two-second shot he's wearing a hat, the next second he's not—no visual continuity at all—but there is a consistent voice track of his speech. John suggested the very great idea of overlaying the word 'P A P E R', very pronounced, over where he said 'shit' which, if anything, serves to only accentuate the 'shit'. A number of years later, John and I met again and he was very flattering. I no longer direct television programmes—I'm an executive, running a couple of companies—but John said it was a great mistake I gave up directing because he felt the two pieces he did on *Peter Cook & Co* were amongst the very best bits of filming he had ever done. I was so touched, I couldn't believe it!

Peter was very dedicated to the show, it meant a lot to him and he was highly professional and meticulous throughout the making of it. The filming was spread over a long time—the location shoots, the studio sketches and the day spent on Lovely Lady. I recall, halfway through rehearsing the Bee Plumber scene somewhere in Docklands, being struck down by a kidney stone—which I'm prone to and are very painful and distracting when you're trying to direct a television programme—so Peter took over rehearsals while I had to go to a darkened room and yell quietly to myself. I had been told before we started rehearsing that Peter was unreliable: 'He may not turn up, he may be incomprehensible'. However, I don't recall a single time when he didn't make himself available when I wanted him.

There was a bit of friction between Peter and I—especially when he sat in on the editing of the location sketches. We were in an editing booth in Grape Street and he was suggesting this and that, whereas I wanted to edit it my way—I was the director, after all, it was my job—and if my version wasn't satisfactory, then we'd re-edit. But Peter's interference was only his desire to achieve as close to perfection as possible for this show was incredibly important to him. He was without Dudley and he had to prove himself to be a solo performer.

It may seem strange only one show was made with no further ones or a TV series. I don't think Peter was very bankable then; I can't remember what his ratings were. Artistically, he was all right. The show won a Gold Medal in the New York Television Festival. But if there were thoughts of a follow-up series, we spent all the money set aside for it in making this one-off!

COMIC'S TRIP

Some years ago Alexander Games was researching and writing his illustrated biography of Pete & Dud, but it wasn't always like that and it's certainly not now.

It's the 8th of March 1999 and to gain some outside insight into the comedian's lot, Alex is interviewing the two-legged-gallery-of-finely-etched-comic-pseuds-slobs-blackguards-and-fools Nigel Planer in a restaurant. Here they will discuss matters of great significance and, after they've ordered some slap-up nosh, they'll whang morsel-spittingly on about peteranddudley things...

NIGEL PLANER: Like Michael Palin, Dudley Moore has the ability to act A Moment Of The Heart, whereas comedians like John Cleese and Peter Cook could not act A Moment Of The Heart. Peter couldn't do that, I believe. But that doesn't mean we don't love him. I mean, in reality he was an extremely warm-hearted man, a generous and kind person. But when the close-up's on, there's something in his eyes, a brittle quality. What made him funny was that certain cruelty, that cynicism. Unlike Dudley, who really conveyed a warmer, 'Cuddly Dudley', 'Oh, that's not fair' aspect.

Michael Palin likewise. Reluctantly, I have to admit I've got a bit of that as well—which is fucking annoying!

ALEXANDER GAMES: So we shouldn't accept preconceptions of how comedians really are simply from seeing them act on TV?

NP: Quite so. All the women say, 'Oh, that Michael Palin—doesn't he look sweet? What a pleasant smile,' but who's to know what he's really like? He may be a right irascible old so-and-so in private for all we know. I don't know him but I know Cleese and, although he's so big and overbearing—it's quite alarming—he is a warm-hearted person, although you wouldn't think so to look at his work.

AG: Who is your favourite out of the two?

NP: What—out of Pete and Dud? I'm a both man. Well, you can't choose, can you? It's like Lennon and McCartney.

AG: You've always written comedy material in collaboration so you'd perhaps have a fair idea about what goes into a double act in terms of chemistry, creativity and imbalances in talent.

NP: Hmm. I've been lucky with my writing partnerships—I wrote a play at school with Stephen Poliakoff of all people—but double acts... They're fascinating, they're like marriages, and all marriages have different combinations of imbalances. Morecambe and Wise, say. People generally say, 'Well, what is Ernie Wise doing?' However, if you pretended you had a stroke and you can't see what Eric Morecambe is doing, his half of the TV screen is blanked out and you just look at Ernie—it's incredible what he was doing, timing-wise. He's not getting the laughs. What he is doing is feeding, helping, aftermathing the laughs. It's amazing to watch him kind of echo Eric, and the spirit with which he did it. He was always mindful of the audience. He would bung in a look at the audience to sort of say 'Are you following this?' and conduct—gently tickle—you through it. The two of them worked together, using all that they each had, as a team to get the laughs.

It's fascinating watching Ernie let Eric run with it, you know, and it begs the question: Would Eric have been A Great Comedian on his own? We're fairly certain Ernie wouldn't have been. But they were a great double act.

Cook and Moore weren't as traditional a double act as Morecambe and Wise. Cook, with The Establishment Club and *Private Eye* and so on—he had so much extra-curricular without Dudley Moore that his impact would have been the same. He would have had less TV popularity because that's tied in with Moore and *Not Only But Also*. Moore, too, was already pretty established as a musician before their coming together. They weren't dependent on each other. Their double-act was a bonus.

AG: But what a bonus, though.

NP: Extraordinary. I remember, as a child, watching Peter going on about Greta Garbo hanging from his windowsill, and that made me sick with laughter.

AG: And was it just you in the *Comic Strip/Young Ones* set-up that thought that of Cook and Moore or was it a general consensus?

NP: Yes, I think Peter Cook's influence is massive. I was very upset when he died at a) the lack of coverage in comparison to the coverage awarded to other people, and b) the nature of it—you know, people calling him the underachiever of the [*Beyond The Fringe*] group. Just because he didn't fart about at awards ceremonies, they call him the underachiever. Actually, his achievements far outstrip virtually a whole generation. The influence on the satire boom, on Python, on *The Comic Strip*—I'm not saying Alan Bennett and Jonathan Miller haven't done fantastic work—but Peter Cook's influence is actual influence: It doesn't need him to be there for it to happen. His was an original mind that influenced everybody else and actually changed things. It's so often the case that the originator of an idea falls at the first post and never makes any money out of it.

AG: The difference in this case of course is Cook was there at the beginning and his presence continues to loom over the party long after he's gone.

NP: Yeah, that's true, but when he died and everyone was saying he was the underachiever—because on paper it looked as if he was; I mean, no one was gonna make him Sir Peter Cook—there was an obituary piece on him at The British Comedy Awards, where Jonathan Ross said, "And now a tribute to—" and we got 20 seconds of indifferent clips before cutting to the commercial break and then back to the show and, "Here's Bruce Forsyth and Liza Minnelli," or whoever. I thought, 'Fucking hell!' I really felt offended by that, considering his influence. And his subliminal influence. It's not a matter of listening to a Peter Cook tape so much as the idea of it. He was The Virus: He is more influential than his actual body of work. It's the virus of the ideas, the very existence of him is so outrageous!

AG: How do you define 'virus'?

NP: Peter Cook is a virus because a virus is tiny—smaller than a germ—but once you've got it, you're incurable. The symptoms of the virus? Well, a genuinely anarchic and witty force with a healthy disregard for established pomposity. Especially when you think of where he's coming from—How Things Were In The Fifties And Sixties, do you know what I mean? And—I can't think of the word, but—whatever the opposite of 'anally retentive' is. Naughtiness is in there, and the flying freedom to rant, too.

I think the inheritor of the mantle is Chris Morris. He's the major virus. He realises that in telly now the difference between the news, a comedy, a game show and a serious documentary is negligible and what he's doing is showing it up so you can't tell what's real and what's not anymore. He's a fucking genius, I think—and it won't do him any good. It won't make him a fortune and he may be completely forgotten in five years' time, but he's the virus and dangerous to have around. Really dangerous comedian. Good luck to him.

AG: Who from your generation of comedians could lay claim to Cook's mantle, do you think?

NP: Ummm...

AG: You?

NP: Definitely not. '*I'm just an actor, luvvie.*' If anything, it was a collective effort. Keith Allen has the naughtiness of Peter Cook. Keith never cared about the outcome of a meeting; what he minded about was whether he managed to fuck everyone up in the meeting itself, which was a Peter Cook-type attitude. But his naughtiness doesn't show in his work. He's a movie star now. What he did was keep the fire burning for Chris Morris.

AG: Speaking of movies...

NP: Yes, I worked with Peter for two weeks in Rye and Hastings and another two weeks in Mexico for a pirate movie. *Yellowbeard.* Peter was behaving like a complete teenager, doing loads of things—and *all for a fucking laugh*. He was a totally non-threatening man and it was fascinating to see his behaviour towards a particular American producer [Carter de Haven]. The way he could talk to this producer—who held all the power—and the English crew were just pissing themselves because Peter was so disrespectful. The producer never twigged because it was too over-his-head.

Peter was always very generous. If you can imagine it—me, pretty young, totally in awe of working with my comic heroes, and getting paid for the privilege. There was no need to feel inadequate in terms of wit with him, because he wouldn't be withering about you putting your oar in, not in any way. He'd pick it up—whatever you were saying—and run with it.

AG: And that's the ultimate in generosity, really, isn't it?

NP: Yeah, he wasn't a cruel person by any means, I thought. Who was it I read [in the newspapers] who said of Peter, 'Oh, another person who we all thought was funny but totally wasn't'?

AG: A.A. Gill?

NP: Yeah, probably A.A. Gill, yeah yeah, just to stick the boot in.

AG: Just to be a cunt.

NP: Yeah. And he's wrong, isn't he? Because Peter was funny. I mean, he really was funny. Even in a hotel room. In fact, he was funnier in the hotel room than he was in the film.

AG: I just can't work out why Cook was such a bad actor.

NP: Probably because he couldn't be bothered. I mean, it's such a stupid thing to be good at, isn't it? I suppose the advantage is it means lots more work—but work's so boring! Filming's so boring. Acting's just pretending: 'Pretend you're angry with me and I've got to believe it.' Pretending emotions for twelve hours is so dumb. Where's the intellectual satisfaction in that?

SHIP SLOG

Bernard McKenna on the writing and filming of Yellowbeard

Keith Moon, Graham Chapman and I were getting drunk one day in the mid-70s when Keith said he always wanted to be in a film with lots of superheroes—Spiderman, Wonder Woman, Desperate Dan—and he thought that would make a terrific, wild film of some sort. Although I was a mate of his, I didn't think Keith could act. He definitely had presence but he couldn't act at all. He appeared as a poofy hairdresser in Mae West's last film, *Sextette*, and he told me he had slept with Mae West, who must've been about 80 years old by then. I don't know which is the more revolting—Keith or Mae West. He was never fussy, Keith.

Back to the pub where Keith's talking about this mad film: Graham and I said we'd been toying with the idea of a pirate spoof. Keith immediately said, 'I love it! I'll pay you to write it.' He called his minder, who's holding a briefcase, over. 'What, five 'undred each—will that do for a storyline?' He opened the briefcase and gave us all this money—a vast amount for 1976 or whenever—and had us write out a contract on a bit of paper in the pub: 'We, Graham Chapman and Bernard McKenna, do hereby agree for the sum of £500 each'—et cetera. Keith had a case absolutely stuffed with readies. Thousands. Usually, he was skint... So Keith Moon commissioned a script and wrote a story line about pirates because the legal hurdles one would have had to overcome to gain the rights to use all the comic superheroes he wanted would have been sky-high: Keith's chemically-changed brain came up with a totally unworkable idea. Keith, of course, died before the script was finished but, in tribute to him, there is a character in *Yellowbeard* named after him, played by Peter Boyle.

Graham, by the end of the '70s, was living in Los Angeles and he found a producer, Chris Mankiewicz, who was interested and would pay us to write the screenplay. I went there in 1980 and got a flat to live in that was near to Graham.

I often wonder why I work with people who can be very difficult—such as Peter and Graham—and I suppose it's because I want to and because I admire their talent. Graham at this point was officially 'dried out' and loving living in the states for tax reasons. He also loved hobnobbing with the rock fraternity—Harry Nilsson, Ringo Starr and Ron Wood were around a lot. Graham was terribly enamoured of the glitzy, shallow side of life, whereas I hated L.A.

We were pitching our 12-page synopsis to a Warner Bothers exec at a restaurant whilst, at another table, Charlton Heston was being bothered by two women who wanted autographs. When they sat down for their meal, Graham went over to pester them for their autographs. Anyway, I was two pages into the synopsis when the executive says, 'Cut to the chase! What happens to the young couple at the end? Do they fall in love?'—'Er, yes.'—'Oh, OK I like that, good.' On the way out I asked Chris Manckiewicz, 'Have we got a deal? I didn't notice any decision being made'. He said, 'Yeah. He said he liked it. So we got a deal'.

Warner Brothers let us see all these old pirate movies—Erroll Flynn, Burt Lancaster, Douglas Fairbanks Jr.—in private viewings so we could take notes and get the flavour. There were problems trying to get a cogent story; Graham liked an easy life and found it hard to buckle down and concentrate. He would say, 'Come by

in the morning and we'll make an early start', but he wouldn't
be up when I got there. I'd be losing patience for, by midday,
when he had gotten up, he would then say, 'Oh, let's go out for
lunch; I think the Polo Lounge might be nice'. So we go to the
Polo Lounge and then, 'Harry Nilsson's just up the hill, let's pop
round'. We then visit Harry's earthquake-proof house in Bel Air
where Harry would crack out the vodka or the cocaine and that'd
be it—another day gone and nothing's been done. I never was a
great drug freak and I found that, after a month of being in L.A., I
had had cocaine every day and hardly written a word, so I stopped
taking it. Everybody in L.A., it seemed, was on coke. It was the
time of people having coke spoons round their necks. I took coke
for fun for a month but I stopped because I wasn't really me. I'm
not a showbizzy type, but I was on my own and I had to belong to
something out there.

The personal differences between Graham and I made for some
very uncomfortable writing sessions. A screenplay is a tough nut to
crack and Graham was taking it all too lightly. Monty Python's *Life
Of Brian*, for example, is a very tightly-plotted, coherently-struc-
tured film script because of the masses of research and re-writing
that they all put into it. Their *Meaning Of Life* film, however, was
just a lot of loosely-connected sketches—good sketches, but the
discipline required for maintaining a narrative was lacking there.
And Graham in L.A. couldn't find any discipline; he was distracted
by his showbiz pals, and drugs, and his gay lifestyle—he was
living with two guys and there would be rows and mood-swings-
and-roundabouts. Once, in a writing session, he said he would be
flying out to Australia the next week to make some commercials so
we had better get the script finished by next Tuesday. We wrapped
the writing up and I typed it all out and then presented it to Warners—who couldn't make head nor tail of it.

The script eventually ended up with Denis O'Brien and George
Harrison of HandMade Films in Britain. Dennis and George had
produced *Brian* and were interested in a solo Python project. Chris

Mankiewicz came over and 'did deals' with HandMade. What HandMade wanted was another draft of the script and changes made. I said, 'Well, who's going to pay me?' and they said, 'Oh, there's no money'. Well that wasn't a problem for Graham, who was getting a large and steady income from Python royalties, but it was a problem for me as my earnings weren't as solid. I couldn't afford the amount of time it takes to spend on a screenplay. I bowed out of the project at that point, stating I had to make a living, and so I went back to television.

Graham, faced with not having a co-writer, calls Peter Cook. Now, here you had two very undisciplined people getting together to work on a mutual project, both of whom had been pushed to write by me at various stages, except now I was the missing element. And they were missing from my life as well. What was odd about their writing together was that Graham would start calling me up to tell me how it's progressing—as if I was still involved. Later, Peter would start ringing me up, too. But I was keeping it at arm's length. However, Peter had an idea that I thought was very funny. He wanted to be in the film and knew what kind of character he wanted to play, so he wrote for himself a Donald Wolfit-type actor-manager who led a troupe of actors who were press-ganged aboard a ship. He would be in charge of this terrible bunch of people who would be performing plays on the ship as it went off to look for treasure.

Despite my claims of not wanting to be involved, I did actually see the Cook/Chapman second draft. The script was about 240 pages long! People used to joke about me in my years of script-editing where I would weigh a script in my hand and say, 'That's two minutes over length'. But you don't need my experience to know that 240 pages is way too long. That script would have played for over three hours! When it arrived I said to Peter and Graham, 'This is ludicrous! You can't possibly expect anyone to read a script this big. You should be reaching the conclusion by, say, page 140, so what the hell is all the rest about? Where's the dross?' It amazed me that Peter and Graham, despite all their years of writing, were never hard enough on themselves to take stuff out.

Graham had a very dilettante way of working. In the early '70s he was working with John Cleese in the morning for Python, then with Barry Cryer in the afternoon for another TV series, and with me on the *Doctor...* series in the evening. Basically, he would see each of us, discuss some ideas and leave Cleese, Barry and me to write it all up. The next day I'd say to Graham, 'That scene we did yesterday was all over the place, so I've cut this bit and added whatever', to which Graham would puff on his pipe and say, 'Hmm, very good'. He was earning triple what John, Barry and I were getting, but it would be us shaping and re-working the material. Graham had the wacky, off-the-wall ideas but he needed others to mould it. An example: There's a scene in *Yellowbeard* where Eric Idle sees the Queen—Peter Bull—about extending *Yellowbeard*'s prison sentence. Graham thought it would be really funny if everyone in that scene leaned at an extreme angle towards the Queen. But without some kind of reason, it wouldn't be funny, just odd. Peter could be slightly similar to Graham like that, so their getting together produced a pretty oddball script.

There was an awful lot of the theatrical troupe in their draft. So much so that Graham would see me privately and say, 'Peter's got some wonderful ideas, but they all feature this Wolfit-like character', who does take over the film. I don't know who—maybe Graham's boyfriend, David Sherlock—but someone had to step in and cut the script down. Then HandMade pulled out and it was all up for grabs again. Suddenly I was involved again, partially to act but I think mainly to help fix the script up for the shooting in Mexico—it was an acknowledgement that I had had some input. It also meant I was finally getting paid. My contribution included going round to Peter's and trying to bash the script into some shape with him and Graham, although Peter was still very insistent on retaining the theatricals. I'm afraid it was me that suggested we cut the theatrical troupe out altogether because I reasoned that that would bring the film in at an acceptable length. Had we kept the troupe in we would have had to take everything else out and would have had a totally different film. Which might have made a better film, maybe.

I didn't attend the location shooting in Rye, Sussex, because I had lots of script development work to do at LWT, but luckily that ended in time for me to join the crew for Mexico in October-November 1982. I must admit, I didn't monitor the progress of the film like I cared. I enjoyed the company, the hot weather, surfing and swimming, drinking tequila, having lots of fun with Peter and the cast and crew. Graham was a bit distant; he was involved in a producing capacity, too.

There was an amazing cast list... David Bowie turned up for a few days. James Mason was absolutely terrified of meeting Cheech and Chong, who he believed to be horrendous junkies, leaving a trail of syringes in their wake. I said, 'No, they just smoke dope', as did everyone in Mexico. Everybody! The hotel manager, the chambermaids, everyone was totally out of it. You couldn't move without someone offering Acapulco Gold. You'd walk past a barbeque and you'd be stoned.

One of the things Peter loved was playing golf on a course there which had a sign saying 'BEWARE OF ALLIGATORS!' He was dying to see one and fight it with a golf club.

The whole shoot was like a bizarre happening. Harry Nilsson flew in and found that, at the drop of a 500 peso note, you could hire a mariachi band. So Harry had a mariachi band following him round the hotel playing their hearts out, thinking he's terrific and not having a clue who he was. We were in a wonderful Aztec pyramid-shaped hotel where everybody had their own hammock on their veranda. You could lay there on your hammock, sipping tequila, watching the sun go down—you know, working very hard on your film.

By day, we filmed on The Bounty, where Marlon Brando and Trevor Howard had strutted their stuff 20 years before, and after work, Peter and I would get stuck into the margueritas and tequilas with the worms at the bottom. One night we came back to the hotel, the lobby of which was on an epic scale, and where they always had canned music piping away. We came in and heard the canned music—it was the *Chariots of Fire* theme—and we spontaneously went into Faggots Of Fire, running in slow motion—like the film—but in a terribly camp way. A group of American tourists loved it and applauded, saying, 'Are you doing that again tomorrow night?' As if that was our job!

Peter's role in *Yellowbeard* was supposed to be a Squire Trelawney-type character but it wasn't well developed. He, Graham and I attempted some script meetings to try and improve things but these meetings were 'herbal smoke-attended', shall we say, and we would end up talking total gibberish. Peter had a 'naughty boy' aspect to his psyche and his thinking in Mexico was, 'What does it matter? It's only a film. It's costing some other bugger thousands. We're being paid. Who gives a shit?' That was also my attitude to the film. I knew it couldn't be saved. It might seem cynical my being there and having a great time, but that was my reward for suffering during the writing and not being paid and being generally farted about.

Peter was feeling so wildly free in Mexico. He and I both spoke Spanish and could mix with the locals, who we got on well with. If anything, the filming got in the way. When we were in Mexico City we chanced upon this fabulous cantina that sold Mexican cider, which we had to sample. Above the bar was the price list where, if one bottle of Mexican cider would cost, say, 10 pesos, two bottles would be 18 pesos, ten bottles would be about 70 pesos and so on. These bottles were the size of champagne bottles. Peter's reading this and he says, 'Think of the discount if we buy 300 bottles!'

After a few drinks, we decided to split up in the market and meet up again back in the cantina after half an hour, after having bought the worst gifts we could find. I returned with a pair of the shoddiest, most hideously-made puppets imaginable. They weren't deliberately bad but something had obviously gone wrong in their making and they were just ineptly made—eyes hanging out, bits missing... Meanwhile, Peter came back with what was supposed to be a wrestling ring, but what was actually little more than a box. The ropes of the ring were just elastic bands. The wrestlers were two plastic models wearing masks. The thing was, wherever you went, people would try and sell cheap jewellery, usually a signet ring of a couple copulating. The man's hips were on a hinge so he could be moved in a copulatory fashion. We were pretty fed up having these things thrust at us—'Senor, senor buy sexy ring, watch'—so when they approached us, trying to palm their copulating key-rings or whatever to us, Peter would respond with, 'No, senor, watch this', set his wrestling ring down and have the two masked wrestlers copulating. The traders would run a mile—'You crazy..!'

  Both of us actually knew quite a bit about bullfighting. Not now, but in the past I did follow bullfighting, and so did Peter, and there is a lot of knowledge that goes with it. I know it's a very distasteful sport and I wouldn't go now, but I had in the past. Peter, as a child, had lived in Gibraltar and gone to bullfights. So we went to the world's biggest bullring, which is in Mexico city. We were sitting there, watching the novilleros—young bullfighters who were fighting for their first time and therefore very keen to impress everybody so that they would be written about in the papers as being the bravest and the best. One of them did something which was either foolhardy or very courageous, which was to hold his cape out and go down on one knee in front of the gate so when the bull is released, it will charge straight at him. So he has got to be able to get away as quick as he can. It's an incredibly brave thing to do and you don't often see bullfighters do it because it's so dangerous, but it can make a reputation. So this guy knelt down, cape out, the gate flew open and the bull went straight at him, knocked him over, and Peter jumped up and shouted, '*You stupid cunt!*' The American tourists around us were so shocked at Peter's total irreverence and for shouting the dreaded 'C' word, which they regard with total horror, even more than in this country.

Marty Feldman died the day before he was due to film his death scene, which was very weird. If you see *Yellowbeard*, you will see that a double is used in a scene that had to be altered. Marty wasn't at all well, suffering back problems. We kept saying, 'Go to L.A. and get it treated'—L.A. was a couple of hours away by plane—but he was determined to stay and finish the film. But a heart attack finished him. He was on a lot of pills—he was a bit of a hypochondriac—and he'd have a pill for going to bed, a pill for waking up, a pill for the middle of the night to make sure he was still asleep. That aside, he was fine company. We shared a car when we moved location to Acapulco. We were told it was going to be a very hot journey, a four hour drive, so it would be wise to take cold drinks. Marty and I obtained a bucket full of ice and bought lots of beers to sup as we drove through the beautiful Mexican countryside.

On the morning of the drive, Peter saw us holding our bucket between us and said, 'That's a brilliant idea!', and disappeared. It later transpired that Peter had gone to his hotel room and emptied the entire contents of his servi-bar into a huge bucket. He travelled with Sir Michael Horden and his wife with all these miniature brandies, tequilas, beers, lemon juice, peanuts—he took the lot. When I saw Michael Horden in Acapulco, he was just shaking his head in shock: 'He... drank... the... lot. He drank everything!' After, I saw Peter in the hotel where he was shouting at the receptionist that he didn't like his room. I thought I would try and mediate. I asked Peter, 'What's the problem?' 'I jus' don' like my fuggin' room.' The receptionist then said, 'But you haven't even been up to your room'. What Peter had done was, he had gone and sat in the café of the hotel, which was very quiet, and he must've assumed it was his room—and he didn't like it.

But the day Marty died was very sad. The film company wanted to ship his body back to L.A. but I insisted on escorting him by plane.

I had his hand luggage with me on the flight and I couldn't resist looking into his notebook—we had been talking about collaborating on a script—and all the stuff I read in there was concerned with death, destruction, mortality, immortality, resurrection. He knew deep inside that he probably didn't have long left.

You can speculate why wasn't the film cancelled, but film company economics are such that it would have cost a fortune to stop production. Cast and crew had been hired, hotels booked, sets and costumes made, locations prepared... When that much progress is made, the film company will want the film made even if it means having it written off as a tax loss some way or another.

Peter was quoted in a magazine some years after, saying that *Yellowbeard* was 'a great script that was damaged by the director'... I assume from that he had never read it, which wouldn't at all surprise me. Or he meant that it had a nice binder on it. There were a few amusing moments but it was not 'a great script' by any stretch. I don't think Mel Damski was a good director. He didn't have the right sense of humour. Mel just shot it as it was in a very straight manner. Being American, he didn't grasp British Humour well. What *Yellowbeard* really needed was someone like Dick Lester—he's American or Canadian, yes, but he has that sensibility and would've been more in tune—or Joe McGrath. Someone who could've brought some comedic vision to the proceedings.

NEVER MIND THE WALLOPS

Picture a journalist in your brainframe and what do you get? A shapeless, shabsome raincoat spurting breath of purest gold watch, shunny, with a flappy, fleshy bonce bearing a five o'clock shadow of carpet tacks perhaps? Or an Auschwitz tin rib chisel head, perma-yakketyyakking who, when he sneezes, has Bob Marley falling out of his Peruvian Persil'd nose? Odd, then, that Stephen Pile, despite two decades of journalising, fits neither caricature. A trim, fit, young country vicar-looking chap—'Ah yes. Non-smoker, you see.'—he elegantly strode ourmaninhavana-style through Bethnal Green's streets of knuckle-dragging, flat-skulled crispmunchers, their cat's-arsed gobs punctured by high tar verymuch lungfuckers, to the crumbling lair of Wisty Towers where he sat by the Holy Dragger's ruby-encrusted luxury life support machine and told his tale of how Peter Cook and Mel Smith belly flopped as synchronised swimmers.

These are his words as heard by The Dragger through his customary morphine haze. Speak, thou Press Pass-wielding varlet. Speak!

I met Peter Cook once in 1980 when I was doing a Diary column on *The Sunday Times*. It had a regular item in it about spending time with the famous, doing their hobbies with them, and one of these was going to see Spurs with Peter Cook. It was very enjoyable. Peter was very outspoken, very vociferous, on the terraces. A lot of hooliganism and shouting, but he loved that. We had a meal beforehand and he suggested we have different courses in different cafes and restaurants because it was the only exercise he got—walking between courses.

I next came into contact with him at this Nether Wallop festival. How Nether Wallop came about was, I went to the Edinburgh Festival in 1983 to review it and the problem was how to cover all of these events; there were thousands of them all on at the same time all over Edinburgh. You couldn't do it. One year I didn't go to see anything at all and just wrote about the confusion of people with the brochures trying to work out what to see.

What I had written about the Festival was a quarter of an inch short so the office rang up, saying, 'Can you write a couple of sentences to fill it out?' So I just wrote, 'Why have they got all of these artistic events in Edinburgh at one time of year and we can't possibly see it all? Why not siphon half of it off and have it somewhere else in April, somewhere like Nether Wallop?' Now, I'd never been to Nether Wallop, it just sprang out of nowhere.

A week after Edinburgh I went into work and there was an envelope with spidery, elderly handwriting on it and it was from the treasurer of the Parochial Church Council of Nether Wallop. It read, 'We have noticed with interest your suggestion that there should be an international arts festival to rival Edinburgh and Salzburg in Nether Wallop, and the Parochial Church Council have authorised me to write to you to appoint you Artistic Director.' I didn't seriously think there any chance of doing it because I'd never organised a festival, but I phoned him and he said, 'Well, just come down to lunch and see what can be possible.' So I went down there just for the fun of it and it was a wonderful place. If it had been an Ealing comedy it'd have been perfect. The treasurer had spent his life in Brazil insuring Brazilians—which I imagine is quite a demanding job! The chairman of the council was a man called Billy Jepson-Turner. He was the village squire, a bluff farmer and Army sort of chap. A Herbert Gusset type. He had a butler called Gussidge, who served everyone vegetables but omitted to give any to his boss: 'Don't I get any vegetables, Gussidge?' I thought that was a wonderful thing to say.

During this lunch—lots of sherry, very amiable—we talked ourselves into having a go at doing a festival. Their plan was to raise money to restore their church roof. Eventually we decided on the programme for the festival. It seemed to me the best thing was to have a programme of events going over a weekend combining the best of Nether Wallop local art—the vicar's magic tricks, the doctor's farmyard-impressions song, the Danebury Players, an amateur theatrical troupe who gave a generous selection of an author's lines in any performance but not necessarily in the order which he intended. I asked the Major, Billy, if the village had any connections with famous artists. 'Oh no, no, no. Nothing like that here!' But deep in the recesses of his mind he came up with the name Popovsky. 'Tchiakovsky?' 'No, no. Popovsky.' He was actually thinking of Leopold Stokowsky who conducted the music for Disney's *Fantasia*. Stokowsky had lived in the village so we contacted the Stokowsky Society who were very excited about holding an event in his old house. That was our first event. And then Lynn Seymour, the ballet dancer. It transpired she was living outside the village—she had retired and was living under her married name.

For the record, I was not the organiser of the Nether Wallop International Arts Festival of 1984. Jane Tewson was the motor. She worked for Charity Projects and I approached her, saying 'I'm in big trouble. How do I raise £20,000 to repair a church roof?' Jane set the wheels in motion, got London Weekend Television to make the film of it (*Weekend In Wallop*) and so on. But the important thing about that festival was on the last night Jane was talking to all these comedians who had realised that they had the power to raise enormous sums of money for charity. Out of that, Jane got the idea for Comic Relief which she now runs.

Then it was just a matter of writing lots of letters to the great and the famous, asking them to perform in this village hall, a tiny place made of corrugated iron. I wrote to comedians first: I thought they might be an attraction for other people to come. The first I contacted was John Cleese who said, 'Yes, I'll come so long as my diary permits.' He couldn't come because he was filming *Silverado* but the fact he said he would come encouraged others to say yes. So, in the end, everyone except John Cleese came along. The second person I phoned was Peter Cook. He always has his answer-machine on—'Leave a message'—but amazingly he rang back: 'Yes, I'm interested in this.'

What I wanted for the festival was for people to do things for which they weren't famous. Wayne Sleep, for example, sang opera. He was *enthusiastic*, let's say. He gave it a good go. Another thing was asking performers whether there was someone they'd always wanted to work with. Surprisingly, Bill Wyman of The Rolling Stones said he'd always wanted to work with Stanley Unwin, the comedian. So they wrote and performed a sketch. Peter Cook wanted to perform with Mel Smith with whom he had not worked, I think, at that stage—he had an admiration for him.

I kept vaguely in telephone contact with Peter, during which time he hadn't worked out what he was going to do at all. There was a slight scare when he said, 'Erm, I've had a telegram saying America has picked up my pilot'—a phrase that amused him. I don't know what he was talking about. [*Most likely, another series of his U.S. sitcom* The Two Of Us—Ed.] There was a possibility that he might have to cancel us and go and work in America. Happily for us, it didn't happen and he came to Nether Wallop with Mel Smith.

Nether Wallop is down the main road to Portsmouth, turn left and you arrive at a crossroads. To your right is Over Wallop and Nether Wallop is on the left. Nether Wallop actually means Hidden Valley of the Anglo-Saxons, and it really does feel like that, because you can't see it from the road. In 1984 it looked like nothing had changed for a very long time. Thatched, beamed buildings, very pretty, very 1950s. It's probably got a skyscraper plonked in the middle of it now.

On the day of the festival, this large car—I remember it as a Rolls Royce, is that possible?—drove up and in the back of it were these two—*these two*—who had clearly had at least a very good lunch, probably countless bottles. Smith was sitting comatose with an enormous cigar. He didn't even move. Not a muscle, not a flicker. I was just walking down the lane when their car arrived. Car window opened and out leaned Cook and he said [*drunken shout*]: 'Tell them I won! I won the bet! And we're not performing tonight. 'Cos I won!' [*See Mel Smith interview following this to find out what Peter was shouting about.*—Ed]

But these two deciding they were having too much fun to perform a sketch—which they said they hadn't even written at that stage!—just caused a lot of problems for everyone else. So the programme was shuffled around and they did the sketch the following night. But first they spent the afternoon before, sitting out in the sunshine, outside the picturesque thatched cottage of the village council treasurer, who looked like Richard Wattis, and they sat there writing. They may have been winding me up, trying to scare me somewhat, when they said, 'Oh, we 'aven't written it yet'—but I do recall them working on a script in the afternoon. All we knew was it was about synchronised swimming which is less popular than it was but once it was immensely popular on TV. They were sober enough to perform it the second night. At that stage Peter was at his most overweight and he looked very peculiar in a swimming hat and goggles. He didn't look well at all. But then, with Mel Smith next to him, he didn't look *too* bad.

After the weekend festival, in a big country hotel situated in a cluster of houses called Middle Wallop, there was a huge party. At this event I remember Peter saying, 'The trouble with this festival is—there are *no women*! You've got to bring your own women!' I apologised to him for this omission. Then he said that he'd managed to find one. There was a waitress at the hotel who had taken a shine to him and vice versa. At the end of the party—it was gone one in the morning, possibly very much later—I left the hotel, leaving Peter with the waitress sitting on his lap. I came out to see Lin—not Peter's wife then, but his serious girlfriend—walking down the path, asking, 'Is Peter in there?' It's very difficult to know what to say in such a situation. So I tried to stall her, shout him, but all to no avail because she just marched on. They had a row. A serious row. As opposed to a comedy row.

The other thing Peter did at that hotel was at four in the morning he had woken up hungry and instead of calling room service, which is what you're supposed to do, he decided to potter down to the kitchen and make himself a boiled egg. However, he wasn't a great cook—never mastered even the simplest of things—and couldn't find all the stuff but emptied out lots of pots and pans and eggs and boiling water, causing complete chaos. Did not succeed in sorting out something to eat. The next morning they weren't sure whether the mess was due to a poltergeist or a strange burglary. Peter told me himself he had failed in his endeavour to boil an egg.

Peter and drink... You wonder how Richard Ingrams really felt about Peter, because Richard went teetotal in the late '60s or sometime, whereas Peter just carried on. I suppose he just had to accept Peter because he was so important to *Private Eye*. He was the spirit of it, if that's the right word. You just had to make an exception for Peter, really, in the circumstances. I mean, he was a very charming drunk, wasn't he? He wasn't abusive, didn't hit people. He was just funny. That's how I remember him. He must have been quite drunk on the last night of Nether Wallop—well, because *everybody was*!—but he was very pleasant to be with all the time.

I did meet him once after that, when he was even drunker, and that was at the launch of the *Derek and Clive Get The Horn* video. 1993. There was a press launch 'do' and Peter and Lin were having a party afterwards at Perrin's Walk and they said, 'Would you care to come?' I was very touched because I hadn't seen Lin since that terrible night ten years before. It was a bizarre party in that it was a combination of his neighbours, who were normal mortals, and people like Keith Richards, whom you wouldn't have thought to be his close buddy but obviously was. I remember the two of them—well gone in booze—just monkeying around, not talking like adults at all, more like very young children playing. There wasn't any language involved. They were just groaning and grunching and '*WHERGHH!*' and pulling faces. There didn't seem to be any point but they were having a fantastic time...

THE WAGERS OF SIN

What better way for a huge dinner—consisting entirely of one roast ant—to go down than to retire to the smoking room and have a damned good chat about Peter Cook?

What follows is such a blabfest between Mel Smith and Harry Thompson, conducted in 1995 for Harry's biography of PC.

MEL SMITH: He liked to have a bet, he liked the idea of a bet. I went racing with him, probably only with a handful of cash, but I never saw any methodology at all, although he used to have the occasional winner. I mean, he knew all the obvious things—things that you'd learned from reading the back pages of *The Sun*, but I think the only newspaper that Peter didn't read was *The Sporting Life*. He liked to bet on soccer 'cos he did know a bit more about that.

HARRY THOMPSON: From an expert point of view.

MS: Yeah, from knowing a little more about it 'cos he used to go and see Tottenham play when they were at home—and, of course, a big Torquay fan from his old days—so, yeah, he used to bet on soccer and he used to win. The funniest bet I ever remember him having was on the last General Election. I think he had £1,000 on the Conservatives to get back in at about even money—this was a couple of years before the election actually happened. He was round my house watching the election that night, and when Basildon went Blue, Peter, to the annoyance of the left wing contingent there, went absolutely cock-a-hoop which annoyed everybody to death; he was running around waving his fists in the air.

HT: Purely from a financial point of view?

MS: Purely from a financial point of view. Actually, I don't think it made much difference to Peter who was in, to be honest, as long as he could have a cheap laugh at their expense. I never went to a casino with him, but we've had a couple of days at the races where we all just get completely smashed, you know, and mainly do our money. It was just a laugh and it was another fun thing to do, really, than take it seriously.

HT: What sort of sums did he—?

MS: Oh, you know. Fifty quid, maybe, at the most.

HT: Quite restrained, really.

MS: Relatively, yeah. He never went completely mad. I think he used to go to Aspinall's casino, think he used to take four or five hundred quid, like that would be for the whole night.

I had a couple of funny bets with him. The first thing we ever performed together was a charity show at Nether Wallop. We had bets on exactly when we'd arrive. We were in a limo and it was fifty quid to who was nearest by 10 minutes, and he purposely, absolutely, he was the only person who theoretically knew where we were going, and of course, in order to win, he actually misdirected the limo. I couldn't believe it, because it's late at night, so we wanted to get there, and it wasn't for the sake of fifty quid—I mean, who cares?—let's get to the hotel for fuck's sake. And he's going, 'No, no, I'm sure it's, I'm sure...' You know—because you know there's Lower Wallop—

HT:—And there's Upper, Nether, Over and Middle.

MS: Thank you very much. Well, we basically spent about half an hour piddling around in the other Wallops until he won his bet. And seeing how long he could keep an ice cube balanced on a baby's head was another bet. That was in my house. Oh, it was sort of like seconds, you know. You hold the baby, you've got the ice cube and you put it on the baby's head, and it's a question of trying to keep the ice cube balanced. That's a typical Peter Cook idea, that is. He sees a baby and an ice cube and he immediately wants to balance the ice cube on the baby's head.

HT: You performed with him at Wallop; were you like a double-act onstage?

MS: Yeah, it was a double-act, yeah, so we wrote together—with significant help from others, I have to say. John Lloyd, I think, was involved.

HT: Did you improvise with a tape recorder, or did you—?

MS: Er, I think we did it with pens, really. But the truth very much really is that you let him ramble. As soon as we had the idea then Peter was off and running.

HT: What was the sketch?

MS: We were coming on as two men in swimming caps, pretending we were a synchronised pair of swimmers who were, er, lesbians and, er, who wanted to declare our lesbianism, er, um, so that people weren't affronted by the fact that we were chasing after young girls all the time. But it was just like a huge smokescreen for the fact that we wanted to behave like randy young men. It was a very funny idea, it had quite a good comic spin on it, but it did involve us in doing some synchronised swimming onstage, which was, er... Peter's stagecraft—it's very funny, when it came down to it—was absolutely appalling. I mean, the words were no problem, except he'd go on and make up new ones on stage. That was alright because if he was getting laughs he just used to carry on: what should've been a two-line speech with me coming in neatly on cue became a monologue while they were pissing themselves but I had no complaint about that at all. The funny thing was trying to do this little bit of synchronised swimming onstage, which we kept as simple as possible, including the sort of smiling at the audience as if we were coming up through the water. That took longer to rehearse than the rest of the thing took to write. He never got it right. It's very funny. I've got it on tape, actually, and I look at it now and he's still hanging on by his fingernails to the choreography. Choreography would never have been his strong point, I'll say that.

C.P. KNOWS

A feature of the early issues of Publish And Bedazzled *was the regular interview section "Who The Fuck Is...?" Let's go back in time to 1995 to read and relish once more PCAS founder The Chief Rammer's opening sally to an unsuspecting interviewee...*

JOHN WALLIS: Ciara Parkes, who the fuck are you?

CIARA PARKES: I am a publicist. I have my own company called Public Eye—nothing to do with *Private Eye*—and I do PR for entertainment and leisure products, and people.

JW: How and when did you first meet Peter Cook?

CP: I met Peter when I was eighteen years old, thirteen years ago, at a film editing company I used to work for in Soho—The no-longer-with-us Post House Productions in D'Arblay Street. He came in off the street, no introduction to the company, up the backstairs, knocked on the door and said 'I've got some 16mm footage that I'd like edited'. It was *Letter From America*, or his sort of version of *Letter From America*. [*Apparently something to do with a bloke called Alistair Cooke, and absolutely sod-all to do with* bespectacled *Scots warblers The Proclaimers*—Ed.] It was new stuff, and it was Peter sat on a park bench discussing various things. I don't think it got anywhere because it was just him being really silly.

JW: Peter as E.L.Wisty?

CP: Well, I think it was. You see, there was two lots of film, and I can't remember what the other film was. We said, 'We'll put it up and just have a look at it', and it was just rambling but very funny. So we edited it and he came in for about three days.

JW: Before he walked into the office were you aware of Peter and his work?

CP: Yeah, because I used to have a couple of Derek and Clive albums. I knew those. I think we found them in a friend of mine's father's briefcase when I was a child. We were looking for chocolate! We liked to listen to it because it was so rude.

JW: So he came in for three days?

CP: Yes, then he said he wanted something typed up, and I was sort of secretary/runner at the time so I said I'd type it for him. I started typing and it went on for hours and hours. Ended up about 8, 9 o'clock at night. The next day he came back and it was more typing! I mean, we never discussed money or anything, everyone was just so bemused that Peter Cook had brought this stuff in. He then told me he was starting a Political Party called The What Party, and he told me about his neighbour, George Weiss—Rainbow George. My mother became Minister for Lifts. He said I was Minister for Ladders, which I wasn't, I was actually Secretary of The What Party. Peter was obviously in charge, and George was Minister for Confusion.

JW: How did your Mum become Minister for Lifts?

CP: He phoned up one day and demanded! He was looking for

me and I wasn't in, wasn't home from work yet, so he got on the phone to my mum and she was in hysterics 'cos she knew that Dad wouldn't approve of him phoning me up, and more to the point, she couldn't get him off the phone because he was laughing so much! She knew who Peter was but I don't think she ever knew his work. I came home and she said 'Peter's given me a job'. I said 'Oh my God! What are you doing?' and she said 'I'm Minister For Lifts!' He thought I was a child and that she would uplift children, she 'uplifted' me 'cos she was my mother. Anyway, this went on for weeks and weeks, then finally he rang me and said 'Right, I've got The What Party sorted, I'm going on Wogan!' He was phoning about eight times a day at this point, on What Party business, and he rang and said, 'I'm going on the show tonight and I need What Party badges made for everybody to wear.' So I had to get these sort of school badges, colour them all in, and do What Party logos. Then he phoned again and said, 'I can't go on the show on my own, you'll have to come on with me.' This is two or three in the afternoon. I said, 'I'm not going on the show', and Peter said, 'I've told them, I've insisted that you're coming on the show to talk about The What Party'. I said, 'But I don't *know anything* about The What Party!' Peter said, 'That's exactly right, there's nothing to know!' I'm going, 'Well, this is ridiculous!'

Anyway, eventually I said I'd go and sit in the audience, but I didn't go. I'm sure he went on, I'm sure he did it, 'cos I had to write all those What Party badges. I'm trying to think if it was cancelled. We became friends after that, and I used to go to Peter's soirées quite regularly. He'd ring up and say, 'Are you coming over?' I'd say 'No.'—'Oh come over, we've got business to discuss.' Rainbow George, Peter's neighbour, would be there, and about ten other people. Nobody I knew. Nothing to do with The What Party, people I'd never seen before, and never saw again. They would just be passers by, I'm sure. There was usually the three of us, drinking and eating.

I was only 18 at the time. I was commuting. I had to get the train back to Reigate in Surrey. Peter would send a car to pick me up, and I'd go out and it would be 'Peter said, can you go over?' He'd get the car to take me home 'cos it was late at night and I had no way of getting there. I think my parents were very cross though because Peter would phone in the morning, for no reason whatsoever. Mum was going, 'What on earth is Peter Cook doing phoning you?'

JW: Didn't Peter try and get The What Party on TVAM?

CP: Peter was trying to get on the programme and they wouldn't have him on. Peter said, 'Go round there and try and get The What Party on.' I'd never worked with TV at all at this point, but he said, 'Oh never mind that, just go, alright!' So he got a car and George and I went down there. We spoke to the security guards, saying, 'We've got to get this programme on tomorrow morning'. We stood around and no one came to see us. After about twenty minutes we went back. There was no way they were having it, so we never got on.

The other thing he used to make me do was, if something he didn't like was on TV, he used to make me and whoever else was there call up the duty officer and register huge complaints. He had two phones, for incoming and outgoing calls. He used to put on a voice, ring up and really let rip, then he'd get me and George, and we'd all be somebody different. We'd sit there endlessly—about eighteen calls sometimes! He had all the duty officers' numbers, all of them. Like the Sven stuff, it was the same sort of thing. You know about his TV fascination. Peter would watch TV all night long and he'd know everything that was going on, and he'd read every single paper every day. There were lots of things like that, things he was making George and me do, and we were saying, 'We don't want to!'

JW: So you were a regular visitor to Peter's house in the early '80s.

CP: On a few occasions I'd go to the house and it would be such a mess, I'd just start tidying it up. He used to have this beautiful Tiffany lamp, and a chair in the corner. He used to bet every day, £100 a day or something. One day I was messing around and I moved the chair. '*Don't move that chair! That's my lucky racing chair!*' He sat there and picked his horses out on his chair. I came round one morning and I said, 'Peter, what on earth is all this white stuff?' White powder all over the carpet. He'd just sacked his Portuguese cleaner and she was halfway through doing the Shake and Vac. He'd sacked her. She'd just left it, and he couldn't be bothered to do anything about it. On another occasion I went round and I fed the fish, he had these lovely fish round the back, and he turned the light on outside and music started blaring out. He'd rigged it up. I said, 'Where are all the fish flakes?'—which Peter said he had imported from America—and he said, 'I got so hungry last night that I ate them.'

You could never sit on a chair 'cos it was always piled up with newspapers. One time Peter threw this radio to me, there was a few of us there, and I said, 'What are you doing?' He said, 'Playing catch the radio. Let's see who drops it'; this big heavy radio.

JW: Do you think he was bored?

CP: Yeah, there was probably a lull in the conversation for about two seconds. Hitting golf balls into cups was a great hobby, just endlessly. If I had dinner at his house, we used to send out. Peter used to tell them to bring food from the Italian restaurant on the corner.

JW: That'd be La Sorpresa?

CP: Peter never knew how to operate any cooker. I offered to warm up some croissants I'd bought him one day for breakfast: 'I've no idea, you sort it out.'

JW: What about drinking and drugs?

CP: Well he wasn't sniffing Shake and Vac, that's for sure.

JW: Or if he was he was spilling a lot. Between this time and the time of the *Derek & Clive Get The Horn* video launch, in September 1993, did you keep in touch?

CP: We kept in touch for about two years, then I moved jobs and didn't give Peter my number, so we lost touch for a while. Then I met him again. One of our clients, PolyGram—we used to do all their public relations—they phoned and said, 'Do you know anything about Derek and Clive? Do you know Pete and Dud?' I said I knew Dud through [his TV series] *Orchestra* and I knew Peter Cook of old. Then they said, 'We're having lunch with Peter Cook in two days' time. Will you come and see him?' I said 'Yeah', but I didn't think Peter would remember me. It had been about five or six years. I walked in and he went, 'Hello, red fluffy jumper'. I used to have this tiny Mohair jumper, very trendy now, he used to love it, and I remember him saying at the time of the Wogan thing, 'Don't forget to wear your red fluffy jumper'. It was really funny, we had a long lunch and got no work done. Talking about things. From then on we saw each other a lot.

JW: So what was your job from then on?

CP: My job was to get Dudley involved, which was difficult but we managed it eventually. Dud came in and did some P.R. at the beginning of the week, then Peter, and then on the Thursday night we had the launch party, which was, I've got to say, one of the best showbiz parties ever. Peter was looking for a funny venue, and we spent days going round. We found a working men's club (Cobden Working Men's Club) and it was, 'This is *it*, this is *Peter*!' You had to have been a resident of the Kensal area for something like 100 years to get membership to this place! The party was upstairs, and the old men, all about sixty or seventy, sitting round the downstairs bar with a quiet jukebox playing, then suddenly Peter and all these people piled through the door. Aaah! Singing and dancing, Dave Stewart, The Stones, sportsmen, everything, and the old men were sitting there going, 'What the hell is going on?'

The guest list for that party, we had like 53 'top flight celebs'. The Stones turned up, Messrs Richards and Wood, with wives, every comedian in the world was there. Jonathan Miller, Alan Bennett, I think, everybody was there. Lin worked on the list, a lot of it was Lin's input. The pictures from that party are the best I've ever seen of Peter. Peter was happy. He was really pleased about the video, it was out, and more importantly he was surrounded by so many people that he cared about.

Afterwards about eight people went back to Peter's house, the Stones and that, and there was a party 'till about eight in the morning. It was a great party, and the sales went mad, a page in the *Evening Standard*, so much press.

Then Peter and I did the *Golf Balls* video PR together. In November '94 we did Ken Andrew, and Richard Littlejohn on Sky TV. Took Peter up to Hampstead Golf Club and took him round the nine holes there. He was never a member there, though. He was doing some PR. Around his birthday, and there was a surprise party for him. Stephen Fry gave him a trilby. The next morning, he had egg all down his front and it was, 'Are you going out like that?', and he said, 'Yes, because I've got my green trilby on and it's one of the nicest presents I've ever had'. He loved it.

I saw him another couple of times throughout November, and we spoke on the phone, but I didn't see him after then. When he was in hospital I sent him some red Satanic balloons. It was a joke we had about being a Satanist. We had like a secret sign, like the Red Rum thing from *The Shining*. [*See Eric Daley's digit-bending entrance on* Clive Anderson Talks Back—Ed.]. We'd been talking about Satanists at the PolyGram lunch for Derek and Clive. He wrote a letter about how Satanism would work through the TV. He wanted to do a message on the video, so that if you played it backwards you got this message!

SAMUEL BECKETT DEPT PRESENTS: CRAP LAUGH TAPE

Since 1995, when Peter Cook popped his clogs decorated with the masks of comedy and tragedy, his Perrins Walk neighbour Rainbow George 'Weiss' has been touting his booty of homemade recordings from 1984-7 as a treasure trove of the private Cook expounding hilariously on matters political, spiritual, trivial and sexual. It sounded tantalising, positively ear-watering. In 2002 a selection of the much-discussed (by Weiss) tapes, two hours' worth, have been made public as a double CD, Over At Rainbow's. *Sadly, it is my opinion that, instead of the hoard of crazy diamonds promised by Weiss, we have been palmed off with paste, fugazis. Fool's gold, pardner.*

Past attempts at quizzifying Rainbow George about his tape stash proved futile because of his tendency to bilge out some herbal verbal droppings about 'Peter the Wizard waving his magic wand in Rainbowland.' Much better to approach John Hind, the only slightly less potty journaliser and author of a fascinating book of comedian profiles, The Comic Inquisition. *Resembling a*

JOHN HIND   331

steroid-stuffed Shaggy from Scooby Doo and possessing the voice
shape of Northern campy, the late Russell Harty Plos, John Hind
liberally peppers his speech with a frankly alarming barrage of
gobnoise—squeals, pops, raspberries, lipflappery-a-go-go—some
of which have unavoidably been retained in the following inter-
view.

   The Holy Dragger met John Hind at The Bagpipes And Steel-
drums, a Stratford juicehoose, on the 19th August 2002. This is wot
woz sed...

PAUL HAMILTON: How did you become involved with *Over At Rainbow's*?

JOHN HIND: I got to know George a bit, went round there, Perrins Walk. Then Proper Records contacted me and said 'Will you write something for this record?' So I went to see them; they were very worried about George.

PH: Why?

JH: *WEEEELLLL!* They didn't know what to do with it. I had to mediate and find a balance between what they wanted and what George wanted. George wanted it to be the story of *him*, really. It could have been completely different. It could've been all about Peter and had only a tenth of George. This record, to me, is a documentary, really.

PH: How many of George's tapes were you compiling tracks from? Did you have the whole lot?

JH: He went in there and they copied off loads of stuff. But there's still a hell of a lot of material where Peter's sitting there with George playing records and Peter's becoming melancholic, or falling asleep—as one might in George's company—or there's a very loud radio playing. So, essentially, 70% of it was unusable for copyright reasons or technical reasons.

PH: None of those tapes are dated or identified as to who's on them.

JH: Not really. Bits. Little bits written like 'Bronco'. Erm... I've played it to people who really like it and other people who—Well, I fall into that camp that deem everything Peter Cook does is marvellous. I'm interested in *him*. And the aspect of him as a neighbour, you know, what he did; what he was doing at that particular time. And he chose to spend his time with George. Quite why he did do that is an interesting question.

PH: Almost as interesting, maybe, is the fact that the Dud and Pete dialogues and Derek and Clive LPs have these awful characters popping up, invariably called George. There's George The Wanker, George Riddles the vampire shit sucker, George Spiggott (of course), George Noades who plays Gregory Peck's bum—all these dismal, pathetic Georges, and Peter ends up with a George as his neighbour. Do you think he intrigued, fascinated Peter?

JH: Yes! I think. Maybe. I think what perversely interested Peter in George is the fact that George is always stuck on the same thing. Whereas Peter would take an idea and drop it after a minute—if there's no comic potential there—George would spend 20 years on the same idea. On these tapes, made 18 years ago, Peter's saying 'For fuck's sake, shut up about the Rainbow Party,' but he's still burbling on about it today. Even Bronco John, the tramp, tells George to belt up about it because it's so boring. He never will. But I perversely like the idea of a record with a person who sounds like Denis Norden—

PH:—who thinks he's a prophet!

JH: But I want to hear Peter talking. When I interviewed Peter for my *Comic Inquisition* book, one tape we did in Kenny's restaurant in Hampstead. I wanted to ask him about comedy, really, being a comedian, but he was more interested in music. Sixties records were on in the background and every one was a memory to him. I should have interviewed him about them because each record fired him up in some direction. He was floating off on the memories of seeing black singers in New York when he was there doing *Beyond The Fringe*. But is it of interest to hear what Peter says? To me it is. But whether it should be on record... I mean, why *shouldn't* anything be on record? [*John grins manically.*]

PH: Don't smile at me for the benefit of the tape! This CD, it's just—I dunno... What if all the unedited Watergate tapes were suddenly issued as a boxed set, they'd be fucking boring, wouldn't they? Totally unfocused. Why didn't you try to edit *OAR* down?

JH: It was edited down!

PH: Oh, that Bronco thing! Come on. I mean, you're talking of twenty-five minutes of Peter, George and Bronco trying to heat up a tin of baked beans. Fuck me! A year on a grain of rice is endurable but 25 minutes on a baked bean! You could have trimmed that down to five minutes.

JH: But does it need the 'air' in? Meaning, do you want to hear the pauses in something like that? Do you want the sense of Peter sitting there? I would be quite happy if Lin put a tape out of Peter in the garden, or if someone in the off-licence puts a tape of Peter out: I'd be happy to hear that.

PH: You'd be quite satisfied spending your entire existence listening to recordings of someone else's complete life?

JH: Yeah!

PH: You'd happily do that?

JH: Absolutely. I'm that sort of person. I've got about 300 Rolling Stones bootlegs, of them rehearsing rubbish and developing songs. I'm interested in rubbish and trivia and outtakes, so I don't mind this record being on the shelf, really. I don't mind being credited as the producer of it, either. It's what interests me.

PH: But *OAR* is not a thing I would return to for repeated listening pleasure. You can't tell me when you were going through the tapes in the studio you were jumping out of your seat and punching the air, shouting 'Yes! This is the stuff!'

JH: Most of the enjoyment was in hearing George stutter. I laughed when Peter was taking the piss out of George. That was essentially Peter's character. George pushed Peter into becoming more conservative in some strange way.

PH: How?

JH: Well, Peter's reaction to George's desire to bring everything down is interesting. George is a person who pesters people to do things so Peter spends a lot of time keeping him at bay.

PH: Do you see Rainbow George as the A.J. Weberman to Peter Cook's Bob Dylan? [*Weberman was a notorious fanatic who formed The Dylan Liberation Front, organised demos outside Dylan's house, searched through the Mighty Zim's dustbins for 'clues'—thus inventing 'garbology'—and issued bootleg CDs of his taped telephone conversations with Dylan. Matters came to a head in September 1971 when, after months of harassment, Dylan physically attacked Weberman in a Greenwich Village street—Ed.*]

JH: Possibly.

PH: In that Dylan wanted a quiet life with his family but was being harried by Weberman who denounced him for not being on the barricades and leading the counter-culture revolution?

JH: Yeah, there's a wonderful bit on *OAR* when Peter snaps at George, '*I don't want to buy fuckin' farmland!*' That's Peter being pretty dramatic and stern to stop George from roping him in to some scheme. And that happened a lot.

PH: What other stuff would you have liked to be on *OAR*?

JH: Well, there was Checkpoint Perrins where Peter discusses the idea of setting Bronco up in a box with a barrier at the top of the mews to stop Jewish people getting in. Because it became a religious thing, a sort of Gates To Heaven. Peter had this obsession with Jewishness. One tape had Peter talking about a Jewish woman he went out with and he had bad dreams of being eaten by a Yentl two weeks afterwards. Nightmares. He was fascinated, obsessed by Jews and whether he himself had Jewish roots. There was his Sylvester Stallone song. That's good. It's all about Peter getting fucked by Rambo. Have you heard the tape where Peter's a Samaritan? Peter was both worried about this guy but also trying to wind him up so he and George rang him up, saying they were from the Samaritans and that they had calls from people they couldn't take the names of saying they were worried about someone. It was half a wind-up and half a genuine worry for this person. It's odd.

PH: It's absolutely Peter, isn't it, for him to express concern by way of humour. It's touching and creative.

JH: I think partly the reason why Peter went round to George's was because there used to be women there, 19-, 20-year old women. There were two lesbians who stayed there for a while and you can hear on the tapes that, essentially, Peter is there to see them in bed together. He's trying to find a way to get upstairs. He gives this line about 'An absence is stronger than a presence'—e.g. 'Is Dudley's absence stronger than his presence?' His idea was to knock on their door, wait a while, then go in and ask them whether their presence was stronger than his absence. He wanted to see and interact with women.

PH: Hm, he makes a complaint at the end of the second CD, about how there used to be women in George's house but now it's just boring stoned men yanging on about politics all the time.

JH: Yeah, yeah. But the thing is, Peter is, in a way, talking on various things about wanting a woman like George. Which is masochistic.

PH: Why would he want that?

JH: Oooh, you tell me!

PH: A bearded woman?

JH: A bearded woman.

PH: One aspect of Peter I'm surprised and impressed by on this CD is his almost heroic politeness and modesty in the face of nigh constant rudery. He nearly never loses his temper or good manners, does he?

JH: He doesn't, no. It's almost masochistic of him to go there and endure, y'know, abrasive Americans saying, 'You haven't done anything since *Beyond The Fringe*: When are you going to do something?' It's a tragicomic thing. Peter was heartbroken by Dudley ending the partnership, and what he was left with... was George. [*Laughter*] Is that not funny?

PH: Exchanging Dudley Moore for Deadly Bore?

JH: I think it is funny.

PH: George doesn't get many of Peter's jokes, does he?

JH: George often doesn't pick up on things. A bit I like is when Bronco says 'Maybe George is right' and George asks 'Maybe I'm right about what?' and Bronco leaves a pause of nothingness—i.e. 'Is George right about nothing?' [*Laughter*]

PH: Wouldn't it have been more entertaining if all the George piffle were dumped and instead just have all the Sven calls out on one CD?

JH: Hmm, could've done. There was a legal worry about whether any of them would be on at all. I know George bores the pants off you but, give him his due, would Peter have done the Sven things and would they have been preserved on tape if it hadn't been for George?

PH: Granted. True. OK then, gold star for George. Actually, how do you feel hearing the tapes of George's visitors rudely treating Peter like a back number? Did you think, 'God! I must have inflicted similar hurt when I was interviewing him about his past for my book'?

JH: Welll, there's a bit of that, there's a bit of that. But I adored him, I think he was wonderful. I liked everything he did, really. I'd've liked him as a neighbour. Who wouldn't, really? I spoke with Peter after my book came out and he was quite pleasant about it. Peter's suggestion for a title to my book on comedians was 'Fuck 'Em All' and John Lahr, reviewing it, agreed it was a great idea. Peter particularly identified with Jerry Sadowitz. He said, 'I find him very endearing.' Peter really liked Jerry's last line in his chapter—'I wish I kept my mouth shut'—and Peter said to me, 'I wish in my life I had kept my mouth shut.' I wonder what that meant.

PH: How do you feel about George—who is very upfront about this—using Peter's name and reputation as his meal ticket to line his own pockets and further his own ends?

JH: Well, I see the record as a documentary of something that happened in the past. I was surprised when other things ended up on the record. But George was kept at bay a lot because he'd be constantly saying he wanted this phone-in: You know, going through the whole genesis of the Rainbow Party with Peter as merely a kind of sideline. And maybe it should have been that. Maybe it should have sold on that.

PH: No one would have bought it.

JH: Well, exactly. He was upset because he wanted his story in the CD booklet. And he didn't like me calling him Gefilte George in the notes, either. You know, I wasn't suggesting he was a fishy character or anything.

PH: He smokes gefilte tips, though.

JH: Yeah. I wish Peter's postcards to George were included in the booklet. Everywhere Peter went he'd send him cards with messages like 'Keep doing nothing'. Sweet little communications. Peter told George he would never have married Lin had George not been in prison, and George got a card in prison from Lin saying, 'This is to inform you we got married yesterday.' That was her great dig at George.

PH: Has there been any reaction from Lin about this record yet?

JH: I was hoping Lin would go round and kick him in the nuts, really. George, I think, really wants her to try and get it banned—like she once prevented the tapes from becoming a radio series—because of the resultant publicity. What is she thinking? Is she being sensible enough to ignore it? But do you feel the CD damages Peter's reputation?

PH: Yes, because of the non-availability of the *Not Only But Also* LPs, *Here Comes The Judge* and so on, if someone comes to *OAR* expecting swooping flights of comic invention and unsurpassable delivery, they're gonna be left sorely flattened.

JH: Yes, well, those records should be out. But this record is a placebo, isn't it? I'd like that pointed out—it is a placebo. And in a way it is the real Peter, though.

PH: You said earlier you didn't mind being known as the producer of *OAR* as if the credit was a surprise to you. What was your role as producer?

JH: Was I the producer? I influenced it. I influenced George being cut out of it. [*Laughter*] I'm fascinated by the idea of Peter being surrounded by Jews.

PH: 'Have I Got Jews For You.'

JH: Yes. And having people accusing Peter of not doing very much without even asking him if he was up to anything.

PH: A neat inclusion was the snippet of Peter giving George a quick précis of the Arthur Grole sketch which he performed on *Saturday Live*. It's refreshing to hear Peter amused by the work he does.

JH: Ah, but George isn't. George was off in another world at that point.

PH: Do you think Peter, were he alive and kicking right now, would have sanctioned the release of *OAR*?

JH: Ahm, interesting question. Would he have sanctioned the release? Well, I don't know if they would have been so interesting if he wasn't dead.

PH: But if he were alive?

JH: He might have stepped back and ignored it.

PH: Hmmm. Tell me about this Bronco bloke, the tramp.

JH: He looks amazingly like E.L. Wisty. He's got the hat and the coat and he wanders around Hampstead. But I think there's more to him than meets the eye. He's smarter than he lets on. What is he? Secret Service? Why is he round George's so often?[5]

PH: Why are you interested in the private lives of comedians, John? Isn't their work enough for you?

JH: I was on holiday with my parents in Malta—the Corinthia Palace Hotel—and I was a kid, standing in the swimming pool, my head just above water level. I was alone in the pool—everyone else had gone to get ready for dinner or go out—and the only people left were Ernie Wise and his wife.

PH: Mrs. Wise.

JH: I was there unbeknownst to them and listened to them having

---

5 Bronco John died on Boxing Day 2004. John Hind wrote a long obituary of him in *The Observer*, and a funeral service was held at Hampstead Church, attended by a large number of locals and celebrities. After his death, he was found to have kept over £5,000 in plastic bags.

this God Almighty argument. Ernie was just mental, he was freaking out, really. He wanted love and was really mad. And that was the start of it. I've been fucked ever since. That was the defining moment for me, when I started becoming interested in comedians. I'd collect books of Stan Laurel's postcards, I'd listen to a tape of Oliver Hardy buying groceries. It's the fascination inherent in most men, I think.

PH: You actively seek to get bored, do you?

JH: I actively seek to get bored... and this is why I got to know George. [*Laughter*]

FOOTNOTE: CRY BARRY FOR SAINT GEORGE

There were some who felt possibly, just possibly, we here at Pub & Bed *were a little harsh about George Weiss' release of* Over At Rainbow's. *Barry Fantoni saw art in the artifice. "OK then," we said, "tell us how you feel about it." So he did.*

During the last ten years of his life, Peter Cook seemed never to sleep. He had a small group of close and understanding friends he knew who he could phone, totally pissed or totally sober, at four in the morning and not find the answering machine switched on. I was one and George Weiss was another. George was more privileged than most. He lived a few doors away and had the pleasure of seeing Peter as well as listening to him at such times. On an unashamedly and purely personal level this CD gives me back something of those early morning conversations. The point to remember, especially if you never met or knew Peter, is that he was always funny. No matter when, no matter where, no matter who with. Funny like no one else.

PC World has given its own verdict on *Over At Rainbow's* and the interview with John Hind in the last issue gave a good account of the technical problems of editing reels and reels of sometimes unissuable material. And there is nothing in the canon of recorded sound that is remotely like it. Nothing more revealing. Nothing, in some ways, more ridiculous: a kind of contemporary version of Boswell's life of Dr. Johnson in hi-fi, with the tape machine acting as a silent and uncritical scribe.

Although the existence of the tapes has always fascinated me, I nevertheless shared the reservations of some, including Cook's widow who tried twice successfully to smother them, about making their contents public. My main concern was that George's Rainbow nonsense might swamp everything else. Well, George and his Party feature but in a very limited context. What we get is quite a lot of comparatively mediocre stuff intermingled with moments of Cook brilliance, such as the late night phone-ins with presenter Clive Bull acting as surrogate Dud to Peter's lovelorn, fish-faced Sven. These episodes are worth the price of the disc alone.

But the indisputable highlight is a long and extraordinary Pinter-esque episode, The Comic, The Mystic and The Tramp. It involves George, Peter and a hungry bum called John, a.k.a. Bronco. The Comic, The Mystic and The Tramp is a unique masterpiece of improvised, unintentional theatre: there should be a name for this new art form – TAPE (Theatre Accidentally Performed Electronically) possibly, or Reel Life.

If you know Pinter's *The Caretaker*, you will get some idea of the plot, which is uncannily mirrored in The Comic, The Mystic and The Tramp. Bronco turns up at George's starving hungry and, between them, Peter and George feed him. Peter goes and gets some beans and bread, presumably from his own kitchen next door, while Bronco tells George about a really heavy bloke who chucked him out of his last place when he was about to have beans on toast, or egg on toast, and how in this other place, the bloke there bought his beans from Budgens, and that Heinz beans are the best and that beans on brown bread is alright but you can't toast brown bread, not like white bread, and so on. The plot's key subtext is that George can't cook. He doesn't even know how to turn on the grill. Bronco has a roll-up. Cook reads the instructions on the baked bean tin so that George can cook them. Each line is perfect. The performers excel. Pinter, eat your heart out, or better, your beans on toast.

An enterprising director should transcribe it and put it on stage. It really is that good.

The similarity with Pinter is not, come to think of it, entirely accidental. Cook and Pinter both closely observed and wrote distinctively about isolated people, mainly men, who create their own and often impenetrable worlds. Indeed, the links between Cook and Pinter are numerous and some anorak researcher might find such research worth his while. The best tracks on the Derek & Clive albums are when these particular kind of men are speaking, men who live beyond feeling. *Over At Rainbow's* echoes much of this and is a triumph. The fact that George Weiss led the daft and slightly murky Rainbow Party is not important. That he had a tape machine on twenty-four hours a day, expecting to pick up messages from higher beings, is. And it did pick up messages from at least one higher being: his friend and neighbour, one P. Cook.

THE BACK PASSAGE

It's a page. It's got letters on it. Bugger me, it must be the letters page!

Hello there,

Thanks for another belter of an issue. I especially enjoyed the 'Justify Yourself'-style interview with John Hind. I too bought *Over At Rainbow's*—hmm. I have listened to it but, possibly because George has been banging on about them for so long, it just wasn't as good as I wanted it to be. I agree with you about Peter's heroic politeness, though. It's nice to know that some things are true.

ALISON HEATH, Cheltenham.

Dear Clintistorit,

[...] Rainbow George comes across as a basically decent aging psychiatric patient hitching a ride on Peter's astral coat-tails. The idea for the CD is good but there just ain't anything there! It's the equivalent of flogging PC's toenail clippings. I'm sure they'd be top grade keratin but they still wouldn't be funny.

RICHARD GEORGE, Herts.

Dear Chief Rammer,

At last, after years of squandering his talents working with pure zillionth-rate neverwillbeez like Dudley Nimmo, Christ Boris and Clyde Hungerford, our Peach has found a partner every millimetre his equal in comic invention. *Over At Rainbow's* is the funniest record I have ever heard! All hail the publicity-shy George Wheeze, who matches Cocky quip for quip. Fantastic!

I also believe that *The Deer Hunter* film is two hours too short, the *Bedazzled* remake was a vast improvement on the original, that The Who didn't make one decent record until after Keith Moon died, and black people can't play reggae very well.

LENNY BOLLOX, Ferts.

[*A message of world-shaking significance from Captain Sensible of The Damned now...*]

Dear Scumbags,

get your wallets out and lend us a fiver—the *Happy Talk* dosh has run out and I need to buy more beer.

Your Captain, xxxx

ALL MOD CONFABULATIONS

If ever you, gentle reader, are fortunate enough to spend a day with gentleman dandy stand-up poet and Bard Of Salford John Cooper Clarke, you will swiftly realise that it's not a Monday or a Tuesday, a Wednesday nor a Thursday or any other day. It is a holiday. Fact! This is the finding of the PCAS's mobile film unit when he consented to abandon his quill and parchment and hot-cuban heel it to London's Wardour Street in November 2001 to shoot his contribution for the PCAS's all-star Goodbyee video which he did in the doorway of kinky kecks shop Agent Provocateur, appropriately enough. All other plans for the day went AWOL in a sea of vodka martinis.

So turn up your eargoggles, you hipsters, flipsters and finger-poppin' daddies, you cool cats and hot dogs. JCC recalls PC just for you.

This was about 1984. Back in my junkie days—'My Junkie Hell'—the worst bit of luck and mistiming I've ever had in my life was the moment I was leaving the Charter Clinic in Chelsea just as Peter was walking in. Where's the Charter Clinic? You go down the King's Road and it's where the Chelsea Potter is, the pub on the corner. It's all kinds of blue bloods in the Charter Clinic, you know—Princess Margaret. A better class of waster. I'm in there, coming off smack, and one of the things you do is Group Therapy where a load of recovering addicts sit down and gripe and mither about their situation: My Booze Hell by Anthony Hopkins or whatever. Really horrible, Group Therapy, but you had to do it. I was on my way out as Peter Cook was on his way in. I thought: 'Christ! If there's ever a guy that could've done me any good, you know, it would have been that guy.' We could have helped each other, ha ha!

Before I seen him coming in, you know, they were saying to me: 'You've got to come back here every day for After Care,' and I was like: 'Fuck that After Care! I'm outta here, that's it.' But then he came in, you know, it was like every day of the week: 'Oh, I've just come in for a bit of After Care, as it happens.' Changed my tune.

Fucking wonderful. He looked great, he looked great. He had grey hair but he had the face of a fucking adolescent. A fanny magnet. All them chicks in there, after seeing him, they'd all be falling off the wagon, having relapses, anything to prolong their stay. Ha ha ha! Fucking Cooky, he looked fucking fantastic, man, really did.

It's very rare having someone who's both funny and handsome. Will Hay—forget it. There's only two I can think of: Lenny Bruce and Peter Cook. Every other comedian is ugly as fuck. Comedians to a man are ugly. Because, I mean, if you're going in to show business and wanted to pull chicks you wouldn't be a comedian, would you, because you've got to tell jokes and that's not very sexy. Les Dawson—you can understand why he was a great comedian: timing, great imagination. He has a shave every morning and he looks in that mirror and he can see what he looks like, you know what I mean? He's got that dichotomy of What They Want and What They Can Get. Ha ha ha! There you've got that rich vein of humour. But the likes of Lenny Bruce and Peter, they have a shave in the morning and they're pretty tasty fuckers, so they're getting their humour from a different place.

Peter was as good looking as George Harrison, the best-looking Beatle. He coulda been a rock star. In *Bedazzled* where he does that totally unenthusiastic number—it's so effete. He pre-dates David Bowie by ten years. The knowingness of the guy. Nihilistic but still with a rockin' beat. It's completely rock 'n' roll but it's the antithesis of rock 'n' roll too, in the Elvis sense of enthusiasm to the point of rapaciousness. Whereas *Bedazzled* had the same music but voicing total indifference. It's like using music of one thing for the expression of the complete opposite. Amazing, pre-dating the likes of Jarvis Cocker, Iggy Pop, Lou Reed, Bowie. And he looked as good as all them guys—better than Lou Reed, not quite as good as Iggy, but in the league.

The thing is, he watched telly all the time, Cooky, and that's why I like him. Because I get all my ideas from the box, for what they're worth. We've got the same gene pool. I can only speak for myself here because I clicked into Peter at a very impressionable age. I was about fourteen—1963—when the generation gap kicked in. For people like the Ben Eltons ad nauseam, you know, it's Monty Python. But for me E.L. Wisty was the first time I ever found myself laughing at something my Dad didn't find funny. Because up until then me and my Dad shared the same sense of humour. But he didn't really 'get' Peter Cook. And that was a generational thing. He got the Goons; he got that because it was against the officer class. Any victim of conscription would have got the Goons. It's a very delineated class structure, the armed forces. I'm not saying it's a good thing or a bad thing but generational humour began with Peter. It's a phenomenon, a fact and definitely a generational ghetto humour.

My Dad could get along with satirical comedy but Peter left him cold. Because it wasn't left/right, right/wrong, it wasn't that simple, was it? Cooky had a world view that you come upon on a daily basis but had never been expressed by one person. E.L.

Wisty, like Alan Bennett, is someone who actually listens to what people talk about. And the obsession with boredom Peter actually had, it's actually the antithesis of boredom because he could see a world-shattering importance in the most mundane event. 'Isn't it fascinating that the Royal Family are so boring?' Fantastic. Now it seems like a commonplace, it's a rich seam of humour being mined by the usual suspects but he really was the first guy to tap into it. And he was the first guy to bring Lenny Bruce over. They were both ploughing the same furrow! Lenny was harder hitting than Peter but America's a harder place. There's no welfare state, or fuck-all else.

But saying that, I love the Derek and Clive stuff. The sheer unacceptability of it! Fucking hilarious. That Parking Offence one: 'Do you know what technicality they done me? Murder.' What a punchline. There's no coming back from that one. That's fucking funny.

RAGE RAGE RAGE AGAINST THE DYING OF DELIGHT

The 1980s. The decade that could make a country priest bark. All that buzzword doublespeak; Go For It, Greed Is Good, Kushti, Loadsamoney, Natural Wastage, Freedom Of Choice, There Is No Alternative, On Your Bike. Margaret Thatcher's government selling us back what we owned in the first place. Seasonally adjusted figures. People turning into statistics. Heaven knows it was miserable then.

And where was the so-called Godfather of Satire during this State-approved madness? On the golf course, most likely, letting the New Breed of comedians learn the hard way that political comedy doesn't alter voting allegiances at all; rather, it reinforces them.

Peter Cook's greatest contribution to the 1980s was perhaps his becoming a slouchfast symbol of What We Were Not Supposed To Be. The 1980s model citizen was to do aerobics, do work, do working lunch, do sport, do work, do home, do family. A lot of do-do. The sight of an increasingly sprawled Peter, in the shoes of indolence, sparking up another cigarette on some TV chat show, gleefully recounting how much of nothing he had been getting up to, was an astonishingly huge raspberry to the Tory New Work Ethic. He was a merry child, a naughty cherub, thoroughly irrepressible in those states, but that attitude was adopted in earnest in the second half of the decade, after stepping into the arena for one episode of *Saturday Live*: Channel 4, 22nd March, 1986.

That show saw Cook, perhaps unconsciously, return to the source of his creative Nile. His special rider had been faithfully waiting and his gifts to the transmitted programme were as incongruous as they were subtle, suprisingly poignant and pinpoint accurate. He was also very funny. (The input of Bernard McKenna in the co-writing and editing of Cook's sketches should not be underestimated for a billisecond.) Cook's return to his comic roots isn't indicative of a drying up of his talent. The child being father to the man, it makes imperative sense to revisit the places where one's inner strengths and beliefs took initial shape. Hence the Macmillan reinvention, the resurrection of Arthur Grole, the mention of hamburger stands (a crucial totem from *Derek & Clive Come Again* and, further back, *Bedazzled*), the echo of *A Spot Of The Usual Trouble* in Grole's debating female movie stars. Basically, the 48-year-old Peter Cook was suffering that universal malaise, the 'mid-life crisis'.

Cook opening the show as Ferdinand Marcos was a daring gambit. (A week being a lifetime in politics and all that, here is a nutshelled Marcos: President of the Philippines, 1965-86. Imposed martial law, 1972-81. Strict authoritarian rule. His wife, Imelda (she of the shoes), held two govt. posts concurrently and gave relatives lucrative jobs. Benigno Aquino Jr., opponent of Marcos, was assassinated in 1983, apparently on Marcos' orders. Huge protests. In 1986 Marcos called for Presidential election, beating Aquino's widow, Corazon Aquino, by massive voting fraud. At US urging, Marcos fled country on Feb 25th 1986. Exiled in Hawaii. Later transpired that Marcos embezzled Philippines economy of billions of dollars. The crook dies to wild public acclaim in 1989.) Dar-

ing in the manner of interpretation. Had Ben Elton, say, 'done' a
Marcos, his liberal sensibilities would have hammered home the
point about him being a Baddie, thus precluding the opportunity
for any wit or creative thought. What Peter Cook did was display
sympathy for the Devil. One watches Cook-as-Marcos chatting
on the phone about nighties, and the money kept in his pink vault
('next to the porno videos') and one thinks, 'Where's the lacerating
satire, then? OK, Marcos is a bit of a tosser but he's not that awful.
He could be me on a bad day.' Perhaps that is the point Cook is
making. Rather than being 'soft' on dictators, isn't he being 'hard'
on us? If you were given the chance, the power, an army to back
you, no one to say no to you, wouldn't you be just like Marcos?
Cook-as-Marcos doesn't speak of torture squads. That's because
when it's been part-and-parcel of your life for twenty years, it has
ceased to be a lively topic of conversation. It's just another trivial
thing. (Significantly, all of Cook's turns here dwell on the trivial, as
if downplaying his own status in the comedy firmament. Cook here
like nowhere else plays on perceptions of obsolescence until such
perceptions are rendered obsolete. He could imagine a scathing
press review on his Harold Macmillan revival: 'Forgotten Sixties
Has-Been Plays Forgotten Sixties Has-Been.')

John Bird, talking about Peter Cook on BBC2's *Newsnight* on
9th January 1995, said: 'He had a tremendously strong bullshit
detector. For example, he actually liked political monsters because
he thought at least they were being upfront about it. He liked Harold Macmillan. Didn't like Harold Wilson because Harold Wilson
was a hypocrite, in his view. I remember him saying to me at the
time Ferdinand Marcos was deposed—and Marcos was some kind
of hero of Peter's because Marcos was a right bastard... They had
just found this mountain with Marcos' face, which was going to
be carved into it; about half of the face was done. But then he
was overthrown by Mrs. Aquino, who was this liberal heroine, the
tortured widow, and the democrat. And Peter wasn't having any
of it. He said, "Oh no, you wait. In five years' time you'll find

a mountain somewhere with Mrs. Aquino['s face and her] BIG GLASSES sticking out of it.'"

Peter's other roles in *Saturday Live* are more traditional. The Builders sketch, enacted with Bird, has a lot of the flavour of vintage *Not Only But Also*. It's the one item where the verbals are delegated fairly. More than fairly in fact, since John Bird gets nearly all the funny lines. This is Bird playing Moore in both line delivery and in the physicalities; the way he looks out the corner of his eye, the way he leans back—rather than forward—to listen to Cook. Was this an intentional salute to lost-in-Hollywood Moore?

James Last is a surface composite of two past Cook creations. The voice is a modified, less hysterical version of Globnick, *Peter Cook & Co*'s world authority on ants, and the pointy beard and long swept-back barnet harks back to 1968's *Goodbye Again* investigative reporter Herman Hermitz. The physical resemblance Cook has to James Last is startling. (Last, as any fule kno, was born in Bremen in 1929, and became a big, middle of the road cabaret bandleader of phenomenal Continental popularity and zero artistic credibility. He had fifty two UK hit LP's from 1967 to 1986, including *Polka Party*, *Violins In Love*, *Non-Stop Dancing*, etc.) Last's brand of posh easy-listening pop may have tickled Elvis fan Cook and certainly Last is a splendid target to hit for points about disposable culture and the trash aesthetic. However, the state of pop music by the mid-80s had degenerated to such an amoebic state of slick, click-tracked, predictable perfection, James Last could have been construed as Jesus more than Judas. (Obsolescence again.)

Arthur Grole, Peter's pre-Cambridge creation, returns in pristine condition, and the school reunion vibe is reinforced by it being John Fortune who plays the chap who just wants to sit in the park and read his newspaper. It is joyous to see Grole approach the bench, seat himself and sidle rightupagainst Joe Public, blatantly disregarding people's unspoken right to 'some space'. Grole is yer actual Personal Space Invader.

The highlight of *Saturday Live*, for this pukesack anyway, is Lord

Stockton (Harold Macmillan as was). Peter Cook made his fame with *Beyond The Fringe*, partially for being the first person to play a current Prime Minister on the stage, and this 1986 revival may stem from the merest piece of word-association from the original monologue:

'I went first to Germany, Herr... Herr and there, and we exchanged many frank words in our respective languages...'

In 1986 'Herr' becomes 'hair' and the withered, decrepit old bore obsesses about bouffants in the realisation that, since he is regarded as a museum piece, no one will find any modern relevance to him and so does it matter what he says, anyway? (These words are meant to describe Stockton but they could be equally applied to Cook in the Yoof-obsessed Eighties.) Stockton's sense of powerlessness is compounded visually by his long, dangling, useless legs extending from a high but narrow chair that appears to be eating him. Cook convincingly plays the octogenarian but for one miniscule flaw: Stockton's eyelids, by then, hooded his eyes like a pair of flesh sombreros, whereas Cook's eyes are glow-in-the-dark alert. Other than that, an absolute masterclass of comedy acting.

There is an inescapable sense of disappointment, though. Because Cook was billed as the host of *Saturday Live*, the Marcos and Stockton sketches had to be curtailed without real endings in order that Peter introduce the next act. Shame. I'd have liked Marcos to venture down the US TV alley more (alluding to the sensibility that anybody's OK as long as they're famous; as The Clash once yelled, 'If Adolf Hitler flew in today/They'd send a limousine anyway') and Stockton's plans for playing Las Vegas (a continuation of Cook's Elvis Presley fascination). Brilliant though they be, their inconclusivenesses are akin to a joke article in *Private Eye* where, once the point has been made or the potential exhausted, it's brought to a quick close with a (Cont'd p.94)

THE JACKSON FILE

The CV of producer/director Paul Jackson scales the dizzy heights of British TV comedy: The Young Ones, Filthy Rich & Catflap, Red Dwarf, The Appointments Of Dennis Jennings, Cannon And Ball—*these are but a smidgeon of the shows where he aimed an Uzi at a studio of comedians and said "Make me laugh you bastards, and RELAX!"*

At this very *moment (1999) Paul Jackson revels in the Orwellian job title of Controller Of Entertainment for BBC TV, where he has initiated 20-minute smirk breaks for all Television Centre staff. Paul Hamilton was gracious enough to surrender his precious time to allow Mr. Jackson to talk to him.*

PAUL HAMILTON: So, *Saturday Live*, 1986—a one-and-a-half hour live comedy and music show. Who on Earth thought of that idea?

PAUL JACKSON: I did, unfortunately, much to Peter's annoyance when he came to do it. Mike Bolland, who was running Channel 4 Entertainment at the time, had sold Jeremy Isaacs on the principle of an alternative entertainment show. Saturday night was the big entertainment night on the BBC and ITV and Mike had said, as part of our counter-scheduling, we should be offering an alternative version of that concept.

He came to me with the idea and I said, 'Yeah, great, we should do it live'. The American *Saturday Night Live* show was the very basic model although we didn't buy the format as such. And nearly everybody we approached to host it would say, 'I'm sorry, I am not doing it live'. But Pamela Stephenson did it, Barry Humphries, Steven Wright, Fascinating Aida, Tracey Ullman, Lenny Henry, Ben Elton—so you know, we got quite good people hosting it, actually.

PH: So how many nervous breakdowns were you having a week?

PJ: It was probably one of the top three toughest pieces of work I've ever done, under the intense difficulties of doing an hour and a half every week, with persuading people to do live stuff, with the huge legal problems of approving the material before we went on air, a vast studio. It was great fun, too, although we struggled for the first few weeks. Actually, because we worked in such a massive studio, sometimes performers didn't quite get the laughs they should've got and you couldn't tickle it up because it was going out live—

PH: Yes, that studio was absolutely enormous. It looked like there was an audience of millions.

PJ: Right, and there was stuff moving around, multiple stages, videotapes playing. Pamela Stephenson hosted one show and did some near-the-knuckle stuff which caused some complaints and John Birt, who was my boss then at LWT, got very edgy: 'I'm taking this off the air unless you get it together'. So we did the next three under the threat of cancellation until he relaxed and said, 'OK, I believe you've got it sorted now'.

By the time Peter Cook did show 8, I think, 8 or 9 of the series, we had gotten a grip on the show. But, having agreed to do it, he did say to me several times during the week and certainly on the afternoon [of transmission], 'Just give me *one fucking good reason* why we're doing this live'. And, of course, he gave one of the best reasons himself on the night, because when he was doing Harold Macmillan, Lord Stockton, a lightbulb went—exploded—and he came out with a brilliant ad-lib: 'Am I being assassinated?' Great ad-lib. He was a great pleasure to work with—but he did not want to do it; he was very nervous.

Bernard McKenna wrote with Peter most of the stuff and he'd got this idea for doing a film of James Last on tour which was an idea that just made Peter laugh. It was a very funny film.

PH: Do you think some of Peter's jokes were a tad too cerebral and went over people's heads? I mean, I got the feeling watching the Marcos scene that the audience didn't know who Marcos was.

PJ: I thought the sketch was very good actually, but it just didn't get the response I had hoped for. Peter was just so clever sometimes people didn't pick up quickly enough.

PH: In that sketch, John Wells plays a Generalissimo, and he's wildly over the top, yelling his lines at the top of his voice. Did he play it like that in rehearsal?

PJ: No. John had done a couple of shows before but, if I remember rightly, on film both times. This was his first time in the *Saturday Live* studio and what you must remember about that bear-pit—actually, that was why Ben Elton performed in the way he did, that's why he *worked* in it. You really had to grab them, you know? Because there was a fucking Ferris Wheel, giant inflatable elephants, camera crews—it was a big fandango—and whilst he's doing his bit we're setting up Slade or whoever to play on another stage. You had to get the audience's attention, and I think Peter had the professional chutzpah to do his own performance, but I think John—not necessarily having that confidence—played it very big.

PH: Another thing I noticed about the show was Peter works with

John Wells, John Bird, John Fortune—well, basically anyone called John. In short, comedians of his own generation. Was that Peter needing familiar faces to be with him?

PJ: It was more to do with the material that came up. As Peter and Bernard produced that material it became clear that we needed to surround him with players of a certain age and playing a certain kind, so we therefore turned to John and John and John. But they had appeared on earlier shows, they weren't brought in especially as, y'know, The Oldies.

PH: How was Peter on the writing side? Because he hadn't written much new material for a while, had he?

PJ: Bernard was heavily relied upon as a writer. That was implicit from the moment we signed Peter up, weeks before. Bernard took the bulk of the writing weight on and, because he needed Peter's input, it was quite a slow process, and we used every word that we got. It wasn't as though we had lots to choose from, like you would get from Ben Elton, say. From Ben you would get an hour of material and you choose, like, twenty minutes. With Peter, no, we used everything he came up with but, conversely, everything he came up with was good, so you wanted to use it anyway. There were no discarded sketches. I mean, to be honest, because it was Peter, if he had written some more we would've done it and cut another item from the show. We wanted as much of Peter as possible, because we wanted it to be Peter's show.

PH: Coming back to his performance of Ferdinand Marcos... He uses a very strange voice there. The only voice similar I can think of is Peter Sellers' in *The Magic Christian* film, where he's buying a 'hot doggy' from a vendor at a railway platform. It's an extreme, drawling upper-class caricature. I'm sure Marcos never spoke like that.

PJ: No, I'm sure he didn't. The very interesting thing about that was you expected a pretty bog-standard Latino accent. Harry Enfield was on the show doing his Greek 'Hallo Peeps!' and maybe Peter thought, 'I'll go a different way', and it's more rasping and unpleasant.

PH: Oily.

PJ: The way he played it, yes. That was a stroke of genius, a brilliant way to play Marcos, not some 'Hey, me no speek-a-de-Ingleesh'. And since absolutely nobody knew how Marcos spoke anyway, Peter was free to make it up and make him a much more interesting character. Whereas Macmillan, of course, he did perfectly. And two big lookalikes, there, all done on the night. But again, how did James Last talk? I've no idea but I'd be surprised if he had a voice like the one Peter used—that sort of strident Hitler character.

PH: You said he was initially reluctant to do *Saturday Live*, so what was the carrot on the stick that tempted him?

PJ: I think Peter still looked for challenges. It seemed to me, working with him through the week, that he was confronting a fear—the issue of live TV. He never said these words but, to me, he was thinking, 'I have been the best, I am good, this is a hot happening show, they want me to do it, I'll go on there and show them I can do it and I'll make it really good'. And he really cared about it. I mean, he could have phoned it in, you know? He could have done an old E.L. Wisty from memory and a small bit of topical stuff, but he didn't. He absolutely wanted to do it, do it good, and worked very hard indeed on it.

PH: *Saturday Live* was the first show in about half a decade where Peter was performing and writing. And I'm wandering why that was. Was it Peter's sense of being in a rut as in, 'Comedy bores me but what else can I do? Oh, nothing', or was it TV producers thinking he's a bit of a lush and therefore unreliable?

PJ: I think, and this show proved it, that when Peter wanted to do something, he would have been the most professional person you could possibly hope for. He would be committed to the work. If there was writing to be done, he'd get it done; if there was a rehearsal, he'd be there. He was never late for anything, he never let you down. The only difficulty was in getting his interest, quite frankly, because most of it seemed—I'm guessing now—so easy and predictable to him. He'd been there, done that, and never wanted to do it again. He was missing his lifelong partner in a practical sense—Dud was in Hollywood and unavailable for joint work—so Peter was always looking for a solo project.

Occasionally one would come up, like those wonderful [*Life In Pieces*] films. That was a challenge and Peter rose to it, writing something very funny in a very rigid format. And the chat shows, he would be brilliant on them—wipe the floor—when he could be roused. But that would be too easy for him, almost.

So people would go to him with what he must have thought were pretty boring offers and he must have thought, 'I can't be arsed'. Most times he'd just say no but occasionally he'd say yes to something, only to be bored by it, and that's where the reputation came from. 'Oh, he's unreliable'—but that's only because he wasn't engaged. But if you engaged him, then he was fantastic. Peter, though, would never tell you he was bored. Instead he would suggest something so deranged and unfilmable, knowing full well the idea would be impossible to execute. That was his way of saying, 'You're not saying anything that's interesting me at the moment, so I'm not doing it.' He did need to be constantly stimulated.

PH: Did you work with him on anything else?

PJ: No, not really, apart from the Amnesty show.

PH: Was that *The Secret Policeman's Biggest Ball* [1989]?

PJ: Yes, that was the one.

PH: I went to see that show at the Cambridge Theatre. Peter and Dudley together on stage for the last time.

PJ: Yes, they did 'Spiggott by name, Spiggott by nature'—the Tarzan sketch.

PH: How was Peter there? Because that show is like three years on from *Saturday Live* and Peter looks physically radically different. A reporter in *Time Out* described him as a dyspeptic dirigible.

PJ: Yeah, there came a point where your commonsense told you that—and you didn't want to believe it—even if you managed to get him interested in something, could he be able to actually physically do it anymore? I mean, when we thought of asking him to do *Saturday Live* there was no voice anywhere saying, 'Are you sure about this? Is he all right?' Whereas, yes, three years later and Peter's weight had gone completely out of control, his brain was slowing, and his speech was quite often, if you got him on anything but a good day, a slur. And, at that point, you would hesitate to commit to a whole project around him because, in all fairness, such was his physical condition, would he be able to do it? It's a physically demanding game. He could still make you laugh but his mouth would be slightly dry and sticky and dribbly, and he'd be talking in that kind of hangover-y way. You couldn't see him doing Marcos, Macmillan, Wisty and James Last on the same night by that time.

PH: It must be said though, that despite his vastness of fleshy substances at the *Biggest Ball*, I've never seen anybody with such a spring in their step.

PJ: Yes, I agree. He was incredibly sparky in his physical movements, in his eyes, in conversation. Peter was never 'Oh fuck, this is never gonna work' and worried about things. He was always positive.

SATURDAY LIVE EXTRA: MARK THOMAS

Q: So when did you first become aware of the existence of Peter Cook?

MARK THOMAS: Probably when he made *Hound of the Baskervilles* with Dudley Moore, erm... I thought it was really funny. I've forgotten when it was made but I remember seeing it as a kid. There are several bits I can still recall from the film—one scene in a brothel with Penelope Keith, where she says, 'Of course you could have our Roman Special with a free grape', and he says, 'My dear, you don't spell grape with a 'o'. And there's a really silly bit with Dudley and a bloke with these little dogs who start pissing everywhere! There's also that great thing where Dudley meets the Devil woman—she flashes her chest and shows 'LOVE ME' flashing in lights and her head swirls round. It's very funny. So possibly then...

I must've been aware of him. I suppose the main stuff I was interested in was the Derek and Clive stuff which I thought was hysterically funny. When I was about 13 or 14 I could quote it word for word... Most of my friends could quote Peter Sellers or Tony Hancock, I could quote the Cancer Olympics and stuff like that. I was watching that *Heroes of Comedy* and if that had been me talking about Peter, I'd say, 'Oh it was fantastic; I used to love all that stuff he did about coming!' It was the pure, unadulterated filth—and the fact that you knew most of it was improvised, 'cos Dudley used to just piss himself. I thought it was brilliant!

Once you start noticing Cook you'd notice him in other stuff he did. Like *The Bed Sitting Room*, which has every comic known in it—Arthur Lowe, Milligan—it's really weird. I think most people idolise Peter Cook and regard Dudley Moore as this dwarf drunk but there are bits where Dudley is just brilliant. There's that famous Father and Son sketch about this boy coming home and Dudley's doing the dad saying, 'You're a who-er! Nothing but a who-er!', it's brilliant. 'The word is "Whore" father.'

Peter Cook was a genius, Dudley Moore was just very good... I remember the series of *Saturday Live* with Ben Elton—in fact, Ben Elton didn't host it then, they had a different host each week, and Peter was on and did this really funny sketch about Imelda Marcos, and a lot of it went WHOOSH!—straight over people's heads. And then he would pop up on Clive James' shows and talk about strippers. What I thought was brilliant was his ability to talk about anything, and I think also the fact that generally, I don't think he gave a fuck. At the end of it there was this attitude that... 'I've made this money, I own *Private Eye*.'

I like the legend of Peter, I like the way that when [Robert] Maxwell was taking him to court he would follow Maxwell around and have lunch where Maxwell was having lunch, and wave money at him. I like that, that ability to upset people, and I think that was him at his lowest point! He'd been on too many vodka benders. John Cleese said, 'Peter was the gatekeeper to the fields in which we now all play'. I think Peter Cook kicked the doors down!

Mark Thomas was raving to Milly 'Regretti' Shilton

HELLO CHEEKY

Barry Cryer is an incredibly industrious cove, with books and gigs and his I'm Sorry, I Haven't A Clue *radio thing. Very, very busy indeed, so Paul Hamilton decided to phone him up and waste his valuable time.*

BARRY CRYER: ... I knew Kenneth Williams but I didn't meet Peter through him, although he was writing for Kenneth.

PAUL HAMILTON: *Pieces Of Eight*?

BC: That's right. He was writing for Ken when he was about twenty. He told me he wrote the one-legged Tarzan when he was very young and he said, 'I haven't written anything better since! It's all been downhill.' And he always had this strange preoccupation with snakes, bees, insects. One of the things he wrote for Ken Williams was about an asp. An asp in a box on a train. [*K.W. voice:*] 'Got an arsp.' Brilliant word for Ken Williams, made for him.

PH: The other great word he wrote for Williams was 'looming': 'The war clouds are leeeeeooooooooooooooming.'

BC: I started meeting Peter a lot when he did tellies and when he guested [on chat shows]. I've got a big photograph upstairs of him, me and Kenny Everett. Very sad photo because I'm the only one left now. We did *A Christmas Carol* together with Everett as Scrooge and Peter as one of the ghosts. The other two ghosts were Willie Rushton and Spike Milligan so it wasn't a bad cast.

PH: This happened in 1985, didn't it?

BC: Probably. Rory Bremner played Bob Geldof, knocking on the door and being blasted away by Scrooge with a shotgun. I love that photograph of Peter just posing in this awful Victorian graveyard set. A strange time I worked with Peter was a very unhappy time for him, when he did the Joan Rivers show [*Can We Talk?*]. We recorded six shows in seven days and he was very unhappy. Joan wanted him as 'British class'—she'd seen him. And they stuck him on the settee, if you remember. He did two minutes at the top of the show—which he didn't enjoy and didn't devote much time to. It wasn't him at his best.

PH: What did he do there?

BC: Just a monologue about something or other in the week's news. He was very uncomfortable. Then he was banished to the end of the settee, and asked questions that demanded the answer Yes or No. You know what I mean? A complete waste. He realised very quickly that it wasn't working and he, of course, got very depressed and didn't try very hard in his bits. He'd given up on it. He admitted to me he gave up on it. He rang me in a very emotional state one night: 'More people have seen this fucking show than anything else I've ever done!' The irony in doing something he enjoyed least and didn't want anyone to see being seen by a lot of people. He affected not to care about things but he did, and it really upset him. But he rallied as he always did.

PH: So what was your role? Writing jokes for Joan?

BC: Yes, I was just one of the gag writers for Joan, really. Peter used to sit and chat with us during the day. That was when he was most relaxed. He was just dreading the show coming up. But sitting around, nattering, he enjoyed that. And, of course, he came to life when Dud came over and did one show. Dud said, 'I can't do "Funny" anymore.' Peter was coaching him: 'Funny. Fuu-nny.'

PH: Kenneth Williams, in his diaries, wrote about that show, and said to Dudley that it's hard to talk to Peter now on anything other than a superficial level.

BC: Who was saying that?

PH: Kenneth Williams about Peter.

BC: Look who's talking! This is Kenneth Kettle talking about Peter Pot. They were two of a kind, probably, which is why Peter could write so well for him. Because no one got to know Kenneth either, really. Peter was certainly much more accessible to talk to on a social level, I thought, and not *always* joking. Kenneth you always felt was very much on his guard.

PH: How did Peter react to the reviews of *Can We Talk?*

BC: He was devastated.

PH: It must be hell when you're stuck in a show and there's no way you can change it for the best.

BC: Peter was a commitment. [Writer] Neil Shand and [producer] Jim Moir flew out to see Joan Rivers. She said she wanted a side-kick, like Johnny Carson had Ed McMahon, and because it was being done in London she wanted somebody British and 'class'. She said, 'I want Peter Cook'. So they said, 'You *got* Peter Cook!' And of course she *hadn't* so they had to fly back and 'get' Peter, and, quite rightly, his agent asked for a lot of money for six shows in seven days. Peter thought it was splendid until it hit him. We did one, then two, and—oh dear, what a waste of Cook. It's criminal.

PH: Did he get more and more depressed with it?

BC: Yeah, but he wouldn't wish the depression on you, if he was working with you. You were his mate so that was all right. He would laugh and talk during the day but you could tell it had got to him.

PH: Sorry but I've just realised a terrible trend developing, which is dwelling on the failures. When I interviewed Auberon Waugh we talked about *Where Do I Sit?*

Those shows are wiped now. Do you think Peter wished the same fate on *Can We Talk?*

BC: I can't speak for him but I don't think that would have been any pain to him at all! To have it erased as if it never happened at all. Because he was him there were one or two moments of real joy because he was so good but overall it was a complete waste of him...

He got insulted by Bernard Manning on one show. Peter had had a particularly bad night, and Manning came on, looked down the line, down the settee, saw Peter and said [*Manning voice:*] 'You were very funny, Peter, ummm', and pulled a face into the camera. 'He can't remember the lines, y'see. I work every night.' He was so insulting, it was awful. To see that made you go hot and cold. He also insulted Rupert Everett: 'University actor. If brains were dynamite he couldn't blow 'is bloody hat off.' And Everett went for him after they finished the recording! And Peter said he felt like joining in. But Manning picked the wrong one when he picked on Peter 'cos the audience were still on Peter's side.

APOCALYPSE TROUT

David Renwick does the usual things. He cries at wildlife documentaries, he falls asleep on the train and snores blithely on past his appointed stop, he fills in the Guardian *crossword with rude or Polish-looking words, he runs into fire stations shouting 'Cinema!' A regular chap, in short. But stick a pen and paper before him and he is transformed into a comedy-writing colossus, as a nanosecond of his* One Foot In The Grave *will amply testify.*

Paul Hamilton probed David lightly with thoughtsticks about—well, have a guess...

PAUL HAMILTON: The last series of *One Foot In The Grave* made mention of a character (unseen) called Spiggott. Was that a deliberate tip of the hat to Peter Cook?

DAVID RENWICK: Of course. Mrs Warboys had a plotty speech to deliver referring to her dentist. It's one of those little bits of colour you throw in to take the curse off the exposition. Because of its associations it made me smile every time she said it, but it would have been lost on most people.

PH: What were your comedy tastes in your formative—i.e. professional writing—years? Did *Not Only But Also* have an effect?

DR: I was born in 1951 so although I was aware of things like *TW3* in the early Sixties they were still a bit past my bedtime. It was really around 66/67 that everyone at my grammar school started getting into Pete and Dud and *The Frost Report*, and then, of course, subsequently Python. So *Not Only But Also* was very much the cutting edge comedy of its time for us, spawning all kinds of references and catchphrases. In hindsight one can see that something very fresh and exciting was happening on television in those days—the emergence of a rather literate, intelligently quirky kind of humour—but at the time you don't put it in that kind of context, we just found it very funny.

And so inevitably by the time I started trying to write comedy sketches myself a few years later, Cook and Moore and Cleese and Palin and the rest of them were the gods we all worshipped, and that was the style I tried to emulate. I wasn't aware, of course, until I started going into the history of it, what a totally seminal influence Peter was in that whole Oxbridge school of comedy, and that when you watched a particular kind of Python interview sketch, for example, like the Merchant Banker or the Lion Tamer, with that precise, circuitous use of language, it all stemmed from him and the stuff he'd originated in the Footlights.

And one thing I feel bound to stress, because it's a factor that critics and commentators almost always ignore, is how crucial Peter's performance was to the effectiveness of his own material. I've never quite recovered from hearing a recording of Kenneth Williams doing the Tarzan sketch (from, I think, the *One Over The Eight* revue). Peter's material, word for word, and yet it was utterly and miserably unfunny. A sketch that was so exquisitely based on the humour of understatement was being delivered with overstatement, and killed it stone dead. And so that's something I learnt very early on, that the writing and the acting have to chime exactly or the material just won't work.

PH: The common perception of the clown is of a less-than-buoyant personality offstage/off-screen. From Dan Leno and Grock to Tony Hancock and Peter Sellers, they tend to be portrayed as tragic, neurotic, egomaniac pessimists—in Philip Larkin's phrase 'natural fouled-up guys'. Did this hackneyed 'tears of a clown' type apply to Cook, in your experience?

DR: In no way. But I have to bear in mind that I knew him only in what people have described as his more mellow years, and there seems to be a general acknowledgement that he had softened in the latter part of his life, compared with the early, more ruthless, steelier Peter of the Sixties and Seventies. All I ever saw was a wholly benign, affable character who seemed to be very comfortable with his life and career and had nothing else he particularly wanted to prove.

PH: When *Whoops Apocalypse* was adapted from TV to film, was Peter Cook your first choice to take over from Peter Jones as Prime Minister? Where did the name Sir Mortimer Chris come from? Was there any connection in your minds to his earlier film *The Rise And Rise Of Michael Rimmer*?

DR: As far as Andrew [Marshall] and myself were concerned, Peter Jones' portrayal of Kevin Pork was one of the highlights of the TV series, but of course Peter Jones wasn't a 'marquee' name for a feature film, so we had to re-think the casting. And when we were writing the script we very much had John Cleese in mind, imagining it like the Robin Hood character he played in *Time Bandits*—genially and mechanically patronising, like a kind of spaced-out Duke of Kent. Sadly he passed on the role, and after that there really wasn't anyone else we could think of who would be funny except Peter, and fortunately he said yes straight away. I think Andrew came up with the name Mortimer Chris, Chris having been very much coined by the Pythons, and just, to us, so wonderfully inappropriate as a surname for this stuffy, rather patrician statesman. I'm not sure either Andrew or I had ever seen Michael Rimmer prior to that, though we might have been vaguely aware of it. But certainly there was never any conscious attempt to draw from it or revisit Peter's character.

What you knew you would definitely get with him was 'funny', and that was the number one requirement. There was a triangular focus to the *Whoops Apocalypse* film, with three principal players—the US president, the international terrorist Lacrobat, and Chris. In an ideal world all three would have been funny people but we reasoned that it would still work if only the second two were. In the event only Chris was, and it led to a serious imbalance in the picture.

You can imagine how we were leaned on to play up all the American side of things, and it meant we ended up cutting down a lot of Peter's stuff, which as it happened would have strengthened things. Even at the American test screenings he was the character they enjoyed the most. It was the usual simplistic crap about Americans just wanting to watch Americans—we really should have had more faith in what was our strongest card and gone with it.

PH: Did you tailor-make his lines to fit Peter's persona and abilities better?

DR: I can honestly say that we didn't make any adjustments to the script to suit Peter. Not that we wouldn't have done if we'd felt it necessary, but I think it was just something to do with that whole comic lineage, that I mentioned before, that it was always destined to work with him. Peter influenced The Pythons who influenced us, so inevitably that characterisation was genetically very Peter Cook to start with.

PH: Peter's portrayal of Sir Mortimer is akin to Sir Arthur Streeb-Greebling, only more bone-headed and patriotic. In pre-production were there alternative characterisations tested and explored before deciding on the final choice?

DR: There are certain key inspirational moments when you're trying to construct a comic character that, essentially, define where it's going to go and get you rubbing your hands together with glee because you know it's going to be funny. In the TV series it was the moment we thought of Peter Jones as a prime minister who believed he was secretly Superman. And with Chris it was the moment Andrew came up with the line 'Unemployment is caused by pixies.' Because you can immediately see the reaction all the way round that Cabinet table, and it's a cast-iron comic formula, that goes back to Jack Ripper and the bodily fluids in Dr Strangelove and beyond. Wonderful stuff to react to. And then you can just keep piling it on, more and more.

Of course the entire *raison d'etre*, for us, of the *Whoops Apocalypse* film was the nation's response to the Falklands War—inexplicably, insanely gung-ho and jingoistic, so it felt like the idea of people throwing themselves off cliffs to reduce the unemployment figures was barely an exaggeration, considering the kind of slavish support Thatcher was enjoying by that time. So this was all factored in, and I remember Peter saying that he basically wanted to play the character as Anthony Eden, who had responded in similar monomaniacal fashion over Suez. And when he came in to talk to us about the script most of his analysis of the character, as I recall, seemed to revolve around his moustache.

PH: In the cabinet meeting scene, where Sir Mortimer blames Britain's failings on elves (and 'all manner of goblinry') he makes an aside 'And we've all seen them', which causes Richard Wilson and Pearson to corpse. Was that line an off-the-cuff addition of Peter's, or was it already part of the script?

DR: It's a measure of how gloriously right Peter was for the role that you can ask that question, because re-reading the script I find it was all there on the page. And in fact, if you imagine that speech without those words the rhythm really isn't quite as satisfying and you don't get the same kind of oratorical build to the point he's making. The character and the dialogue just seemed to fit him like a glove, right from the off, and the only line I can ever actually remember him adding, on the take, was at the end of the scene where he's distributing the Union Jack umbrellas which he believes will protect the nation from a nuclear attack—'So simple, and yet so effective.'

There was, in fact, another scene which on paper should have worked wonderfully: at the dinner to celebrate his victory over the Maguadorans Chris delivers a triumphant speech to a packed banquet hall, and then breaks into this diabolical sub-Vera Lynn song, 'There'll be tea and buttered crumpets on the lawn just you wait and see, there'll be fanfares played on trumpets in the morn when this land is free ...' And we had to cut it because Peter really couldn't hold a note when he tried to sing. If you watch the film you can just catch him humming a little reprise of it in the scene where he's sprinkling the acid into his bath water.

PH: What is your verdict on *Whoops Apocalypse* (the film version) now?

DR: We were so concerned, after the TV series, to clamp down on anything that threatened to become too cartoony or comically overblown (cf. Kenneth Williams) that, looking back, I think a lot of it may be a bit muted. While I feel in many ways it's a more mature piece of work than the LWT project I think we may have stifled the sense of fun that series had. There's always a 'dampening down' effect that occurs when you go from tape to film in any case, most of it due to the fact that instead of just recording actors' natural rhythms and timings in a multi-camera set-up you end up trying to reconstitute them in the cutting room, using bits and pieces from all sorts of different set-ups, and 99 times out of a hundred there's never enough attention given to the pacing. The pacing on *WA* isn't bad, although I do feel we should have worked a lot harder on the soundtrack, which is very flat, and a much more spirited musical score would have perked it up no end.

All of that said, it's clearly a very flawed piece of work, partly because too much of the comedy relies upon 'jokes' and set-pieces and not enough on character. Where it does rely on character—as with the Chris scenes—it can be very successful, and looking back you start to wish it could have been much more solidly based at the Downing Street end of things, with that one solid comic perspective which everything else could have served. And then I think it would have been a lot more satisfying.

PH: So, *One Foot In The Algarve*: Was the journalist character written for Peter?

DR: Once again, the answer is no. But this time I think it shows. Martin Trout was far from the kind of role you'd normally imagine Peter playing. I believe I'd originally imagined Ronnie Corbett as Trout but he turned out to be working in Australia and was unavailable. Once again it wasn't like you were just looking for an actor who could make the part believable, it was all about being funny. So that inevitably narrows the list down to a few select people in this country.

It was a pretty traditional kind of device, just to have this running character as the victim of ever-escalating violence, and it wasn't at all the kind of thing you associate with Peter, so in a way that gave it a certain freshness. He wasn't, at this stage of his life, blessed with great physical dexterity or lightness of touch, but that very ungainliness when, for example, he's hit in the face by a truck door, is what lifts it above the ordinary for me.

PH: Had Peter changed—in terms of temperament or outlook—in the seven years since *Whoops Apocalypse*?

DR: If anything I think he'd become still more accessible, and I suppose I felt I could approach him with a little more confidence than I had done before—on *Whoops Apocalypse* I'm not sure I ventured to give him many notes, I was too awestruck even to be near him, whereas by 1993 I was a bit less inhibited. I think we were all aware that physically he was more dilapidated than when he played Chris, where in fact he'd been in commendably good nick. And that rather slurry seediness, I suspect, was what led us to feel he would be good as an oily paparazzo photographer.

PH: Do you think alcohol affected Peter in terms of learning the script, keeping consistency in his performance, being physically capable of meeting the demands of the shooting schedule?

DR: The demands on Peter in terms of material weren't so great that this proved a problem. Generally he'd learnt whatever it was he had to do that day, it's just that vocally that precision and clarity of diction that were so much a part of his early work really weren't there any more. But as I say, the character of Trout didn't rely upon that so much as a general sense of this unsavoury, comical presence at the periphery of the main narrative. And I can't say I ever remember him being unprofessional. In fact, on his last morning shooting with us in Portugal I remember him mentioning that his flight back to the UK was booked for one o'clock, and apparently no one else was aware it was that early, and rather than complete all of Peter's shots so he could be released the director was just starting to set up some reverses with Richard. And Peter was so mild and non-confrontational he would have just stayed there and waited if I hadn't gone across and said something. There was absolutely no question of him 'pulling rank'.

Peter was nice enough to be very enthusiastic about the material from the off—typically arriving for our first meeting by saying that any script containing a reference to Susan Stranks was a winner with him—and I just got the feeling he was comfortable enough with it not to feel the need to fiddle. At one rehearsal of the clash with Margaret at the pay-phones he ad-libbed the line 'Are you trying to access my Mercury facility?' which was pure Cook, and I immediately said to keep it in. Also, there was a later scene where he's calling his editor about the photographs and says 'Listen, you'd better wear oven gloves because these pictures are hot.' And instinctively instead of 'oven gloves' he said 'asbestos gloves', which of course was better rhythmically. But beyond one or two instances like that he just got on with it. I have a very simple policy about anyone changing the material—if it's better I'm the first to welcome it, but of course most of the time it isn't. More often than not it's just because someone has a different idea of what's funny to you, and once you start trying to accommodate everyone's sense of humour you're finished. Unsurprisingly, Peter and I found exactly the same things funny, so there wasn't likely to be much disagreement.

In the end I just went to the UK filming and the first week over in Portugal, which was when most of Peter's stuff was done. Typically it pissed down with rain for most of the first seven days, which seriously disrupted our schedule. Additionally, the organisation was poor and the shooting so sluggish I was in a state of total despair very early on, wondering how we were ever going to complete the thing. And I remember it was only Peter's company, endlessly extemporising on this and that as we stood around waiting for something to happen, that kept me sane. Each morning we'd be driven to the location together in this van, and it was about 30 minutes from the hotel, and he was just funny all the way there. Postulating a different kind of travel programme where celebrities are sent to really awful, crap destinations, called 'Wish We Weren't Here'. All kinds of stuff like that.

He arrived in Portugal, I remember, with a large cold sore on his lip and we had to call in a local doctor to come and have a look at it. Cue much confusion when he turned up to find Peter, as Trout, covered with cuts and bruises, arm and leg in plaster and his neck in a brace—the kind of joyously surreal scenario that Peter could then do ten minutes on and have you aching with laughter. That same evening Peter and Lin had gone out for a meal and by coincidence the doctor happened to walk into the restaurant while they were there. Peter's reaction—'My Gosh, this *is* thorough.'

During another interminable lull in the proceedings at Victoria

Station I just remember him talking endlessly about old American cop shows, a subject he appeared to have an encyclopaedic knowledge about, and for some reason that escapes me now he started telling me about the time he'd gone out with Mia Farrow, who was completely mad because she wanted him to make love to her in a phone box. Triggering some wonderful speculation about how it would work in the Mercury bubble booths we'd just been shooting in. Just relentlessly, deliciously funny all the time.

WHOSE LINE IS IT ANYWAY?

Harry Pye watches an old videotape on his microwave oven

When producer Paul Jackson asked Peter Cook to host an episode of a new series called *Saturday Live* in 1986, our hero was happy enough to take part but pleaded with Jackson to pre-record the show and to get rid of the studio audience. We can presume that PC was even less keen on appearing on *Whose Line Is It Anyway?* in October 1988 which involved not only turning up and being funny in front of another audience of young people ('Aren't they awful?') but also actually standing up. (For strangers to this show, the basic premise is that four comedians enact situations suggested by the audience. The ringmaster was Clive Anderson and Peter's partners were Josie Lawrence, John Sessions and Stephen Fry.)

Despite the sweat, the chubby chest and the nicotine-stained hair, the constantly smoking Cook manages to look vaguely handsome. But for most of the show he seems puzzled and even slightly shocked at the amount he's called upon to do. When Anderson gives Fry and Cook acting styles to perform in, Peter queries, 'What—living?' Given the situation of a prospective MP asking a constituent for his vote in a 'gangster film' style, Peter instantly shouts '*Freeze*!' and remains silent and motionless whilst pretending to aim a gun at

Fry's head. There are only a few moments when Cook bursts into life and, as ever, they're all worth their weight in gold.

The first moment occurs in the 'Authors' round. The performers have their own choice of novelist to improvise on the theme of 'A Day At The Races' (chosen by an audience member). Peter decides to be Albert Goldman. According to PC, this 'terribly nice man' who wrote books on Peter's hero (Elvis) as well as his friends (Lennon and Lenny Bruce) has a new project up his sleeve and proceeds to reveal an extract: 'I knew that there were serious problems with the horse when I saw him unable to get up in the morning. Crazed with drink, drugs and women—and tiny little white panties—this horse was never gonna run. But I knew, I knew, that once Shergar died I could make a fortune.'

The next diamond in the dung was Peter as an American National Geographic-type travelogue announcer: 'The Orange Beaver has always been a lonely animal. It mates only in the Spring and springs only in the Autumn. The beaver that provides so much soap for rich women is endangered.' Stephen Fry: 'It has but one enemy.' Peter [*normal voice, to camera*]: 'Me! I hate the bloody things.'

There is a further moment in the 'Rap' round where, to a 4/4 drumbeat, contestants have to improvise a rap to a given subject. Tonight's topic is 'Having A Baby'. Rock the house, Cooky MC!

> When the baby come, you know full well
> That the baby gone to make your life hell
> So you throw the baby out the door
> Say, "I wan' a little bit more"
> Oh, what makes a baby come in the first place?
> [*PC does a floor-clearing 'funky chicken' dance here:*]
> With a boogie woogie woogie woogie
> Woogie woogie woogie woogie
> Woogie wooo.

For some, the most fondly remembered section of the show will be

the heated debate on the dangers of smoking. John Sessions played
the part of Music Hall comic Tommy Timpkins ('Tommy Timpkins,
dame by name, I'm always ready with a joke. 'Ere's one!') and
Josie Lawrence was a deeply confused body hair enthusiast called
Trixie. On the side of smokers were Fry as Richard ('Actually I'm
more of a Dick; I answer to Dick') and—surprise, surprise—Mr
Cook, wearing an RAF officer's cap plus an enormous pink feather
boa draped around his neck.

Peter: I'm terribly sorry I'm late but I got delayed. I was smoking
     and my boa caught fire.

Clive: That does illustrate one of the dangers of smoking.

Peter: And one of the perils of boas.

Clive: Right. Could I ask your name?

Peter: Yes of course you can.

Clive: Well, I'll do that now. What is your name?

Peter: Yes, erm, Arthur.

Clive: Yassir Arthur?

Peter: Yassir Arthur.

Clive: You're an Arab gentleman, are you?

Peter: No, I'm a married gentleman. But if you want me to be
     Arab I will of course, you know... [*Plays with boa*] This is
     just a religious thing I wear.

Although Cook and Fry are a tasty combination (geddit?), as the
debate picks up, it's Stephen's Dick that gets the laughs and mo-
nopolises the conversation rather than PC's sidelined Arthur.

Clive: Do you think cigarettes should be taxed?

Stephen: How can you tax a cigarette? People should be taxed,
     possibly smokers should—but you'll get no money from a
     cigarette. [*To his ciggie:*] "Excuse me, could you give me a
     quarter of your income?" Nothing. No joy at all.'

Fry concludes the conversation with a brilliant comparison of the harmful effects of passive smoking and the far more dangerous ramifications of passive bigotry. However, unlike the other guests on Channel 4's number one ad-lib/improv show, his material had previously appeared (almost word-for-word) on both his radio show *Saturday Night Fry* and in his column for *The Listener* magazine.

Seeing Cook team up with John Sessions for the 'Funny Prop' round is no cause for a street party—Cook's laidback surrealism doesn't mix at all with the Anthony Burgess Of Improv's uberliterate intensities—and, overall, the show doesn't do Peter's less-than-frenetic pace and comedic style any favours at all.

It's a shame Fry and Cook didn't work together again, on something of more substance. It would've been great had Cook managed just one more *Clive Anderson Talks Back* Special. But I'm sure even the most obsessive PC fan would agree that one appearance on the pretty dismal *Whose Line...* show was plenty.

THE MAKING OF A MOVIE

Peter Cook acted in an as-yet-unfinished film, The Jungle Of Jules Levine, *and had collaborated with that movie's director, Michael Mileham, on a script with the charming title of* It Sucks! *Since Michael is all the way over there in Californ-I-A with his screen-writer chum Jeff Craig, and Paul Hamilton is all the way over here, this following dialogue was conducted in early 1999 via smoke signals.*

PAUL HAMILTON: When was *The Jungle Of Jules Levine* made?

MICHAEL MILEHAM: We were out in the Darien jungle outside Panama City, Panama, when to our great misfortune the country's dictator—Manuel Noriega—had a great falling-out with the CIA and the American government. We were guests of the Panamanian government and some Panamanian financial backers. As the Americans launched their military invasion in 1989, there was no way we could be out in the jungle shooting, so that was it.

PH: How did Peter become involved?

MM: I met Peter in Mexico in 1982 on the set of *Yellowbeard* where I was directing and producing the behind-the-scenes documentary, *Group Madness*. Anyway, we really hit it off. A couple of years later, Peter and I got together with Dudley Moore and Susan Anton, and we went out onto the beach in Venice, California, where we shot an E.L.Wisty sketch. It was a great day as it was the first time Peter and Dudley had seen each other in years. It was that afternoon I told Peter about the *Jungle* film and asked him to be in it.

PH: Was the role specifically written for him?

MM: Yes it was. I had Peter in mind all along to play the part of Trevor Backwater, a drunken Australian bush pilot who had some-how found work flying over the Central American jungles with his lucky charm, a poison arrow frog called Queenie, in the passenger seat.

PH: Did he re-write any of his dialogue?

MM: Re-write? I knew that Peter would come up with better dialogue for his character than I could so we had a meeting in which I explained who this character was. I gave him all the elements and Peter came up with his own lines.

PH: How large was his role?

MM: He dominates the first ten, memorable, minutes of the film. That's the thing about Peter, he was so memorable. Look at *The Princess Bride*—he was only in it for, I don't know, less than two minutes, and his Impressive Clergyman was one of the film's high points.

PH: Were all his scenes in the can before hostilities were declared?

MM: Yes, Peter's work was finished before we pulled out of there.

PH: Why has it taken 10 years for the film to be revived?

MM: The entire American/Panama thing had to run itself out. We've gone through several wildly different scripts, all of which we've eventually rejected. Finally, Jeff and I came up with what we think is the definitive take on all of what went down in the jungle. I think the whole project just needed this gestation period. Besides, I spent quite a few years just simply heartbroken over the high of nearly completing the original film, only to have it derailed at the last moment. For some time I didn't want to even think about it. It wasn't until I met Jeff that I found somebody who could see the project from a fresh perspective and make it come alive again.

PH: Do you intend to finish the film as it was originally conceived or are you utilizing Peter's scenes and other salvageable sections in the construction of a totally new film?

JEFF CRAIG: This is a completely new film, using sequences of both Peter and Elliott Gould, which are priceless. Instead of a film about a certain story taking place in the jungles of Panama this is a fictionalized biography of Michael's experiences, struggling against all odds to get his movie made.

MM: This is how we're able to use that precious original footage. At least a portion of it. It works and it's relevant.

PH: When will we see the film?

MM: Good question!

JC: Right now we're polishing the *It Sucks!* script and going into pre-production on another, unrelated, film. Next up is *Jules Levine*.

MM: So if everything goes according to plan, the *Jungle* film should be completed in about two years.

PH: When did Peter pitch the story of *It Sucks!* to Michael?

MM: It was in 1993 and Peter, my wife Marilyn and I were at Forest Mere—a fat farm in Liphook—and we were on one of our fabulous outings, where we usually bought treacle pies and booze, and we ended up at a Japanese-owned golf course country club. I had my Apple laptop computer with me and Peter said he had an idea he'd been working on, so we decided to do a treatment right then and there—you know, write the script and hit the Japanese up for funding at the same time. As Peter and I ran around the bar drinking gin and tonics, working up the story and soliciting funds, Marilyn typed it all into the computer. It was a great vacation. When we checked into the place, they asked us what kind of diet we wanted to go on, and Peter told them we just wanted to maintain our current weight. It was tough, and we had to go on frequent outings, but we managed to get through it.

PH: How much of the screenplay was written before Peter's death?

MM: Sadly, we didn't get any of the first draft completed before Peter died. We just had time to get a treatment finished. With me living in L.A. and Peter living in Hampstead Heath, we had to compose it in just a couple of transatlantic visits and dozens of rather expensive phone calls.

PH: Were you aware that Peter had written an earlier version—same title, same scenario—in the mid-'70s with Claude Harz?

MM: Peter had told me that he'd been kicking the idea around for quite a while and had worked on it with another writer. But he said he wasn't at all happy with what had come of it and had tossed out everything. He didn't even say who it was he'd worked with, he never showed me any of the material.

JC: Michael had told me it had been fully fleshed-out but not written into screenplay format. So that's what I began doing in 1998—taking the Peter Cook/Michael Mileham treatment and turning it into a fully realised screenplay.

PH: Who do you envisage in the lead roles?

MM: It's funny but Peter really wanted Elliott Gould; the main character's even called Elliott. The sooner we get funding, the sooner Peter Cook fans will see one of his last creations—a killer vacuum cleaner ravaging a small American town.

EYE SORE: SONIA SUTCLIFFE

On 24th May 1989 Sonia Sutcliffe, wife of Peter Sutcliffe, the Yorkshire Ripper who killed 13 women, was awarded £600,000 in libel damages in a high court action against *Private Eye*. Editor Ian Hislop famously fumed, 'This award is 100 times more money than for being murdered by the Ripper. If this is justice, I am a banana.' It was later reduced on appeal to £60,000 but it looked like the *Eye* was to close for ever.

Ian and a self-confessed 'ashen-faced' Peter Cook met the Press outside the *Eye*'s office at 6 Carlisle Street, Soho. Peter, hangover banging behind his blue sunglasses, professed to be more worried about his beloved Torquay United's chances of victory over Bolton Wanderers in the Sherpa Van Trophy final. 'Will someone make it clear whether it is the winning players or the losers who'll each be given a Sherpa Van?' he asked.

'I love Torquay,' he added. 'That's where I come from. When I moved to London. I started supporting Tottenham because it started with "To" like Torquay.' Cook cracked jokes about how the *Eye* would henceforward be running controversial stories about kind vicars spending nice days at the seaside, but wouldn't be naming the vicars or committing itself to the weather for fear of comebacks.

'I can't see the point in running a magazine like this if you're going to allow it to become bland,' he said in a moment of what looked like seriousness.'

—*The Guardian*, 25/5/1989

Peter, the next day, vowed to raise the £600,000 by going on a sponsored megadiet and shedding three stone, calculating that he would have to raise some £14,000 per lb. The enormity of his plight sank in painfully as he ordered burgers and chips, plus half a pint of lager, for a late breakfast in Hampstead, London.

—*The People*, 28/5/89

Later, Peter claimed he would raise the dosh by attempting to walk around bouncing Czech Robert Maxwell, but, after due deliberation, conceded that that was too daunting a task.

The Carlisle Street conference ended with the Torquay Tornado stating in best Lord Gnome mode: 'I want to make it perfectly clear that this will not in anyway affect my plans to move into satellite television, which will be absolutely free and can be received with the lid of a used baked beans can and a furled copy of *The Sun*. We hope to have the entire staff of *Private Eye* in outer space very soon.'

OBVIOUSLY DOOMED

Lexington Street, Wl. The offices of Literary Review.

A gibbering, quivering Paul Hamilton sits trembling opposite Auberon 'Bron' Waugh columnist (despite looking nothing like a column), champion pricker of pompous balloons, and ironist supreme (although he refrained from doing any ironing during this interview). In between nibbles at sarnies, puffings on 10,000 cigarettes, and slurpings from a damned impudent bottle of Entree d'Legs, the Dragger attempts to interview the charming, disarming Mr.Wargs, a man of resolute good cheer—nearly every utterance comes with a chock full of chuckles. We begin with PH explaining that he is a virgin in the art of interviewing, 'so be gentle with me'...

PAUL HAMILTON: Who brought you to the *Eye*?

AUBERON WAUGH: That was Richard. I'd known Richard for quite some years. I'd gotten the sack from *The Spectator* and went over the next day to the *Eye*. But I went back to *The Spectator* about a year later as a book reviewer.

PH: Who sacked you?

AW: It was Nigel Lawson... whose Diet Book, oddly enough, is on my desk awaiting a review. [*Smiles*]

PH: Did you meet Peter Cook before you joined the *Eye*?

AW: Once or twice, but not at all well. I never really knew him well, which is rather embarrassing 'cause Lin thinks I was his oldest and best friend.

PH: Well, you share the same birthday.

AW: That's quite true. We used to have birthday parties together from time to time, and in fact the last time I saw him was at my birthday party in 1994.

PH: What did you think of *Beyond The Fringe* and The Establishment in your youth?

AW: It was very exciting and very new, you see, and it seemed to be a great movement for freedom; and the *Eye* was awfully good too but now, you see, everybody does it. But the *Eye* has kept its head above water, it's still got that sharp edge. Liberating, the freedom to be rude in public, but now, you know, *The Sun*'s insulting everybody... This newsletter of yours—what is it called, a newsletter?

PH: A fagazine.

AW: Fagazine—how often do you intend to bring it out? Twice a year?

PH: Hopefully four times a year.

AW: That's quite ambitious. Because, goodness, all these memories are fading.

PH: Yes, I've got to get everyone before they die. That was Roger Lewis' problem in writing his Peter Sellers biography, racing around trying to catch everyone before they died or lost their wool.

AW: I saw Peter Sellers two days before he died. Very odd. Went to see him in Switzerland and came back and wrote my piece. Then the news came through he'd died and they used my piece as an obituary. [*Laughter*]

PH: Did you think he was as mad as Lewis paints him?

AW: I think he was pretty dotty. I think he was actually quite disturbed.

PH: I learnt that Peter Cook, with John Bird in 1965, had adapted your father's novel *Scoop* as a screenplay.

AW [*Surprised*]: Did they?

PH: The film was never made. He was down to play Boot.

AW: I wonder what happened to that? I wonder if Lin's got the script. I'd like to see it.

PH: He never mentioned it to you?

AW: No.

PH: Did you ever go to The Establishment club?

AW: Yeah, only about once or twice.

PH: How did it strike you? Rip-roaringly funny?

AW: No, not really, no. It was somehow very American, don't know why. Perhaps because it was full of Americans.

PH: Tourists?

AW: Yes, hmm, it was like Carnaby Street that had got on to the list for visiting Americans.

PH: Peter's stage appearances were very rare in the last years, weren't they?

AW: He used to make speeches at—he made one speech, brilliant, at the *Private Eye* lunch at Brighton (1987). Ab-sol-ute genius. Every single line was extraordinary. Totally inspired... I can't remember a word of it. [*Laughter*] He presented the *Literary Review* poetry prizes. That would be in '92 or 3.

PH: Do you think there was a book bursting out of Peter?

AW: No. He wasn't exactly lazy; he was just too sort of hopeless and unconcentrated.

PH: Do you think that helps explain his last 15 years where he would do a couple of marvellous pieces and then a long period of inactivity?

AW: Yes, a bit. He'd lost all ambition. He was just a pure artist producing very, very, very occasionally.

PH: There was a TV series he did in 1971 which lasted for all of three shows called *Where Do I Sit?*

AW: Yes, it was terrible, it was terrible. I was on the very first one. I think I was, I was certainly there at the dress rehearsal. Oh, it was awful. It was totally disorganised and didn't work at all and pathetic. [*Laughter*]

PH: What was the problem?

AW: Well, he insisted on being live and he'd had no experience at all in anything like that, so he was just dithering around and standing up and interviewing you badly and walking everywhere. There was no shape or form. He was alright but nobody else knew what was going on. It was just a disaster.

PH: Mary Whitehouse demanded he be tried for blasphemy for a sketch he and Spike Milligan did about God.

AW: He was a red rag to Mary Whitehouse, and intentionally too.

H.D: So *Where Do I Sit?* Isn't a lost comic gem, its loss to be forever mourned, then? It is absolutely awful?

AW: Yes, total rubbish.

PH: What was he trying to do with that show?

AW: Who knows? He hadn't concentrated on it and thought he could swan through it.

PH: Was he trying to be David Frost?

AW: Not at all. He was the antidote to David Frost. Nobody could perform properly and he was too mad to talk to.

PH: Back to the *Eye*. Peter Cook as proprietor: Did he interfere or encourage you?

AW: Absolutely not. He was the all-time hands-off proprietor. All he did was come in once a fortnight and sat upstairs making jokes. There was a general group making jokes to each other, and that would be the basis of the magazine. A very strange person, he was.

PH: In terms of getting to know?

AW: He couldn't be friendlier. There was no conscious urge to distance himself. He was just very different to other people.

PH: Barking?

AW: No, just deeply, deeply eccentric

PH: Now, you've seen this book of tributes, *Something Like Fire*?

AW: Yeah, yeah.

H;D. What, in your capacity as editor of *Literary Review*, do you think of it?

AW: Admirable effort. I think, of all the magazines I've ever seen, it's the most obviously doomed, because to have a magazine, four times a year about someone who's dead...

PH: Oh no! I'm talking about the book!

AW: Oh, the book! I'm so sorry. [*Laughter*]

PH: Thanks for inspiring me with such confidence, though.

AW: The book—I've yet to read all of it. I think they've done a very good job really, although it gets a bit repetitive, as they all say the same sort of things about him. But it is more of a tribute than a critical study.

PH: You're a dedicated smoker. So was Peter.

AW: Oh, but I give up about four times a year.

PH: What—in between cigarettes?

AW: Just for about three weeks. I've only one lung and I get so I can't climb the stairs so I have to stop smoking for a couple of weeks.

PH: It was mandatory for everyone in the '50s and '60s to continually smoke, so why has the tide of opinion turned against the innocent smoker? What should the government do to make life worth smoking in?

AW: Well, the interesting thing about it is that we smokers actually pay for the entire hospital service out of our extra taxes And, also, we die younger so we don't draw all the old age pension. They're worth a colossal profit to the government and they really should encourage us and give us awards, such as Member of the Honourable Order of Smokers. The problem lies with these strident, fanatical lobby groups who are the only people politicians ever get to talk to. Smokers haven't got a proper lobby at all, nor the moral outrage the anti-smokers have got.

PH: Aside from smoking, I doubt whether you shared Peter's love of football, pop music and golf?

AW: No, no, none of those things

PH: So what interests did you share?

AW: That's a very good question and, no, I'd say none really. Except the *Eye* and politics a bit.

PH: He was generally right of centre, wasn't he?

AW: By the end very, very far right.

FOOTNOTE: ON A LITERARY NOTE...

"A year or two before Peter Cook died, I arranged a meeting between him and my editor at Century Books, Mark Booth. Mark wanted him to write an autobiography. They met at Rules. Peter arrived announcing that he had just finished his autobiography, and that he had it with him. 'I'd love to see it,' said Mark. Peter brought out a couple of pages of notepaper with a few rough sentences scribbled over them. 'Is that it?' asked Mark. 'I thought we might flesh it out with a few photographs,' replied Peter, his peerless lack of drive spurred on by his Olympian sense of humour."
—Craig Brown, 1996

EYE SPOTS

It's Tuesday 3rd of June 1997 and it's too damn hot to do anything except talk about Peter Cook, so Paul Hamilton lurches towards Private Eye's *office for a bit of a chat...*

PAUL HAMILTON: Name, rank and cereal bowl?

CECILIA BOGGIS [*for it is she*]: Cecilia Boggis. Classified Advertising Manager, *Private Eye* magazine, circa 1981 to 1997. Very rare name. The Boggisses hail mainly from East Anglia. Boggis—it seemed to go with the job, so I kept it.

PH: A Boggis-standard job.

CB: It's a kind of *Private Eye* name, they use it a lot. There's usually a snooker player called Sid Boggis. So that's my name. Is there anything else you wanted to ask me?

PH: No. I'll go now.

CB: In January 1986 they asked me to create a classified advertising page, because it'd never been anyone's specific job. It'd hitherto been pretty random. It needed someone to revamp it. So I got

Willie Rushton to do little graphics for it, make lots of changes, and that's what I've been doing ever since. It's better than the old days when I used to do all the typing of every word of every issue. You know, Auberon Waugh's Diary was done with him just wandering around the room shouting it at you. No correction tapes or floppy discs, it had to go straight to the page. Nothing was rewritten.

PH: So when did you first meet Peter?

CB: I met Peter straight away. He was there a couple of days after I started. He was looking brilliant, wonderful, thin and handsome, wearing a suit, I think. I thought he was always very debonair. Well, he was in those days. Very dapper, very nice, and he had the same effect then as he did 15 years later which was, the moment he came in the whole atmosphere was different, and it was immediately very funny.

PH: What was the first thing he ever said to you?

CB: I don't remember! What an extraordinary question.

PH: Well, I did say this'd be an in-depth interview. My next question is, 'What was the second thing he ever said to you?'

CB: 'Who are you?' And he still said that to me 15 years later. Nothing had changed. I don't think he ever knew my name the whole time he was there! But there was no reason why he should. He was quite shy, really. He used to sneak upstairs and get on with the jokey bits...While he was waiting for his car to take him somewhere, he would sit on the settee, always with some extraordinary, inventive anecdote that would have us roaring with laughter. Like, 'I just ran over a police car. Do you think it matters?'

But one specific occasion where he and I were together was when I started here. I wasn't making enough money so I moonlighted on another little job for Vidal Sassoon's hair place up the road, South Molton Street area. They would have certificates issued to the people who passed the course in hair design, and my job—because I knew a bit of calligraphy—was to write their names very elegantly, with the dates of the course, on their certificate. So I was given a huge heap of empty certificates, very lavish things, where I would fill in the names stylishly. I'd do them for an hour every evening after work, and someone would collect them the next day. Peter was often here, looking over my shoulder, asking what I was doing. And he made me write one out for him once, so he actually had a certificate saying he's a qualified hair stylist for Vidal Sassoon. He had me put his name in French so it's 'Pierre De La Cuisiniere'.

Also on one of those evenings a friend rang me up and I said, 'Peter Cook's sitting here with me. Peter, would you say hello to my friend who doesn't believe it's you?' So he picked up the phone and said, 'Hello, Richard Ingrams here.'

PH: Richard Ingrams, on the *Cook's Tours* radio thing, said Peter would disappear from the *Eye* for sometimes years at a time. How true is that? Was that an exaggeration?

CB: He did disappear a long time when he did that extraordinary thing in America, being a butler. *The Two Of Us*. We didn't see him for a long time when he did that. When he was doing the chat show with the *Can We Talk?* woman he came in here a lot and was mortified by the whole thing. He hated doing that and he wished he never agreed to it. But mysterious disappearances, I can't really say. Sometimes he'd be in the building and I'd not bump into him at all, being in my small corner.

PH: Tell me about the day *Private Eye* lost the libel case against Sonia Sutcliffe and were ordered to cough up 600,000 quid.

CB: I was on holiday then, on a cross-channel ferry with my mother, and I went to the newsagent and all the tabloid headlines had, er, *Private Eye*, ah, 600,000, and I said to her, 'There's no job when I go home. I've had it. This is it. This is the end of *Private Eye*.' That was a very scary moment, I must say.

PH: Peter was making those Wispa TV ads with Mel Smith that

day, and Mel said it was the only time he'd ever seen Peter really worried.

CB: I remember seeing Peter shortly before he died—about a week—staggering down Carlisle Street. I really thought, 'If I don't find my keys in my handbag quickly and open this front door, this man is going to fall on me and I may not recover.' Because he looked so big towards the end, and to think he was so slender.

PH: He just ballooned, didn't he?

CB: Yes, and he seemed to get taller as well as fatter. Like The Incredible Shrinking Man, he was the Increasing Man.

[*In 1987,* Private Eye *had a party in Brighton—at the Grand Hotel, most famous for being bombed by the I.R.A. when the Conservative Party were staying there during their annual conference. Anyway, at the party, Peter, rather than make a speech, recited the menu...*]

PH: That 'do' in Brighton—did you go?

CB: Yes. Didn't he do that because he hadn't prepared a speech? He read off the menu. Very good.

PH: How?

CB [*Giggles*]: Don't remember.

PH: No one remembers anything!

CB: We were drunk! I wasn't—I'm teetotal—but I'm sure I was under the influence. It was nice, that party, we all went down on the same train. They got quite drunk on the train, didn't they? Steve might remember that menu thing, but, you know, we're not talking about the night before, we're talking about 10 years ago. I think you're asking too much!

PH: Oh, come on... Did anyone make a tape of it?

CB: No, everyone was too insensible. Ask Hilary about that speech.

[*To Hilary, who has just entered the room:*] Hilary, do you remember that party in Brighton, were you there?

HILARY: Yeah. There were two pipes hanging from the ceiling, and Peter said, 'Oh, Norman Tebbit's left his legs behind.'

CB: What about that reading from the menu?

HILARY: Oh, that was so funny! Such dreadful food, wasn't it?

CB: There was Sussex Pond Soup.

HILARY: Awful!

CB: Peter was someone who could make a menu sound funny. [*Loudly into tape recorder:*] Sussex. Pond. Soup. It's the way you tell 'em, really, isn't it?

[*Hamilton is reliably informed that a man called Steve will explain fully the saga of the mirthful menu, so fast-forward tape...*]

PH:...We've been talking about the *Private Eye* party in Brighton in 1987. Auberon Waugh said it was the funniest thing in the world but couldn't remember a word.

STEVE: No. Nor me!

PH: Everyone's been saying you're the one to ask!

STEVE: I don't know why. Was I there? No, I wasn't there.

CB: Hilary thinks Sheila might know.

HILARY: Sheila's very good at remembering speeches. She's up on the second floor.

CB: Go and see her.

[*Two flights of stairs later...*]

PH: ... in Brighton and Peter made a speech from a menu.

SHEILA: Ah, yes. I couldn't hear a word he said because I was at the other side of the room and the acoustics were so bad. I'm really sorry...Wracking my brain...Well, in the early years I was here we would see him in the pub where he would tell stories and have us all in stitches, and then in later years he didn't come in as much, and when he did he went downstairs to write. He was away for an awful lot. Spent a long time in Australia, you know.

PH: Oh? What was that? Golf..?

SHEILA: I don't know. That was probably late '70s, early '80s, because I know there was a lot of correspondence going to Australia. On tour? On holiday? I don't know. Er, um...

PH: We were discussing downstairs the £600,000 award to Sutcliffe... There was a pall of doom around this office that day.

SHEILA: Very much so, but he livened things up with his 'Support Torquay'. That's the thing you miss about him most. He raised spirits. When he came in you knew nothing was too terrible. I recall in court—it must've been the Maxwell case—where he got very bored and started showing off his shirt. He'd just been shopping. And the jury were totally entranced by Cook, watching his every move and laughing.

PH: Was this the shirt that had 'Do fish have lips?' written on it?

SHEILA: I don't know. It was just a very garish shirt, the type he was prone to wear at times, and he had the jury fascinated and they weren't listening to a thing that was going on. The case went against us. Judge didn't like it. He took the whole thing very seriously...

The Dragger realises by now that this whole menu-reading inquiry is like some mad attempt at nailing smoke to water. As they say, 'You had to be there, cocker.' Well , we weren't, but they were—and they don't remember a word of it!

THE GLOOMERIST

'I'm currently in a very questioning state of mind, wondering if there is some meaning to life, a pot of gold at the end of the rainbow,' admitted writer/producer/director and recovering workaholic John Lloyd after finishing the end of our interview, his haunty, seen-a-little-too-much-far-too-clearly eyes gazing beyond the ceiling of an office that wasn't his. Killing another innocent coughin' nail in the Auschwitz of an ashtray, he elaborated: 'I'm in this peculiar dichotomy where I make cheese commercials during the day and read Spinoza at night.' It could be worse, John; you could be making Spinoza ads and reading about cheese.

Life itself is formed by the fervent rubbing of contrasts and Baudelaire (or was it a baldy liar?) defined humour as the clash of opposites, so it seems natural that John Lloyd would be mentally juggling the trivial (Spinoza) and the essential (cheese).

During the pre-interview drinky. Mr. L expressed some doubts as to whether he could remember anything of worth about Peter Cook, but after reading a transcript of A Life In Pieces from an old Pub & Bed, he soon convulsed with laughter, reading aloud some Streeb-Greebling dialogue with Cookian timing and inflections.

Suitably tickled, he then professed himself ready for anything.

   The following yak is culled from a four hour tour of the section of John Lloyd's brain marked 'Peter Cook'.

PAUL HAMILTON: How shall we go about this interview? Chronologically?

JOHN LLOYD: Yeah. Or dart about.

PH: In your *Something Like Fire: Peter Cook Remembered* essay, you mentioned some Duracell battery radio ads that Peter voiced and you produced.

JL: Yeah. They were written by an old friend of mine from college, John Canter, who went on to write for Lenny Henry. They were very well written and funny and I can't remember anything about them.

PH: We've got off to a flying start with that question!

JL: Peter and I kind of intersected at very irregular intervals over quite a long time. It's all a blur. It's funny that you consider somebody a close friend even though we didn't see each other really that often but it was really intensive when we did stuff. The only friends that are worth having are the ones you can go to and say, 'I've just murdered somebody by mistake. Can I live in your wine-cellar for three years?' [*Laughter*] Peter would be such a friend. It's impertinent, really, to feel that about Peter, but there was a kind of affinity—we both smoked too much and drank too much.

   When we were writing the Fergleberger script, he used to some round to my flat initially before we went to Lin's house—because his house was always such a tip—he'd come round and we'd sit there and nothing would happen, you know? I'm thinking, 'Shit! What made me think I could do this because that man's a genius and I'm just a git of a producer?' After about an hour of this and putting it off and having a large vodka, Peter said, 'I'm feeling very nervous because I don't feel, with you in the room, I can be funny enough.' I was feeling the same thing!

It's hard to put in a way that doesn't sound boastful but there's a kind of affinity with people who understand how gags work, really, and have some sort of comic taste. I mean, I don't have a hundredth of Peter's talent. I can't write the lines but I can certainly pick the lines that are gonna work—I can edit the stuff. I felt with Peter that he didn't have enough people he could really talk to, do you know what I mean? He never really talked to anyone about what was eating him. I think Lin asked him once what the matter was and he just said, 'Despair, really. Just despair.' Maybe he recognised me as a fellow despairing person, I dunno, but because he was such a polite bloke who was so funny, he could live most of his life on a level of just being funny the whole time, and he would always laugh at other people's jokes, he was very good about that, very genuine. But you always felt he had something he just wanted to tell you but he never quite got around to somehow.

PH: A sense of aloneness?

JL: Yeah, I think he did feel isolated, but he was just too polite to show it and it came out in other ways. I always felt that when we were writing together—which is something that I feel that I kind of offer as a producer, which is, 'Look, halve the burden. I can take a lot of the weight off you. You don't have to do any typing or transcribing or any shit like that. I'll do all the boring nuts-and-bolts stuff for you.'

PH: Did he make a point of that, 'I hate writing on my own'?

JL: No. Well, I never saw him doing any writing. He did a lot of talking and tape-recording but his penmanship was all over the shop, like an ant with inky legs. Someone had to get it prepared and I took great pleasure in doing that. It's like tackling the washing-up and there it all is in neat lines, the forks all shiny. I was his comedy cleaning lady.

PH: How much of the Morton P. Fergleberger script was written before you got involved?

JL: None. Not a word. No, he was in a dreadful state. Deadline-itis. You know, when you've given yourself nine months to do it and eight-and-three-quarter months have elapsed and they're wondering where it is and you haven't even started.

PH: Was it the shock of staring at a blank sheet of paper and not knowing where or how to start?

JL: No, he had just gone off the idea: 'I've accepted this fucking money and now I can't do it,' and all hateful. But I've been in the same situation lots of times. Like, Douglas Adams struggled for a year to write the first four episodes of *Hitch-Hiker's Guide To The Galaxy*. Got desperate. Couldn't finish it. Had a deadline. Asked me to help—because I shared a flat with him. We wrote the last two episodes in a week and a half. It was all fun, no pressure. I defy anyone to tell any difference in the writing style. It's why so many comedy writers do write in pairs. It helps to have one brilliantly intuitive, zany one—Graham Chapman—and the sensible, logical guy like John Cleese. But they've got to share the same sensibility, they've got to know when the thing is better than just wacky.

  Fergleberger, the writing, didn't take long.

PH: So what was the plot of Fergleberger? What was it actually called?

JL: It was called *The Dark Horse From The Grass Roots*. The plot was about a guy who ran Al Ladd, the Aluminium Ladder Company—devised originally because the film star Alan Ladd was so small he had these ladders. It was the usual Peter Cook bollocks about this guy who became a candidate for the Presidency, a sort of, er—who was that little nerd who ran for it a few years back?

PH: Ross Perot?

JL: That's it. But, apart from some very good bits in it, some rambley Peter Cook bits, we were going to actually take him to real political rallies and get him to pretend to be this character. That was the really exciting part for me, as a director, getting that peculiar interface between a lot of Mid-West Americans who had never heard of Peter Cook who would be pretending to be this Fergleberger character. It was going to be a biopic telling you how the Ferglebergers came to America, all that stuff, and, of course with Peter, he *had* to be abducted by aliens and have titanium rods probed up his arse [*Laughter*]. Peter Cook Eternal Themes.

I remember it having lots of very funny chunks in it. It was a very, very professional, well-structured, neatly done piece of work along the same lines as Harry Enfield's documentary spoof on Olivier, *Norbert Smith—A Life*. If Peter didn't have someone around when he was speaking ex tempore he couldn't really be bothered, a lot of the time, to get it down on paper.

The show never made it because we were ripped off by Gary Trudeau and his American election show, *Tanner '88*. It was a shame.

PH: How did you feel?

JL: How did we feel? Thoroughly pissed off, but what can you do? The guy at HBO—his name was Stu Smiley, I remember—said, 'Aw, it's nothing to do with me,' but we got the impression that what had happened was HBO had given up hope that our script was ever going to show up, but it was a very good idea so they commissioned someone to do a proper series. You get used to that, the fact that people often genuinely have the same idea, and that occasionally someone will rip something off, but what struck me as strange about it was that fact it was Peter Cook: If the show was here, no one would have dreamed or dared to do it, but because it was in America he was just 'some old British guy who was funny a long time ago.' He didn't have any clout there, that's what struck me as surprising. He didn't cut any mustard there.

Something I struggled to express in that book of Lin Cook's was that Peter had the handle on something that very few people go near. He expressed the human condition in a very poignant and very funny way. He once said to me that everything he had done was autobiographical which, at the time, being a lot younger and callower, I thought, 'I don't really get what you mean.' Then someone rang up about that section of *A Life In Pieces* where Peter's talking about being raised by goats and said, 'Well, what he means is he was raised by nannies. He never had proper parents 'cos they were on foreign service and absent so much.' What Peter made was a subconscious connection and you get a very funny sketch about this poor guy in a goat hut.

PH: When you were having these jabber sessions for the *A Life In Pieces* scripts, did Peter's responses to your questions come out fully formed?

JL: Yes. Oh yeah. A lot if it came out like that—you know that expression, 'saw it off by the yard'—and you'd begin [*clicks fingers*] and it'd be about Bollywood or something, and it's a bit like a mining because you'd be digging a lot of shit out of the ground and then suddenly you hit a seam. Then there would be some lumpy, splashy bits, but you dig a bit more and another seam comes up. It's just Peter had a higher frequency than most people do, a higher ratio of gold to ground.

PH: Were there occasions when you and Peter Fincham [*A Life In Pieces*' producer] turned up at Peter's house to write and Peter would say, 'I'm sorry lads, I can't think of anything today'?

JL: No, it didn't really work like that 'cos Peter Fincham, as a managing director of TalkBack, was incredibly indulgent and didn't pressurise us. For months we could not crack the problem of *A Life In Pieces*. Everyone recognised the clever idea of a series based on *The Twelve Days Of Christmas*.

PH: Whose idea was it?

JL: Rory McGrath. Rory wrote all the original scripts—or certainly most of 'em—full of very funny Rory jokes, puns and all that. We all thought they were very good but Peter couldn't do them because they had no meaning. They were just gags.

PH: 'Meaning' meaning what?

JL: Well, if you could work that out then you'll know what The Big Secret was. I mean, we tried Peter out reading Rory's scripts and it just didn't ring true, it didn't catch Peter's tone of voice at all. We were puzzled why not. I had to keep calling Rory and say, 'We can't do it. Can you maybe re-write it?' We were all pals with Rory and he got on well with us—it was a bit of a Mutual Admiration Society—but we couldn't make it work.

Both the Peters and I were very upset because what had started out as a kind of, 'Here's a great scam, lads! We go to the BBC, get a commission for thirteen shows—introduction and twelve five-minutes. Rory's written 'em all; we gotta do is turn up and shoot 'em.'

Peter's like, 'Fantastic. Big fat fee. Pleasant people to work with. Lloyd'll shoot 'em. He can be trusted not make a pig's ear of it.'

So you turn up and you think, 'Oh no, this is a disaster. None of these will work.' And Peter—like me, he backed out of a lot of things. He'd get cold feet; he went off ideas and was very lazy, as I am—but he's also a very loyal bloke and when he said he would do something, he's on for it.

The nut we couldn't crack in Rory's script was, 'Who is this bloke and what's it got to do with—?', and that idea of, 'And what's your next gift, Sir Arthur?' was an add on, that wasn't in the original script, the sort of justification for the format, as it were. After weeks and weeks we eventually decided it'd be quicker to write it ourselves.

PH: Were Rory McGrath's scripts written for the Sir Arthur Streeb-Greebling persona?

JL: I don't know that it was... However, what grew out of it,

agonisingly slowly, is this peculiar combination of very strange
ideas like slow farming, personalised light-bulbs, weird ideas like
the Balinese fighting fish. What was really wonderful about that
strangely moving opening credit sequence with the slow-motion
crashing waves and the Rachmaninov piano music playing, is that
you said, 'Well, of course, this is a fictional character but it tells
you a lot about the awful miseries of life.' And although Peter plays
the same man in each episode, he's distinctly different every time.
The one where he's the awful spy who was at Cambridge—there's
a terrible smugness about him and there's the shifty aspect when
he's the conman. It seemed to express exactly that—a life in pieces.
A whole life, and strange resonances and echoes of Peter's own
life. The spy character was actually based on my tutor at Trinity,
Cambridge. We had to change the name for fear of libel. He was a
pretty powerful character who did a lot of recruiting for the Secret
Service.

PH: Did he try to recruit you?

JL: No, I was always very upset about that. Later, I did have a
very odd experience at the BBC. I was 24, 25, and got a call from
someone with a grand title like Head Of Corporate Affairs and who
never actually did anything but was very highly paid and important.

PH: Sitting in an office and never seeing anyone.

JL: Yeah and I said to my head of department, 'What shall I do
about this invitation?' He said, 'Be incredibly careful what you say.
This is the managing director's hitman.' I was very suspicious about
why this man wanted to take me out to dinner and, having been to
public school, you're well advised to sit with your back to the wall.
I went to this dinner—I got pissed beforehand because I was so
anxious—and decided to answer every question with another question so I wouldn't commit myself. So it would be, 'Do you like...
opera?' 'Erm, do you?' 'Ahh, yes I do rather like it, actually... Do

you like theatre?' 'Do *you*?' This went on throughout the whole dinner and this man obviously thought me completely insane, very drunk and totally unreliable. He never called me again. Years later I learned he was recruiting for MI6 and I'd botched the interview by behaving like an arse.

PH: Was Peter easily persuaded to do *A Life In Pieces*?

JL: Yeah, he was. He liked Rory, thought him a good writer, but there was the horror that the idea wouldn't stick and we had to re-do it. Unlike, say, *South Of Watford*, which is how I got involved with Fergleberger. The original idea was for a show for the *South Of Watford* series called *Peter Cook's London*, which was literally the hundred yards of pavement between Perrins Walk and the newsagent with an off-licence on the way. I called Peter up about this idea, saying, 'This is going to be such a gas—'

PH: '—you'll be on location—'

JL: Yeah! 'You'll go to the newsagent and then a car will take you to *Private Eye* and this will be your life, this pathetic patch of turf and you just chat.' 'Cos he was the sort of person who could just talk to a camera crew for a day or so and it'd be wonderful. It was all content and no form—that was the attraction of it—the reverse of most television. No nice shots. Just a bloke talking, doing something utterly banal. Then whizzing off to *Private Eye* with London whisking past but you don't see anything 'cos you're too busy reading the newspapers and then you come back and that's the end of the programme. He said it's quite a fun idea and toyed with it, but then he said, 'I just can't do it. I've got this awful deadline.' And I had to really draw it out of him, what the matter was. So I said, 'I'll tell you what, I'll come and write Fergleberger with you, we'll knock it off, if you do the programme.' And he said, 'Oh... OK,' and then, 'No, I can't do the programme, I'm under too much stress.' So we did Fergleberger instead. It had just transmuted itself.

PH: And neither show got made. In fact, that *Peter Cook's London* idea sort of reminds me: being an idler at art college around that time, I wrote to loads of famous people about how they spent their day. The plan was to get enough replies to make up the 6,000 words necessary for my final year thesis, thus saving me the bother of wasting valuable time writing it myself. Peter Cook was one of those I wrote to and I didn't get a reply, and I thought, 'A-ha! *That's* how you get through the day. By not frittering away your time opening fucking letters!'

JL: That's right. He never used to do that. He used to be knee deep in letters. Even when he was out of his bad patch, you'd go round to his house and the mat would be covered in these bloody things and you had to kick 'em out of the way.

PH: I cannot understand that attitude, not opening letters. I mean, wasn't he in the least curious to know?

JL: I have the same thing. My briefcase is full of unopened letters. [*This is true*—PH]
About that time—'86, '87—Harry Enfield said, 'I've got a great idea. We should do a show—I play the kid, Lloydy plays my dad and Peter plays the grandfather.' Because we all saw each other a bit and we shared similar characteristics—with Peter it was un-emptied ashtrays that ran over, the unopened letters. I made the assumption—me being obviously more gloomy than Peter—that these things were indicative of a melancholic nature beneath the jokes. Peter, though, managed to make so many jokes that it never occurred to anyone that he might actually be quite sad.

PH: And the reason he never opened the letters?

JL: Why? Because he was frightened, basically. I'm frightened of the work it might engender, or frightened of the bank manager, that kind of thing. I don't know why he didn't open 'em. Maybe it was a not-wanting-to-face-the-world kind of thing... I remember talking to this gay bloke who said he only had unprotected sex and

I said, 'You're absolutely crazy. Why do you do that? You can die.' He replied, 'Look, *you* smoke. What's the difference?' Why did Peter smoke so many cigarettes, why did he drink so much, why did he *kill* himself, basically? He put himself through so much that eventually something was gonna give. I mean, it wasn't an accident, really. It was a sort of accident but you're asking for it, really, if you're living at that level. Smoking's an unconscious habit that gets worse as your system attunes to the intake and craves more.

PH: He was a walking oxymoron, wasn't he? We'd see him on chat shows making merry and marching to his own drum, and you'd think this was a chap totally relaxed in himself and the world, but that would be undercut by the ever-present burning cigarette and, occasionally, deep, heavily-bagged eyes that relayed the fact he was a wired insomniac.

JL: Anxious, yes. And all that stuff about Peter reading 39,000 papers and watching every television show forty times over—it's displacement, isn't it? It's somebody saying, 'I don't want to deal with real life, which is *me*, so I'll push it away.' You see that in people who work too hard. It's too painful for them to look inside themselves and so everything is directed outwards by making people laugh or not going to bed in case you have dreams about it...

He told me once that when Wendy left him he really couldn't see the point of anything very much. He'd done everything, he had won and lost fortunes, and then his wife left him and something snapped inside. After that, the divorce, he felt he was just going through the motions. It's strange too that he was an incredibly good-looking young man but it's the women—Wendy and Judy—that both walked out on him, for whatever reason. That reality must have been very hard for Peter to take. It'd be ridiculous for me to opine on why they left him—I know neither of them—but I suppose he was a wonderful guy who was impossible to live with.

Thinking about it, I don't think it's possible to do really great comedy if there isn't, behind the jokes, meaning, point, sadness and pain. That sounds pretentious but if comedy's just about puns or light remarks then forget it. The stuff that really touches you has got tragedy woven into it. You know, the miner who wanted to be a judge but lacked sufficient Latin—that's a tragic story if it was a real person. It's ghastly. Peter had something to say about the human condition, even if it was dressed up as an upper-class bastard teaching ravens to fly underwater. It was there at the outset with the one-legged man who wanted to be Tarzan and it carried on through to the Streeb-Greebling stuff we did in 1990—this awful smug opportunist, but you feel this terrible tragedy that he's destroyed and wasted his life and made a complete hash of it. And the petty things people get upset about, exemplified by Sir Arthur's complaining that he hasn't got four enormous larks, he just has a lawn de-nuded of larks.

PH: And in the next episode he learns that the man responsible for the enormous larks has been sacked, and he is tickled pink that revenge has been exacted.

JL: It sounds pretentious to say it's about the human condition but it is acutely observed of how bastards behave, isn't it? They get incredibly sulky and upset, and the next moment everything's forgotten, it's fine. It's a man with a huge ego. Streeb-Greebling is very cruel but deeply sentimental, too.

   It's odd but I was reading a book of quotations by Greek philosophers the other night and I kept bumping into things where I thought, 'Oh, Peter would have said that, but he would have put it in joke form,' you know what I mean? I think that, of Peter's work, if we could work out what the code was—if we could crack his code—we could get a new philosophy. Because it's all there—if only we could work out what he was trying to say, then there's nothing else that needs to be said. That'd be the only bible we'd need. I really feel this powerfully. I've met a lot of famous comedians, and some were absolutely brilliant, but I always felt Peter knew something he wasn't letting on. But John Cleese personally knows the Dalai Lama. John's written books on family therapy, he's studied philosophy and read Elizabeth Kubler Ross. He has all the kit, you know? I don't think Peter did any of those things but if I was to choose between the two who to discuss philosophy with, I'd be, 'So, if you could be serious for five minutes, Peter'—he *wouldn't* have been—'could you just tell me the meaning of life, what's it about?' Cleese would probably give you a twelve hour lecture and turn it into a series of best-selling books but I don't think I'd be any the wiser about it. In theory, he knows all the facts but I think Peter had the handle on something that very, very, very few people know. I couldn't for the life of me tell you what it was. It was mysterious to me. I had a terrific sense of goodness, even in an ill-lived life where he made a hash of his marriages and—although his daughters adored him—he was probably inattentive as a father sometimes.

He drank too much, read too many pornographic magazines and so on, but none of those things are important to the innate sense of somebody being on The Right Side. There are lots of people who are famous and very funny who I definitely think work for The Other Side. They're just in it for themselves, ultimately. I can't pin it down, why Peter was different.

PH: Another difference between John Cleese and Peter Cook is that, for me at least, somewhere down the line, Cleese just stopped being funny. *A Fish Called Wanda* and *Fierce Creatures* seem so precisionist, so calculated. The countless TV adverts he does where he's a tool of marketing don't help either. I just get the impression that through self-analysis (and beardy Liberal politics) he has rationalised his capacity for wanting to create comedy out of himself.

JL: I think he'd hate you for saying that. With *Fierce Creatures* I think he reached a point where—arguably and reasonably—he felt that he had never really done a failure and he knew what The Secret Of Comedy was, and that is fatal. Like they say, if you know what makes people laugh and why, then nothing else needs to be said because you will have discovered The Secret Of Life. That is my sincere belief, I promise you, because nobody knows, despite what is said about humour—Freud's theories or Bergson's theories. Nobody has any idea, and that extraordinary feeling you get when you can't stop laughing—it's some strange, magical touchstone. If you're arrogant enough to think you can produce it from a cupboard—and I never got that impression from Peter. Every time he started talking he had no idea what he was going to say, no intention to be funny...

Clive Anderson is similar in that way. He's a straight, serious, slightly anxious guy, in repose—not gloomy, but an unaffected, decent person—but when Clive starts joking you know there's no time to think when he comes up with these razor-sharp lines. OK, he's a trained barrister and highly intelligent but his comedy isn't coming from the conscious part of his brain that worries about railway timetables. Clive comes out with yards of comedy like that [clicking fingers] and that's just the same as Peter, that spontaneous ability.

Much though I like Jack Cleese, there is a tiny little bit of arrogance where he thought he knew everything in that world. My thing is The Universe Does Not Like Smugness and it rewards it with a kick in the teeth, and *Fierce Creatures* was such a kick: 'You're very lucky to have this gift of making people laugh. You should be modest and grateful about it.' When Peter and I were writing Fergelburger and Peter said, 'I'm scared in case what I say to you is not funny in your eyes,' that was an incredibly modest thing to say to somebody who is 15 years younger and who is nobody. That was a sincere statement.

PH: Did Peter regard the physical act of writing as a block to spontaneous invention and therefore needed people to be with him to bounce off ideas?

JL: Well, I don't want to get locked in to these strange ideas of creativity and intuition. If you go to Monty Python's infamous Parrot Sketch, the original sketch was about returning a faulty piece of electrical equipment to a shop; a very Cleesey idea of how annoying it is to try and get your money refunded while the sales assistant is claiming there's nothing wrong with the item. That was how the sketch was until Graham Chapman gets up from under a hail of gin bottles—he'd been lying under these bottles on the floor—and says, 'It should be about a dead parrot, you cunt!' And Cleese, smart bloke, thinks, 'Ah! Of course.' Now it's a classic whereas before it was just The Toaster Sketch and nobody would ever have heard about it again...

So there are two kinds of writer. I'm like John Cleese. I write Toaster Sketches. I'm very neat, thinking logically. Then there is the Chapman or the Cook kind of person who goes, 'No, no, no, it's much odder than that.' So we made a good combination. We did, of course, sit down and say, 'Let's start with this,' but there was never any point, you know? It was like weather. You both sat in the room with the drinks or whatever-it-was, with Fincham or Lin bustling about in the background, and sometimes [inspiration] arrived and sometimes it didn't. It wasn't as though we could call up a thunderstorm or electrical discharge. The idea of him being disciplined in sitting down every day and writing funny sketches—it's a different part of the brain, you know what I mean? It's like the lefthand side of the brain wasn't any use to him and he had to use only the righthand side and that required an intuitive and, er, drinking-too-muchy kind of way of working.

PH: There were a few episodes of *A Life In Pieces* where the Christmas gift in question was barely mentioned. That aspect was often entirely peripheral to the interviews. Did you and Peter find it tough to stick to the Twelve Days Of Christmas carol format?

JL: We did produce a lot and I would take home huge scads of stuff and try to think how they would relate to milkmaids and drummers and partridges in pear-trees.

I've found that nearly all ideas for shows that initially look promising always turn out to be a nightmare. Like Spitting Image: 'What a great idea—a topical, political show with puppets.' But it was quite another thing to get it on-air. A nightmare. *A Life In Pieces* was the same. We had to throw the format away and get Peter to be very funny for three weeks or however long it took to write—and, in fact, the one about the Single European Hen was written by Peter with Peter Fincham in about two hours and we were almost shooting the series by then.

There were some jokes that we held on to till the last minute, thinking, 'At least we can use this joke,' until we eventually had to admit it's the one gag that doesn't fit and we had to cut it. I have endless respect for Rory, who never complained, 'You fucking bastards, you've ruined my life.' A writer not to moan about having his work not used is unheard of. He's been very nice about it and said, 'I think it's brilliant what you did. It's very funny and I can see why my stuff didn't work.'

PH: Let's proceed to the filming of *A Life In Pieces*. Ludovic Kennedy wasn't the first choice as interviewer, was he?

JL: I think he might have been. Who was it then? Do you know?

PH: Well, Harry Thompson's biography of Peter says it was Edward Heath.

JL [*Groans*]: Oh *nooo*. Not a chance. And I'll tell you why. Richard Curtis had asked me to contribute to a Comic Relief night and what eventually came up was The Nose Night Quiz, with clips of politicians from *Newsnight*. Politicians are very wary of saying anything that may be misconstrued or taken out of context so they're all given to spouting bland statements but what they have in common is that they're always quoting numbers, figures—'Three million,' 'Five million'—and I had this total flash of inspiration where Rowan Atkinson is a quizmaster asking this panel of MPs, 'Right, fingers on the buzzers. What is two plus two?' and there'd be a clip of Edward Heath saying, 'I think it's 330 million, I'm absolutely certain!' And David Steel: 'Well, I'm not prepared to answer at this time until all the facts are in but I would guess at 17 million.' Sometimes you do bump into genius by struggle and that is a fantastically funny sketch, particularly Quentin Hogg, Lord Hailsham, every time he's asked a question, saying, 'Was it the Belgians?' [*Laughter*]

We then asked all the MPs used in the sketch for their permission and they all gave it willingly and cheerfully, except for Edward Heath who said it was disgraceful that politicians should be made a mockery of, so we had to cut him out of the sketch. So there's no way I would have asked him. Ludovic Kennedy was definitely the right choice. He was a sort of serious version of Peter Cook. He's a very good man, a man of utter integrity, but also the most wonderful sense of humour. Ludo was perfect because he looks deadly serious and you don't want someone chuckling, 'Ho, ho, very amusing.'

PH: What I thought was great about the casting of Ludovic Kennedy was in his reaction shots. His jowls, upon hearing another fantastic Streeb-Greebling tale, would wobble like an old elephant's bum flaps.

JL: Yeah. I seem to remember that Ludo wasn't there. I think we just shot Peter with Fincham reading him the questions. Ludo came in on separate days, or only for one or two days, and then we had to cut him in doing, you know, nodding—otherwise Peter would've been talking to nothing. Then there was another strange thing: When we came to edit the thing there was no laughter-track—obviously—and when we put in all the Ludo questions it wasn't funny at all because it wasn't [*clicks fingers twice*] pointed out. So we put in all the cut-aways [Kennedy's reaction shots] and that took months, the editing. It's the way you time the cut-away that makes it funny. If you don't have them it's rather dull, actually. Strangely.

PH: And how did you feel about the final result?

JL: I think the scripts were brilliant. Shooting them you obviously can't add much to a two-hander interview, and because we never had Ludo in situ most of the time I just had to shoot Peter and make his performance as good as possible. But you know about film directing: most people who are ignorant about film directing think that the hardest thing for a film director is to shoot a battle scene or the sinking of the Titanic with millions of extras. They are easy! That's just planning. What's really hard is to shoot one person on one camera, because then you are naked. Special effects and flashy cutting don't help you. You must get the performance out of your actor. That's very, very difficult. So it was wearing, the filming, and Peter felt tense. Most of my job was to get him up to speed in the morning, saying, 'You remember when you wrote it, how Sir Arthur was very sunny?' and helping him find the character.

PH: How did Peter rate *A Life In Pieces*?

JL: Hmm, I think when you're right on the edge of something like that and you're used to having a live audience, as Peter was, even when he was writing, as it were, because we'd all be pissing ourselves, then that awful doubt creeps in when you do it to a cold studio and you do ten takes you're thinking, 'Is this funny? I don't know.' And then when it went out to *nothing*—you know, one review or something—being shown at all these strange times of night. Nobody ever mentioned it at all.

PH: Except *Time Out* who said it was one of the highlights of the Christmas fortnight.

JL: Did they? Well, apart from them, it was a thing where we worked very hard on it, we thought it was very good but it just disappeared, so we just forgot about it, really. This is almost the first time in ten years anyone's mentioned it.

PH: That's a great pity because *A Life In Pieces* not only has wildly inventive writing but a fully engaged, multi-detailed performance from Peter. He's not just sat there with a big moustache stuck on his face.

JL: When they say Peter wasn't an actor, I think Rory's script was an acting job and Peter wasn't an actor in that way. What he was good at was creating characters out of aspects of himself. What he couldn't do was take someone else's dialogue and give it any credit. In *The Black Adder* he suffered dreadfully like that. If he had been allowed to write the whole piece I'm sure it would have been brilliant, but it was part of a script and he had to do those lines whether they were funny or not and we only had a week to do it in. Rik Mayall, though, every time he guested on *Blackadder*, insisted he re-wrote all his lines, which is why, when he appeared, he wiped the floor with everyone else—because he took over his scenes.

Peter was his usual, diffident, modest self when we asked him to play Richard III: 'I don't think I'll be good enough,' when, of course, he was. He was perfect.

PH: Did he make any contribution to the script?

JL: In rehearsal, things come up, but not much because he was tense, he didn't really know what he was doing there. He got on well with all of us, he'd known Rowan Atkinson for a long time, but like so many actors who came to do cameos on *Blackadder*—Tom Baker and so on—we treated them appallingly because we wanted a 'house' style, a sort of revue way of performing rather than Great Acting. We had the Stephen Fry sort of acting—[*Fry's bray:*] '*Erghh! Wurghh!!*'—you know, simple. Stephen's wonderful, a sort of genius, but I wouldn't call him an actor the same way I'd call Hugh Laurie an actor. Rowan's not an actor, he's a performer, like Stephen's a performer, Peter Cook's a performer and I suppose John Cleese is a performer. I know he's played Petruchio but that never cut any ice with me. Those guys have to play a version of themselves.

Great comedians like Peter and Billy Connolly have to have to huge element of themselves in their material otherwise they're not telling the truth. Whereas an actor is an interpreter. Miranda Richardson, who played Elizabeth I in *Blackadder* II, is a brilliant case in point. One of her lines was 'Hello Blackadder, how are you this morning?' No one in the world can make that line funny, but she can because she's interpreted it and put something into the performance that isn't apparent in the writing. That's the kind of thing Peter Cook wouldn't have been any good at. He had to have the funny line to begin with. So, as an actor—no. As a communicator of comic ideas—second to none.

PH: After *A Life In Pieces* did you two work together again?

JL: I don't know. You tell me.

PH: Well, in your *Something Like Fire* contribution you mentioned plans for books and TV shows.

JL: Yeah, we spent ages and ages—because we'd had such an enjoyable experience with Peter Fincham—trying to think of doing something proper, trying to think of a format for what we used to call 'The Prisoner With Jokes'. It was gonna be like a huge conspiracy.

PH [*flummoxed*]: 'The Prisoner With Jokes'?

JL: You know, *The Prisoner*?

PH: Er, Prisoner Of Zenda? [*Penny-farthing drops*] Oh, *The Prisoner*! Yes yes, Patrick McGoohan menaced by balloons. 'I am not a number.'

JL: That's it. A big '60s adventure thing, but funny. We were struggling to find the format, what the basic idea of it was. We had reams and reams of jottings—'The False Passport Office' and 'Burberry Apes'—loads of stuff we had written but we never worked out what the bloody idea was!

PH: So you've got all this atmosphere but no gravity?

JL: Yeah, and it was all down to Peter, you see? I'd have lots of ideas but if they never suited Peter's sensibilities they wouldn't go anywhere. The idea was to put some words into the air so then he could go off on a ridiculous tangent, and that would be the funny bit, and it would have nothing to do with what started it... It was all a bit lackadaisical.

PH: We're talking about Peter in the early 1990s but you first worked with him, I think, in 1979 for the *Here Comes The Judge* record. Was he another can of beans then? Did he have a different dynamic?

JL: Well, I never heard him complain or moan, or weep for his lost life or anything. But the fact that he had these press-cuttings from years and years ago on his wall—I mean, his success was important to him, but he never boasted about it. He'd never go, 'I've done this, I've done that,' whereas most comedians boast continually about their novels or their series. He never mentioned it but he must have been very proud of things he had done. This was a guy who, when we'd had too much to drink—and I'm the sort who likes to talk seriously about the nature of things—but Peter would never want to. He would always turn it into funny stuff.

I think he was too intelligent not to have wondered, 'What are we all doing here?' I'm certain he did. That line of inquiry is all over E.L. Wisty. Maybe for some reason he had addressed it and decided it was all futile or had found it too unnerving to think about. Maybe he thought it best to just drink a bottle of brandy or something and watch the telly. He wasn't the type to wear his heart on his sleeve and consequently it didn't get much airing.

PH: It's admirable and noble, I feel, that sense of self-unimportance.

JL: Yeah, he was not a pompous person. Peter would be the person at the Celebrity Party found chatting with the little old lady serving the sandwiches. He didn't have any side. He was just as interested in the waiter as he would be in Henry Kissinger—probably more interested. That modesty is innate and in general social intercourse he was a very sunny, easy-going chap. When we started writing *A Life In Pieces* he came over to my place and immediately began chatting to Sarah, my wife—not in a brusque 'Oh, the producer's wife: better say hello'—but as if he'd known her for years, and the same with our baby, Harry. He'd give everyone equal attention. When people say 'charming'—the thing about charm is that it's a deliberate act, it's people who know they're charming and set out to charm to get a result. I don't think Peter did that. It's just the way he was. People said he was bitchy about Dudley Moore but, again, it always came across as very funny.

PH: What do you think Peter's politics were? Now, I know this is a dodgy area of questioning, asking about the political leanings of a dead man, because the interviewee would like the person they're talking about to share a lot of the same beliefs. Like, when I interviewed Auberon Waugh he stated that Peter was always a right-winger and, by the end, very, very right-wing indeed. Paul Foot has gone on record saying Peter Cook was a libertarian and this is seen in his hands-off approach as *Private Eye*'s proprietor. Richard Ingrams said, 'Peter Cook was a Christian Conservative Anarchist [*Guffaws from John Lloyd*]. Like me.'

JL: [*Ingrams voice*] 'And a non-drinker!' Christian Conservative Anarchist... No, that's Richard Ingrams only. No, I think Peter was a floating voter because you can't be that acute in the way you look at the world and see the funny side and be any kind of joiner, you know? I suppose Peter's attitudes to politics was pretty much like most people's in that politicians are only in it for themselves and there are very few good ideas in modern politics. Everyone says Auberon Waugh's right-wing, but Bron's a completely human person. His trick is to seek out hypocrisy and cuntishness wherever it lies and then address it from a comical right-wing perspective, and he often comes up with truthful things. He's not hampered by political correctness.

PH: The mention of Auberon Waugh leads us logically into the arena of discos and nightclubbing. Did you ever go out on the tiles with Peter?

JL: Once, yeah, at The Limelight.

PH: What was his record collection like, by the way?

JL: Never heard it. Usually he would have the telly on. I never noticed any records.

PH: Oh, OK, I just wondered. Anyway, you were down The Limelight, necked a couple of E's...

JL: We didn't have any drugs, actually. For some reason, I had been given a Gold Card there as a freebie. Peter had been working at my flat and he said, 'Oh come on, let's go out,' and because I had this Gold Card we went to The Limelight. The doorman had no idea who we were—just an old bloke with this slightly shorter, less old bloke. Both pissed, of course. Because I had this card we got shown to the VIP room where there was a particularly delicious class of bimbos and a few pop musicians. I swear to God nobody in that room knew who he was, 'cos a lot of the girls said, 'Who are you? What do you do?' but they were all around him like bees around a jampot. Quite extraordinary, this magnetic pull. They were all around him, one on each arm, laughing, all that stuff, fantastic. I didn't get a look in... *Bastard*. [*Laughter*]

One got the impression from that—you know, two middle aged blokes going out—what fun it must have been to be a friend of Peter's in the '60s. He had a story about how he was in New York once and he decided he wanted some drugs, so he went up to the first black guy he saw and said, 'Do you have any drugs, old boy?' [*Laughter*] The black guy said, 'Yeah, sure, get in the car with me,' and he actually got in and they drove off somewhere and procured some drugs and came back, not a hair on his head harmed, very good deal—not some rip-off, you know? It was that innocence about him. You couldn't imagine anyone beating Peter Cook up. It'd be like, er...

PH: Kicking the shit out of Mother Teresa?

JL: Yeah, it just wouldn't occur to anyone. He was such a nice bloke and that is a terrific piece of armour in those situations because people connect with you intuitively, and that's what the girls did in The Limelight. They thought, 'He's sexy in a way we can't identify.' Because he looked a bit porky and hadn't washed his hair in six weeks, you know, but he could turn those eyes on people and they'd go weak at the knees.

PH: We should discuss your contribution to *Here Comes The Judge*.

JL: That record struck me as a bit of a scam, really, like the way they advertise videos these days as having previously-unreleased material not seen on TV.

PH: Yes, usually for a good reason: It's rubbish!

JL: But it was really good fun, if terrifying, to do, trying to be Dudley Moore and realising how difficult his job was. It was very hard not to laugh, apart from anything else. Plus one felt so stupid in comparison because Peter's mind would be so amazingly agile and leap from one thing to another. I mean, I think I'm reasonably bright but I just felt thick in that situation. But Peter would be very pleased if someone came up with a good ad-lib. He used to play this game—he said he and Dudley used to play this game in the '60s and '70s, where they'd be driving down the street in a car and they'd do this endless dialogue taking in all the names of shops that they passed. It'd be hilarious, unbelievably brilliant, Peter doing this so quick 'cos the car was doing 30, and there would be this endless spring. That's what he was like in everything. You just couldn't keep up with it. Nobody but he could ever do it. My contribution to *Here Comes The Judge* was pretty minor. The important thing about the record was the [*Entirely A Matter For You*] monologue from the Amnesty show, an absolute masterpiece that will stand forever.

PH: You were involved in Peter and Mel Smith's turn at the Nether Wallop Arts Festival. Paul Jackson said he saw Peter and Mel writing the sketch at Nether Wallop.

JL: No, it didn't happen like that. We did it over at Peter's house in Hampstead over two or three afternoons. He came up with this stupid idea and I was acting as the editor, typist and spare ideas person. They worked on it—lesbian synchronised swimming—pretty hard and came up with some funny ideas. It was extremely funny and very well performed in rehearsal—the synchronised *walking*, as it was.

Unfortunately, because Nether Wallop was a completely unique experience and all the events were happening in tin huts strewn all over the village, everything over-ran and there was an awful lot of free alcohol floating about. Peter and Mel were in the beer tent for much too long. What they were drinking, I don't know. A whole mixture of things, probably vodka-based. They both got very drunk. Peter is probably the only person I can think of who could drink Mel under the table. Mel lived a pretty riotous lifestyle but he used to be an athlete, so he's pretty fit under the rotundity. But I think they had each met their match at Nether Wallop and they were both genuinely drunk, almost unable to walk when they came to do the sketch. I was sitting there, a little drunk myself, finding what they were doing very funny but also seeing this marvellous, beautifully scripted and rehearsed piece in absolute ruins. These two drunks blundering around with these silly glasses on, and not much remaining of what could have been the new Tarzan sketch. Not *quite* the triumphant highlight it was intended to be.

THE BACK PASSAGE
Letter spray

Dear Clinty,

Not only would John Cleese take exception to the Dragger's opinions expressed in the (exceptional) John Lloyd feature. I would, too! I actually enjoyed *Fierce Creatures* and I don't care who knows it. But then I also thought *The Hound Of The Baskervilles* was funny. Am I mad?

DAVE TOYNTON, K*nt.

TALKBACKCHAT

The Holy Dragger has packed his poofy shoulder bag
With his tape recorder, clementines, an extra pack of fags
And a 1991 edition of Blitz, a defunct style mag
(A pathetic attempt to keep up with the latest fads).
He's going to see Peter Fincham.
He runs TalkBack Productions, he ain't short of a tanner
But he's not the sort to be seen puffing on a Havana.
His tough-as-a-Dalek's-titness is noted when he scoffs a black
    banana.
Who's got tapes of Peter Cook what we'd love to grab with our
    wanking spanners?
Here's a clue: It's Peter Fincham
Every TV comedy prog that's ever been planned
Seems to have been executively produced by this man.
A poker-faced Venus de Milo, he never shows his hand.
When he croaks there'll be a memorial hatstand
Unveiled in honour of Peter Fincham.
If there were pert derrieres going spare, would he... pinch
    'em?

Is he the one-man KKK of bad jokes? Would he... lynch 'em?
He's not the nut in Network; that was Peter... Finch. Mm...
Has anyone got a good rhyme for 'pinch 'em' and 'lynch 'em'?
I know! I'll go and ask Peter Serafinowicz...

PETER FINCHAM: Peter and I probably first met through Mel and Griff in the late eighties and then first worked together when we did *A Life In Pieces* in 1990.

PAUL HAMILTON: Ah, I thought it might have been earlier, your working with him, since TalkBack began as a radio commercials enterprise—

PF: Yes, Peter and John Lloyd did some Duracell battery ads. That was before I stepped into the frame. Jon Canter wrote those—he's the sort of bloke who keeps his own archives, I bet he'll have the scripts. I could probably get them. There are things you've asked for that are much, much more difficult.

PH: Ah, these hallowed tapes of Peter improvising that I've been whanging on to you about for six years.

PF: Well, Harry Thompson wanted them when he was writing his biography of Peter. Once he published his biography, he never mentioned them again. The thing is, I've moved house about three times and I've never found them yet. There are lots of these tapes in existence of Peter rambling. I'm not claiming that they're special, but Peter rambling was always funny so there would always have been great moments in them.

Sometimes John and I would sit with Peter and we'd lob questions at him... which he'd answer—Very Nice! Sometimes it'd be me on my own, other times John. Sometimes we'd record them—sometimes we wouldn't—usually in my office. Sometimes I'd go to Perrins Walk. Peter preferred working in Lin's house for some reason; perhaps to get out of his own house.

PH: Was he easily distracted from getting down to work?

PF: Ha ha ha ha. Well... You turn on the tape recorder and lob a question at him and there would be quite a long pause, and then he would answer it, never in the way that you'd expect him to do so, and I think that's partly where his genius lay. You would ask him a question and your own rather slow comic brain would think 'Oh, there's a funny answer to that' but he wouldn't come out with that, he'd go someplace else. In fact, the second series I made with Peter, *Why Bother?*, was made that way. Those two series of Sir Arthur Streeb-Greebling—*A Life In Pieces* and *Why Bother?*—were made in completely different ways. Obviously so since *Life...* was on film so we needed it scripted beforehand. But one script didn't work and Peter and I went to this hotel one night to re-do one about Belgium.

PH: The notorious Toblerone complex—

PF:—Yeah, the girl with the Nesquik who had never seen furniture before. I do have a vivid memory of sitting rather tired at the end of a day's filming while he just made that all up. I was just annotating, really. Note-taking.

Whereas the radio series happened much more like the way he would improvise naturally: Chris Morris would just ask a question, like, you know, 'Your Second World War record's been rather controversial, hasn't it?' And he would have had no notice of that question at all and suddenly we would be into something about Japanese prisoner-of-war camps.

PH: What did Peter think of the series?

PF: He liked it and wanted to work with Chris again. *Why Bother?* was very heavily edited and to some degree it's Chris Morris' construct. Chris' background is radio so he took the tapes and went away and turned often quite shapeless things into coherent pieces.

Personally, I think *Why Bother?* is the better of the two series. That may be something to do with the methodology in making it. The filming of *Life...* in some ways made it a bit stiff. I haven't seen it for a long time so I don't know whether the joins show. It had some wonderful passages.

All I ever did with Peter was Sir Arthur Streeb-Greebling. I didn't do anything with Peter where he wasn't Sir Arthur and I think during those series Sir Arthur became more developed and they became the definitive Sir Arthur pieces. Of course, the character's attained this elegiac feel and so they're rather apt.

PH: I met Chris Morris in the street about a year ago and he said that, as a preparation for *Why Bother?*, you had lent him a tape of John Lloyd and Peter extemporising.

PF: Did he?

PH: Yep!

PF: Maybe he's got the tapes.

PH: He insists he hasn't. No one admits to having them! But this tape started off with John asking, 'Evolution, then: What's all that about?' Do you remember this?

PF: Yes!

PH: And Peter went something like, 'Well, in the beginning there was the sea—'

PF: '—and on the sea was an umbilical cord—'

PH: '—and a baby grew out of the umbilical cord, and at the end of the umbilical cord grew another baby who had an umbilical cord, at the end of which grew another baby... And so on and so on until the sea was covered in a net made of babies. A string vest of babies.' It's a startling image.

PF: Yeah, that rings a bell and was very inspired. I think he'd read about the aquatic ape or whatever that thing was we were supposed to have evolved from under the sea. It played on his mind a lot.

PH: Aqua apes. Excellent!

PF: Peter, you see, was very well-informed. He scoured the news-papers and watched loads of telly, so he seemed to be right up to date on a whole range of matters.

PH: The benefit of not doing much work.

PF: Yes, because everyone else is too busy to keep up with everything. What did he talk about? He never talked—or very rarely—about the past.

PH: His own?

PF: His own past. He would if you asked him to: He didn't make a thing of it, you know, 'I'm not talking about *Beyond The Fringe* or Dudley Moore, any of that.' He was always very polite. But he didn't live in the past at all. He lived very much in the moment, in the present. When we were doing *Why Bother?* there was a day in which he turned up with a bottle of champagne to the recording. It wasn't that unusual to see Peter with a champagne bottle in his hand, but he said his fax machine had been delivered that morn-ing. He finally got himself a fax machine so this was something to celebrate. So we all had a glass of champagne. There's a mixture of things in that: An ability in taking pleasure in a trivial event in one's life and then to share it with everybody was a rather endear-ing trait.

He didn't at all have that thing some comedians have—of really wanting to have an industry gossip; who's up, who's down, who's in, who's out, whose latest series has flopped. While I was working with him I had a series on BBC1 which didn't really work, a sitcom called *Bonjour la Classe* with Nigel Planer.

[Blank look from Hamilton]

PF: You see, you can't even remember it. It was OK but it didn't lift off, but because we worked together he kindly watched an episode and he had kind words to say. Kind words: now there are some comedians who don't have a kind word to say about anything or anybody, and only see competition in their fellow comedians, only see rivalry. One of the reasons he got along with, and appealed to, the younger generation of comedians was that he seemed to be Beyond All That. He didn't seem to resent the younger guys coming up behind him. He might have done at some stage but when I knew him, in the last five years of his life, he seemed to be at peace with the fact that his career had... stopped, really. It didn't bother him, as far as I could tell.

PH: So what did you talk about with Peter?

PF: Well, you didn't talk about comedy in a professional way. He was amusing all the time—though, sadly for those who write about him, not very often in ways that translate well to the page. And when you turned on the tape recorder and said 'Let's start work'—for want of a better word—he was happy to do so. He loved stepping into the character of Sir Arthur. Never any trouble getting him to be Sir Arthur, because he obviously saw him as an alter ego. And then he became funnier.

PH: Do you know William Donaldson? The Henry Root chappie and producer of *Beyond The Fringe*, yah de dah?

PF: Yes.

PH: Well, he maintains that Peter's name was poison in television circles through the eighties. Donaldson had approached various producers with ideas for a Henry Root series or one about Major Ron Ferguson. They seemed receptive to the proposals but as soon as he said Peter's willing to play Root or Major Ron, they went cold on the idea. 'Over my dead body' was a phrase Donaldson said he heard.

PF: Hmm. No, that sounds a good idea. Henry Root is a very Peter Cookish character.

PH: You were the first producer to get him a TV series since, er, God, *Revolver*.

PF: Yes, but I'm coming along at a slightly later period when he was turning the corner into A Living Legend and so curiosity at working with Peter Cook was replacing the feeling of 'Oh, he's burnt out' or whatever. We were just starting out with TalkBack; we had made *Smith and Jones*, but we needed to do other things. We were looking for opportunities and Mel Smith knew Peter and so, y'know, 'Let's ask Peter'... Peter, because of his... situation, was approachable. You *could* approach him, and he had time, and he liked Mel and Griff so he was willing to come in.

Another person who played a role in this courtship of him was Chris Langham. Chris was working at TalkBack then and I remember there was a meeting early on when there was almost too many of us present. There was me, Rory, Chris Langham, Mel may have poked his head through the door, John Lloyd. And I was leaving the room thinking, 'We're crowding out Peter here; there's too many people.'

What we were selling to the BBC was very modest. Twelve ten-minute programmes, and the budget wouldn't have been much, so we weren't asking BBC2 for an unbelievably big commitment.

PH: What was Chris Langham's involvement in *Life*...? He's credited as, I think, script editor.

PF: Yeah. He faded out of it and I'm not quite sure why. But he certainly was involved in the early stages.

PH: What's all this rot about you being an art collector, then?

PF: Oh! Daisy—Peter's daughter—is a painter, an artist, and Peter would ring me up and say, 'Daisy's having another exhibition. She's currently in her Expensive Period.'

PH: Did you buy one?

PF: No.

PH: Not expensive enough.

PF: I met Daisy Cook a few times and liked her enormously. She's enchanting. But, er, Peter was with Lin and you could feel the... *tension*.

PH: Did you ever do much socialising with Peter?

PF: Yes. He was a very social animal, Peter. He would come round for dinner, go out to restaurants, but he didn't seek out the world of parties just for the sake of it.

I went away with him for a few days to a hotel in the New Forest between Christmas and New Year—this would be a year after *Life....* It was just me and him. I remember Lin and my girlfriend at the time waving us off as we drove off down to Hampshire. We arrived at this hotel but it was too structured a thing to try to do. It wasn't like 'Let's turn on the tape recorder and see what happens.' We had to get up in the morning and try and work and write, but the discipline wasn't there. Plus it was that weird dead time between Christmas and New Year. Peter, at that time, was a fairly rococo figure to look at, with his pink tracksuit bottoms and his tweed jacket, the fag blazing in one hand, another one just burning out in the other hand.

PH: [*Remembers something and rushes off to delve into his bag*] Carry on, carry on.

PF: I thought the hotel was run by, I dunno, kind of French or Belgian staff who had no idea who Peter Cook was, so I suspected they all thought I was his young gay lover and we had gone away for a, erm, whatever reason.

[*Hamilton shows PF the relevant page of* Blitz *magazine retrieved from his bag—it has a photo of Peter in pink trackie slacks, tweed jacket and compulsory fag on.*]

PF: My God, this is him *precisely*! That is the Peter Cook I knew. That's how he was all the while! Amazing!

We had a great time at this hotel, which we didn't really like.

They were getting a bit snooty and this was at the time when hotels were beginning to worry about people smoking in the wrong bit or whatever. They didn't like *that*.

One day his mother came, and we had lunch, the three of us. She was a very charming lady to whom Peter was extraordinarily solicitous and polite. I remember sitting there trying to see him through her eyes, and thinking, 'What a weird thing to have been Peter Cook's mother'; the extraordinary meteoric success of his student years and early twenties, and the ups and downs and now *this figure*—what was he then, in his mid-fifties?

PH: Yeah, fifty-three.

PF: Although he looked... you know.

PH: How was Peter when he was with his mum? Did he cut out the swearing?

PF: Yes. His mother was charming, reserved, well-bred and seemed to take Peter's eccentricities in her stride. She wasn't the over-emotional type. A bit like the Queen, actually!

Anyway, the tapes I made stem from this time. I can't find 'em. I actually had been given as a Christmas present by Griff a camcorder and I took it with me and did some camcorder filming with Peter that I'd love to find but I know I don't know where it is.

PH [*Laughing*]: You can't find *anything!*

PF: I can't find anything. But that was a great experience—even though nothing came of it. We were trying to see if you could create a sitcom for Sir Arthur Streeb-Greebling. But this was absolutely self-defeating because Sir Arthur was a monologist, pure and simple. All he could do—which was the essence of the character—was to endlessly tell the story of his life and tell lies and bullshit. Putting Sir Arthur in a dramatic...—well, it'd be like putting Dame Edna Everage into something where other people were playing acted parts. The magic would go. You couldn't do it.

But we tried to fit Sir Arthur into that format—possibly in response to encouragement from the BBC. You know, 'These ten-minute shows are all very well; what about something lasting half an hour?' But it all came to nothing.

With the *Why Bother?*, I dunno, it might've been my idea. I started working with Chris Morris on *The Day Today*. As I got to know him, I thought, 'Hm, put these two together...'

The last time I saw Peter was in a thing called The National Perudo Championship and I was on his team—

PH: With Sting?

PF: No, we *beat* Sting! He wasn't on our team! We beat Sting.

PH: Tell me about Perudo. What is it? Lying?

PF: It's a South American liar's dice game and we did jolly well. The rules of Perudo refuse to stay in my mind and I have to be reminded from scratch each time I play it, but you can learn it in five minutes. It's a brilliant game. Stephen Fry called it the second most addictive thing to come out of South America. Another person on our side was Carla Powell. There was a fourth person but I can't remember who. Carla Powell was the Italian, er, political woman who knew Mrs Thatcher.

PH: Charles Powell's missus.

PF: That's it. I was sharing a taxi home with her very drunk to Notting Hill where we both lived, and I can remember saying goodbye to Peter on the pavement in The Strand and that was the last time I saw him. That was a very jolly evening. He was totally at home with that kind of celeb-y, um, sort of weird evening.

And we did beat Sting.

PH: Was the booze a help or hindrance in getting scripts made with Peter?

PF: In the morning, when we were working at his house, he would pop off somewhere to have a snorter of vodka or whatever-it-was rather than do it in front of me, as if there was some, er, some, um—

PH: Like he was letting the side down?

PF: No, more out of politeness. Like, you don't drink in front of someone. But I don't think of Peter as somebody who was drunk. In his speech patterns—and you can tell this from checking interviews—he was seemingly in a continual state that maybe he had had a few drinks, *maybe* he hadn't. Certainly I've worked with him when he was stone cold sober and he still had that slightly *camp* way of talking, you might say. From what I've read about him in the 1970s he must have been a bit unbearable to be around but I never saw it when I knew him. I mean, if he had plenty to drink he'd get a bit more tiddly than if he'd only had a drink or two. He didn't get belligerent. There was nothing problematical about it. It didn't affect the work. When we were filming *Life...* he was thoroughly professional and conscientious. He started drinking earlier in the day than most people. And he did smoke an awful lot. I mean, he sort of never *didn't* smoke—which takes an awful lot of doing. They weren't those weak ones either—those Silk Cut ultra-low things. It was an obscure, er—you probably know.

PH: Superkings, wasn't it?

PF: Yeah, and if he went into a newsagent he'd buy forty, and there aren't many people who'd do that these days. And it wasn't even his smoking that got him in the end, incidentally.

PH: No. All this talk of smoking is giving me a gasp-on. But, er, the writing sessions were invariably in the mornings, were they?

PF: Yes. I don't think he sought to work terribly hard. If things came along—like, whilst we were working, he went off and did that TV series, *Gone To The Dogs*.

PH: No, the sequel, *Gone To Seed*.

PF: And I watched an episode with him and a scene would come on and he'd say, 'Eight o'clock, Tuesday morning.' It'd cut to another scene and he'd say, 'Teatime, Wednesday.' That's all he'd say throughout the whole show. He was *not* a good actor. Acting, in the proper sense of the word, was not his forte at all, but he managed to make the watching of this episode enormously amusing simply by telling me the time of day that every scene had been shot in. He had a vivid recall.

But comedians and acting... I mean, Streeb-Greebling is the most fantastic character but it's not like Peter's acting someone else's words. Streeb-Greebling was in his element when rewriting his own personal history, slightly on the defensive, you may say 'entering a plea', a justification for what he'd done.

PF [*Misquoting*]: 'There are one and a half frames of film footage of me in my POW camp office trying to get the air conditioning to work which proves I did not beat anyone up.'

PF: Yeah, and I don't know where he comes from. He's like some 1940s archetype—the veneer of respectability, behind which he's a complete humbug.

The wonderful one from *Why Bother?* was about discovering the remains of the infant Jesus Christ. I was listening to that going out on my car radio and thinking, 'I'll never work again. The Duty Log at the BBC will be overwhelmed because it's so blasphemous.' But actually there were no complaints because I suspect hardly anyone heard it. It went out in a gap in the evening concert on Radio 3. But if you tried to give it a wider audience today you'd have people from Editorial Policy or whatever tying themselves in knots about it because it's outrageous. But very funny. A wonderful conception.

PH: Apart from the two Sir Arthur series were there any plans to use different personas?

PF: No, because between them there was two years of abortive improvisations and sessions. Maybe he was getting less disciplined but I don't think so. I think the Peter I knew in that five year period wasn't a finisher of things by nature. He was quite easily distracted.

PH: About ill-discipline or simply being unable to correctly channel energies... Comedians such as Steve Martin, say, or John Cleese wouldn't waste a gag in promotional interviews. They'd harness their creative energies for the job itself—writing a screenplay or performing it. Peter's interviews were joyous occasions; he'd be gassing away and making merry. Was that a true reflection of his general demeanour?

PF: Yes, yes. I can't honestly claim to have seen much of a Dark Side, do you know what I mean? Did he have moments when he wondered where his career had gone? Maybe, but he didn't bore me with it. Did he have moments when he worried about being overweight and unfit and smoking too much and drinking? Yep, but I never heard about them. He was endlessly genial and willing to make the social effort to amuse the person he was with—and that's something that's not true of all comedians. And he'd *listen* to you. He didn't want to only talk about himself. He liked talking about things.

PH: You make him sound like a Zen Buddhist in his adherence to living in the moment, seizing life as it happens, not mulling over the past or worrying about the future.

PF: Yes, I doubt that he would have subscribed to that view except in jest.

PH: A Zen Duddhist.

PF: Yeah.

DIFFERENT JOKES FOR DIFFERENT FOLKS

From radio's On The Hour *to TV's* The Day Today *and* Brass Eye *and back to radio for the twisted sinister of* Blue Jam, *Chris Morris causes Grievous Bodily Ha-ha-harm. He is both modern comedy's shining light and darkest star and if you can put a face to the name—it's usually submerged beneath a plethora of snot carpets, chin quilts and scalp-spaghetti—there's no mistaking his kamikaze brilliance and influence. Over cups of coffee and syringes of sodium pentathol Chris is quizzed by the Holy Dragger about his collaboration with Peter Cook,* Why Bother?, *at Munchies snack bar in London's notorious Charlotte Street on Friday 5th June 1998.*

PAUL HAMILTON: Whose idea was it to team you with Peter Cook?

CHRIS MORRIS: It was the idea of the guy that runs Talk-Back—Peter Fincham. He'd had some chatting sessions with Peter Cook and the idea just surfaced as a result of, I don't know, he put two and two together or he thought it would be appropriate in some way because it must've fitted with something that I was doing. He'd heard some radio shows I'd done—*On The Hour* or the Radio 1 series. It came out in early '94, I think, *Why Bother?* So we recorded it during the autumn of '93.

PH: Did it take long?

CM: Three or four sessions. We did a pilot in February '93 then recorded it in November, so there were probably four sessions in all, the last of which was a sort of 'details' session, meaning putting in the beginnings and ends.

PH: How structured were the interviews?

CM: Just shoot from the hip, really. See what happens.

PH: No preparation?

CM: No. I think the preparation that existed existed only in terms of the things we had already done. I was already quite used to going and imposing bollocks interviews on people anyway from any direction so it didn't seem much different, except with him, obviously, you could keep an idea going for much longer. There was an idea that was cut from *On The Hour* which I was still rabidly insisting should get on the air somewhere, about an archaeologist having discovered a fossil of Christ as a baby and what that would mean for the whole Christian religion. So we'd get the tapes rolling and let's talk about Sir Arthur and religion or experiments, whatever. I just said, 'Sir Arthur, you are going to address the Royal Society tomorrow and reveal that you have found the fossil of Christ as child.' From that, he said there came a whole series of larval stages and it developed from that.

It's trying to keep some sort of logic going. It was a very different style of improvisation from what I'd been used to, working with people like Steve [Coogan], Doon [MacKichan] and Rebecca [Front], because those *On The Hour* and *The Day Today* things were about trying to establish a character within a situation, and

Peter Cook was really doing 'knight's move' and 'double knight's move' thinking to construct jokes or ridiculous scenes flipping back on themselves, and it was amazing. I mean, I had held out no great hopes that he wouldn't be a boozy old sack of lard with his hair falling out and scarcely able to get a sentence out, because he hadn't given much evidence that that *wouldn't* be the case. But, in fact, he stumbled in with a Safeways bag full of Kestrel lager and loads of fags and then proceeded to skip about mentally with the agility of a grasshopper. Really quite extraordinary.

PH: Where was it recorded?

CM: Up in Camden, can't remember the name of the place. Some radio studio.

PH: Did you have any preliminary talks about the interviews?

CM: No, just chat. He was such an affable bloke and approached it all in rather a modest way—'Ooh, just ask me, you know, we'll see what happens.' I think we did talk for about quarter of an hour beforehand about, y'know, 'Is there something we could do with the War?', but it was really to find the first question or starting point. We did do a bit of that then to get to an obvious end, normally being gales of laughter, and pause for five minutes and then say, 'Right, tape's rolling again', and it was more fun to say, 'Right, Sir Arthur, you're shortly going to die', and I'd find myself thinking, 'I wonder what he's going to say to *that*?' It was quite odd because I felt I was half-interviewing him and half-interviewing Peter Cook. Sometimes he'd be horrified at where it was going. We'd find we'd been talking about something that had started innocently and had gone, er, you know... He had imported a tribe of 12-year old girls and dressed them up—or *something*, I can't remember.

PH: I don't remember that one.

CM: No, it wasn't on tape because it didn't go anywhere. It was Sir Arthur's experiments with some child-nurturing scheme. We'd get to the end of a recording and he'd be like, 'My God!', and just be appalled at himself about where he got to. But the sessions were pretty merry.

PH: *Why Bother?* is like Peter Cook as an Alice wandering in a Wonderland composed of elements of *your* comic universe—the mental and physical tortures, the drugs, public figures being weirdly humiliated, like Leon Brittan whizzing around on a food trolley—and he does rise to the challenge.

CM: Completely. That's a good analogy. As we got to know each other through the sessions it seemed less divided like that. He pulled Leon Brittan out of nowhere. And the good thing was—and the thing that made us enjoy it—was the fact that we found the visual cartoons and people being ridiculous was something we both found very difficult not to laugh at. People will look at my stuff and say it's Dark and Death and stuff, but that's where it *starts*. But what it is is always laughing at something—not because it's mentioned, i.e. just raise a subject and it's shocking, but because you get something to live in that situation until it pops in a ridiculous way. And, after all, Derek and Clive—you don't get much bleaker than...

PH: 'Raping a nun' or—

CM: '*Stoop* to rape a nun.' That's fantastic but it's clearly a well of dark stuff. I mean, in his head, he was absolutely capable of appreciating where it was going and why. I don't think I shocked him at all. He may have shocked *himself* occasionally, probably because he hadn't been down that route for a while and he was thinking more about his mother than he was when he was off his head in the '70s. He was seriously thinking that—not 'What would my mother say if she heard it?', but it was a thought that was at least half there. He did have a sense of propriety—the only evidence Derek and Clive show of that is that they have to have a sense of it to know they're ignoring it or driving a coach and horses through it.

Whereas, he felt, in 1993, at least some compunction to pay a due sense of propriety. But he quite enjoyed not doing it.

PH: RCA were supposed to have released *Why Bother?*, weren't they?

CM: Yes. There was a lot of rather hopeless pottering about and it just evaporated. There was a difficulty when he died of seeing the wood for the trees in terms of a simple transaction. Suddenly everyone started rushing out 'Peter Cook this' and 'Peter Cook that'. We were thinking of doing another session when he died, which was what? Christmas?

PH: January the 9th, '95.

CM: God, was it that long ago? Ninety-five! Jesus... So, we must've been thinking of meeting up in February, a wintry kind of thing, and exploring it a bit further. But the RCA thing came and went, then the BBC thing came and went and then has come back again and I think it is on their list [of releases] for the autumn.

PH: Are there any good, salvageable outtakes that could be included in the released version?

CM: Well, I was pretty sure when I edited it first time round that we got everything of worth there was. In fact, the last programme—the fifth—had three different stories.

PH: Yes, it started with violence—the Heseltine Handy—and then the Queen's Speech. But the opening question was about plans for the BBC Orchestra, but that was completely forgotten as you two got sidetracking.

CM: I think we were playing with the idea that in the pre-'On Air' bit all sorts of things could happen—from dealing with a cough to a subject that never got raised in the interview itself. But that last programme being in bits and pieces is because, by that stage, I couldn't find a complete narrative. So I put it together as a bits and pieces thing. I don't think there's anything else from those rushes. There are about eight hours of rushes to hack down. But when you are shooting like that, a lot of it is straining for quite some time to get into the right ball-park. Then you get there, you'll find a fertile bit and that produces a good ten minutes and then you move on and go somewhere else. Some of it's funny at the time but not funny afterwards; some of it's funny in bits but it doesn't hold together. There's quite a high wastage but you could do that on radio.

PH: Was the pilot ever broadcast?

CM: I think the pilot was the one about eels and Eric Clapton. I don't know if you can tell but I think it probably did get more complicated. I certainly wouldn't have asked him about dropping dead in the first session... What was the first one? Eels...

PH: Louis B. Mayer's casting couch...

CM: That's right; getting letters from someone who was 'rather like Alma Cogan but without the bounce'. What was she called? He mentioned her name a lot: 'Lita, Lita, Lita, Rosa, Rosa, Rosa'. And, ah, L.A. Riots. [*Laughs*] 'I like to think I mowed down as many blacks as I did whites. The Koreans did very badly out of the whole deal'. Yeah, that was the staggering thing—hearing fully-formed jokes just coming out. And that gave the lie rather to the impression that by the end he was a sack of old useless potato. He was not. It was very evident that whatever he did to his brain he could still get things out fully-formed.

PH: Like Gavin the hairdresser's pre-snipping ritual, was there a pre-taping ritual you and he went through?

CM: No, he'd just turn up. Doing the first one, he was in high spirits, came in with a bottle of champagne, celebrating the fact he'd just bought a fax and he'd been up half the night faxing world leaders with various bits of advice as to what they should do. And he'd just chat—'Have you seen what they've done in this week's *Private*

Eye?' or 'I saw that Dave Baddiel thing, it was rubbish.' Then we'd wander through to the studio, sit down and get the fags out, and only paused to open the doors to let the smoke out so I didn't suffer from carbon-monoxide poisoning. He was really getting through them in a sealed studio with no ventilation, air-conditioning off so it doesn't get picked up on tape. A complete fog I was wrestling. I've taken up smoking up again now but at that time I was not used to that carbon monoxide concentration.

PH: And after the session you'd both go your separate ways?

CM: I think so. But, er, the first time I met him was at a lunch, and he'd meticulously ordered what I thought was a *suspiciously healthy* bit of poached cod, a big lot of spinach and some mashed potato. And he left the spinach and the cod and just ate the potato and drank wine and smoked. Obviously, he was trying. Somebody had said to him 'Eat a few vegetables' and he'd got as far as putting them on his plate, but then thought, 'Ugh, don't want that'. Somebody had said, 'Oh, he'll probably be pissed when you meet him', and, in fact, he wasn't, but he spoke with a slur which seemed to me to indicate somebody who could speak perfectly well but just *couldn't be bothered* to articulate precisely when articulating in a sloppy way did just as well. He had reached that level of 'Ah, fuck it!' kind of thing.

PH: So, when he burst into the studio brandishing his sack of lager, you weren't filled with optimism?

CM: Well, I'd already met him informally for this meal so I kind of knew what to expect in terms of physical presentation. He did burst in one time with a mightily bloated arm. He'd stumbled around in his bathroom, and the builders had been building, and he'd fallen over a stack of tiles and he'd cracked his arm. It was in a messy state. An enormous bruise. It was already a two-week-old wound which clearly should've been going away quicker. In fact, we did remark that you were never sure if he was going to turn up; he always *did* but you always thought you might just as easily get a call saying, 'Sorry, he's pegged it'. Because a knock on the arm doesn't blow it up to the size of a leg unless the immune system is licking its wounds in its own corner.

But what struck me was that, at his memorial service, Alan Bennett said, 'And even in later years when he lost his powers and was evidently not the man he was...' and you thought '*Bollocks!*', actually. He may have presented a more shambolic figure and I'd be the last one to maintain a sentimental notion, but there was clearly a lot still going on there. And God knows what else is going on in there, but in terms of that ability and joy in ridiculous ideas, it seemed completely genuine... *completely genuine*. He seemed a very twinkly sort of person. You know, very conspiratorially amused, and not the classic hardened cynical figure that a late-in-life alcoholic tends to bring to mind. You can cross that out if it sounds too sentimental, but that's what struck me. He came in looking like a boozer, he came in looking like someone who could well have chosen to give up—*and why not?*—but in fact there was an alarming amount of neural activity still traceable...

My memories of him are sort of broken and diffused and fragmentary. He was incandescent with indignation at having been told to stop smoking when he went to Hat Trick Productions because they have a slightly Born-Again attitude—all mineral water and no booze—and he just couldn't believe it. He was beside himself and unable to speak. He'd be, 'Oh, I'll just put this one out and I won't smoke again' and then have another. That was about the time of *Clive Anderson Talks Back*, where he did the football manager: 'Motivation, motivation, motivation—the Three Ms!'

PH: And as Norman House, abducted by aliens.

CM: Yes. Yeah. Otter. Good use of otter in that. [PC's drawing of] the shape of an otter! It was like a Greek letter.

PH: He drew two exactly alike and pointed at one saying, 'That's the one that took me'.

CM: Yeah, very, very good! He'd obviously conserved his energies for the session and didn't do anything crazy like mount a double-decker from the top deck.

PH: So, no drugs involved making *Why Bother?*

CM: No. No evidence of drugs. No trackmarks on the arms.

PH: No bugle dust or ponce powder? Martian Marmite on blitz-cuits?

CM: No, none of that. You always get suprised by a fat coke-head, but no. [*Fat coke-head interviewer laughing*] Well, you do, when you see Chaka Khan or Barry White, you think, 'It's an appetite suppressant! What is going on?' But I suppose for Peter, the booze would've accounted for it. But there's all kinds of rumours, aren't there? People saying he was a heroin addict right until the time he died.

PH: *Who* said?

CM: Fuck knows. I've read people saying that about Peter Cook... He did go through a stage when he did look like he was taking a lot of coke in the '70s, around the *Revolver* period. He looked very hard-beaten. But no, there was no trace of Ecstasy on his breath... He wasn't sprightly enough to be on coke. He was at an even. Sort of laid-back... I knew someone who was a waitress in The Dome or something similar, and he used to go in there for a coffee some time in the '80s.

PH: The Dome?

CM: No, it pre-dated The Dome. It was on the Kings Road. It was one of those pale interiors, you know, espresso coffees type places. He would never give a tip but he always left an immaculately rolled joint at his table after he'd gone. Which she thought was *class*...

PH: I'm just absolutely amazed that *Why Bother?* took next to no time to make with so little pre-planning, 'cos I think in years to come people will say that, after Dudley Moore, this was a brilliant, albeit short-lived, partnership.

CM: Well, I found it so stimulating and it gave me a sense of being able to risk staying up there with things till they happen. The Dudley Moore collaboration was propelled by the organic heaven-and-hell of their relationship. I think, had we gone on, it would've gone further and tried lots of different things, but I was very pleased that there was something very good about the instant way you could do something like that, and it's a cliché that's worth repeating: 'You can only do it on radio'.

When I saw *A Life In Pieces* you can tell he's reading out the autocue answers from a previously worked-out session. And I just know that, often with improvised stuff, it happens the first time you do it because it's happening exactly in time with the thoughts that make it, and then it falls apart for a very long time, and if you manage to rehearse it well enough it can sort of return. It's never quite the same but it can be effective enough for that not to matter. But you know that Peter was never going to last from Improvisation #1 to Rehearsal #40; he'd never do that, would he? I believe the Clive Anderson Special was prepared but there was a degree of leeway involved, so he had the space to come up with things at the time.

One of the most impressive things about the show was not so much the ideas, though some of them were very funny, but the way he performed it. You could easily be forgiven for thinking he was in was in the World's Bottom Ten Actors. In many of his performances he didn't really do anything, he was being 'Peter Cook' and had a strange way of shrugging lines off, but in that show I was thinking, 'I've never seen this before; he's right inside these characters.'

PH: And each one has their own physical lingo.

CM: Yeah, and you're tempted to say 'crafted' although it probably wasn't.

PH [*Mishearing*]: Crafty?

CM: Crafty if it looked crafted and wasn't—very crafty. It was character-acting with a real sense of character. But the thing about *Why Bother?* was it meant you could go off with an idea and stay there as long as the idea deserved it, rather than just so long as the camera would tolerate it. That's the difference. Because if you're in the middle of Lake Ontario you're in the middle of Lake Ontario and that's where you are. That's what you've been told. You're not in the middle of Lake Ontario plus 'Is that moustache he's wearing real?' or 'I like the way he raised his eyebrow when you said that.'

PH: Real fan-club question now: Was Peter a hero of yours?

CM: Well, it's very odd. The temptation is to create an ideal football team of all-comers but I don't find it works like that. I particularly enjoyed the way he could rip a chat show to pieces in the same way Spike Milligan could, by breaking all expectations of what you're going to say. So it was more just leaping at the chance to work with him for that reason. I mean, I didn't see much of *Not Only But Also*. I recall seeing *Bedazzled* when I was about 12 and liking that. And seeing him on *Revolver* and thinking, 'That guy's wrecked'. And hearing Derek and Clive when I was at school and liking that because of all the swearing.

PH: Do you think Derek and Clive stands up now?

CM: It depends on what you listen to it *as*. I think it represents a stage a lot of people get to. It represents a lot of things happening at the same time. It's like you're completely bored with what you've already done; not wanting to do that again; not quite knowing what to do next; knowing there's a sensation in going massively down-hill like a burning bomber; being fuelled by the curiosity of what that would feel like...

It's like a massive mixture of mainly negative forces that takes you there, but 'stands up'? For God's sake, I dunno. I still enjoy it, most notably when they're enjoying it. It's not so much the ideas, it's the degree to which they're taken. It hasn't got anything particularly delightful about it to savour, but sometimes their sheer rage at something they don't like... There's an absolutely rubbish pastiche of Bruce Forsyth—'I can't dance, I can't sing, wurgh wurgh wurgh'—and it's borne out of looking at a television screen and going 'ARGHH!' Or the things where they're just beginning to crack up because they can't believe where they've got to. And then just going "Fuckingcuntfuckingfuckingcuntcuntfuckingcunt-youfuckingcunt", the fact that it stops being a sketch and becomes two guys in a studio doing this becomes funny for that reason.

But the best thing was Jonathan Miller—who is given to ridiculous pronouncements and God-knows-what—on some TV programme describing what happens when you're trapped into being a clown or comic. I think he was saying the desire to be a comic is primarily a young man's thing which tends to be through by the time he's 30 and, in Peter Cook's case, he had done a lot by the time he was 30—of everything—and if you're intelligent, like he was, you just realise that you haven't anywhere else to go. You are landed with this gift which has reached its sell-by date—not in terms of people wanting to listen to it but in terms of your own mentality, so you're stuck, saddled with this blessing that's become a curse. That's the way Jonathan Miller looked at it, which seems to make sense because you see how people fossilize if they try to occupy the same area...

I try to keep ahead of it but it's a sort of race because you're trying to keep yourself interested because your biggest fear is being trapped with something you hate, or grow to hate... But tell me, do you slavishly adore everything Peter's done or—?

PH: God, no. We're not uncritical. I think I can tell when Peter's coasting and when he's roasting.

CM: Good. Because the worst thing that could ever occur is the sanctification of Peter Cook as the Princess Diana of Hampstead.

THE BACK PASSAGE

What, apart from a toupee, is on your mind? Despatch your brain patterns for immediate analysis to The Back Passage...

Dear Dragger,

Rip-roaring jaw session with Chris Morris. Great to read sensible, sycophancy-free remembrances of Peter Cook. I wonder, would it be too much to ask for a copy of the tape of your interview with Chris?

Grovellingly,

IRVING MOSES THE BOOTLEGGER

[*Yes, it would be too much to ask. Fuck off!*—Diplomatic Ed.]

Dear Captain Thundercrack,

I have just found this FILTH of a mag in my dirtbox and am totally disgusted that Professor Morris has the impertitude to suggest that Peter Cook is not the Princess Diana of Hampstead. During her lifetomb I placed Princess Diabordumb on a pedestal (so I could look up her dress). As a skidmark of respect I now place YOU, Dragger, on a pedestal—and look down on you.

Sex'n'shrugs'n'ho-ho-ho,

STANLEY SPOON, no fixed underpants

Dear Ed,

The next person to threaten physical violence is gonna get their bastard teeth kicked in.

[NAME ILLEGIBLE DUE TO BLOODSTAINS]

GLORIOUS SWANSONG

What is it about the *Clive Anderson Talks Back* Xmas Special 1993 (let's call it *CATBOX* for short, eh?) that makes it a highpoint in Peter Cook's career? I mean, it was this show, not anything from *Not Only But Also*, that made the list of the 1999 Channel Four/*Observer* newspaper's Top 100 Greatest Television Moments, sharing the platform with historic occasions like the Moon Landing, the collapse of the Berlin Wall and Oliver Reed being pissed. Are we to think readers of *The Observer* as fickle fuckwits? Hell, no! So, then, what's so good about that show?

One reason is the sustained invention of Cook's four characters who appeared as guests on the show. Cook's work in the preceding decade had been invariably unsatisfying, haphazard and erratic—muted supporting roles in films like *Supergirl* and *Great Balls Of Fire* gave little, if any, indication that this was the best improviser of wayward, random, freewheeling comedy; a lot of TV commercials helped pay the bills but effectively neutered him; a slew of TV chat show appearances where he could strike an occasional spark of absurdist brilliance when he wasn't having to rattle his brains trying to come up with new, or evasive, answers to an increasingly familiar litany of dull, or intrusive, questions. His bewildering acceptance of the job of second billing co-host to Joan Rivers' *Can We Talk?* prattling chat show where, shockingly, Peter, for perhaps the first time, couldn't talk, sitting it out, fixed smile, on the end of the studio sofa, ultra-thin, grey, smart-suited, looking for all the world like Kenneth Williams' shyer brother. Of course, there were the isolated triumphs—the last ever renditions of 'The Frog And Peach' with Dudley for *The Secret Policeman's Biggest Ball*, his acting the baddie in the TV comedy drama series *Gone To Seed*—but the F & P sketch was written in 1966 and Peter had no hand in concocting *Gone To Seed*. The hope that Cook would write something new, something relevant, something if not better than, then at least equal to, the quality of *Beyond The Fringe* or *Entirely A Matter For You* looked more and more like the folly of a fervent follower. (That's the name of the game. Any perceptible drop in the set standards and everyone's pinpointing the sorrowful decline, where it all started to go wrong. Orson Welles used to publicly laugh off the public's—or, rather, the media's—image of him: 'I started at the top [*Citizen Kane*] and have been slowly working my way to the bottom ever since.' He spent the worst part of 40 years scrambling for money to make his films and died leaving a prodigious array of unfinished movies, scripts, projects doomed to collapse because the money men believed Welles' cavalier bluster to be the true nature of the man. Cook and Welles, self-destructively, could never take their art or themselves—or at least any pretentious perceptions of their art or their status—seriously for long.)

Peter, to all outward appearances, seemed to care not one whit. His one major work as writer/performer in that period, the *A Life In Pieces* TV series, went largely ignored or missed by box-gogglers in the cramped Christmas schedules. It looked like Peter would just amble on in his own sweet way forever, making the most of not doing very much at all, becoming a role model for idlers, seeking and seizing the moments of elation in the mundane, lighting up some TV chat or game show with his natural, undiluted wit and charm. Yes, he could have done that, no sweat.

Why then did he pull himself together at the dog-end of 1993 and make *Why Bother?*, the radio series with Chris Morris, and *CAT-BOX*? Eleanor Bron, in the 1995 tripartite BBC radio documentary *Cook's Tours*, contends money—or the need for it to finance his loafing lifestyle—was the primary factor. Sure, Cook lived off and on his wits, but simply citing a serious sheet shortage does Cook a disservice as a creative artist. He could have earned enough to keep him coasting for another year if he did a TV advert. (It's a measure of Cook's modesty and sheer perverse contrariness that he would probably have 'agreed' with Bron's assertion.) So let's try and clamber into Cook's brain in 1993 and rummage in the smokerings of his mind...

In September that year he and Dudley Moore reunited on a PR blitz for the launch of the *Derek and Clive Get The Horn* video, filmed 15 years before. Three years previous, in 1990, they performed a similar function for *The Best Of... What's Left Of... Not Only... But Also* videotape and TV series. It may have been these events—celebrating decades-old material with an ex-partner who was never going to work with him again—that jolted Peter into action. No one wants to be seen as a Yesterday Man, and *Horn* and *TBOWLONOBA*, plus the CD releases of the *Derek & Clive* trilogy, effectively painted Cook as a back number. All the newspaper articles publicising the reissues couldn't help but mention the aged (as if one has a choice in growing old), bloated Cook selling the public the wasp-waisted model of his youth; they must have hurt his pride. How could he ignore it? He read all the papers. What could he do to prove to his critics, and himself, that he was still in the game, that he could cut it with the best, that he was still the wild card in the pack?

A tough question. Certainly no TV channel was going to risk a vast budget on another *Peter Cook & Co*. Why? 'Well, he's getting on a bit now, isn't he? Over-fond of the ol' falling-down juice.

Probably stoned out of his tits, too, most of the time. And he's so fat and health-free—I mean, he's an insurance risk, so we can't have him doing anything remotely physical. The man's got no self-discipline. He can't write anymore—when's the last time he contributed to *Private Eye*, eh? Does the great British viewing public out there even vaguely remember what he's supposed to be fucking famous for? I mean, don't get me wrong here. I love the guy—love him to fucking death—but I'm not risking my reputation and our money on some fucked-up ancient sozzled heap of blancmange. No fucking way, guy! Jeez, he hasn't even got a catchphrase to fall back on.'

Why Bother? was an unexpected choice—it was Cook's first (and only) radio series—but it was an inspired decision because Cook was always a verbal-based comedian. He didn't have to worry about his shambolic appearance in a sound studio. (Careful listening reveals the comforting clicking of Cook's lighter.) All that mattered was the voice and the masterful timing to conjure ludicrous imagery, colluding with fellow maverick Chris Morris with such mutual empathy one would think that that double-act had been going for years rather than hours. (Brilliant though it is, Cook and Morris are exploring new ground in old comfortable shoes. Were they to have branched out away from their familiar roles and the Q & A format they were both so superlative at, and experimented with different scenes performed in new guises, they may have come unstuck. We'll never know now. This is the playground for dreamers.) *Why Bother?* as a project might have tickled Cook in some private way: For so damn long, chat show hosts and journalists had been almost pleading with him to do some new work and now here it was, buried away on BBC Radio 3 with less-than-minimal fanfare in-between yawning stretches of miserable classical music and Croatian nose banjo duets.

CATBOX was a more obvious choice of vehicle for Peter and probably the right one in terms of safety for the TV company. Nothing physically strenuous here—the days of Cook haring up three flights of stairs, like in *The Rise And Rise Of Michael Rimmer*, remote now—all he had to do was walk the few yards across the studio to Clive Anderson's desk, plonk himself down and start talking.

Peter's years of watching a frighteningly high pile of junk TV paid off in spades in his *CATBOX* performances. He knew the laws of the chat show jungle as both active participant and as semi-passive viewer. He had seen enough dried-out, drug-free rock stars embarrassingly recant on their hedonistic youth and he noticed how these rockers of his generation, these working-class boys made good, looked slightly shifty in their designer threads. Rod Stewart, Phil Collins, Eric Clapton, Uncle Rog Daltrey and all, they shared a habit of rolling up the sleeves of their Versace jackets as if to say, 'Yes, I may look flash but I'm still working class at heart; I've rolled my sleeves back because, beneath all the glitter, it's just a job, innit? And 'ooever done work with their sleeves down, eh? Success ain't changed me at all'. When Cook, as Eric Daley, tries to push his sleeves up, it's the recognition of the guilty body language, the confirmation of the class he's escaped from and the generation he's forever chained to.

John Bird, another uniquely gifted improviser/comedian, in the *Something Like Fire: Peter Cook Remembered* anthology of celebrity reminiscences, wrote perceptively of Peter's performances in *CATBOX*, how strong and deep and true they were, and he was right. What Cook may have lost to tobacco love in terms of vocal dexterity—compare the sound recording of *CATBOX* to the Lol Creme and Kevin Godley 1977 triple-album *Consequences*, with Peter at his most virtuoso chameleonic, and there is a tight constriction, the former elasticity snapped—he gained in new, mature subtleties of speech. It is worth hearing and comparing the 1966 and 1989 versions of 'The Frog And Peach' to illustrate what I'm banging on about. The 1966, original, take of Sir Arthur Streeb-Greebling's exploits with the world's worst restaurant has Cook whipping like a dervish through the material, spinning out more jokes and situations on the premise than anyone could reasonably expect. It's funny, very funny, totally cherishable, but one doesn't believe for an instant that it's anyone but Peter Cook putting on a silly-ass voice.

The 1989 performance from *Biggest Ball* is another thimble of hippos entirely. He's stately and eminently convincing in the role. He is Sir Arthur. He's learnt the power of the pause in comedy. He's slowed it right down so that every word counts, every gesture and inflection matters. Instead of being instantly squashed by a giant brain packed with jokes, as we were in '66, Cook could now slowly bulldoze us with the accumulating revelations of a man who, for all his privileged upbringing, is totally lacking in the knowledge that a) he is a fool, and b) everyone knows he is a fool. This fundamental absence of self-awareness makes the 1989 re-making/re-modelling of Streeb-Greebling a more well-rounded human, and all the funnier for it. Cook's creative cleverness, perceived by certain professors of the craft as a coldness, is subdued by the warmth of his character acting. (A-ha! But isn't hiding one's cleverness itself an example of clever-cleverness?)

These new actorly considerations were developed upon in *A Life In Pieces*. Peter's portrayal of Sir Arthur was no longer a basic outline of an upper-class twit wasting his life on futilities.(Was that how Cook saw himself in the Showbiz world, one wonders?) Now he emerges highly-detailed as a man struck and altered by the changes wrought in society since the supposed carefree '60s. He has become a deeper, darker, more mercenary prospect. All that matters in the end is money, seems to be the subtext: People are expendable; self-preservation is all. In the '60s Sir Arthur was happy in his idiocy. In the '90s he has made the change from one of life's losers to one of the undeserving winners, a cad who expects everyone to 'play the game' and 'act the white man' while he is ripping them off left, right and centre. It's a penetrating, devastating portrait, full of nuance and reptilian slipperiness. Peter Cook's declining years? Drink my shorts.

There is a moment in *CATBOX* when Cook, as Judge Beauchamp (pronounced 'Beecham'), is explaining how his wife suffered a fall when a woman in the audience suddenly shrieks with laughter. The Judge slowly closes his eyes, turns his head away, slightly curls his lip in contempt and in sorrow that the youth of today could behave in so heartless a fashion. Other comedians may have 'corpsed' at this outburst but Cook never slipped out of character for a second. It was a completely natural response for the Judge and succeeded in adding a new layer, another dimension, to the persona.

Let us not forget the contribution of Clive Anderson himself in all this. Most readers will be familiar with the cut of his jib. A deft prober with a quick wit, sharp tongue and a fine-tuned bullshit detector (e.g. his cutting-short of Jeffrey Archer's listing of his own achievements: 'Is there no beginning to your talents?'), his most notorious interviews a bout of mental and verbal jousting where his guests/victims are generally reduced to perforated gurgling slabs of jelly.

To Anderson's everlasting credit, he tempers his natural urge, in *CATBOX*, to reclaim the limelight from Cook, to stem the flow of Cook's creativity by quippy interjections of his own. He displays a rare sympathy in dispensing with his usual rapid-fire manic style of presentation for once and playing at Cook's chosen speed. Like John Wells, who played interviewer to some Cook creations on *Private Eye*'s *Blue Record*, he manages to act the straight man whilst retaining enough of his own individuality. It's a difficult tightrope to negotiate—play it too straight and there's the danger of bogging the thing down, Cook playing to a brick wall; try to be funnier than the oddball you're interviewing and the audience can be left wondering just what and who is supposed to be funny, and why. *CATBOX* succeeds by virtue of Anderson being alert and responsive enough to anticipate Cook's ebb and flow.

CATBOX was and remains a comedy revelation. Peter Cook—a man fucked and buckled by his perfect gift of comedy, who (to paraphrase another '60s icon) made shoes for everyone while he went barefoot, who had reasons to be fearful but refused to explain, refused to complain—against any rational hope produced four brilliant, multi-layered portraits. Self-portraits, really. Norman House was a manifestation of the bore Cook found within himself, Alan Latchley reflected his obsessional nature, and obsessives are always the maddest bores (Latchley was also a stick with which to beat the hated work ethic), Sir James Beauchamp duplicates the self-satisfied, smug, reactionary, blinkered mouthpieces of the privileged classes—a mindset Cook could fall into at will to attack the Establishment he was groomed for; and Eric Daley was the elegantly wasted rock'n'roll star Cook had oft professed he wished he could have been—the satirist as satyr. Remember Cook's quote about satirists being like spiders, 'they are always devouring each other'? Here, Cook devours himself.

This show is just too much and not nearly enough.

DAN PATTERSON PHONES BACK

Dan Patterson is the dynamic, thrusting, stark naked producer of various TV Hat Trickery including Whose Line Is It Anyway?, Room 101 *and* Clive Anderson Talks Back. *He flew back from America for the sole purpose of giving The Holy Dragger a tinkle and spilling Cooked beans. This is what he said:*

I first worked with Peter Cook when he appeared on one edition of the 1988 series of *Whose Line Is It Anyway?* Despite it being an improvisational comedy show we do have a run-through—more of a warm-up, really—in the afternoon before the evening recording. We go through some of the games, although in the evening it all changes when the cast are given a set of different situations to improvise in. Peter was right on the money in the afternoon run-through, great, brilliant, and then he went off afterwards and had a few drinks. His performance for the actual taping suffered a bit from it. He was good but not quite as good as he was in the afternoon.

There is enough testimony from the likes of John Cleese and Stephen Fry that Peter was the funniest man they'd ever met, and I'd go along with that. He was indeed a comedy genius but the question was, 'How can one harness it?' How does one capture his brilliance on film, on tape? There was an instance when he was the guest on *Room 101*: He turned up at the studio about an hour earlier than expected and he was in the Green Room passing the time, amiably chattering away and being so on-form—just consistently funny. He was in hilarious form and I thought, 'It's a pity no one outside this room will ever know about this. We should've brought a film crew in to capture it!'

He had made a few appearances on *Clive Anderson Talks Back* prior to the 1993 Christmas thing. Some chat shows are rigorously prepared. A guest will be interviewed by a researcher beforehand and the resulting TV appearance will stick very closely to the informal interview. It's particularly true in America where chat shows are almost scripted because everything has to be tightly scheduled. Clive's shows are much looser. He prefers to work in vaguer areas rather than rigidly-adhered-to perimeters because that gives Clive and his guests a certain freedom, an opportunity to manoeuvre from the brief, the chance for a bit of unexpected spontaneity. The preparation for Peter's appearances on Clive's show was utterly loose. We knew he was into a wide range of popular culture, so we'd ask him what he's been intrigued by recently in the news or on the telly—he was sort of famous for watching television, which is a bit bizarre—and he'd go, 'Oh, I've been watching cable telly, the shopping channel—QVC, or whatever it's called—especially. Get Clive to ask me about that'.

The Christmas '93 show was Clive's idea. He broached it to Peter at a party, I think—'Fancy doing a chat show where you are all the guests?' Usually, these ideas come up, are talked about, but the next morning everything's forgotten. But Peter remembered the conversation, was really into doing it, and so the wheels were set in motion. Clive purposefully took a backseat in the pre-production run-up to the show. He left it to Anne Marie Thorogood, Ruth Wallace and myself to liaise with Peter and the roles he wanted to play. We were there to help Peter in his developing the characters. Clive felt it would work best if he was told of the characters' backgrounds as near to the recording time as possible, like they were real people, real guests. This, he felt, would give the proceedings an element of freshness.

It was decided to invest a lot of background spadework into the show because my sense was, although Peter was an astonishingly inventive improviser, he needed some firm foundations to build on, given how short the show was. I could have had Peter improvising with Clive on the spot but then I would have had to shoot some 30 minutes of action just to get a worthwhile 10 minutes of quality where everything gelled, made sense and was really funny into the bargain.

The real tragedy is that originally we were set to do two shows on successive nights with Peter playing seven or eight separate identities. As discussions progressed, however, Peter said, 'Let's just pick the best characters and do one show'. Anne Marie, Ruth and I would meet Peter for breakfast over the course of a week, maybe ten days, where he would go into a character and we would question him. I can't recall all the other characters he tried. We made audio recordings of these breakfast meetings but, very annoyingly, they have gone missing. I can't remember where they are. But one unused character I do remember was this foreign dignitary which I felt was ripe for some satire of British foreign policy or the European Community. It was Peter who suggested he be dropped. What he was doing in that role was great but he felt that there was only so far he could go with it. With the roles he did play on the show, we had immersed ourselves deep into their backgrounds to the extent that Peter could tell you what they would eat for dinner, what cars they drove, what their beliefs were. He built up very quickly a huge store of data in his mind about these four people. We achieved a lot in a short time because, although

Peter was focused and excited about the show, he would get tired after two or two-and-a-half hours of constantly improvising with me in the role of interviewer. But once he had developed a large enough reference base for a character and was familiar with it, he could carry on embellishing the material and keep on spinning.

Peter played four roles on the show as an insurance: *Clive Anderson Talks Back* was a half-hour show, which meant we could quite comfortably include three interviews. Four chats were shot to cover ourselves just in case one of them flopped. As it turned out, they were all of such a sufficiently high standard that I had them all included. That meant some trimming in the editing suite and the show being extended to 35 minutes. I don't know why that show has never been given a video release. If it ever were, I think we could restore some cut footage. Not all of it, obviously. There are a few moments of stumbling around but I think there are two or three good usable minutes from each chat. There's some ten worthwhile extra minutes that could be re-incorporated into the show.

I remember a very happy time of Peter in Wardrobe, picking out and trying on different costumes. It was work but also lots of fun. Whilst he was playing about, trying on hats and coats, I saw 20 years drop from his shoulders. He was a kid let loose in a sweetshop. He was how I recalled him from watching *Not Only But Also*; an infectious fun person. He loved going into character, trying on disguises, experimenting, working on the fine details. He was trying out clothes for the Alan Latchley part, saying, 'This man must wear a cheap suit but he would never know it was a cheap suit'. He was also working out the Latchley walk—that ape-like advancing determined strut. I don't think Latchley was based on any one particular footballer; he was an amalgam of all those miserable football managers droning on from *Grandstand* and *Match Of The Day*.

Because Peter was playing all the guests, the evening's taping went on a bit longer than standard editions of the show to necessitate Peter's costume changes. To fill in time whilst Peter was off getting changed, Clive would keep the audience amused with a bit of stand-up comedy, and there was also a very fine a capella group there called Jonah And The Whalers. All right, they weren't that fine, it was just me and a few friends. It wouldn't be right to have had a proper, professional group in to play between Peter's spots: They could be mid-song and I'd be, 'Right, Peter's ready now so get off!' We were filling in between the Latchley and Judge sections—the interviews were shown in the same order as they were filmed—and we thought Peter'd be about 15 minutes in make-up. We're singing away when Peter appeared in his Judge clothes. 'Oh, Peter, you were quick.' 'Well, I had to save the audience from any more of you.'

What Clive had on his clipboard was a series of signposts, words that would trigger Peter off on the subjects we had discussed with him over the preceding ten days. Anne Marie, Ruth and I made copious notes but he never seemed to. He improvised it all out. That Norman House interview, for example, where he talks about the planet Ikea: That idea had surfaced in the breakfast meetings but in a very different form. On the night he re-phrased it all in a new way. I loved Norman House—he was pretty close to E.L. Wisty. That final line of House's is a killer—'An experience like that—in fact, that experience—made me realise... just how insignificant they were'—a brilliant twist on a tired, over-used phrase. A lot of good material that had been prepared unfortunately never made it to the show, however.

It's pretty apparent that, by the last interview, the rock star one, Peter was getting tired. Concentrating for that amount of time is pretty wearing but I think Peter got away with it because that role was intended to be pretty spaced-out anyway. It's hard to tell with that last interview what was Peter Cook and what was Eric Daley.

After the show Peter was completely knackered—but happy. It really took it out of him. He came in that day nervous but full of positivity and energy and, though he was alert and responsive and inspired during the breakfast sessions, it was in front of a live audience that he truly came into his own. The adrenalin was coursing through him.

It was a privilege—not in some fake showbizzy way—but it was a real privilege to work with Peter and it's gratifying that we managed to bottle some of that genius.

A GUNNY MAN

'This is a delightfully "Peter Cook" touch; suitably surrealist,' opined Clive Anderson of holding an interview in Noel Hennessy's designer furniture shop that used to be at 6 Cavendish Square, London W1. Slimmer and more hairy of head in real life ('It's the wrong way round, isn't it? You should look your best on television in front of millions of viewers and be a hideous wreck off-screen'), Clive is a self-confessed Man With No Insight (hooray!). His sense of the ridiculous coupled with a healthy dose of self-effacement resulted in a bit of a chat high in good humour.

PAUL HAMILTON: I want to talk to you about talking to Peter Cook.

CLIVE ANDERSON: Well, I first met him when I was writing a radio pantomime—*Black Cinderella II Goes East* (1978)—and he struck me then as a very amiable person. There were quite a lot of stars in that show and most of them gave us—me and [co-writer] Rory McGrath—a hard time, but he was very generous, and very diffident, saying, 'I wonder if it would be better if I changed such and such a line', instead of saying, 'It's *rubbish*!' It amounts to the same thing but he did it in a very polite and pleasant way...

PH: When were you at Cambridge?

CA: Between '72 and '75.

PH: Oh, so you'd have been in straw boater, kipper tie, stack heels.

CA: I don't remember the straw boater but definitely the fashion nightmare—loons, flared trousers. Erm, don't know about stack heels. Everyone had long hair—longer than the '60s—and I had prodigiously and very unpleasant long hair, which I'd rather like; I'd have that now if I could. It was a poor decade, the '70s, for being a student. In the '60s they'd had revolutions and protests about Greek colonels and Biafra and Vietnam, but when I got there we'd run out of things to protest about. There was a sit-in in my first year about Economics degrees and whether second-class degrees should be divided into upper-second and lower-second or not. I felt like, 'Do I want to get arrested for *this*? I don't even *do* Economics!' It was a dull decade, I think...

PH: How did you get in to Footlights?

CA: The way it was done was there'd be these shows called 'Smokers'—a term used by army regiments and other pompous people—to which you could go along and perform a song, sketch or monologue you had written. Quite a tough audience, actually, because everyone thought they knew all about it. If you weren't booed offstage you'd be allowed to join. They wouldn't go into great debates about your comic timing or anything, it'd just be, 'He wasn't bad, that fellow singing that song dressed as a penguin.'

PH: Who were your contemporaries in Footlights?

CA: Griff Rhys Jones; Douglas Adams, who was just finishing as I was starting there; John Lloyd; Rory McGrath; Jimmy Mulville.

PH: More or less the TV comedy mafia of the last 10, 15 years.

CA: We-e-ell, sort of. At the time you think, 'All the great people were in the past'. It's much harder to be impressed by your contemporaries. And years go by and one or two become famous and it's 'Oh yes, it was *marvellous*! We had all the *greats*!'

PH: The fact that Peter Cook and John Cleese had been in Footlights—did that cast some kind of intimidating shadow? Was it tough to live up to?

CA: It's a mixed blessing. A couple of years after I left I returned to direct a show and I made a feature in the programme of going through the reviews of past Footlights shows because it amused me that they'd always refer back and say, 'Oh, these spotted 19-year-olds can't compare to—' you know, whoever subsequently made it as a star. There'd be write-ups saying 'John Cleese is rubbish. He's nothing like as good as Peter Cook or Clive James', which sort of puts things into perspective because, in the end, it's only a student revue group with a slightly elevated reputation.

PH: Your name cropped up in the '80s as one of the writers for *Alas Smith And Jones*. You wrote Mel and Griff's Head-To-Head things?

CA: Yes, did quite a lot of that, working with Griff mainly.

PH: I thought the Head-To-Heads were very much inspired by the Pete and Dud duologues in that you have Mel as the informed idiot and Griff as the uninformed idiot.

CA: I think they are very similar but Griff in particular always says 'No, no.' It's sort of inevitable in a way, if you have two men talking—the difference in television terms, and what I liked about Head-To-Head, was the fact it was a single shot of two profiles speaking with no funny shots from the director or props getting in the way. It wasn't a deliberate copy of Pete and Dud but you couldn't fail to be influenced by them. I think Pete and Dud were more surreal, weirder, whereas the Head-To-Heads were, as you say, the stupid person and the even more stupid person. From there, Griff got me into writing for Frankie Howerd.

PH: It's odd how Frankie Howerd, like most comedians, had a set stage act, enacting an extension of himself, whereas Peter never did that at all. He never went onstage as himself doing a 'Funny thing happened on the way to the theatre' routine, did he?

CA: He was probably more comfortable in impersonation. When I'd interviewed Peter as himself, he wasn't somebody you could get to talk about himself. He'd be reasonably comfy talking about some funny thing that had happened or he had seen, and he could then go spinning off. Yeah, you'd normally see him as E.L. Wisty or a judge or something. He was never quite playing just Peter Cook. He did have a certain reticence. I always found him to be a nice, kindly person. A lot of comedians tend to be competitive, putting each other down, getting quite cruel about other comedians. I only knew him in his later years—as it turned out—and he may have settled into a comfort zone. Maybe when he was younger he was as competitive as the next man but then had a lot of success and thought, 'Well, I'm not going to bother with *that* any more'.

PH: Now there's one subject that can *not* be avoided: Peter adopted Tottenham Hotspur as his football team—

CA: *Yesss...*

PH:—whereas you are an Arsenal fan.

CA: If I had to identify a deep flaw in his character I think that'd be it. It was *really sad* to see an otherwise great man brought low.

PH: Do you think it might have been a satirical attack on football?

CA: I think it might have been. Now you mention it, it was probably a huge joke because it's so unlikely that anyone would like Tottenham.

PH: But you support the Gunners. You're a Gunny man.

CA: I'm a Gunny man—rather than a funny man. But, to be honest, if he got interested in football in the early '60s, then Tottenham—for a *very, very* short time—were the top club. They won the Double and that must've made a deep impression on him. He must've wandered along to a game, thought, 'Oh, they're good', and once you choose a team you're sort of stuck with them forever. He endeared himself to Tottenham fans by once saying that [Arsenal's ground] Highbury smelled like a toilet.

PH: The only reason I found for Peter supporting Spurs was his saying that, like his home town Torquay, Tottenham began with 'T.O.'

CA: People *do* support teams for mad reasons, like, 'Sunderland used to wear purple strips and I liked purple when I was five so now I go on 500-mile round trips to see a home game.'

PH: I wonder whether Peter supporting Spurs could be tied in to his comedy—all his creations wasting their lives on futile schemes.

CA: Like Sir Arthur Streeb-Greebling spending 30 years trying to teach ravens to fly underwater? Teaching Tottenham players to play football—it's similar, isn't it? Yes, your theory is good: It was a long and extended joke. It's always better for a comic to support a poor team, like Jasper Carrott supporting Birmingham City. He calls the ground to ask, 'When does the game kick off?'—'When can you get here?' You know, taking a lap of honour when you get a corner.

PH: 1992 I think it was; there was a single by Right Said Fred—

CA: Oh God, yes...

PH:—for Comic Relief called *Stick It Out*. The video had you, Hugh Laurie and Peter dancing around dressed as gamekeepers.

CA: Oh yes! Now this is a personal grievance for me. Somebody decided for this pop video that Peter, Hugh and I would be the dancers—we were probably the last names on the list: 'What can we do with *them*?' We were shown into this room and told to get into some tweedy clothes. We tried on these tweed jackets, trilbys, deerstalker hats, and we all looked ridiculous. Nothing fitted right. Ten minutes later we walked out again and Peter and Hugh looked great. They looked like extras in Brideshead Revisited and I looked like someone who had just staggered out of an Oxfam shop. It's because they were both tall, slim, elegant and had a natural flair for dressing, so they looked marvellous and I looked like the git who turned up late for the costume fitting.

PH: Do you recall Peter's line from the song? 'Who said white people haven't got rhythm?' followed by a burst of Elvisly gyrations.

CA: I remember that, yes. If I ever saw the video I probably had my fingers over my eyes—which isn't the perfect way to watch TV. *It was for charity!* An awful lot of dreadful things are committed in the name of charity. You know, it's good but one doesn't wish to be reminded of it necessarily. Thank you. Peter Cook always worried that his obituary headline would be 'Zsa Zsa Man Dies' and I certainly don't want to have 'Tweedy Old Git Snuffs It' as mine.

PH: The Christmas '93 Special of your show; how did that come about?

CA: It's unusual for me to have an idea and for the idea to then be filmed and transmitted. Most of my ideas are sneered at. I was at a *Private Eye* party—

PH: What, one of their dinners at The Coach And Horses pub?

CA: No, it was a big Christmas party, and I was talking with Peter about mucking around with the chat show set-up. I put it to him that he could play all the guests on it. I couldn't work out whether to do the one show or two or a whole series with Peter as the guests. Also, I couldn't decide whether I should be someone else—'John Smith's Interview Show'. But I said, 'Look, I know you don't like chatting about yourself much, but this is an option where you can improvise away as a character'. He said, 'Yeah, yeah, very good', the way you do when either a good idea is put to you—or a *dreadful* idea is put to you. What was impressive—I mean, it took us a year to get it done—

PH: So this is Christmas 1992 that this happened?

CA: Yes, but he phoned me the next morning. He didn't have my number and he had to call around to get it. I mean, there was plenty to drink at this party so he woke up sufficiently bright-eyed and bushy-tailed to think 'Clive Anderson... that idea...' and then find me. By then, he had already gotten about 20 characters that he was suggesting he could do. They were quite freaky, off-the-wall, along the lines of a man who had been shrunk to a tiny size to go through a human body. We eventually settled upon four fairly straightforward characters—for him—to play. Those he did were close to aspects of his own character or characters he had previously done. It was shown with no advance fuss being made about it, which I thought was nice. It's actually my favourite bit of broadcasting that I've been involved with, in that I'm imagining there's someone watching who doesn't like Peter Cook and they've just worked out at the end of the first interview it was him—'Oh, that was just a silly pretend interview. I'll, er, stay up to see who's the next guest...'—and it would be Peter Cook again. Lots of publicity can destroy a show so we downplayed it. We were quite purist about it.

PH: Dan Patterson said there was a second show planned for 1994.

CA: Yes, but what with one thing and another it just didn't get done. Who knows, it might've been a disaster to do it again but I think it would certainly have been better. For one thing, we would've overcome the impracticalities of Peter playing four characters in one session. It's so stupid that we never got round to following it up. Because the absolute, best thing to have done was to have him come along to a few separate recordings, doing a different role each night. We could have done that over a series and then edit them together for a special edition. We could have done that with each series but, of course, no one had thought of it.

PH: It's a shame this show happened so late, isn't it? I mean, this idea, like many brilliant ideas, is so devastatingly simple. Why hadn't anyone thought of it before—a Peter Cook chat show where he's the guests rather than the host?

CA: I don't know. Years ago, Mel Brooks did a similar thing as *The 2,000 Year Old Man* with Carl Reiner interviewing him... Although I say it myself—I mean, it's not like inventing the wheel—the idea was a good one, in the context of all my other ideas are normally rubbish.

PH: You described Peter, in the *Something Like Fire* book, as a 'perpetual undergraduate'.

CA: And now I'm supposed to sustain my fatuous remark! What I meant by 'perpetual undergraduate' was Peter was very worldly-wise, bright and ahead of his contemporaries when he was an undergraduate and he *stayed* like that. He never became staid or middle-aged in his thinking; he was always larking around and being amused by the world the way people are in their 20s. When most people reach their 40s or 50s they start to become all 'I know it seems awful that people are starving on the streets' and kind of understand things world-wearily and are neither amused by it anymore nor affronted by it.

PH: Also mentioned in your essay is a picnic in Regent's Park. How does this sort of thing come about? Who arranges picnics?

CA: John Lloyd was there but I'm not sure if it was he who suggested it. Someone invited Peter and Lin along so along they came. It was one of those things one should do more of, one of the most entertaining things you can do and years go by and you think,

'Why didn't I do more of that?' You spend a lot of time queuing up for things, walking in the rain, all the dull things in life, and yet, a simple thing, it doesn't require much. You just phone up two other families and say, 'Bring some sandwiches, a flask of tea and a ball'.

PH: You had a cricket game there that day.

CA: Yes, it was just a surreal thing. I didn't know this other family picnicking—might have been Indian, might have been Pakistani— but somehow or other we all ended up having a sort of cricket challenge.

PH: Was Peter batting or bowling?

CA: I can remember him bowling with that sort of angular, lollopy style. He had a natural elegance. I don't recall him batting but I im- agine at some stage in his life he would have made an elegant—if casual—batsman; a David Gower type more than a Mike Gatting. I'm sorry I can't provide you with a ball-by-ball account of the match. I'm not even sure if we were using a ball, it was that level of cricket. I think Peter may have been bowling a bread roll...

THE BACK PASSAGE

It's almost time for this issue to go to bed—see, it's already donned its moustache net—but not until we read your screeds...

Dear Dregs,
   When will Chanel No.4 issue a video of Pater Cake interviewing Clive Henderson, with Coon playing some trappy slaphead geezer? [...]
   Yours, live from the snug of The Flare And Bicycle Chain, fish- ing the peanuts out of his pint of Holy Friarwater,
   LENNY BOLLOX.

Dear Mr Hamilton,

Thank you very much for your recent letter regarding Peter Cook's appearances on *Clive Anderson Talks Back* and *Saturday Live*. Regretfully, we must advise that these Channel 4 titles have not been chosen for commercial release on video. Nor, due to our limited resources, are we able to make one-off copies for viewers or societies. We are sorry to disappoint you on this occasion but hope you and the rest of the Peter Cook Appreciation Society continue to enjoy our programmes.

[SCRIBBLE], Information Officer, Channel 4 TV, London.

Dear Reg,

[...]

I met Peter a couple of times. On one occasion he was recording the soundtrack for a Roger Mellie video. A producer greeted him at the studio with typical showbusiness insincerity:

'Peter, you're looking great. You've lost weight, haven't you?'

Peter smiled politely, then as the producer turned away he muttered to himself, 'Yes, another few stones and I'll be a Sixties cult figure again.'

I got the distinct impression that, unlike so many people in his field, Peter's main priority was to amuse (and, of course, to enjoy) himself.

I kept a beer bottle he drank from that day as a souvenir and will treasure it as long as I live.

All the best with your society and magazine.

CHRIS DONALD, Viz comic.

ABSOLUTE BALLS

"Give a man a mask and he will tell you the truth"
Oscar Wilde (or someone disguised as Oscar Wilde)

There are a number of chinstrokers who contend that Peter Cook, like Orson Welles, started at the top and worked his way down, citing *Beyond The Fringe* as the apex of his performing/writing brilliance and his subsequent career being exactly that—sheer careering—collapsing at the bottom on the crashmat that is the *Peter Cook Talks Golf Balls* retail video, released in the autumn of 1994. Overweight, out of inspiration, almost literally out of breath, a comic god is reduced to the nadir, mumbling inconsequentialities about the middle-class pastime of golf. On the other hand there's a fist. There are also sages who know their onions, and they will stamp their feet and protest the case that everything Cook did was merely preparation for this final attack and declare it the master-work. They would argue that he had to get utterly brain-addled and lose all his good looks (in the same method-actory way Robert DeNiro employed to lose all that weight for the early scenes of *Raging Bull*) in order to convincingly capture the true nature of the sport and convey Man's inevitable stroll towards time-wasted doom. Is *Golf Balls* a ghastly mess of incoherent inanities of less-than-single-molecule-of-redemption or is it the finest blast of class satire from the master? ('Possibly both, probably neither'—Sir Arthur Streeb-Greebling.)

Peta Button was the set designer for *Golf Balls*, as she has been for exactly many films and TV productions, and Paul Hamilton met her on a sunny March Monday at a Swiss Cottage rub-a-dub to find out about the background to Peter's Last Stand. Her husband just happens to be Joe McGrath, director of the first series of *Not Only But Also* and the London run of *Behind The Fridge*. Peta had lent Joe her copy of the *Golf Balls* video a couple of days before and 'he might drop in a bit later to deliver his verdict.'

For the Peterphiles who have never seen *Golf Balls*, a swift résumé of its contents is required: Peter Cook appears, absolutely solo, delivering four monologues in different guises about various aspects of the game originally known as 'flog'. First up is retired caddie Alec Dunroonie, reminiscing through a red foot-long beard about his glory days. Nextly, Doctor Dieter Ledbitter, all bottle glasses and white coat, theorises in his laboratory how fish are better adapted to golfing than humans. Then we're off to the Antler Room of an un-named club where chief secretary, pederast and ninety-per-cent-proofter Major Titherly Glibble discourses on the existence of women and on golf club etty-quetty. Last is U.S. golf commentator Bill Rossie, who reveals the actual, secret contents of the successful player's golf bag.

Anyway! Let us float in to this Spring afternoon sot shop interior and hover like fat lazy blue-bummed flies above a man and a woman, and vice versa. The man is asking the woman about the existence of a script, bzz bzz SWAT!

PETA BUTTON: There was just a discussion about what props were needed. There was no script as such. When I talk about 'script' I mean there was no dialogue. One knew what each of the sequences was going to be about—but that was it. When I watched it, that whole first sequence with the bloody stuffed dog—which I got from some taxidermist—you could hardly hear a word he said, could you? Terrible sound quality.

Can you remember anything about it? When did you last see it?

PAUL HAMILTON [*sheepishly*]: Last night, actually.

PB [*bursts out laughing*]: Good researcher, you! It's *awful*. The whole thing is *dire*.

PH: Seeing it again, it's disturbing how he's sometimes really straining, struggling to come up with a good line: 'Oh, there's Nick Faldo, looking like a right... Nick Faldo.'

PB: Hmm, what did become apparent is that, in the sequence where he's playing the secretary of the club –

PH: Oh, the Antler Room, Major Titherly Glibble.

PB: Yes, and I know that that was completely unscripted because that was in fact the very last scene—half-day or day that we did it, a Friday, my last day, so to speak—so by that time I could go and sit down and relax and watch everybody at work. It was the first time I really had the chance to talk to him. It was because of some things that we were talking about when he was waiting for some new set-up to be prepared that we ended up talking about young boys. It started off talking about holidays and I'd said one of my favourite holidays that I had was in Sicily, and I mentioned that one of the most extraordinary things I'd seen—I was in Termini—was that all the shops had got these photographs of angelic young boys with blond curly hair, ivy in their hair, wonderful little gay angels, and he immediately knew all about these photographs. He knew the name of the photographer—I can't remember the name now but he was apparently quite famous. But that got us chatting about young boys, as this was the first time I'd seen young boys walking down the street hand in hand. And I said the next time I saw it was in Morocco, and that's how I know where that whole Morocco dialogue comes from. He may have already had some ideas jotted down on a bit of paper about what to say, but once a new idea entered his brain he just went with it. And this is what makes me think that, because that sequence is intercut with shots of young boys holding hands in the sand –

PH:—and camels –

PB:—exactly, that in fact what they did was get Peter on the post-production, adding commentary. He must have had a strong hand in the editing. What's fascinating is on the video the director isn't given a credit. The guy who directed it was Rob—I can't recall his surname.

PH: Maybe he was Welsh: 'Rob The Director'.

PB: You wouldn't think that there was a director, would you? I can't believe that we actually stopped from time to time to re-light scenes. Where were the lights? It's extraordinary.

PH: Yes, especially the opening monologue—Alec Dunroonie, the old Scottish golf caddy. It seems to be shot in pitch darkness.

PB: It was done in a pub a bit like this but, obviously, dingier and a lot darker. And they must have given me quite a budget because there was a lot of props so I re-dressed this corner of the pub.

PH: Stuffed dogs don't come cheap.

PB: They don't. More expensive than living ones. So I made the scene to look like a, a Scottish... cottage.

PH: 'Scottish cottage'. Say *that* without your teeth in.

PB: Scottish cottage. It was covered with plaid throws over the chairs, lots of detail, but all to waste because you couldn't see a thing. The director must have been completely desperate because he kept on zooming in on the stuffed dog's face when they needed to do a cut-away. It was such a shambles!

[*Joe McGrath enters the pub with Peta's video of Peter Cook Talks Golf Balls in a bag.*]

JOE McGRATH: Gad, it's almost impossible to find your way in here.

PH: We've been trying to get *out*!

PETA [*going to the bar*]: Well, since you've seen it, I'd better buy you a drink.

PH: To steady his nerves.

JM: The video? I liked it.

PH: You liked it?

JM: *Yeah*!

[*Halves of cider are procured for Peta and Joe, whilst The Dragger opts for yet another flagon of Foamy Scrotum*]

PB: I'm trying to remember how the golf video was initiated. It all came about after his last appearance on *Clive Anderson Talks Back* when he suddenly reappeared out of nowhere, and everyone was phoning around saying, 'Did you see Peter Cook last night? He looked absolutely wonderful! The amount of weight he's lost, how good the show was, how fast he was.' And then this video idea came out of the blue and what was interesting was that, because everyone had seen Peter in the Clive Anderson show, including— obviously—the producer and Rob The Director, and the costume designer... When we all met for the first time at a costumiers in Camden Town we were all expecting to see this svelte Peter Cook, and he rolled in looking *huge*. And she had put these costumes to one side for him and he couldn't get into any of them. So they had to completely re-costume him.

I must say that he didn't drink alcohol at all until the last day. It was a five-day shoot. And the very last day was the Antler Room scene, shot at *his* golf club –

PH: Where was that?

PB: North Hampstead—and that was because no one else would have us.

PH: Why?

PB: Shortly before there had been a fly-on-the-wall documentary set at a golf club. It was shown on television and everyone was absolutely outraged at the gossip that goes on, the terrible anti-women jokes, and the drinking. So, immediately, every golf club in a sixty-mile radius of London closed their doors to us, saying, 'No way, we'll never allow a camera in here again.' So Peter obviously clinched the deal of getting us into his own golf club. He must have had a great deal of input throughout.

PH: What do you think of the final piece—where he's Bill Rossie, the American commentator?

JM: 'In Scotland, England.'

PB: I think that was probably the best sequence of all but that was probably—a) you could *see* it, and b) you could *hear* it. [*Laughter*]

JM: But, even then, under the tree—you can't see his face. It's absolutely in shadow in both the wide and the close shot. And what was all that awful business, when he's the caddy, of him craning his head to look at a camera that's behind his left shoulder?

PB: They must have had different camera positions, or two cameras going, but there was no coordination.

JM: Definitely two cameras because at times he's looking in the wrong camera, then he suddenly realises and then turns around to talk to the correct one –

PH:—and then the *first* camera starts filming.

JM: And the angles! They're filming up his nose.

PB: Well, to be honest, the director was so bad... I know they kept doing the same scenes over and over again –

JM:—oh, so it might be bad editing.

PB: Yes, because what actually made it a lot more fun to all of us than what appears on the film is the very fact that once he got going and he'd done a scene once with dialogue he was virtually making up as he went along, each time he did the sequence again, of course, he did a completely new lot of dialogue. We were all having a great time, corpsing with laughter, because we never knew what he was going to do next, and neither did the director. I think Peter and the director had more or less fallen out—they weren't even talking to each other by the last day.

JM: Ah yes. Is that why there's no director's credit?

PH: Not even Alan Smithee would want a credit for that one.

JM: The scene where he's in the Antler Room, that's very funny. 'Young boys in the bunkers... naked if they wish... Naked if *I* wish.' [*Laughter*]

PB: They probably did that scene four or five times. I think it really took shape in the editing suite with all the film footage of camels traversing the desert. There are other bits of stock footage, of Spiro Agnew and of Nick Faldo, whoever, and they must have called Peter in to extemporise a commentary over it.

PH: Yes, one of my favourite bits is of a caddy who's puffing away on a ciggie behind Seve Ballesteros or someone, and Peter's Major voice proudly says, 'See that young chap over there? I taught him to smoke.' [*Laughter*]

JM: What was brilliant about the Antler Room chappie was that I've just come back from Edinburgh, teaching Film Studies, and when I was there I went to a gentleman's club, The New Club, which is affiliated to The Savile Club in London, y'see? And this guy comes up to me and says, 'Hello, I'm the bloody fucking secretary of thish club.' What I found funny was Cook, at the end of the Antler Room scene, suddenly goes into that whole black, 'I'm the bloody secretary, you'd better fucking understand it.' That's exactly how the guy in The New Club was after a few drams: 'I'm in fucking charge here!' Screaming and shouting. He informed me that the windows were bullet-proof because, 'Oh, someone took a pot shot and blasted out one of the panes.'—'Who did it? Anarchists?'—'Oh, I think it was one of the members' wives.' [*Laughter*] Like a golf widow, you know? Cook expressed that mentality brilliantly in that scene.

PB: You see, Peter was a golfer and he knew these types–

JM:—who'd spend all day drinking.

PB: It might sound dreadful but there was nothing really exaggerated about any of his characters.

JM: The very essence of *Golf Balls* is its rambling quality and once you get into that you can accept it for what it is. It's not tightly structured.

PB: The terrible mistake, really, was in their putting the worst sequence first. That's got to be the ultimate switch-off. It doesn't really cngage you in at all.

JM: I like Hamish. A few shots of him talking to the dog would be all right, that'd be enough.

PB: I'm surprised you remember the name of the dog!

JM: Yeah, I liked him. [*Laughter*] 'Hamish! To heel!'

PH: There was a scene where Peter's a Prussian scientist, explaining how fish were better adapted to playing golf than humans.

PB: That was another instance of him rambling on and on and on.

PH: Good drawings, though.

PB: Oh, they were funny.

JM: His drawings were ridiculous. That fish!

PH: Yeah, it looked like an arm with the fingers at the wrong end.

PB: But that, again, was all improvised. We were in a laboratory but I had to bring in all the skeletons, Bunsen burners and the giant fish that he throws.

PH: Was that an inflatable fish?

PB: Yes. Absolutely. But when he was describing how the fish would hold a golf club and the difference between that and a man's swing with the little skeleton, and then he was swinging his golf club around and it looked like he was going to take a swipe at everything. Fortunately, he had the brain to say, 'Well, I can't wreck the place in case we have to do another take.'

JM: What I do like about the film is that nobody's made any attempt to edit it so that he's moving quickly from one gag to the next. He's allowed to simply ramble on and, you know, he comes up with absolute gems. I love it.

PH: I wonder whether it'd be better in a way if *Golf Balls* was simply a sound recording rather than a video, because his physical condition is such that it detracts –

JM: It does worry you, yeah.

PH: Especially the Major Titherly Glibble bit where he's sweating profusely.

PB: You wouldn't believe it but he was sweating because there were a lot of lights on. [*Laughter*]

JM: Yeah—but not on *him*!

PH: They're on the director.

JM: He's trying to find the script.

PB: But, to Peter's credit, he was putting on the whole act in the golf club. So he knew he was sweating; he could've had the make-up girl tend to it; but he was very happy to go on and be more and more outrageous.

JM: Yeah, he wanted to look like a total piss artist.

PB: Exactly. He was never shy about looking absolutely grotesque, was he?

PH: How was his mood during the shoot?

PB: He was charm, he was calm, he waited patiently for—don't laugh—the director and the lighting cameraman to re-set, start again. People left him very much alone. He sat very quietly in a chair, watching everything that was going on; would speak when he was spoken to; and that was it. I never had the opportunity to say hello until the last day because I was always somewhere else, dressing the next scene. We had a chat about *Behind The Fridge* because I met him and Dudley when Joe was making the films for that show. We had lots of laughs reminiscing and nobody seemed to mind that we were joking away in the corner, and when Rob said, 'We're ready for you, Peter,' he would just get up and go. He was very organised. I remember I was getting fed up with try-ing to mix fluids so it would look like a brandy, trying to get the colour right. Mixing brandies for film is Tizer and Lucozade and God knows what, and holding it up to the light all the time and comparing it to a real brandy because you *know* someone's going to notice. And Peter just said, 'Oh, forget it. Why don't we have a *real* one?' [*Laughter*]

So I raided the golf club bar and, yeah, we had a couple of brandies at the end but, to be honest, when I saw that sequence he looked pissed all the way through, You couldn't see him deteriorating as the afternoon went on. It was all a big act, all of it.

The most fun was when he was the American on the course.

JM: Oh, that was wonderful. All the stuff he kept bringing out of his bag.

PH: Yeah, the rabbit!

JM: Swinging the rabbit. And the barbecue.

PB: Yes, that was the wonderful thing about it. He wanted the biggest golf bag one could possibly find and there was a discussion about what would go in it. Everyone was chipping in ideas and, because it's on film, we didn't have to cram everything in at once. There'd be one take of Peter pulling out these essential golfing accessories and commenting, then cut to refill the bag with more items.

JM: It was like Tommy Cooper.

PB: What was tremendous was Peter didn't always know what was in the golf bag and he would occasionally bring something utterly unexpected out whereupon he would have to improvise a response to it instantly.

JM: The editing's very poor. He'd talk about something and they'd cut to what he's mentioned a couple of seconds *after*, when they should have cut to it when it's mentioned. Very casual editing. No feeling for the material. It struck me as if there had been a falling-out with the director and the producer and it was subsequently put together by an editor who's been brought in, y'know? Someone who wasn't there during the shoot and hasn't been given any guidance by the producer who's probably distracted by some other project.

PB: Ah, my feeling is, since Peter's talking all over the inserts in post-production, he would have had a strong hand in the editing. Or was he not like that?

JM: Oh no, when we did *Not Only But Also* it was the three of us discussing it and Peter always had lots of suggestions, he was very good like that.

PH: Maybe by 1994 he relied on people more to deal with the nuts and bolts. Because the year before he made that radio series, *Why Bother?*, with Chris Morris. Chris has said that they improvised about eight hours of stuff but it was left to him to get fifty minutes of broadcastable material. Peter did what was required of him and he left the situation. He played no part in the editing whatsoever.

JM: Yeah, maybe he didn't care. He told me he hated making feature films. He was so bored by it because everything takes ten times as long as a TV show. A close-up, one single close-up shot, can take up to two hours. That killed it for him. Dudley, of course, loved it.

PB: Well, Dudley was always happy to have a joke with people, whereas Peter, like on this, would just sit quietly. He never appeared to get frustrated. He would never look at his watch, you know: 'Why is this taking so long?' He was always buoyant, such fun, that the last thing on my mind was, 'Oh my God, he's massively overweight.' It certainly never occurred to anyone that he might be very ill.

PH: It's strange that on the cover of the video there's a pretty slim Peter –

JM [*inspects videotape*]: There *is* no cover to this.

PH: No, you can't see it. Well, that's how slim he was. He was *too* slim.

JM: He's invisible.

PB: What is on the cover?

PH: It's a photo of him, shock of white hair, pulling a long face. It doesn't prepare you for how he actually looks in the film.

PB: A-ha... Marketing.

JM: Yes, the first one, as the caddy, he's wearing a Shetland sweater that doesn't cover his stomach.

PB: But he didn't mind, you see, looking completely outrageous. He was quite happy about that.

JM: He looks so uncomfortable throughout.

PB: Well, it was in a very cramped space, you know, supposedly set in a –

JM:—bothy. B-O-T-H-Y. Not a *botty*.

PH: What's that?

JM: A small Scottish house. But you couldn't even see the fire in the fireplace.

PH: It was underlit. [*Laughter*]

PB: Underlit flames!

JM: He had some funny lines, Peter's caddy.

PB: A great one was, 'Golf is my wife, my mistress, my secret love'. [*Laughter*]

JM: 'My one-night stand'. [*More laughter*]

PB: Another one I loved was, 'I've had some laughs over the years... Well, three actually'. [*Renewed laughter*] There *are* some gems, and the more you talk about it... what you do... by the end of an afternoon we would actually have created a far better video than what is, from the material we're talking and laughing about.

PH: It's like the delayed response one finds with Monty Python sketches. Like, you see 'The Spanish Inquisition' sketch and you don't think much of it—the acting's all over the place, the writing's forced. It's actually only *afterwards*, when you discuss it with your mates a few days later, it becomes a fantastically funny piece. All the imperfections are forgotten and you are relishing the *idea*. It grows in the mind.

JM: You see, the thing with Cook is—he's not an actor, so a lot of good stuff is thrown away by him. You know, there's absolute gems in there but he'll mutter it away. There's wonderful lines spilling out of him but a professional actor would have made more of them.

When he was with Dudley, we imposed a discipline on him. And a lot of the stuff he did on *Not Only But Also* was reading straight from autocue. Dudley memorised the lines but Peter had all his lines typed up on the teleprompter, he never gave it enough attention.

PH: I knew that his Wisty monologues for *On The Braden Beat* were performed that way because he wrote them the night before the show, but this is news to me. I thought they just had subjects, single word prompts, cues on boards to guide them through the dialogues.

JM: No, it was all on teleprompt; it was actually going up. He was looking straight in the lens and reading it. That's why he has the glazed eyes.

PB: I don't think many people have enough... *respect*, if that's the right word, for what Peter was doing on this video, which was getting up without any script at all—it was all in his head –

PH:—no one to act to—

PB:—no one to act to, no director to respond to, and he just rambled on and it's lovely, the fact that he does literally ramble, and then suddenly think of something else. Which is why every take ended up completely different. He couldn't remember what he had done before but also he didn't want to remember because he was thinking of new ideas.

PH: One aspect of Peter never diminished and that was his love of disguise.

JM: Exactly. He loved dressing up as Dracula—which we did on *Not Only But Also*—and Marlene Dietrich. He was so good.

PH: And you see his joy when he's the American commentator in the ridiculous headphones with the antennae.

PB: The more I think about it, I think that's the best sequence of all. He's very good in it.

JM: It's certainly the funniest. Belly laughs.

PB: Yes.

JM: Most of them his. [*Laughter*] It just shows you directors don't matter a fart. It's still funny. You can't fuck it up.

IS THAT AN ACT?

Paul Hamilton on Cook's legendary acting skills

It's been trumpeted for so long and by so many, that 'Peter Cook was an awful actor', that it has become a given, a thoughtrail for the imagination cripple. This screed is an attempt to redress the balance in Peter's favour and pooh-pooh naysayers like John Cleese, Dudley Moore and all the other Gielgudian titans of the thespian persuasion.

For what is an actor anyway? Somebody who puts on an act, pretending to be another person who then twists knots, and chokes the emotions and sympathies of his audience (who, essentially, collude in the pretence). The actor is a fabricator, a chameleon, a trickster. The actor earns his dough making meat of lies. You will recall the scene in Mel Brooks' film *The Producers* where Zero Mostel (as third-rate theatrical impresario Max Bialystock) encourages Kenneth Mars, a.k.a. Nazi playwright Franz Liebkind, to exterminate with extreme prejudice the cast of his wrecked masterpiece *Springtime For Hitler*. Gene Wilder (as Bialystock's junior partner Leo Bloom) intervenes, ever the outraged liberal: 'You can't kill the actors,' he pleads, 'they're not animals!' 'No?' harrumphs Mostel, 'You ever eaten with one?' The late Hollywood star Robert Mitchum—who was as much an insouciant poet of the laidback as Cook—was under no illusions of the importance of being an actor: 'Movie acting's a job of work, like plumbing or fixing a car, only with more make-up.'

It's true, of course, that Peter Cook was always the first to recognise his shortcomings in that respect: 'Whenever I made movies I used to suffer Cook's disease, which involved a terrible glassy-eyed look... I belong to a school of acting which consists of doing nothing in particular. The variety of my expressions between shock, joy and terror are very hard to define.'

A possible reason for Cook's reticence as an actor, outside of any personal unwillingness to stamp his foot and rent his clothes and cry and holler before the cameras or a theatre audience, may lie in his formative appearances in The Footlights Club at Cambridge. The hallmark of the Oxbridge revue comedians is their ironical style of performance—they simper, shriek, prance and gurn, overdoing it rotten to relay to their fellow University graduate chums now in 'proper jobs' who may be tuning in, that they are totally aware that it's utterly beneath them, this acting crap. John Wells, John Fortune and John Bird—devastating satirists all—are unconvincing as actors, and The Goodies barely register at all on the acting effort-o-meter (their TV shows are refreshingly daft end-of-term school pantos), but I think Eric Idle and Terry Jones of the Monty Python mob are probably the worst offenders of that generation, with nary a molecule of subtlety or credibility in their garish, over-the-top, furniture-chewing caricatures. (Cook is a model of restraint by comparison.) Not to say that they were completely joyless in the myriad of skits they wrote and performed, but there lurked a faint disgust, a trace of contempt in and for their acting, and an inability to subsume their self-conscious embarrassment. Of course, Terry Jones was included in the line-up of *Peter Cook & Co*, but this may have been a satirical attack on casting.

One comedy colleague of Cook's to stand aside from the pack and defend his performances is Mel Smith who, in the 1995 BBC

Omnibus documentary *Some Interesting Facts About Peter Cook*, said this:

> "He wasn't an actor, right? He was doing the lines and making the moves but he was always slightly removed from it—which was kind of wonderful. It's like a Brechtian technique all of its own. He was just enough in it to get through the plot and the narrative and say the lines, but just slightly kind of just a little further away from it than that.
>
> "It's a very unusual technique to watch on film. In fact, it's not a film-acting technique at all. I mean, you could almost say it's like Supposedly Not Very Good Acting."

This opening to what could have been an enlightening debate about *What Makes Good Acting Good Then?*, and *Can Comedians Act?* is swiftly blocked with Dudley Moore's consensus view that Peter Cook was 'a terrible actor. I think he was strange. A strange actor. He was very awkward with other people's lines. He was fine with his own—which he found highly amusing and beautifully formed—but with other people's stuff, he couldn't deliver it at all.' Well, I'd like to return to Moore's comments about Cook's handling of scripts not written by himself in a while, but firstly let's examine Smith's not-at-all-pretentious comment about Cook's semi-Brechtian acting technique.

Bertolt Brecht was the revolutionary—in all senses—playwright who introduced 'alienation effects' in the productions of his plays to highlight the artifice therein: spartan sets, visible scene changes, unhistrionic acting styles, workaday costumes. (Reminiscent of *Beyond The Fringe*, eh?) Instances of Cook subverting the audience's suspension of disbelief, highlighting the pretence, abound throughout his work. In The Fairy Cobbler sketch from the *Not Only But Also 1966 Xmas Special*, Cook's ears are plainly visible behind the false pixie ones he's wearing. Flash forward to 1989 and the film *Getting It Right* where he plays a bewigged manager of a hairdressing salon: note the infinitesimal adjustment he makes to his syrup. Again, in the TV series *Gone To Seed* (1992), when he is gunned down the bag of fake blood is clearly outlined beneath his white T-shirt. The *Derek & Clive* records have their share of Brechtian nuances too, not least in *In The Cubicles* (from ... *Come Again*) when the dramatic set-up of our zeroes indulging in public loo knobgoblinery is violently destroyed in a hurricane of screaming invective and insults. Perhaps Cook's most brilliant, chilling piece of theatrical sabotage is in the last shot of *The Rise And Rise Of Michael Rimmer*, where Cook, as the democratically elected President of Great Britain waving to the lines of cheering Britizens at the forefront of his victory motorcade, ignores the 'fourth wall' (the invisible barrier separating a dramatic spectacle from its audience) and looks hard and cold into the camera eye and, by extension, at—and into—us.

Peter Cook's obsession with words, phrasing, ('beautifully formed') language—his subject at Cambridge was Languages—meant that something had to give, and that was body language. His most successful pieces are those that rely solely upon The Voice and The Word, his body invariably rigid, statuesque. The Wisty monologues, *The Dagenham Dialogues*, *A Life In Pieces*, *Entirely A Matter For You*, *A Bit Of A Chat*. All classics, all still funny, and not a frame of film reliant on visual comedy—no twitches, facial tics, tongue poking, arm waving or physical jerks of any kind to provoke or promote laughter. It's disconcerting that a man so confident with his voice should be so diffident and meek physically. Cook is so unsure of how to comport himself in, say, Hello, the opening sketch of *Behind The Fridge*, he can barely move a finger. (His confidence returns in that show's Mini-Drama where he is seated, holding a steering wheel and wearing tinted glasses. Do you notice that Cook's almost always at his best when he's parked his carcass? Truly, he is our best sit-down comedian.) And when he isn't centre stage or has nothing to say—e.g. *Find The Lady*, *The Adventures Of Barry McKenzie*, *Supergirl*—he renders himself invisible, he is that negligible a presence. Or worse, as we find in the Beryl Reid-dominated Bee Plumber scene from his own *Peter Cook & Co* show, he's left staring madly, his body frozen in a semi-stoop, like one of his own crouching toads caught in a snake's gaze, unwittingly disrupting the natural flow of the action by doing too much of nothing.

This matters not a jot, his Captain Scarlet-like premonition of rigor mortis, when his performances are collected on soundtapes, LPs, CDs. When we hear audiences laughing uproariously at Dudley's corpsing, choking, face-pulling and unidexterous hopping, we feel alienated—we don't know what's occurring. (Likewise on *Monty Python Live At Drury Lane* there are irritating stretches of raucous laughter unexplained by any stage banter. Are we supposed to be laughing at laughter itself here?) We don't get that from Peter who paints his pictures in sound. From the *Beyond The Fringe* LP to *Why Bother?* he proved time and again the freakishness of his surreal, engaged creativity without recourse to mime or to visual gags. And it was a record that provided him with his finest acting opportunity.

Consequences, the triple album by the wandering, wondering Jews of 10cc, Kevin Godley and Lol Creme, devoted 64 of its 114 minutes playing time to a playlet written by Cook who also voiced all the male characters (four major ones and a small army of cameos—black and white Americans, a BBC newsreader or two, bullhorny coppers, soldiers of all ranks from Japan, Germany, France, Australia and good ol' Blighty). A thoroughly surprising display of virtuosity, it sounds like Cook's homage to his beloved Goon Show of his Radley sickbed youth and his wonderment at Peter Sellers' bravura performances sprinting from, say, pre-pubed Bluebottle in one breath to older-than-God Henry Crun the next. (For the writing, however, there are scant traces of continent-hopping Milligoonery. The bulk of the action takes place in a solicitor's office and the scenario has all the claustrophobia and simmering menace of prime Pinter.)

496 HOW VERY INTERESTING

God is in the details, they say and *Consequences* displays Cook at a personal apogee of miniaturist attention. Mr. Haig, one of the two solicitors, slowly but surely gets more drunk. It's done by the subtlest of degrees—there's no sudden crash from stone cold sobriety into full-blown slurry-gobbed, sack-headed reeling and roaring. Such is the naturalness of his alcoholic progress; one hardly registers it happening. And Haig's panic-stricken howls as the building collapses ('I don't want to DIE! I don't want to DIE!') is unnerving in the extreme. Whereas the action up until then has been dramatic and heavily laced with Cookian wit, wordplay and comic tangents, this scream comes directly from Cook's heart. It's a profoundly moving moment, akin to Spiggott's rejection from Heaven at the end of *Bedazzled*. It almost breaks the spell of *Consequences*, such is the intensity of feeling. Cook, if your antennae are attuned to his wavelength, can summon up the most breathtaking responses, sometimes more than any legitimate actor trying for a similar effect, probably because Peter Cook is such an unexpected out-there source.

It doesn't take much more than a nun's one-inch leap to see the dramatis personae for *Consequences* springboarding from the *Beyond The Fringe* line-up. We have a passive, withdrawn Northerner, Walter Stapleton, with a mangled cliche for every occasion ('You can't bend muck,' 'You can't teach ducks to dance'); the loudmouth, hyperventilating bullyboy coward Jewish solicitor, Malcolm Pepperman; the upper-class English drunk, Haig; and, in the flat downstairs, a pianist, Mr. Blint. Typical of Cook, he takes the template of Bennett, Miller, himself and Moore and distorts and exaggerates them like plasticene models or a hall of mirrors—the Bennett character's dialect is more Lancastrian than Yorkshire, Miller's yiddishness is overtly Fagin-heavy. Interestingly Cook opts for an opiated, sonorous version of E.L. Wisty to voice the pianist with rather than adopt/adapt Moore's Essex-via-Oxford accent. Moore is suggested by the visual clue of having him living a floor below the others, shades of his Joanna jazz janglings in The

Establishment Club basement maybe, so literally the Cook/Miller/ Bennett axis are taller and head-in-the-clouds and figuratively Moore/Blint is more down to Earth. Tellingly, it is the Cook character, Haig, who breaks down first when faced with the prospect of death. This attitude towards death—'Courage is no good: It means not scaring others. Being brave/ Lets no one off the grave./ Death is no different whined at or withstood.' (Philip Larkin, *Aubade*, 1977)—is made explicit in the same year's *Derek & Clive Come Again* LP:

DUDLEY: You gonna go out laughing, are you?
PETER: No, I'm gonna go out fucking—
DUDLEY:—shitting yourself with fear—
PETER:—shitting myself with fucking fear and fucking cancer which God so kindly provided.

Consequences is a master class of comic acting which repeated playing yields only further pleasures and layers of resonance. It's the closest thing we have to living in Peter Cook's head. The minor miracle is, as we hear it, we completely forget that this is not a natural, organic performance. We're not listening to four actors in a studio at the same time, interacting, bouncing off, feeding off and measuring up to each other—it's Peter Cook and Peter Cook and Peter Cook and Peter Cook. Layers upon layers of Peter Cook compacted on to multiple tracks of recording tape. Think of the takes, the re-takes, the re-writes, the comic and dramatic rhythms reliant upon split-second timing, vocal inflection and timbre, and then consider Cook in celebrated chat show mode as the laissez-faire idle idol: Were those 'relaxed and spontaneous' appearances in fact his greatest acting performances? (Actually there is one minor flaw in *Consequences*, a misreading of the line 'Oh, look at that, Lulu,' which comes out as 'Oh, look at that loo, loo.' Lulu Stapleton was sensuously played by the second Mrs. Cook, Judy Huxtable.)

The concentration Cook gives to The Voice puts one in mind of the Samuel Beckett play *Not I*, composed for the actress Billie Whitelaw who is in shadow throughout her monologue apart from two lights from close-up and below focussing solely on her mouth. Whitelaw performed the piece—all non sequiturs and gabbled half-phrases—in a frantic, frightened paranoid stage-whisper, but it's easy to read the text in Cook's trademark drone—'what a position she was in!... whether standing... or sitting... but the brain... what?... kneeling?... yes... whether standing... or sitting... or kneeling... but the brain—... what?... lying?... yes... whether standing... or sitting... or kneeling... or lying...'—and replace Beckett's existential angst with Cook's. (Their outlooks have similarities but Cook's is funnier and makes the burden of The Misery Of Life, as Sven puts it, lighter to carry.)

It's worth comparing and contrasting Cook's portrayals of Jews, for the painful-to-behold *Hound Of The Baskervilles* film was (fatally) shot a few weeks following the conclusion of his stint on *Consequences*. Why is his Malcolm Pepperman a fully-formed being, irascible, belligerent, excitable, cunning and also capable of making small talk with Haig in a relaxed tone ('No, no—d'you mind if I smoke?'), all of that, whereas his (unfathomably Jewish) Sherlock Holmes is a one-dimensional, flat, rasping crass stereotype—one of Cook's most embarrassing forays on the saliva screen? It is indeed wretched—a more toe-curlingly unfunny performance would be hard to contemplate. Especially after one fleeting glimpse of brilliance at the beginning of the film: Cook, as Holmes, is in a dressing gown, depleted aesthete's chest and xylophone ribs on display, a crappy hairnet covering his bonce, reclining in a chair and enjoying a ciggie. At the sound of someone at his door he bungs the cigarette into an enormous pipe and begins puffing away on that, every inch the Holmes we know. The promise in that sublime few seconds evaporates as the film swiftly degenerates, an all-star cast of British Comedy Grates mugging and flailing uselessly in their endeavour to bring a twitch of life to the abortion of a screenplay.

So why was he so on-song in *Consequences* and off-key in *Baskervilles*? It could be down, quite simply, to enthusiasm. Cook's career flourished on whims and spontaneity, on challenges. The challenge of a professionally staged revue (*Beyond The Fringe*); of writing and starring in a motion picture (*Bedazzled*); of scripting and performing a multi-layered musical-comedy-drama (*Consequences*); of improvising a radio series (*Why Bother?*); of being four different guests on a TV chat show (*Clive Anderson Talks Back Xmas Special*). When faced with a fresh, daunting task Cook is like Edmund Hillary facing Everest. However, returning to the rock face for a second or third ascent increasingly filled Cook with inertia. Climb every mountain? No, one will do nicely, thank you.

Baskervilles shatters in a single stroke Dudley Moore's contention that Peter 'was fine with his own' scripts. He plainly isn't. So, by the same token, can Cook be found to be successful performing in non-self-penned works? Well, yes, quite a few, actually. Orson Welles once described himself as a 'King Actor', meaning that due to his imposing bulk and presence he was best suited to playing tycoons, despots, figures of authority, cardinals and kings. Peter was similar in that he shone best in roles of power which he could then undermine. His Beelzebub, Prince of Darkness in *Bedazzled* has been justly acclaimed, as has his Prime Minister in *Whoops Apocalypse*. Add to these his late-career gallery of rogues, scoundrels and rotters that pop up and enliven some films of variable quality: The Archbishop in *The Princess Bride* is inextricably woven into the fairy tale tapestry, the ambulance-chasing journalists of *Great Balls Of Fire* and *One Foot In The Algarve*, the hitman and fluffy toy magnate Ralph Jolly in *Mr. Jolly Lives Next Door*, lending a gravitas and greasy, B.O.-stained authenticity to a near non-existent script, and so on through *Without A Clue*, *Getting It Right*, *Gone To Seed* to his all-too-brief lord in *Black Beauty*.

An early example of Cook as effective comic actor is *Monte Carlo Or Bust*, the 1969 sequel of sorts to *Those Magnificent Men In Their Flying Machines*. Centred around a 1920s Monte Carlo car rally, it is a perfect opportunity for cheap laughs at those odd foreigners and silly women. The Germans, for example, are humourless perfectionist efficiency freaks, their nationalistic pomposity signalled on the soundtrack by raucous farting brass band music every time Gert Frobe appears on screen. Italians are excitable, sex-crazed predators who spend most of their time stalking a team of French women who in turn are first seen twittering at high-speed and swerving their car all over the road (terrible drivers, y'see?). Indians, too, are depicted crudely ('Halt! Who is going there?' singsongs a turbaned sentry of Cook's regiment of Lancers). It's all crude, lewd, loud, offensive stuff but, given the era it was made, probably no worse than the racial or sexual stereotypes one would find in any Monty Python or Benny Hill show.

Tony Curtis is cast, with an eye on U.S. residuals, as a jivetalkin' fingerclinkin' daddy-o capitalist with the irritating catchphrase 'Zowie!'—an unfortunate reminder of Curtis' career apex, *Some Like It Hot*, a full decade prior to this mess. (This occurs infrequently but noticeably with comedians in movies, the harking back and self-referentialism to old catchphrases—e.g. Dudley Moore's opening 'Funny' line in *The Wrong Box* and Steve Martin's 'Excuse me' in *All Of Me*. Whether these distracting inclusions are at the behest of the performer or producer I know not, but it serves to break any internal belief in the drama. It smacks of desperation.)

Terry-Thomas, as always, is the cad, the scheming Dick Dastardly stinker, a character well past its sell-by date by the onset of the cynical '70s. T-T is savvy that his cardboard persona is fraying at the edges and this may be his last hurrah so he gives it his best shot. He is nimbly assisted by Eric Sykes who possesses a comic physical dexterity, a rubber-limbed balletic quality that Cook for one could never match—but then practically nobody else could, either. Sykes is in a class with only Tati and Keaton, he's that good and delightful to watch. (Peter occasionally indulged in physical comedy, however: he wasn't just a talking head on a stick. His diving in to a swimming pool as Emma Bargo and his puppet motions in 'Superthunderstingcar' are priceless in their hilarity value. Just as unforgettable—especially to those who saw it and remember the occasion—is his gangling, dangling St. Vitus dancing schoolmaster in *Behind The Fridge*. The overtly gymnastic display is baffling, oddball—like he's taken the exuberant leg-crossing of Sir Arthur Streeb-Greebling to an absurdist extreme. If it's a response to John Cleese's silly walks then it's an extremely strange one since his ungainly shape-throwing has no context to work in or against.)

How does Peter fare in this multinational, all-star crassterpiece? Bloody well, since you ask. He is Major Dawlish of a regiment of English Lancers stationed in India and he sounds and acts like he's been out in the sun too long without his sola topee. He, with his faithful subaltern, Barrington (Dudley Moore), enters the Monte not only to win (that's for certain, in Dawlish's mindset) but also to show off his array of inventions that will make him a million—The Dawlish Snow Stoppers, The Dawlish Anti-Pedestrian Klaxxon, and so on. Despite being only thirty years old during the shooting, Cook radiates the attitudes, breeding and unwavering sense of superiority ('There's no doubting whose side The Lord's on... Ours, naturally.') you'd expect to find in a member of the officer class some two decades his senior. That he achieves complete credibility as a fifty-ish army officer with little more than a debonair moustache to protect him speaks volumes for his acting talent and his excellent comic timing.

For all of Moore's bitchiness about his partner's screen work, it is in fact Cook's ice-cool underplaying and resolute glassy-eyedness that tempers the shrieking, burbling, hyperactive effervescences of Moore. Without Peter, Dudley would be an intensely irritating brat. They complement each other wonderfully. Throughout this overlong film, it is the Cook/Moore scenes one hankers for. Who could care less for the preposterous gesticulating Italians or the boring romancings of Tony Curtis and Susan Hampshire? Of course, Dawlish and Barrington don't win (Cook and Moore weren't sufficiently Big Box Office to guarantee that). At the last part of the race their car explodes as a result of another malfunctioning ludicrous Dawlish brainstorm. Cook's last line is a classic. He and Moore sit, black-faced, in the smoking heap of their wrecked motor. Cook, stoic to the last, states, 'I think the weather was against us.'

Cook proved with *Monte Carlo Or Bust* that he could involve himself in a very different style of comedy (Keystone Kops with cash) and not be swamped by the running, jumping, bug-eyed, arm-flapping freneticism of it all. In truth, he emerges with credit and dignity. He'd obviously been studying the pre-heart attack films of Peter Sellers and noted how he stole scenes by not seeming to do very much at all. Flash forward fourteen years to the premier episode of *The Black Adder* TV series to see how he fares guesting on a product conceived by Rowan Atkinson and Richard Curtis, chaps raised on a diet of Python, who in *their* youth were fed on three square meals of Cook and Moore a day.

The Black Adder: The Foretelling finds Peter retracing the steps he deftly made in So That's The Way You Like It from *Fringe*. Cast as King Richard III and resplendent in a black mop wig of a type rarely seen, except when worn by Olivier in his 1955 film of Richard III or by Sellers (again) who parodies Olivier in a nightmare sequence in *What's New Pussycat?* Cook is in his element. You can sense his boyish joy in the opportunity he's been given to jump into silly costumes. We see it time and again down the years—as a nun (*Not Only But Also*, *Bedazzled*); as a police superintendent and querulous old geezer (the *Herman Hermitz Reports* film from *Goodbye Again*); the sky-pilot in *The Princess Bride*; Eric Daley, the rock star, in *Clive Anderson Talks Back*. Even in shabby macs and hats as Arthur Grole ('Mr. Interesting Facts'), 'Pete' and E.L. Wisty, he delights in the dual game of obscurity and revelation. It's when he most becomes something other than himself that he paradoxically reveals most of and about himself. He relaxes more in someone else's shoes. His own are too tight for him to go anywhere. This probably explains why Peter was never a stand-up comedian as such, standing on a stage for an hour ranting on about his genitals like most comics in this post-*Derek & Clive* age. Peter Cook was also one of the more successful drag comedians for, whereas the likes of Dick Emery, Kenneth Williams, the Pythons and Dudley Moore would overplay the fact that they are wearing dresses and women's wigs and make up by clumsily tottering about in high heels, playing with their funbags and giving camp, exaggerated winks and smirks to the audience, Cook would play it dead straight. His sexually-repressed lady magistrate in the *Herman Hermitz Reports* film (who sentences young, virile male offenders to 'a spot of light dusting' at her home) is very funny not least because of the absence of self-awareness and the tiresome signalling to the audience of 'Ooh, I'm wearing women's clothes, isn't that hilarious.' Cook was special because he didn't resort to crass stereotyping. His finest creations are imbued with a surplus of sympathy and compassion—from Mr. Spiggott the unidexter to George Spiggott, the devil, and beyond. It's when he's handed roles like Nigel the Warlock in *Supergirl*, simply a two-legged narrative device with no background and even less foreground, that he becomes unstuck and floats off indifferently.

The Foretelling, though no classic (it's pretty dire in parts), is fascinating viewing, principally for Cook's innate sense of comic rhythm. Producer John Lloyd explains: 'The sets were so big we couldn't fit into the studio a bleacher for an audience. The series consequently had no audience, which meant the cast had no focus. Rowan is used to performing to an audience. That's what edits his performance and makes it real.' The finished, edited programme was screened to an audience and their subsequent reactions were dubbed on to the soundtrack. A result of this method is that lines uttered by Atkinson, or bellowed by the roaring beard known as Brian Blessed, are submerged by the laughter track.

The one participant not to fall foul of this post-production method minefield is Peter Cook. His timing is such that he has worked out what lines would provoke some laughter but—more than that—the exact length of the laughing time down to the split-second.

This knowingness of an audience's reactions goes beyond good luck or canniness—this is in the realm of E.S.P. and it served him (and, therefore, us) well through many creations where audiences were not physically present: the *Private Eye* flexidiscs, *Bedazzled*, *Derek & Clive*, *A Life In Pieces*, *Why Bother?*, *Consequences*, the *Here Comes The Judge* studio sketches.

When this talent failed him, it was deplorable. *Peter Cook Talks Golf Balls*, the 1994 video, unsparingly, unfeelingly exposes Cook in his worst physical and mental condition. Brando-bloated, perspiring, wheezing, it's a sorry spectacle indeed. The man whose reputation was founded on incisive, satiric recitatives that produced a sea-change in comedy so violent that it helped topple a government and change the social and cultural thinkmap irreparably—now reduced to under-rehearsed, barely-written, shittily-shot (so often he's acting into the wrong camera), fumbling mumbling monologues about fucking *golf*. What misplaced sense of duty made him agree to undertake such piffle? It's almost impossible to find anything truly funny here. Any quip or jest is undercut by Peter's poorly appearance. The eyes that were once so piercing, so bullshit-detecting, so blazingly alive, are now dulled, sunless, funless. If the eyes are the windows of the soul, Cook's have had the curtains closed. Not even dressing up as a ginger golf caddie, a Prussian scientist and an outlandishly-attired hi-tech golfing expert can save him. But we're getting ahead of ourselves. Let's retreat eleven years—back before the weight of oblivion crashlanded on his face and into his mind.

Let's return to *The Black Adder* where Peter's kingly crown sat comfy on his head. As for his performance, Cook is memorable. He makes a mad, merry King and relishes the cod-Shakespearean flourishes ('Consign their parts most private to a Rutland tree!') but oftentimes one senses the frustrations that are bubbling within him at having to partake in such tosh. His grace and good manners prevented him from insisting he rewrite his own scenes. Recall again the jokey insults he is given to say: 'Horrid little scabby reptile,' 'smelly little dog's pistle.' Absolutely pathetic. (And their witlessness is exposed in all its puniness when placed beside two Cook insults from *Entirely A Matter For You*: 'A self-confessed player of the pink oboe' and 'loathsome spotted reptile.') That Peter could eke out any audience laughter at all spouting this puerile drivel is more a testament to his genius as a performing artist than to Richard Curtis and Rowan Atkinson's writing abilities. What makes Peter Cook burn into the memory cells with his guest turn in *The Black Adder* is the sense that you are watching somebody near self-combustion from being straitjacketed by substandard material. Like an alchemist, he can transform the base into gold, and he has the self-deprecation and tolerance requisite for camp. His generosity of spirit is infectious. You wish it was Cook that had cut off Atkinson's head instead (and maybe Curtis' hands too while he was about it) and taken the show in a deeper, darker, weirder, wilder direction.

Coming to an end now so, perversely and naturally, let's proceed to the beginning and to Sitting On A Bench, Peter's monologue (as Arthur Grole) about the miner who would rather be a judge, from *Beyond The Fringe*. Cook recited this speech on theatre stages from 1961 to 1964 and revived it on occasion throughout the 1970s and 1980s. There are three recorded, publicly-released versions. One from London in 1961, another from Broadway in 1962—they are both collected on *The Complete Beyond The Fringe* triple CD—and a revived, revised performance from the first Amnesty International gala, *An Evening Without David Frost*, in 1976, confusingly included on the following year's *Mermaid Frolics* album-of-the-show. All are similar, all are different—like a river, Sitting On A Bench is forever changing, forever same. It's Cook's dealing with the natures of repetition and invention that fascinate. The polarity held Cook in its sway—the comfort and safety of a successful piece of comic writing and an assured, fail-safe technique of making it live, versus the creative urge to tinker, to adapt, to edit, expand or wholly inject fresh diversions into the text and to then invent new voices with fresh and adventurous risks for the sake of it.

Grole (and his successor E.L. Wisty) are always found seated on park benches unloading their mindtrash. A loner, a drifter, homeless but comfortable seated on the same piece of public property. His mind wanders everywhere but physically he remains rooted to the bench. I imagine it's a response of Peter's to his peripatetic upbringing, a longing to belong. (In a 1977 Parkinson interview, Cook said, 'I've got no roots. I'm a rootless person.') And if the acquisition of material comforts brings with it its own brand of fear—hence the market for insurance policies, burglar and smoke alarms—then perhaps the greatest security is in having nothing at all, except perhaps a viper in a box.

This character, Grole or Wisty (not even Peter was entirely sure of when one of them turned into the other), is straight out of Philip Larkin's 1962 poem, *Toads Revisited*: '... one of the men/ You meet of an afternoon:/ Palsied old step-takers,/ Hare-eyed clerks with the jitters,/ Waxed-fleshed outpatients,/ Still vague from accidents,/ And characters in long coats/ Deep in litter baskets.'

When I played Sitting On A Bench (the London '61 take) I found myself checking the CD booklet to see if Kenneth Williams hadn't made a guest appearance. Cook sounds at first hearing alarmingly like Williams. Peter confessed to a liking for 'grotesques' like Williams and not simply because Williams gave Cook his first break in to Showbiz by using a slew of his sketches in his *Pieces Of Eight* West End revue. Cook revelled in the trash aesthetic—TV cookery programmes, dismal soaps, mongoloid game shows, gaudy clothes, shlocky films and tacky records, all the ghastly ephemera—and Williams is part of that. He was an awful actor (his only genius was in the infinite scorn he poured on imagined adversaries in his nasty *Diaries*)—if he was a smidgen of the talent he believed he was, how is it he couldn't get an acting job outside of the tatty *Carry On* films? Indelicate, cawing like a wounded crow, he was the worst kind of amateur dramatic 'Look at me!

Look at me!' megalomaniac, upending and ruining the realism of every *Hancock's Half Hour* radio show with his appalling, affected impersonations—none of which sounded like anyone you had ever met, or were likely to. His sheer dreadfulness—he truly was a shocker, bereft of any sensitivity or the simple mechanics of comedic and dramatic delivery (check those old albums again where he screws up sketch after sketch of Cook's)—was warrant enough for bad taste-loving Peter's approval.

So Cook performs Sitting On A Bench in a verisimilitude of Kenneth Williams, and it's astounding, really; he was never noted for his impressions. So why do I like it? I think a lot of it's to do with soul—an indefinable quality, I know, but it's there. (Williams, as his *Diaries* testify, was heartless and mean.) Listen to the way Cook says 'All this knowledge is useless.' Williams would have enunciated it archly, nostrils at full flare, leaning manically into the front row, and have meant the line as a blanket condemnation of State Education or even something universal. When Peter says 'All this knowledge is useless,' it is a simple lament for time wasted, opportunities missed. Cook's characters have a humility about them and they share the experience of failure ('Dare To Fail'). It's such a subtle point that Williams would never notice the difference—probably because he never really listened to much else other than his own voice.

A year on and a continent away, we find a radically altered Sitting On A Bench. Absent are the ramblings about Venezuela—the country that was 'implicated up to the hilt in geography'—and about working from five to nine for nine-and-five. Gone too is Cook's artistic crush on Kenneth Williams. Instead we find Grole—or Wisty, for it is the self-same voice, that 200-year-old wittering dunce with shades of Wilfrid Hyde White in the vocal inflections. (Hyde White later played Cook's pater in the U.S. sitcom *The Two Of Us*. Coincidentally, both were gambling men, Hyde White dying broke, Cook dying broken hearted.)

What is staggering—and we must thank George Martin and

Alexander Cohen for recording the shows (I'd like to hear more show tapes to track the transmogrifications)—is the total overhaul of the sketch and the flowering of the persona. This is what I meant by Cook being a performing artist. He was never content to adhere to a script faithfully night after night. (Who else is like this? Bob Dylan constantly rewrites, edits and changes the emphases of his songs to fit the way he feels in the moment—his gigs are like a constant diary in flux. But in comedy? Maybe only Billy Connolly, Richard Pryor and Lenny Bruce had that capacity and ability to remake, remodel and refresh—and even dare to be dull.) A lack of professionalism comes into play here but more so Cook's terror of tedium (the U.S. album cover of *Fringe* notes that the cast get 'bored quite easily').

Some comedians, having developed an act, can tour with it and never change a word for years, decades. Tony Hancock, up until his death in 1968, was performing the same shtick onstage since the early 1950s. The routines were worn threadbare—jokes about teddy-boys and Gaumont Picture Newsreels, impressions of long-dead Robert Newton and George Arliss—and, though sick of them, he stuck limpet-like to them through sheer fear of trying out fresh material. A new joke is akin to leaping blindly in the dark, not knowing whether you land on your feet or your face. Cook was fearless in that respect and you can hear that fearlessness in the Broadway version of Bench.

The audience are tentative, edgy, subdued when he begins. They are on their guard. They have never before heard a voice so strange, so alien. Undaunted, Cook perseveres, droning on and on and on about the boring conversations one is subjected to down the mine and dropping lumps of coal on his foot until gradually the audience surrender their laughter. Resistance is futile. Four decades have barely diluted the power of Cook's comedy.

The third version of Bench dates from 1976 and is included as an annoyingly truncated segment of the *Pleasure At Her Majesty's* film. As another sideline, it's worth mentioning two sublime

Cook moments, one occurring offstage and one on. In the cramped dressing room, Peter is in speaks with John Cleese about a Python courtroom sketch they are set to perform (it's a composite of various Python high court skits that makes little linear sense but is enjoyable nonetheless). Cook nonchalantly suggest a minor alteration of one line to Cleese who almost faints at the mad comic brilliance of it. The other is the look of barely-suppressed elation on Cook's face as he watches Jonathan Miller ripping through his 'Get thee to Gloucester, Essex; Do thee Wessex, Exeter' speech in So That's The Way You Like It. Cook occasionally lamented Miller's retreat from comedy performance and he can't believe his luck that Miller has acquiesced to tread the boards once more. It is evident Peter is a huge fan, and who wouldn't be? Jonathan Miller is a barking uninhibited asterisk of explosive energy—Peter can only stand by and watch as the good doctor hurls himself over the stage in a fantastically over-the-top death scene. Maybe Cook's own death scene in the *Herman Hermitz Reports* mockumentary and the Moody filmed sketch for *Behind The Fridge* are homages to Miller. In both cases the deaths involve much flailing of limbs and tossing-backs of head, are overly theatrical, purposefully bad and go on for an inordinate amount of time. Coincidentally, Cook expires in a hail of machine gun bullets both times.

The person telling us in 1976 he would much rather be a judge than a miner is not Grole or Wisty. It lacks the instantly recognisable higher-pitched drone we would expect from the Fringe version or the *Misty Mr. Wisty* album. Here, Cook has been possessed by the spirit of his alter-ego for *Derek & Clive (Live)*, and not just in the voice. The mind of the character has also been infested. It makes for a strange hybrid, the collision of two characters in the same body, but it also adds a hitherto untapped depth and a fresh, visceral quality to the performance. The Grole/Wisty surreal rambles about ghastly minnows and golden string have been obliterated in preference to more social concerns. Cook's sensibilities fight jadedness and cynicism to the so-called Permissive Seventies. He has written a book, 'Sex And Violence Down The Mine', about three ladies who with each successive day become more nude and more violent. The conclusion of Bench ('being a miner, as soon as you're too old and tired and sick and stupid, you have to go. Well, the very opposite applies with the judges.'), in the Clive voice, has a sharper bite to it, too. A sixteen-year-old joke suddenly attains a fresh, harsh relevance.

An observation: when the PCAS screened *Bedazzled* at the National Film Theatre a few years ago, there was not the usual teeth-grindingly irritating scenario one expects at screenings of, say, *The Rocky Horror Picture Show* or a Python film—namely, the audience en masse reciting every line of dialogue along with the actors on the screen. Why do they do this? As a form of owner-ship? To prove they are bigger fans than you? To make themselves think they're just as funny or outrageously camp? It's a joyless experience sitting in a cinema with a couple of hundred people squawking 'He's not the messiah—he's a very naughty boy' et fucking cetera. It's a communal sketch-parroting sketch. Now, I've seen *Bedazzled* many, many times—and isn't Peter amazing when he plays Eleanor Bron's husband? He's so loving and giving and effortlessly sunny, the absolute opposite from the Spiggott char-acter—and huge tracts of text have been memorised, but I would never chant along with the film. Why? Because I love the way Peter Cook does it. His performance, by turns sparkly and dark, is one to be relished again and again. There's always a new facet or nuance that reveals itself with Cook. Whereas with Python's Parrot Sketch the stage performance are set in stone—hysterically shouted versions of the, by comparison, muted TV original—and the lines very rarely changed (Python are conservative in their rigidity), Cook is fluid, graceful and exploratory. It wouldn't be impossible to edit sections of Parrot Sketch from Python's 1974 Drury Lane album into the *Pleasure At Her Majesty's/A Poke In The Eye* performance and have nobody notice (they're facsimiles). The same could not be achieved of Sitting On A Bench because of each reading's startling differences—and Peter Cook was startling different.

'But was he a good actor?' I hear you continually bewail. To help answer that I'll quote Laurence Olivier from a press conference held on October 17th, 1967 in Montreal for the Expo '67 World Festival Of Entertainment. He wasn't being entirely facetious when he boomed: 'For what is acting but lying, and what is good acting but convincing lying? The whole theatre is a bloody lie from beginning to end.' If we take that as read and then consider the truths exposed and certainties and cosmologies questioned and undermined in his performances then, yes, Peter Cook was a terrible actor. And thank fuck for that!

HUNGARIAN RASPBERRY

As everybody knows all too well, Miklos Galla is Hungary's premier comedian, and, to quote Derek from Derek & Clive Come Again, *can 'speak good English (for a cunt)'.*

In 1993 he, as leader of the Raven Theatre quartet of comedic performers, translated nine sketches of Beyond The Fringe *and* Not Only But Also *vintage for a TV show that was seen and acclaimed by three million Hungarian viewers (bloody good for a population of ten million).*

To obtain permission to use the material, Galla ventured to merrie England in August 1992 for a meeting with Peter Cook who was then filming for the ITV comedy drama series Gone To Seed *where he played crooked businessman Wesley Willis, the majority of his scenes shot either in a hospital bed (which Peter liked) or in a neck brace (which he didn't). This interview was taped on the 7th of that month in a dressing room on the GTS set after the day's filming. In between the usual questions, PC manages to pay tribute to Harold Pinter and Kenneth Williams, and reveals some of his own favourite sketches.*

Things go nicely haywire when Galla seizes the once-in-a-life-

time opportunity to try and engage Cook in some comic jousting. Peter, in laidback Why Bother? *mode, seems to relish a chance to talk bollocks rather than parrot stock answers.*

MIKLOS GALLA: I'm very pleased to meet you, it's one of my ambitions fulfilled.

PETER COOK [*sounding intensely proud*]: Very good!

MG: Could you please tell me how old you were when you wrote the first sketch that was performed professionally?

PC: Erm, the first sketch of mine performed professionally—I was eighteen, I was at university... at the Footlights Club. I wrote stuff for myself, and a London producer called Michael Codron wanted to incorporate it in a revue for Kenneth Williams, called *Pieces Of Eight*. So I wrote most of that. And Harold Pinter was the other main contributor—he wrote comic sketches in those days and very good they were too.

MG: In fact, I'm a bit surprised because I would think that Kenneth Williams is a very different type of comedian to you. He's sort of, you know, *Carry On* things and you seem to be more into the absurd.

PC: Well, he was very good. He did it in a completely different way than I did but certainly as funny. Yes, he was always playing grotesques of one kind or another. But all my characters are grotesques but I deliver them very deadpan, like the miner who could have been a judge if he'd had the Latin. I said it very seriously whereas Kenny Williams would exaggerate everything a great deal more. So, I do deadpan stuff on the whole. I dunno whether it's 'cos it's less effort [*wheezy laugh*], I don't know. I do lots of sketches with this character just sat on a bench and staring straight out, and you can do that at seventy and people won't say, 'Isn't it *pathetic* he's still doing that stuff he used to do when he was young?' because I started off being about 65 years old with this character, I should think.

MG: How do you remember those times when you were doing these sketches like 'The Ravens' and 'The Psychiatrist'? What are your recollections of the era?

PC: Well, Dudley and I had got back from New York where we'd been doing *Beyond The Fringe*, and we were the only two who really enjoyed performing. We weren't wracked by guilt about whether we ought to be doctors or historians. So Dudley was asked to do a show for BBC2, I think it was, and he invited me as a guest, Sir Arthur Streeb-Greebling who was in charge of the ravens and teaching them to fly underwater. He was on the first show, and we also did the first Dud and Pete, which was about [*Cockney accent:*] 'all these bloody film stars that keep pesterin' 'em and bangin' at their window; bloody Greta Garbo, 'ad to poke her off the window sill—stark naked apart from her dark glasses and fishnet tights, or whatever.' And Arthur Streeb-Greebling—one of my favourite lines of his is: 'Do you think you've learnt from your mistakes?'—and he says, 'Oh yes, I've learnt from my mistakes and I'm sure I could repeat them exactly.' [*Smoky chortles*] A very optimistic man despite everything in his life having failed. I like that character, Sir Arthur. 'Cos Sir Arthur could take on anything but whatever he took on, it wouldn't work.

I don't know if you've ever heard any of the *Derek & Clive* records we—

MG: I have them all.

PC: You have? I like the one about Squatter And The Ant, with this very upper-class man talking about how 'There they were—all they had was nuclear weapons and howitzer guns, and this one-legged half-blind ant was advancing to them [*Chortling*] at about one mile every decade. So, a bit of a perilous situation.' [*Derek & Clive (Live)*] seems like a bootleg tape, but in fact it's absolutely legit. We made quite a lot of money out of sitting around for an evening being drunk and stoned. [*Giggles*] Oh, it was great fun. You have

to be in a certain mood—or I have to be in a certain mood—I've
not heard it for years, but sometimes I think, 'I couldn't—did I
really say that? How disgusting!' But other times, if I'm in the right
mood, I think, 'This is exactly what I was trying to say!'

We're thinking of doing another one—we haven't done one for
fifteen years or so. [*Laughs*] Production values are not what makes
the record so we thought we'd do one on the phone. He could be in
Los Angeles and me in London.

MG: Interesting idea.

PC: Well, it'd be quite easy... But I'd miss him.

We made a film of the last record we did, but the company who
put the video out went bankrupt. But it's being re-released this
Spring. Called *Derek & Clive Get The Horn*... The video will be
out in the Spring if we can ever trace the master tape. [...] I saw a
really shitty film I made a few years ago with Graham Chapman
and Marty Feldman and Cheech & Chong called *Yellowbeard*.

MG: I wouldn't say it's very good. I quite like it.

PC: Well, it's disappointing because it's a wonderful cast and it
could have been very good. But it was very badly edited. I mean,
this is nit-picking but I'd sort of co-written the script and it could
have been a hell of a lot better with a bit more work. But I saw it
[dubbed] in German on satellite television, and it works in German.
'Cos the humour is so gross and violent that it actually is funnier
in German. It's more realistic in German, 'cos the German sense of
humour ... [*laughing*] is, ah, not exactly mine. I remember going
to see political cabaret in Berlin and the jokes were just pathetic:
'Herr Adenauer is very old, ha ha ha,' or 'Oh, he's got a long nose,
ha ha ha.' I mean, *pathetic*. Still, they're very good at other things.

MG: Thinking of 'The Frog And Peach' and 'The Ravens', the Sir
Arthur sketches, can you tell me how many times—I would need
an exact figure, actually—how many time the word 'the' is used in
these two sketches combined?

PC: The word 'the'? Have you got a bet on?

MG: No, before I translate it, because the Hungarian government has restricted the number of 'the'-s allowed on television because they're using it quite a lot.

PC: 'The'?

MG: 'The'.

PC: T-H-E?

MG: T-H-E. The Hungarian government uses it quite a lot on their statements, you know, and they don't want to get boring so they're restricting others.

PC: You're kidding? [*Chuckling*] No, but I've heard of many ridiculous things but you can never be quite sure.

MG: So you don't know the exact figure, how many times—?

PC: No. No, but if you tortured me I'm sure I could come up with an approximate one.

MG: If I tortured you?

PC: Have you got your equipment with you?

MG: Er, unfortunately no.

PC: Well, just mental torture would be... Just regular, run of the mill mental torture.

MG: No, I'd like this answer without any pressure.

PC: Oh? *Volunteered*, do you like it?

MG: Yes, yes exactly.

PC [*Big cough*]: Seventy-three in the first sketch and eighty-one in the second.

MG: Thank you very much.

PC: That's quite all right.

MG: You're very helpful. Now, do you go back to Torquay ever?

PC: Well, I went back there to get married, actually. Got married in a registry office in Torquay.

MG: Even though your wife is not from Torquay?

PC: She's from Kuala Lumpur. She's Chinese but she came over here when she was about eight, and was brought up over here. And Torquay was nearer than K.L. so...

MG: But you don't go back there regularly?

PC: No, no. It used to be—what was it called? The Queen Of The English Riviera. We had palm trees down there. It's a very nice town, actually. It's now the drugs capital of the South West, I understand, so I might go back.

MG: When you were doing these sketches such as 'The Ravens' and 'The Psychiatrist', did you have a bicycle?

PC: Not as such, no. I had one at Cambridge, come to think of it. But no, I got rich when I was young, with *Pieces Of Eight*, and I bought a car. A Hillman Convertible.

MG: And you got rid of your bicycle?

PC: I, yes, I gave it to—

MG: And when did you have a bicycle? Where did you ride it?

PC: Rode it around Cambridge. It's very flat.

MG: And when you were a child did you have a bicycle?

PC: Yes, I had a tricycle to start with. And then I was staying with a dreadful family during the War and their idea of teaching me to ride a bicycle was to put me on the top of a hill and make me ride down it.

MG: And what happened?

PC: I learnt to swim. I went straight into the pool.

They were the ones who told me I had to eat up my spinach. I said, 'If I eat spinach, I'll be sick.' I wasn't being naughty: I hated spinach, and it made me sick. I just couldn't stand the taste of it. So they forced some down me and I was sick, so they thought I was being deliberately sick. And I'm pleased that when I was about 20 I suddenly got to like spinach, actually, but I never came round to swedes or turnips. I can't stand them.

MG: And how would you describe your present activities? What are you doing at the moment?

PC: I'm writing for television with, um, a guy called—

MG: Are you busy all the time?

PC: No, I'm not very busy. But *Private Eye* is still going after 30 years. I'm still doing jokes there. I'm very good at having holidays. I really am. A lot of people can't. I could have been born rich without having any of the horrible consequences. It wouldn't have bothered me. A lot of people have to go and work, but I'm actually quite good at leisure. That's probably my major skill. And also I find—I don't remember jokes as such—but when funny things come out the first time they're immediately far more [better], and once I try and repeat them it's really boring. I get most of that from conversations with people but there isn't a profession of just, you know, having conversations. I think I deserve a State Income just for being alive, but I think you should retire at 20, and you get a huge pension until you're about 70 and then start a bit of work.

MG: What do you consider your best work? What is your most hilarious sketch?

PC: Well, I don't think there's much wrong with 'One Leg Too Few' which is one of the first ones I ever wrote. I was performing it at Cambridge and then Kenneth Williams did it in revue—he didn't really like it; thought it was a bit bad taste. And then I did it with Dudley who was wonderful at doing it. I don't think I've ever written anything much funnier than that. It's such a stupid premise—and the guy's so optimistic. And then I saw on television the other day—it wasn't a comedy thing—they showed a guy with one leg, a war hero, who was doing a dance routine to American martial music. Shouldering arms, doing this, that and the other, hopping up and down. And that was pretty funny as well.

MG: Can you tell me—this thing you're shooting now, is it by someone else?

PC: Yeah.

MG: And you tell me you're going to write with someone?

PC: Hm, John Lloyd.

MG: How many offers do you accept where you have to do someone else's material? What is it like compared to doing your own?

PC: Well, this is a pretty good script but I feel easier with my own in that if I forget the lines I can say I'm rewriting it, but if it's someone else's I can't really say I'm improving it. Erm, it's fine. I mean, it's a nice part—I'm playing such an out-and-out bastard. Um, I don't like the stuff in the neck brace just because it's uncomfortable but the, um, premise is I'm trying to screw my children out of their inheritance. It's fun to do. It's a much better atmosphere than doing a movie movie in that it's not so grand. And Alison Steadman and Warren Clarke and Sheila Hancock are all very good actors, so I'm really quite enjoying it for all my grumbling. But I prefer my own stuff because I know that I can say it. I never really think of myself as an actor. I mean, I can do certain things but I'm not—

MG: You're a performing artist that does his own—

PC: Yeah. On the whole.

MG: Can you tell me about the times when you were hired to play drums with The Beatles?

PC: Oh yes. I had to turn that down because I was already contracted to do lead guitar for The Everly Brothers. So there was a clash of—

MG: I thought you recorded a few albums, you know, after they fired their old drummer, Spike Milligan.

PC: Yes, that's true. That is true. You're very well informed. Spike was fired because—

MG: Lack of musicianship?

PC: No, *presence* of musicianship, not lack of it. It was having it there, so it conflicted.

MG: And then they hired you?

PC: Yes, this was the time when I was Golda Meir's toyboy. That was hushed up by Mossad. But, again, conflict of interest: I was also Indira Gandhi's live-in lover. But hectic times, the Sixties.

MG: You were touring a lot with the boys.

PC: Touring a lot with the boys and touring a lot with Indira Gandhi on her whistle-stop tour of the Asias.

MG: And did the boys allow you to do some stand-up comedy between the songs?

PC: Occasionally, yes. I allowed them to do some sit-down music between my—it was a very fine balance between my stand-up comedy and their sit-down music, but there's not much in it. The original posters said—well, we eventually settled on 'Peter Cook And The Beatles' for the billing, but we went through all sort of permutations: 'Peter Beat And The Cockles' was the compromise... Betamax. Um, I did actually know them quite well. [*Liverpudlian accent:*] 'John Lennon was on one of our programmes, I don't know if you've seen it.' Have you got the videos?

MG: I've got, ah, *The Best Of What's*—

PC:—*Left Of Not Only But Also*, right.

MG: And I've got some other films, like, er, what box is it?

PC: *The Wrong Box*.

MG: *The Wrong Box*, yes.

PC: Which has 798 'the'-s in it that we utter. I don't know how many Ralph Richardson gets through but we've been fairly generous with our 'the'-s. Or thees.

MG: Oh yes, I read somewhere that originally your name was the other way round. You were—

PC: Cookpeter. Cookpeter, Struwellpeter.

MG: ...Pardon?

PC: Struwellpeter. Saltpeter.

MG: So your surname is Peter—?

PC: Pieter. my father was a Norse. A wet Norse. I'm from Norwegian stock. In fact, that's what the original Beatles song was: 'Norwegian Cook'. [*Hums refrain of* Norwegian Wood.]

MG: Great song.

PC: But then I sued because of the use of the word 'Norway'. I actually own copyright of the word 'Norway'. So that's why you'll never hear Norwegians mention their country because they have to pay me three krone.

MG: Did you sue Monty Python as well for the use of 'Norwegian blue'?

PC: We settled out of court. Well, Monty Python had to pay me for use of the word 'm', which I also copyrighted many years ago.

MG: The *letter* 'm'?

PC: The letter 'm', yes. Not the capital 'M', just the small one. Because Robert Maxwell had the big 'M'. I suggested to Robert we incorporate our two ventures in Panama so all that working-out whether it's a big 'M' or a little 'm'—just send the whole thing into a holding account in Panama and split it down the middle. In fact I earned a lot more money from the small 'm' than he did from the big 'M', but he's fucking boring. You see where it got him.

MG: I see. But you had to pay Maxwell because Dudley Moore uses a capital 'M'.

PC: He uses the capital 'M' but his money goes to Dudley Moore... But Robert Maxwell, I always deliberately spelt him with a small 'm' and he had to pay me.

MG: Oh, that's a clever idea.

PC: I used to call him 'mr. maxwell' with a small 'm'. So it's very intricate but that's why business works, as I'm sure you know.

MG: Oh I see. Now, finally, can I ask you a little favour? You see, my birthday's next May... and I ask you a little favour that you would learn Hungarian—

PC: No, I don't think I'm going to do this little favour! [*Chuckles*]

MG: Please. Please do learn Hungarian and by May you would come over and perform a sketch that you have written in Hungarian at my birthday party and maybe bring one of your old-time—

PC:—mistresses—

MG:—comedy partners with you, like Eric Clapton—or Jimi Hendrix maybe.

PC: Certainly. Jimi. And we'll perform the sketch with no 'M'-s in it 'cos, erm... Who owns 'H'? I think it's a holding company in Andorra.

MG: So you have to leave out 'H'?

PC: Yes, it would be in Ungarian.

MG: But you don't have to say the word Hungarian in the sketch.

PC: No. I thought, to give people the impression that we were talking Hungarian we'd mention—

MG: But you say Magyar. [*Magyar is Hungarian for Hungarian.*—Ed]

PC: Magyar. Then you're into the 'M' problems again.

MG: Oh, but if you spell it with a small 'm'—

PC:—a small 'm', then that would be all right.

MG: But if you say it no one knows if it is a capital or a small one.

PC: Well, this is an interesting legal case, of course. The spoken word being totally different from the print. [*Chuckles*]
  Right. I would quite like to join Mrs. Cook—small 'm'—who is waiting for me for a bit of lunch.

MG: Thank you very much and give my regards to Jimi Hendrix please when you see him.

"HAVE THOSE BASTARDS MENTIONED ME?" DEPT. LOUDLY PRESENTS...

No man is an island (except Barry Island, of course) and the *Publish & Bedazzled* fagazine was not the sweated labour of a solitary garretted geek. For anyone crazed with info-lust for the origins of The Peter Cook Appreciation Society it's there to glare at on www.stabbers.org, Tom Hedonist's wondrous, if excessively orange, Cooky website.

John Wallis, alias Reg Futtock-Armitage, a.k.a The Chief Rammer, edited the first four issues. Under the pseudoplume of The Holy Dragger, Paul Hamilton co-edited No.5 with Le Rammeur, as the French would foppishly have it, and commandeered the rag for a further fifteen editions. Enigmatic art curator Harry Pye guest-edited No.8 and in July 2000 Peter Gordon, The Clintistorit Of Wintistering his nondenym, made himself at home in the editor's hammock, redesigned the look of *Pub & Bed* and succeeded in hauling it bawling into the 20th century over the course of fifteen issues.

Peter, Harry, Paul and the ghost of John hereby thank the following decent/rotten/hardboiled/scrambled eggs for contributing material, photos, info, vids, tapes, interviews, typing prowess and Cooky-doodle-doos down the years. In order of appearance we salute: *Private Eye*, Ellis Crees, Lenny Bollox, Dave Toynton, Knox, John Hutcheson, Harry Thompson, Sarah Seymour, Milly Shilton, Sarah Otto, Steve Grant, Vince Miller, Nicholas Price, Geoff Lucas, Joe Dator, Jesse Boparai, Mike Scott, Albie Gibbs, Joe Blob, Jane Otto, Wendy Gosland, Becky Beasley, John Lawton, Elizabeth Cook, Roger Wilmut, Bernard McKenna, Steve Walker, Karen Morden, Mark Wareham, Jo Hilling, Nicola Scadding, Alexander Games, Michael Kemp, Bill Lewis, Jimmy Phyall, Roger G. Smith, Anne-Marie Thorogood, Lisa Boggis, Mobeena Khan, John Lloyd, Peter Tatchell (not that Peter Tatchell), Michael Winner (yes, THAT Michael Winner), Mike Gower, Eddie Kramer, Ramsey Campbell, Keith Grant, Patrick Johns, Gayl Gordon, Phill Jupitus, Marc Haynes, Clive Zone, Andrew Collins, James Gilbert, Michael Fishberg, Matilda McKellen, Miklos Galla, John Dowie, John Hind, Kurt Scharf, Zena Barrie, Howard Jacobson, John Lewis, Hannah Dyson, Frank Martin, Richard Jolley (RGJ), David Payne, Mark Cunliffe, Barry Fantoni, Joe McGrath, Richard Ingrams, Jem Roberts, Clare Pollard, Huda Abuzeid, Robert Heading, Irish Jack Lyons, Eric Hands, Gillian Greenwood, Tim Morrison, Edward Ward, Ralph Steadman and Andy Thomson. There's a drink at the bar for you all (with 82 straws in it).

For being gracious and amenable to having their skulls rolled back and their memories dredged up with a brainrake we fling our silken cheesy toppers Godward to our interviewees: Rainbow George Weiss, Barry Fantoni, Harry Thompson, Ciara Parkes, Mel Smith, Auberon Waugh, Joe McGrath, Barry Cryer, Richard Lester, Mark Thomas, Matthew Perret, Cecilia Boggis, Kevin Godley, Hugh Padgham, Malcolm McLaren, Chris Morris, Bernard McKenna, Paul Smith, John Bassett, Michael Mileham and Jeff Craig, Dick Clement, Marian Elliott (Poly Styrene), Elvis Costello, Tom

Robinson, Pete Shelley, Chris Hill, Paul Cox, Martin Lewis, Clive Anderson, Dan Patterson, Will Self, Paul Jackson, John Goldstone, John Lloyd, Eddie Kramer, Humphrey Carpenter, Trevor Baylis, Eleanor Bron, James Gilbert, Nigel Planer, Maurice Murphy, Stephen Fry, Kenneth Griffith, Stephen Pile, John Antrobus, David Renwick, John Cooper Clarke, John Street, John Fortune, John Hind, Jon Canter, John Cobbley, Robyn Hitchcock, Bryan Forbes, Terry Jones, Peta Button and Peter Fincham. On reflection, maybe it wasn't such a time-saving device to interview you all at once.

The Rammer's editions of *Pub & Bed* were Year Zero El Punkoid photocopies whizzed off at a Kilburn newsagent. The first couple of Dragger-led issues were printed in a secret location by Enigmatic Deirdre, Chris Tymkow and Dave Toynton. Thereafter, all the rags from No.7 onwards were professionally printed by Jill and Carmen at The Printing Centre in London's Store Street. The occasional colour covers were created by Clare Kelly at Upstream in Sar Feast London.

The PCAS held not-very-annual general meetings involving live turns, dead stills, lashings of pop'n'tuck at numerous locales and rare screenings of Cookfare at the National Film Theatre. Take a bow, you succulent hams: Elvis Chan, John Cooper Clarke, The Bastard Son Of Tommy Cooper, Patrick Casey, The Harpee, Jonny Blamey, Dolly Dupree, Mark Thomas, Jonathan Miller, Hilary Smith, Dick Fiddy, John Dowie, Arthur Smith, Al Murray, Ricky Gervais, Phill Jupitus, Mel Smith, Stephen Frost, Gordon Beswick, Harry Pye, Milly Shilton, Karen Morden and the Clerkenwell Literary Festival.

The first PCAS-fuelled website was created by Jim 'Trash' Mowatt who one day suddenly disappeared. Wherever you are, Trashmeister, we thank you. Vaughan Green was the emailfuhrer of the Cooky chatroom until October 2004. We will dance for eternity in your honour.

A special Thank You to Peter's sisters, Sarah Seymour and Elizabeth Cook, for their continued warmhearted support throughout the nine years of this endeavour. Aren't they a pair of sweeties? Yes.

Were it not for the Herculean efforts of James Bridle at Snow-books you would be staring at your hands right now. We thank him for his faith in and commitment to this book and, in so doing, averting a mass outbreak of amateur palm-reading.

Is there much more of this? We've got a bed to catch... Oh yes. Hosannahs, ceaseless ear-shattering ululations, hundred year standing ovations and hiphiphooraise-the-roofings to all the former throbbing members of that most seductive of brethren, the PCAS. The constant deluge of supportive and sincere messages, invariably written in block capitals with crayons saying 'This is awful' and 'I want my money back, you chiselling bounders', kept us going through many a dark day.

Finally, if you feel you've been cheated out of a well-deserved credit, then this bit is for you...

AND, OF COURSE, WE WOULD BE LESS THAN MINUS ZERO WERE IT NOT FOR THE ONE PERSON TO WHOM WE OWE EVERYTHING IN THE UNIVERSE EVER. OUR ROCK OF GIBRALTAR, OUR SCALES OF JUSTICE, OUR GALES OF LAUGHTER, OUR CONSCIENCE, OUR MORAL FIBRE, OUR FATHER FIGURE, OUR MOTHER HEN. EVERYONE PLEASE CLAP YOUR HEADS TOGETHER FOR THE ONE AND ONLY

.... (insert name here)

Keep Greebling,
Paul Hamilton, Peter Gordon and Dan Kieran

COLOPHON

A note on the type

The cover, title pages and chapter headings in this book are set in Bedazzled, a typeface generated from Peter Cook's own handwriting, as it appeared in the cartoons he drew to illustrate his 1977 Monday Morning Feeling columns for the Daily Mail.

There are 11791 occurences of the word 'the' in this book.

INDEX